All Things Shakespeare

All Things Shakespeare

An Encyclopedia of Shakespeare's World

A–I

Kirstin Olsen

Greenwood Press

Westport, Connecticut • London

Library of Congress Cataloging-in-Publication Data

Olsen, Kirstin.
    All things Shakespeare : an encyclopedia of Shakespeare's world / Kirstin Olsen.
      p. cm.
    Includes bibliographical references and index.
    ISBN 0–313–31503–5 (set : alk. paper)—ISBN 0–313–32419–0 (A–I. : alk. paper)—
ISBN 0–313–32420–4 (J–Z : alk. paper)
    1. Shakespeare, William, 1564–1616—Encyclopedias. I. Title.
PR2892.O56 2002
822.3'3—dc21   2002069732

British Library Cataloguing in Publication Data is available.

Library of Congress Catalog Card Number: 2002069732
ISBN: 0–313–31503–5 (Set Code)
       0–313–32419–0 (A–I)
       0–313–32420–4 (J–Z)

First published in 2002

Greenwood Press, 88 Post Road West, Westport, CT 06881
An imprint of Greenwood Publishing Group, Inc.
www. greenwood.com

Printed in the United States of America

The paper used in this book complies with the
Permanent Paper Standard issued by the National
Information Standards Organization (Z39.48–1984).

10 9 8 7 6 5 4 3 2 1

For my mother, Nancy Olsen, who taught me how to read,

For Nancy Goodyear Rice, who taught me how to write,

For Geraldine Warren, who taught me why both matter,

And for all other good teachers everywhere.

Contents

Acknowledgments

The study of Shakespeare's works has such a long and fruitful history that I have had the benefit, and the curse, of a wealth of excellent scholarship in compiling this volume. It has been a benefit in that almost every word of every text has been perused with such diligence that someone, somewhere, has explained virtually everything. It has been a curse because no one could possibly digest all the material available in ten years, let alone the two in which I needed to complete this book. I have therefore the constant, nagging suspicion that I have undoubtedly missed the one academic article or the one perfect illustration that would have made all the difference. Nevertheless, to all the scholars who have dedicated their careers to elucidating a set of centuries-old texts, thank you. The format of this book prevents the inclusion of footnotes or endnotes, but there is a bibliography that I hope will enable readers to pursue subjects of interest to them, and when quoting primary sources I have attempted to mention the name of the author so that readers can locate the original work.

I am indebted to the staffs of several fine institutions. In particular, I would like to thank Kate Harris of Longleat House, Mary Lineberger of the Cleveland Museum of Art, Michael Bates and Sharon Suchma of the American Numismatic Society, and the staffs of the Rare Book Collection, Map Collection, and Photoduplication Service at the Library of Congress, especially Daniel DeSimone, curator of the Rosenwald Collection, for their assistance. They have been extremely patient and helpful. Thank you also to my editor, Lynn Malloy, and to everyone at Greenwood.

On a personal note, I would like to thank my husband, Eric Voelkel, for not saying "I told you so" and for being, astoundingly, the most decent man I know, the funniest man I know, *and* my best friend. My children,

Emily and Devon, as always, have been extremely patient with my disappearances into my office to write, and I am immensely grateful. I am also aware that they have been sneaking extra TV time while I've been writing. Guess what, guys? You're busted. I am grateful every day of my life to have had parents who encouraged me to read, teachers who taught me to look at books with a critical eye, and anyone who uses the English language with grace, precision, and enthusiasm. Thank you to Dave Mackie for the ball, box, and stick remark quoted in the Games entry, and to Erica Olsen for researching the saints. Thanks also to Mindy Klasky for providing housing on a research trip and to Bill for starting it all.

Introduction

For those interested in the physical surroundings of Shakespeare's world, this book is an invaluable reference. More than 200 entries illuminate such subjects as the coins, clothing, food, drink, animals, occupations, architectural methods, symbolism, agriculture, and rites of passage of the Renaissance. From the most common gifts at a baptism to the elements of a funeral procession, information about the objects and customs of Shakespeare's world are gathered in one resource in an unprecedented combination of scope and detail. A wealth of charts and tables explains the symbolism of animals and birds, the properties attributed to the constellations of the zodiac, the meanings and derivations of Shakespearean insults, and the names and uses of the heraldic devices found on coats of arms. The appendix contains an extensive chronology that details the historical events mentioned in the plays and places them in their proper sequence so that readers can understand Shakespeare's manipulation and compression of the historical record. More than 200 illustrations depict Renaissance coins indicating their actual sizes in diameter, unusual animals, farming methods, items of clothing and jewelry, weapons, armor, household tools and furnishings, craftsmen's workshops, and many other items. Illustrations include copies of rare photographs and many original renderings that allow readers to appreciate detailed aspects of the items. Maps pinpoint many of Shakespeare's settings and geographical allusions.

While there are shelves and shelves of useful books and journal articles about Shakespeare's works, none has addressed his physical world in quite this way. I have attempted to compile a reference that is both comprehensive and easy to use, for not every reader has access to a university library or the time to wade through those aisles of books and journals. Most public libraries, due to limited space and acquisitions budgets, do not have all the resources that readers require if they are to discover the details of shillings, ships, witches, warfare, cucking stools, and butter churns. Summaries of the Shakespearean world have been published before, notably the monumental two-volume *Shakespeare's England* (1916), which is still a useful resource. However, much has been learned about Renaissance England since 1916, and *Shakespeare's England* omits many topics that are addressed in the present work. Many recent books describing the same historical period tend to be overviews, excellent at sketching the broad outlines of a topic but weak on detail. The really interesting material—how beer was brewed, pewter was made, weapons were fired, and furniture was built—tends to be found in primary sources or in specialized texts or articles that can be challenging to locate.

This book, *All Things Shakespeare*, attempts to summarize much of the interesting but sometimes less accessible material available about Shakespeare's world. Throughout, the primary concern has been the convenience of teachers, actors, directors, audiences, and readers of Shakespeare's works. This text can be used by students writing essays on either Shakespeare or Renaissance England, by book clubs trying to understand a particular play, by instructors explaining *Macbeth* or *King Lear* to their students, by audiences who want to be well-informed before heading out to their local Shakespeare festival, and by theater companies seeking to stage a play with a better understanding of how the original audiences would have reacted to certain lines.

This book is not primarily a work of literary criticism or biography. Shakespeare's dramatic techniques, the traditions from which they arose, his use of poetry and figurative language, the known details of his life, speculation about the aspects of his life that remain a mystery, and the evolution of his skills as a playwright are sources of ongoing and interesting debate, but they are not the subject matter of this volume. This book purports to explain what the *things* in Shakespeare's works are, leaving it to the reader and the critics to determine what the things mean. If you want to know about clothing as metaphor in the plays, this is not the book for you. If you want to know the difference between a doublet and a jerkin, however, or what a bodkin was, or what a clock looked like, or who could legitimately be called "Your Grace," then you have come to the right place.

There are multiple ways to read and use this book. Those interested in a broad content area, such as warfare or government, can consult the bibliography and topic list. This list includes not only suggestions for further reading in the subject area but also a complete list of relevant entries within this book. For a more specific topic, such as breeds of dogs or types of chairs and stools, readers may prefer to consult the index to find applicable entries. The organization and grouping of these entries proved to be one of the most challenging aspects of writing this book. For example, under the heading "Clothing," Shakespeare uses more than 120 different terms, including pomander, doublet, farthingale, smock, caddis, inkle, and round hose. If each of these terms were defined separately, this book would resemble a dictionary more than an encyclopedia, and valuable information about the way the pieces were worn together would be lost or needlessly repeated in each entry. If all terms were included in the entry, it would resemble a chapter more than an entry, and readers might become bogged down in the details of ruff-making when they only wanted to know how hose were different from breeches. Accordingly, most of the terms in this category are discussed under the heading "Clothing," with supplementary entries wherever necessary. For the same reasons, most of the fauna mentioned in Shakespeare's works appear in the Animals and Birds entries, while animals mentioned hundreds of times and requiring much fuller descriptions, such as deer, dogs, and horses, merit their own entries.

At the end of many entries, cross-references to supplementary entries appear. For example, at the end of the Clothing entry, the reader is referred to additional entries on doublet, fabric, gloves, hair, hat, inkle, jewelry, pomander, ruff, and tawdry lace. The best procedure for readers interested in a topic likely to include a multiplicity of terms is to find the most general heading, such as clothing, food, weapons, animals, or entertainment, and proceed through cross-references to related or more specific entries, such as ruff, dishes, sword, dog, or games.

Readers looking for a particular Shakespearean word, such as "tester" or "targe," should head directly to the index. Here they will find the words for which they are most likely to need definitions. Those interested in researching particular plays should also refer to the index for discussions of major themes in particular plays, such as debt, Jews, marriage, or witch-craft.

This book is intended as a companion to any Shakespeare text. Therefore, it tends not to repeat the material likely to be found in almost any well-edited edition of a work by Shakespeare. Most such editions begin with interpretation, character analysis, the date the work is assumed to have been composed and a justification of that assumption, the reliability and provenance of the text itself, a brief biography of Shakespeare, and, inevitably, a description of London theaters in his lifetime—their construction, stages, audiences, actors, and use of props and costumes. In the case of history plays, a discussion of the resemblance of Shakespeare's text to the historical record is also customary. I have touched lightly or not at all upon these subjects. I have instead focused on the sort of material not typically found in introductions to individual plays, such as the difference between a carpenter and a joiner, the text and translation of the inscriptions on contemporary coins, the composition of different grades of bread, and the manufacture of ink, movable type, and paper.

As for the citations found within the entries of this encyclopedia, my concern was to offer a variety of points of reference without attempting a concordance, and without permitting the citations to be more intrusive than necessary. I have therefore tried to include citations that are relevant to the words near which they appear, to include only the most representative or interesting references to a particular concept, and to keep the citations themselves as brief as humanly possible. Most contain only two or three letters, numbers, or symbols, followed by act, scene, and line numbers, so that (*Cor* I.i.26–28) stands for *Coriolanus* Act 1, Scene 1, lines 26 through 28. A complete list of abbreviations can be found on page xxiii. I have, on occasion, omitted the title from the citation when the title of the work concerned is clear from the context. Citations in series should be presumed to refer to the same work unless a new title is introduced, and to the same act and scene unless a new act and scene are listed; thus (*2GV* IV.iv.21, 23, V.i.1; *Oth* I.iii.330–31) refers to *The Two Gentlemen of Verona*, Act 4, Scene 4, lines 21 and 23; *The Two Gentlemen of Verona*, Act 5, Scene 1, line 1; and *Othello*, Act 1, Scene 3, lines 330 and 331. That a scene is set in a particular location is indicated by the word "set" in the citation, as in (*Oth* I.iii.set). Stage directions are abbreviated as "s.d.," and references to characters in a particular scene are abbreviated as "ch." For example, a discussion of meat processing or occupations might include a reference such as (*2H6* IV.ii.ch.), meaning that a butcher appears as a character in *2 Henry VI*, Act 4, Scene 2.

Line numbers, and even scene divisions, can be a problem when quoting from Shakespeare, since the innumerable editions of his works often differ in both respects. I have chosen to use *The Complete Signet Classic Shakespeare*, largely because its copious notes are of great help to readers. Readers using one of the other fine editions of Shakespeare's works should, if they cannot find a relevant word in the line(s) cited, search back or forward a few lines to find the appropriate passage. When Shakespeare's wording differs significantly enough from the language used in my text that I am concerned about readers searching for the wrong word, I have tried to list the key word or phrase in parentheses along with the citation. I apologize in advance to anyone who has difficulty in finding a specific quotation; this is a problem common to all Shakespeare concordances and references.

Where other primary sources are concerned, I have tried to strike a balance between sixteenth-century and twenty-first-century typographies. The former can be obtrusive, even incomprehensible, to modern readers unfamiliar with its quirks, such as writing the number *four* as *iiij* and the word *that* as *y*ᵗ; the latter saps some of the life out of the texts it corrects and, I think, brings the reader closer to the ideas of the text while distancing her from the atmosphere in which Renaissance readers and writers operated. I have therefore retained irregularities of spelling and capitalization but have modernized the use of *i* and *j*, *u* and *v*, and the "long s." The word "upon," which often appears in Renaissance texts as "vppon," will therefore be written in this volume as "uppon," "rea∫on" as "reason," and so on. Readers who remain confused by the spellings should try saying words that mystify them aloud; often this enables an immediate identification of the word, for Renaissance writers were often attempting to write more or less phonetically.

Measurements are given first in U.S. units and then in metric equivalents. However, it should be remembered that Renaissance measurements were seldom consistent from one place, or even one person, to another, and that there is, therefore, a certain amount of inaccuracy built into the system. Since I am an American, I have used the terms first, second, and third story when referring to building levels, rather than the British terms ground, first, and second story.

In choosing illustrations, I had great latitude, for Shakespeare's works are set in times that span two millennia. However, it is not clear how much he really knew of the artifacts of ancient Greece, Egypt, Rome, or Britain, or even of medieval Europe, especially since his plays are littered with anachronisms and since we know that his actors were dressed in more or less contemporary costume. I have therefore tried to select illustrations from the late sixteenth and early seventeenth centuries, and have concentrated only on artifacts from that period unless there is good reason to expand the discussion. I have rarely continued the discussion of objects or ideas past the year of Shakespeare's death.

Many debates about Shakespeare focus on intriguing but ultimately unresolvable questions about what he believed. Usually, these controversies arise when a modern-day reader who fully appreciates Shakespeare's dramatic and poetic gifts runs smack into a very sixteenth-century attitude about Moors, Jews, or women. For example, a female reader may feel uneasy about the conflict between her admiration for Shakespeare's language and her disgust at the racist, sexist, or ignorant statements that come out of his characters' mouths. There are several ways for her to resolve this conflict. She can conclude that Shakespeare fully believed the worst views expressed in his plays, and then determine whether or not this attitude spoils the plays for her. She can decide that Shakespeare's tendency to give even his most stereotypical characters comprehensible motives and emotions makes him ahead of his time, perhaps even a sympathizer with more progressive views, but also a realistic businessman who knew that audiences preferred and expected a barbaric Moor, a greedy Jew, and a shrewish woman. This eternal question—how much is art, how much is personal belief?—has been the meat of countless books, theses, and doctoral dissertations, and ultimately remains largely a matter of speculation.

It is possible that Shakespeare believed every word of his writing, that he believed none of it and simply wrote what brought people to the theater, that he believed only the views of the sympathetic characters, or that he thought he was saying one thing and actually ended up conveying another. What an author intends to say, what he believes, what he thinks will sell, and what he actually gets on paper are often very different things. In most cases, however, the bulk of the evidence implies that Shakespeare shared, or at least was willing to echo, some of the least appealing beliefs of his society. This assessment will doubtless meet with disagreement in some quarters. But in the case of Shakespeare, we are dealing with a distance of 400 years from the present day, and though human emotions have changed little in that time, society has changed substantially. It should not surprise us that Shakespeare's values, and those of his contemporaries, are different from our own. What is surprising is the length to which lovers of Shakespeare will go to ignore or explain away those differences.

I adore Shakespeare and have done so since my first encounters with him in the eighth grade. Yet all my affection for his obvious genius cannot blind me to his appalling views regarding the second-class citizens of his society, including women and Jews. As a woman, a Jew, and an admirer of Shakespeare, I have had to find a way to appreciate the man's work without sharing or accepting all of his opinions. All his genius cannot disguise or erase the fact that he had (or at least perpetuated) many strong prejudices, and I attempt in this volume to explain the prejudices without minimizing them, apologizing for them, or pretending that they do not matter. I have attempted to outline the prevalent views of the time and to assess, briefly, how the works reflect or differ from those views. I have not attempted to enter into a lengthy discussion of all the arguments about whether and how much prejudice is evident in the works, for that has been done much better and more thoroughly elsewhere, and in any case is beyond the scope of the present work. I feel that it is ultimately the reader's decision whether the plays are racist and sexist, whether Shakespeare himself was a racist or a sexist, and whether the answers interfere with one's enjoyment of the works.

As to the authentication of certain plays, or scenes within plays, I am not inclined to disagree with majority opinion. *Henry VIII* and *The Two Noble Kinsmen* are generally acknowledged to be collaborations, and *Pericles* is thought to be an adaptation of another text, partially revised by Shakespeare and then rendered in a corrupt quarto by a person (or people) who recorded it from memory. Some editors have recently adopted another play, *Edward III*, into the Shakespeare canon. The present volume is not concerned with these controversies, but with making the objects of

Shakespeare's time and works accessible to people today. Therefore, I have chosen to include references to all parts of *Pericles, Henry VIII,* and *Two Noble Kinsmen,* on the grounds that readers and audiences of these plays would like to understand everything in the texts, regardless of whether Shakespeare was the author of any given line. Likewise, I have not included any material from *Edward III,* since only a minority of readers are yet likely to come into contact with it, and much of its historical context is already addressed in the entries that follow. When making decisions of this sort, my criterion has been the convenience of the majority of readers, rather than the requirements of Shakespeare scholars.

Alphabetical List of Entries

Alphabetical List of Entries

Abbreviations for Shakespeare's Works

A&C	*Antony and Cleopatra*
AW	*All's Well That Ends Well*
AYLI	*As You Like It*
CE	*The Comedy of Errors*
Cor	*Coriolanus*
Cym	*Cymbeline*
2GV	*The Two Gentlemen of Verona*
1H4	*Henry IV, Part 1*
2H4	*Henry IV, Part 2*
H5	*Henry V*
1H6	*Henry VI, Part 1*
2H6	*Henry VI, Part 2*
3H6	*Henry VI, Part 3*
H8	*Henry VIII* (also known as *All Is True*)
Ham	*Hamlet*
JC	*Julius Caesar*
John	*King John*
LC	*A Lover's Complaint*
Lear	*King Lear*
LLL	*Love's Labor's Lost*
MAAN	*Much Ado About Nothing*
Mac	*Macbeth*

MM	*Measure for Measure*
MND	*A Midsummer Night's Dream*
MV	*Merchant of Venice*
MWW	*The Merry Wives of Windsor*
Oth	*Othello*
Per	*Pericles*
PP	*The Passionate Pilgrim*
P&T	*The Phoenix and the Turtle*
R2	*Richard II*
R3	*Richard III*
R&J	*Romeo and Juliet*
RL	*The Rape of Lucrece*
S	Sonnet (followed by sonnet number, as S 22)
TA	*Titus Andronicus*
T&C	*Troilus and Cressida*
Temp	*The Tempest*
Tim	*Timon of Athens*
TN	*Twelfth Night*
TNK	*The Two Noble Kinsmen*
TS	*The Taming of the Shrew*
V&A	*Venus and Adonis*
WT	*The Winter's Tale*

Adamant

Adamant (*MND* II.i.195–97; *T&C* III.ii.177; *1H6* I.iv.52) is not any one specific substance. The word variously denoted the lodestone (magnet), something attracted by a magnet, a diamond, corundum, white sapphire, or any very hard substance. In Shakespeare's time the diamond and lodestone appear to have been the most common meanings, but confusion remained until the seventeenth century, when the lodestone meaning was generally dropped and the word came to mean diamond or anything else that was very hard.

Alarum

Derived from Old French and Italian terms that meant "to arms!," *alarum* was used by Shakespeare to denote sounds of frantic preparation for battle and warning noises, especially bells. The term appears often in stage directions (*H5* III.Cho.33 s.d.; IV.vii.53 s.d.; *JC* V.ii.1 s.d., V.iii.1.s.d.; *John* V.iii.1 s.d.), and might consist of ad-libbed cries, bells, or trumpet calls. The direction "alarums and excursions" (*3H6* V.ii.1 s.d.) would include some or all of these noises, combined perhaps with cannon fire and certainly with "excursions" of the actors onstage, pretending to be involved in a battle. *See also* Army.

Alchemy

The forerunner of chemistry, alchemy was a science dedicated to the perfection of base materials, most famously the transmutation of lead into gold. It borrowed from and intruded into a vast array of disciplines, including astronomy, botany, medicine, geology, prognostication, and theology. At the core of alchemy's exceedingly complex practice and terminology were a few basic ideas, and these, when he refers directly to alchemy, are the ones with which Shakespeare was apparently most familiar. (Other terms and concepts occur in his references to such alchemically influenced topics as astrology and medicine.) The first of these core ideas was that all matter was composed of a mixture of four elements (*Per* III.i.33; *H5* IV.ii.5–7): earth, air, water, and fire. Each of the elements had its own pair of properties. Earth was cold and dry; air, hot and wet; fire, hot and dry; water, cold and wet. Shakespeare refers several times to this division of the world into four elements, as in Sonnet 44, which ends with the "so slow" elements of earth and water, and Sonnet 45, which begins with "The other two, slight air and purging fire." He again distinguishes between "pure air and fire; and the dull elements of earth and water" in *Henry V* (III.vii.20–23). The alchemists' conception of these elements was different from that of the common person's; alchemical "water" was an abstract concept and not the same thing as seawater, for example, but Shakespeare, like most of his contemporaries, did not distinguish between them.

According to the sixteenth-century Swiss alchemist and physician Paracelsus, these four elements were mixed together in every substance, but in each substance only one element was dominant and capable of reaching a perfect state. This search for perfection is the second core principle of alchemy. Alchemists sought through various means—chiefly by burning, distilling, dissolving, sublimating, melting, and otherwise manipulating metals and stones—to purify and perfect substances. The aims were to alter base metals into precious ones and to extend the human life span by discovering perfect medicines.

Alchemical medicinal methods, however, were usually no better than quackery. Paracelsus, who was better than most in his regard for empirical evidence and his actual medical discoveries, such as a mineral component to goiter and his description of congenital syphilis, still believed that people could survive without food for decades if their feet were stuck in the earth or if they strapped a clod of fresh earth next to the skin and replaced it whenever it dried. In the field of chemistry, alchemy did provide some interesting theories of matter and a good deal of practical metallurgical experimentation. Unfortunately, the practical and theoretical contributions of alchemy are hidden behind a confusing jargon, in which a simple term like "mercury" may mean the planet, quicksilver (*2H4* II.iv.231–32; *Ham* I.v.66), a varying essence found in all metals, a solvent, a white stone, or a spirit imbued in the entire universe; and may be referred to, according to Paracelsus, as red mercury, dissolving mercury, crude mercury, universal mercury, white mercury of the sages, "permanent water, the spirit of the body, unctuous vapor, blessed water, virtuous water, water of the wise, philosophers' vinegar, mineral water, heavenly grace, virgin's milk," and so on. Metals, for example, were all presumed to contain mercury (by which alchemists meant the moisture given off when the substance was burned), sulfur that made it burn, and salt—not table salt, but the ash left after burning.

The principal chemical failure of alchemy was its search for the "philosopher's stone" or elixir, which was thought to have the power to turn base metals like lead into gold. A better "grant proposal" could not have been written, and generations of alchemists were provided with funds by monarchs who were ultimately disappointed in their hopes for augmented treasuries. It was this spectacular failure, however, and its wider context of a search for perfection, that were probably uppermost in the minds of Shakespeare's audience when they heard the word "alchemist." Direct Shakespearean references to alchemy (*JC* I.iii.158–60) are few, but they always involve transmutation, as in *King John*:

To solemnize this day the glorious sun
Stays in his course and plays the alchemist,
Turning with splendor of his precious eye
The meager cloddy earth to glittering gold. (III.i.3–6)

This is an especially appropriate reference, since gold was identified in alchemical texts with both the sun and kingship. Other Shakespearean references to alchemy include mentions of the philosopher's stone in *2H4* III.ii.334 and *Tim* II.ii.117; the "You are an alchemist; make gold of that" in *Tim* V.i.114, and the sun's "Gilding pale streams with heavenly alchemy" in Sonnet 33. *See also* Astrology; Astronomy; Disease and Injury; Medical Practitioners.

Alehouse

A 1577 survey of twenty-seven counties discovered 14,000 alehouses (*2GV* II.v.48; *H5* III.ii.12) in existence, and this was almost certainly an underestimate. The alehouse was one of the indispensable structures of any cluster of houses with a pretension to being a village. In theory, alehouses had to be licensed by the quarter sessions of the justices of the peace. In practice, England was a nation of women who knew how to brew and men who liked a drink away from home, so there were plenty of illegal establishments.

Several features distinguished an alehouse, at least a legitimate alehouse, from an ordinary house or shop. In the first place, there was often a sign (*TA* IV.ii.98; *2H6* III.ii.81) identifying the building. This might have words, but more frequently, in this time of low literacy, simply a picture, such as a mermaid, a fox, a compass, or a star. A common kind of alehouse sign—not a "brand name" like the Sun and Moon (which existed in Aldersgate, London, in Shakespeare's day), but a generic sign identifying the type of business conducted within—was an "ale pole." This was a long pole, extending in medieval illustrations out and upward from just above the front door, and ending in a green shrub. The window lattices of alehouses were often painted red (*2H4* II.ii.77–78; *MWW* II.ii.25). Inside, the alehouse was usually just a room with a table or tables and a small chamber, called a buttery (*TS* Ind.i.102), where the liquor was kept.

Alehouses, as their name implied, specialized in ale and beer rather than the wine of taverns or the rooms and food of inns. They might house and feed travelers too poor to stay in an inn, but mostly they were for drinking. The alehouse staff was headed by the alewife (female—*TS* Ind.ii.21; *2H4* II.ii.80) or ale draper (male), who was in charge of the brewing. There were some men who ran alehouses, but it was primarily a woman's business, and the stereotypical proprietor was a hostess (*2GV* II.v.3–9; *T&C* III.iii.252–54; *TS* Ind.ii.86). Illustrations usually pictured her with a tankard in each hand as a sign of her calling. Some brewed extremely good beer, but others served an adulterated or spoiled product and were punished by being tied into the village's cucking stool and ducked in the local pond or river. The alewife seldom had a large staff, but she might have a "drawer" (*MWW* II.ii.154) or tapster (*2H4* I.ii.172–73; *MWW* I.iii.10–21; *Tim* IV.iii.216–17) to help tend bar.

The patrons—mostly but not exclusively men—were frequently rude, rowdy, and very drunk. The less intoxicated told jokes and wild stories (*Oth* II.i.136–37; *H5* III.vi.71–79), gambled, played games, and sang (*TN* II.iii.88–92). The inveterate "mault-wormes," according to the moralist Phillip Stubbes, practically lived in the alehouse for days at a time, "so long as any money is left, swilling, gulling & carowsing from one to an other, til never a one can speak a redy word." Possessed by "the spirit of the buttery," they staggered, stammered, reeled, vomited, urinated under the table, cursed, wept, drooled, shook, babbled, fought, and forgot all their behavior once sober. Stubbes was a stern moralist, but his observations were confirmed by others, including William Harrison, who said that drunks, whom he called "aleknights," would go from one alehouse to another until they collapsed under the "board" (table) or fell into a stupor, sitting and blinking, afraid to move, until they sobered up enough to drink again. If too much of this drunkenness went on at a particular alehouse, constables might raid it (*MAAN* III.iii.42–47), and the justices might shut it down. Not all alehouses were disorderly, however, and sometimes the patrons were courting couples, groups of married couples, or groups of women.

The best alehouse scene in Shakespeare is unquestionably the first scene of the Induction of *The Taming of the Shrew*, which is set in an alehouse and contains a memorable portrait of an alewife. Both scenes of the Induction turn upon an elaborate prank played upon a drunk by the other patrons of the alehouse. *See also* Drink; Inn; Tavern.

Alms

Charity in England took many forms. One of the most common incarnations was the parish poor box, which collected community contributions on Sundays and holy days. Churchwardens and justices of the peace were responsible for ensuring that every household paid its fair share and fining defaulters. Clergy were not exempt from donating; nonresident ministers, for example, who made less than £20 a year had to tithe at least one-fortieth of their income to the cause. An act of 1572 placed these collections, known as the "poor rate," under the control of the justices of the peace, who appointed rate collecters and overseers of the poor.

A less formal way of giving to the poor was the distribution of alms (*MAAN* II.iii.159; *3H6* V.v.79; *MM* III.i.35; *Cym* II.iii.115), either in the streets to beggars or at the kitchen door to the poor, who were entitled to the "broken meats" (table scraps—*Lear* II.ii.15; *LLL* V.i.39–40) after they had been taken from the master's table and been picked over by the servants. There was a certain amount of suspicion regarding beggars (*Lear* IV.vi.154–55; *2GV* II.i.27). It was feared that they were undeserving of charity, loved idleness, or spread plague in their wanderings. William Harrison wrote of fraudulent beggars who used substances like arsenic, spearwort, or crowfoot to cause ulcers to make themselves appear diseased. Others, he said, pretended to be shipwrecked sailors because such sailors, along with the lame and blind, were among the few entitled to apply for licenses to beg (the "passport" of *AW* III.ii.56–57). Many, if not most, of the beggars seen on the streets were unlicensed. These, if caught and proven to be over fourteen years old, were whipped and branded by the beadle (*Per* II.i.92–97). Those under fourteen were also whipped, but were then apprenticed to a craftsman, whether they wanted an apprenticeship or not.

Harrison, when discussing alms, spends very little time describing ways of giving to the poor and a great deal of time describing about two dozen types of criminal vagrants. He admits that the handicapped, diseased, aged, orphaned, injured, and unlucky should have their woes relieved by almsgiving, but draws the line at the willfully idle, whose numbers he estimates at about ten thousand. These include thieves; "hookers," or anglers who fish for goods through windows; horse thieves; collectors for false charities; fake lunatics, sailors, deaf-mutes, and fire victims; thieving tinkers and peddlers; license forgers ("jarkmen") and hedge priests ("patricoes"); and girl and boy beggars ("kinchin morts" and "kinchin coes"). These rogues, he says, speak a slang called "peddlers' French," "a speech compact thirty years since of English and a great number of odd words of their own devising, without all order or reason." John Fitzherbert, in his *Booke of Husbandrie*, emphasizes giving more than censure in his passage on alms, but even he notes, indirectly, the presence of many unworthy poor. He advises giving alms when possible, offering kind words when money or food cannot be given, and including forgiveness and chastisement as different forms of charity.

Another type of charity was embodied in the almshouses (*H5* I.i.17). These were authorized by the 1547 Vagabond Act and became popular institutions for collecting and housing the poor. Between 1570 and 1600, more than one hundred, ranging in size from tiny buildings capable of housing a handful of paupers to magnificent structures with grand courtyards, were founded, usually by wealthy individuals or trade guilds. Individual or corporate bequests and endowments were also used to build hospitals and schools or to provide apprenticeship fees for poor boys or dowries for poor girls.

Anatomy and Physiology

The story of Renaissance anatomy (*R&J* III.iii.106) and physiology is, with few exceptions, the story of ancient Greek anatomy and physiology, for Renaissance physicians and surgeons based much of their knowledge on the centuries-old works of the physicians Hippocrates (ca. 460–377 B.C.) and Galen (A.D. 129–ca. 199). Human dissection, after over a millennium of nearly complete absence from medical study, was making a slow comeback. As a result, some of Galen's anatomical errors had been discovered, though some were overlooked due to the widespread reverence in which he was held. However, whatever the defects of Galen's anatomical treatises—a few extra liver lobes here, a nonexistent bone protrusion there—he, and thus Renaissance physicians, had a fairly good understanding of the mechanics of joints (*2H6* III.ii.319), the structure and number of bones, the purpose of tendons, and the number and placement of the internal organs.

It was in physiology, the study of how these various systems and structures worked, that Galen made his most dangerous errors. He divided physical substances into four elements (earth, air, fire, and water) with four "prime qualities" (hot, cold, wet, and dry). The human body also had four humors (black bile, yellow bile, blood, and phlegm) and three souls: the rational, governed by the brain and controlling thought, sensation, and movement; the irascible, governed by the heart and controlling the emotions; and the concupiscible or vegetative, seated in the liver (*WT* I.ii.304–6) and controlling nutrition. The dominance of these three organs in Galen's thought explains why Cymbeline calls Belarius "the liver, heart, and brain of Britain, / By whom I grant she lives" (*Cym* V.v.14–15; see also *TN* I.i.38). Further, there were three kinds of pneuma or spirit, each gen-

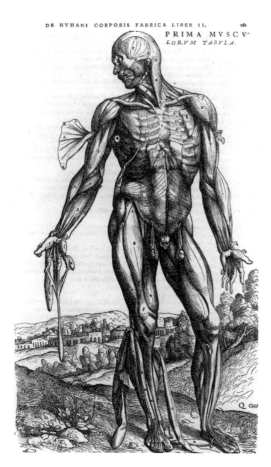

DE HVMANI CORPORIS FABRICA LIBER II.   181
PRIMA MVSCV-
LORVM TABVLA.

One of several illustrations of human musculature from Andreas Vesalius's revolutionary work, *Humani Corporis Fabrica Librorum Epitome.* In a series of pictures, Vesalius strips the flesh and muscles away from a vertical corpse until only a few bits of connective tissue remain. Then he reverses the corpse and shows the flesh of the back side melting away, layer by layer, in the same fashion. The corpse is shown standing, or in some cases dangling as if suspended on strings, not solely for aesthetic reasons but because corpses were often hung vertically for dissection. Reproduced from the Collections of the Library of Congress.

erated in one of the major organs. Each organ in turn had a set of "faculties," including an attractive faculty that drew in what it needed, a retentive faculty that held the nourishment until sated, and an expulsive faculty that rid it of what was no longer needed.

Galen's explanation of the nervous system was actually quite astute. He understood that the brain (*1H6* I.iv.109; *LLL* IV.iii.321, 325) controlled it by means of sensory and motor nerves, which differed from each other. He distinguished between the thick membrane around the brain (the dura mater) and the thin one (the pia mater; see *T&C* II.i.71–73) and described the effects caused by injury to different parts of the nervous system, including the severing of the spinal cord in various places, the severing of the recurrent laryngeal nerve, and lesions of the cerebrum and cerebellum. He did a splendid job of describing the parts of the brain and what happened when things went wrong with it, but was considerably less accurate when it came to explaining how the brain did what it did. For example, he believed that the pituitary cleansed the brain of impurities by draining them down the throat, causing coughing, asthma, and bronchitis when the volume of impurities became too great. "Purging of the brain" thus remained a common treatment for these ailments well into the Renaissance.

Galen's explanation of the cardiovascular and digestive systems also was flawed. It was extremely complex, but a simplified version follows. The process began in the stomach (*Cor* I.i.123–24) with the introduction of food, which the stomach changed into a substance called chyle. The stomach (using its expulsive faculty) sent the chyle to the liver and the waste products to the intestines (*H5* II.i.53; *T&C* II.i.49–50, II.ii.11). Liquids went to the kidneys (or "reins"), which separated the useful matter from them and expelled the leftover fluid (*MWW* III.v.21–23, 110). It was believed that digestion took place because of the body's natural heat, which in some sense "cooked" the food within the stomach, and the association of this organ with heat led it to be associated with the heat of anger (*1H6* IV.i.141; *2H6* II.i.54; *MAAN* II.iii.250; *JC* V.i.66).

This brings us to the liver, which is no longer an organ that captures the popular imagination. Galen thought it was the first organ to be formed in the fetus and the source of the entire venous system. He also thought that the liver wrapped around the stomach, warming it for the process of digestion (*A&C* I.ii.25; *MV* I.i.81–86; *2H4* I.ii.175–78); this was one of the errors that later made it clear he had dissected only animals, not people, for the liver is not structured this way in humans. The liver continued the process begun by the stomach, heating the chyle and separating the yellow bile or choler from the black bile (a nonexistent substance). Yellow bile was expelled to the gallbladder (*2H4* I.ii.175–78), while black bile traveled to the spleen and then back to the stomach to aid retention of food. The remaining purified blood, now imbued with "natural spirit," the pneuma generated by the liver, was released into the veins. However, Galen did not perceive the circulation of the blood; that was left for William Harvey to deduce in 1628. Instead, he thought of the blood as washing slowly through the body in a gentle tide, which explains how he thought that it could congeal or grow to excess in a particular body part, resulting in a need to bleed the "extra" blood away.

Some of the purified blood rose to the heart by means of the vena cava, and here it was altered yet again by the heat of the heart. It was distilled into a thinner, purer form and given the heart's pneuma, "vital spirit." This blood wafted into the lungs (*MV* IV.i.140; *Cor* I.i.110), where it was fanned and cooled by the air inhaled. Blood also flowed to the brain, where it was changed into "animal spirit" and sent back to the nerves. The blood ebbed and flowed, moving from one organ to another in a complex pattern. It changed character from one part of the body to another and could become "corrupted" (*Lear* II.iv.222). It could be increased by some actions (drinking, for example) and diminished by others (*MAAN* I.i.240–44).

In some respects, Galen was very close to the truth. He knew, for example, that blood moved, that arteries (*LLL* IV.iii.302–3) arose from the aorta, and that the heart valves can close and open. In other respects, however, he missed the mark entirely. He thought of the heart not as a pump (*MND* V.i.296–97) but as a furnace, with lungs as its bellows and fan. Normally so astute at anatomy, he missed the heart's atria entirely and thought of it as a two-chambered organ, divided into the right and left ventricles. He also thought that air from the lungs mixed with blood inside the heart. Nonetheless, he was still so influential more than 1,300 years after his death that even the Flemish anatomist Andreas Vesalius (1514–64), who exposed Galen's animal-only dissection scandal in his groundbreaking *Fabric of the Human Body* (1543), stopped short of questioning Galen's physiological theories.

By the Renaissance, Galen's theories had been expanded, so that every organ had not only a function but also a kind of personality. Thus the bowels became the seat of compassion and the spleen (filled with cold, dry, black bile) the seat of irritability, momentary passions, and impulses (*3H6* II.i.124; *1H4* II.iii.79–80; *AYLI* IV.i.210; *MND* I.i.146; *John* IV.iii.97). A person given to fits of temper could therefore be "spleenful" (*2H6* III.ii.128) or "splenitive" (*Ham* V.i.261). Such imagery, in which a "spleen" can be not an organ but a caprice, leads to passages in Shakespeare that are unintentionally funny today. For example, there is the torment of the conflicted and passionate Venus in *Venus and Adonis*, in which "A thousand spleens bear her a thousand ways" (*V&A* 907), calling to mind an angry mob of tiny internal organs traipsing about with a bewildered goddess on their backs.

The liver, too, had a personality. Its assumed role as the origin of veins meant that those lacking in courage presumably lacked the courageous humor (blood), and thus had pale livers (*H5* III.ii.32–34; *Lear* IV.ii.51;

MV III.ii.86; *2H4* IV.iii.103–8; *TN* III.ii.59–61). As the seat of the concupiscible (desirous) soul, it was also the source of passions, particularly
love and lust (*2H4* V.v.32–33; *MAAN* IV.i.230; *AYLI* III.ii.416–17; *TN*
II.iv.97–98; *RL* 47; *Temp* IV.i.56). The heart, too, was a fount of emotion, but generally of purer, less bodily emotions, such as true love or grief
(*2H6* III.i.198, III.ii.409; *JC* III.ii.107).

During the sixteenth century a few bold souls dared to challenge Galen
on one or two points. Vesalius took issue with his anatomy; Paracelsus,
with his physiology and theory of treatment. However, they were a distinct
minority and suffered from vitriolic attacks by those who took Galen as
gospel; and, as noted above, even Vesalius agreed with most of what Galen
wrote. Not until centuries after Shakespeare's death were Galen's errors
rectified entirely. *See also* Bleeding; Disease and Injury; Humors; Medical
Practitioners.

Angel

The angel (*CE* IV.iii.39; *1H4* IV.ii.6; *MV* II.vii.55–57; *MWW* I.iii.51–52)
was a gold coin, first issued by Edward IV in the 1460s and worth 6s 8d,
making it one-half of a mark and one-third of a pound sterling. The dominant gold coin for several decades, it had a portrait on the obverse of the
Archangel Michael, standing on and spearing to death an open-mouthed

The gold angel of 1558–1603 [1 3/16"/3 cm]. Obverse: ELIZABETH D G ANG FRA
ET HIB REGINA. Reverse: A DNO FACTVM EST ISTUD ET EST MIRABI. This specimen is
possibly from 1582. © 2002 The American Numismatic Society. All rights reserved.

dragon. The angel was haloed and winged, and in later versions his garb
was refined so that he was wearing chain-mail hose and a doublet or muscle
cuirass with feathers showing at the shoulders and hips. The legend around

the rim gave the king's name and the lands to which he laid claim; in the case of Henry VI, who continued to mint angels during his brief restoration in 1470–71, it was some variant of "HENRICVS DI GRA REX ANGL Z FRANC," a series of Latin abbreviations that meant "Henry (Henricus), by the grace of God (dei gratia), king (rex) of England (Anglie) and (et, sometimes written out, sometimes represented by a Z) France (Francie)."

The reverse of the coin showed a ship with the royal arms (quartered with the English lions and the French fleur-de-lis) and a large cross in place of the central mast. On either side of the cross was a small device reminding the participants in a financial transaction of the king's identity; frequently this was a royal rose on one side and the monarch's initial on the other. In the case of young Edward V, removed to the Tower and replaced on the throne by his uncle Richard III, his "E" on the reverse of the angel was sometimes simply overstamped with an "R." Around the ship ran the legend "PER CRVCEM TVAM SALVA NOS XRISTE REDEMPTOR": "Save us, Christ our Redeemer, by your cross."

Henry VII improved the art and engraving of the angel somewhat, but except for these and the minor name-and-device changes of each succeeding monarch, the coin remained essentially the same until the reign of Henry VIII, who added HIBERNIA (Ireland) to the list of countries under his sway and determined in 1526 that the coin, without any increase in weight, would be worth 7s 6d. In 1544 the currency was again devalued, with the angel's value being set at 8s. Edward VI improved the innate worth of the currency and at the same time reset the angel's value at 10s, where it remained throughout Shakespeare's life. Half-angels of 5s existed, looking very much like their larger cousins, and Elizabeth followed her father's example by minting a quarter-angel after 1561, a 2s 6d coin so tiny that the claim to Ireland had to continue onto the reverse of the coin. Beginning in Mary I's reign, the motto on the reverse was changed to "A DOMINO FACTVM EST ISTUD ET EST MIRABILE IN OCULIS NOSTRIS"— "This is the Lord's doing, and it is marvelous in our eyes"—and this legend, in variously abbreviated forms, was retained during the reign of Elizabeth I.

By James I's time, the angel was relatively uncommon, but it was still minted, and toward the end of Shakespeare's writing career, its reverse was redesigned. The ship was made more modern, with gun ports and three massive masts. The royal arms were moved from a shield to the ship's sails, and the shield and cross were eliminated.

Animals

Shakespeare lived at a time when it was possible to walk from the center of London to farms and fields, when the vast majority of people in England were engaged in farm work of some kind, and when even those who did not live or work on farms knew the birds and animals of England, either from having seen them or from having eaten them. Since there was interest in the people and geography of faraway lands, there was also interest in the animal life of those places, and even animals not native to England were commonly discussed and popularly believed to have certain qualities. Just as any schoolchild today knows that lionesses do most of the pride's hunting or that whales are mammals, so the people of Shakespearean England knew the habits and properties—or the ostensible and sometimes incorrectly attributed habits and properties—of animals they had never seen. Therefore, when Shakespeare spoke of a pelican, a raven, an owl, or a nightingale, it meant something very specific to his audience. Each bird, each animal, had its own symbolism and significance. (As noted in the Introduction, birds are discussed in a separate entry.)

There are dozens of animals mentioned in the plays and poems, so many that a complete catalog of them, their habits and appearance, and their treatment in Renaissance literature would comprise an entire book of its own. Therefore the list here is necessarily brief. The animals are grouped by type, accompanied by brief notes and Shakespearean references. Domestic animals are listed under their own headings (Cattle, Dog, Horse, Sheep) or in the Farming entry.

Amphibians

Amphibians are treated almost universally in Shakespeare as despicable creatures. They are slimy, wet, and cold, associated with the night and with poison. Newts are banished from the vicinty of the Fairy Queen (*MND* II.ii.11–12) and are listed, along with lizards ("wall-newt"), frogs, toads, and tadpoles, as loathsome food that would be eaten only by an itinerant lunatic (*Lear* III.iv.127–28). Similarly, toads and "Eye of newt and toe of frog" are ingredients in the witches' brew of *Macbeth* (IV.i.6, 14), and a pregnant woman who brought forth moneybags instead of a child was said to have had a bizarre craving for "toads carbonadoed" (*WT* IV.iv.265).

Toads in particular are singled out for opprobrium (*TA* IV.ii.67; *T&C* II.iii.158–59; *Lear* V.iii.140) because they were assumed to be venomous (*3H6* II.ii.137–38; *Cym* IV.ii.90; *R2* III.ii.14–15; *Mac* IV.i.6–8) and because they were associated with witchcraft and the devil. Perhaps some people were aware that the skin secretions of toads can contain a hallucinogenic toxin. Some folk beliefs about toads are mentioned by Shakespeare's characters, who "say the lark and loathèd toad change eyes" (*R&J* III.v.31), that toads can "live upon the vapor of a dungeon" (*Oth* III.iii.270), and that a coveted jewel, the toadstone, grows in the toad's head (*AYLI* II.i.13–14). Toadstone was assumed to be proof against poison, and was thus incorporated into magical jewelry by people concerned about assassination.

Fish

When Shakespeare refers to fish, he seldom uses individual species as metaphors. Since fish lived most of their lives out of human sight, it was hard to compare their feeding techniques, for example, to human behavior, and there were few omens or legends associated with fish that made their way into the plays. When fish appear, it is usually in their contact with humans—that is, being caught and eaten. This leaves us with a few references to specific types of fish, most of which concern the appearance of the fish, but some of which concern behavior.

Fish	Citations	Notes
Carp	*AW* V.ii.19–22	As living in a fishpond.
Dogfish	*1H6* I.iv.107	Schooling shark found near shore, where it devours large numbers of fish; used here as an insulting term for the French Dauphin (Dolphin).

The dogfish, from Konrad Gesner's *Icones Animalium Aquatilum in Mari* (1560). Reproduced from the Collections of the Library of Congress.

Fish	Citations	Notes
Eel	*LLL* I.ii.26–28 *TS* IV.iii.175 *2H4* II.iv.54 *Per* IV.ii.144–45	Mentioned with unusual frequency, probably because it was common, much hunted, and prized as a delicacy. It is noted in Shakespeare for its quickness, thinness, and supposed tendency to be awakened by thunder.
Gudgeon	*MV* I.i.102	Proverbially stupid. A song by Thomas Campion, written in 1617, says it is the only fish foolish enough to be caught by an unbaited bent pin.
Loach	*1H4* II.i.22	Noted for its rapid rate of reproduction.
Minnow	*LLL* I.i.246 *Cor* III.i.89 *TNK* II.i.4–5	Small and insignificant.
Pike	*2H4* III.ii.335 *MWW* I.i.15–21	Popular legend said that if a pike was caught, slit down the belly, and then tossed back into the water, it would be tended and ultimately healed by the tench. The pike was a ravenous eater that had different names depending on the stage of its growth. It began as a fry, then was called a gilthead, a pod, a jack, a pickerel, a pike, and finally a luce.
Shark	*Mac* IV.i.24	Ocean-dwelling; one of the foul creatures incorporated in the witches' brew.
Tench	*1H4* II.i.14–16	Marked with small red spots, as if flea-bitten.

Insects and Other Small Creatures

Unlike fish, insects, worms, and arachnids could be observed on a daily basis. Some were perceived as pests, but others, like ants and bees, provided models of industry. The most irritating of these small creatures were not the bugs that ate the crops but the fleas and lice that lived on human bodies.

Creature	Citations	Notes
Ant	*1H4* I.iii.238 *Lear* II.iii.66–67	Industrious, as in Aesop's fable of the ant and the grasshopper; stinging. Ants are sometimes called "pismires."
Beetle	*Mac* III.ii.40–43 *MND* II.ii.72 *MM* III.i.78 *Lear* IV.vi.13–15 *A&C* III.ii.20 *Cym* III.iii.20	Lowly, black, small, and loathsome.

Creature	Citations	Notes
Breese	*T&C* I.iii.48 *A&C* III.x.14	Gadfly or horsefly, a pest that stings cattle.
Butterfly	*MND* III.i.172 *Cor* IV.vi.95 *Cor* V.iv.12 *Lear* V.iii.13	Shakespeare mentions its bright colors, its metamorphosis from a "grub"-like form, and the tiny scales on its wings, which he describes as "mealy," meaning powdery (*T&C* III.iii.78–79).
Caterpillar	*2H6* IV.iv.37 *2H6* III.i.90 *1H4* II.ii.85 *V&A* 797–98 *Per* V.i.60	Because of its voracious hunger as it prepares for metamorphosis, and the resulting damage that it does to plants, a symbol for rich parasites who take all the wealth for themselves without doing any useful work.
Cricket	*Mac* II.ii.15 *Cym* II.ii.11 *TS* IV.iii.110 *1H4* II.iv.91 *R&J* I.iv.63 *Per* III.Cho.2–7 *WT* II.i.31	Nocturnal; its chirping is either "merry" or noisy, depending on the speaker's mood.
Fly	*1H6* IV.vii.76 *3H6* II.vi.16 *LLL* V.ii.409–10 *Lear* IV.vi.111–13 *Oth* II.i.166–67 *Oth* IV.ii.65–66 *A&C* V.ii.59–60 *Temp* III.i.62–63 *Ham* IV.iii.23	Associated with death for its breeding habits. It lays its eggs on carrion, an action known as "blowing," and the eggs quickly hatch into maggots. In some cases, they reproduced so rapidly that flies were said to be born pregnant. Flies are also mentioned as the prey of spiders. Sometimes they are called "water-flies" or "night-flies"; in the latter instance they are noted as an irritant to the poor, who cannot, like the rich, keep their windows closed and freshen the air with expensive perfumes.
Gnat	*TA* IV.iv.82 *R&J* I.iv.64 *A&C* III.xiii.166 *RL* 1014	Small, buzzing.
Grasshopper	*R&J* I.iv.60	
Grub	*R&J* I.iv.68	Empties nuts.
Ladybird	*R&J* I.iii.3	Ladybug; used as an endearment.
Mites	*AW* I.i.144–46	Here, infesting cheese.
Scorpion	*Mac* III.ii.36 *Cym* V.v.45	Loathsome.
Silkworm	*Lear* III.iv.102–4	One of the rare insects actually cultivated by people. Its cocoon was unwound to yield long strands of silk.

Creature	Citations	Notes
Snail	*LLL* IV.ii.335 *AYLI* IV.i.49–60 *Lear* I.v.27–28 *V&A* 1033–36	Lowly, slow, timid.
Spider	*2H6* III.i.339 *R3* I.iii.241–42 *R&J* I.iv.59, 61 *MND* II.ii.20–21 *T&C* II.iii.15–17 *Oth* II.i.166–67 *R2* III.ii.14–15	Industrious, disgusting, venomous, web-weaving.
Tick	*T&C* III.iii.312–13	On sheep.
Wasp	*2GV* I.ii.106–7 *TA* II.iii.132 *WT* IV.iv.790 *H8* III.ii.55–56	Mentioned for its sting, its nests, and its raids on honeybee hives.
Worm	*R&J* III.i.109 *R&J* V.iii.109 *Ham* IV.iii.20 *Tim* IV.iii.182–83 *1H6* III.i.72 *R3* I.iii.221 *R3* IV.iv.386 *LLL* IV.iii.151 *TS* V.ii.171 *MND* II.ii.23 *R&J* I.i.154–55 *R&J* I.iv.65–66 *Cym* III.iv.35	Not the benign garden earthworm, but almost always the worms and maggots found in corpses, and thus a symbol of death. Sometimes a serpent or any low creature. Worms were said to grow in the fingertips of idle maidservants. Certain specific kinds of worms are mentioned, including the canker worm, which ate flowers (*1H6* II.iv.68, 71). The maltworm, not really a worm at all but a weevil that could infest malt, was also a name for a person who drank too much (*1H4* II.i.77; *2H4* II.iv.340). The glowworm was not a worm but a luminous insect larva (*MND* III.i.170; *MWW* V.v.80; *Per* II.iii.44–45).

Mammals

Renaissance people had no concept of an environmental movement, and animals were not usually admired for their virtues but feared, reviled, and likened to the worst aspects of human character. The wilderness and its creatures—apes, bears, wolves, and hyenas—were to be conquered or extinguished, not preserved. Accordingly, most of Shakespeare's mammals are emblems of fierceness or of the animal kingdom's intellectual inferiority to humankind. A notable exception is the lion which, as the "king of beasts," was deemed braver and more laudable than all other mammals. Oddly, the animals most closely related to humans, and those with the greatest intellects, such as monkeys and apes, are frequently used as symbols of idiocy, wickedness, incompetence, or ridiculousness.

Mammal	Citations	Notes
Ape	*R3* III.i.130–31 *LLL* III.i.84, 88, 94 *LLL* IV.ii.128 *1H4* II.iii.79 *2H4* II.iv.219 *R&J* II.i.16 *H5* V.ii.144 *JC* V.i.41 *MM* II.ii.121–22 *Temp* II.ii.8–10 *Temp* IV.i.248–49 *Ham* IV.ii.18–20 *Cym* I.vi.39–41	Small, chattering, antic to the point of madness, idle, imitative, nimble, foolish. Shakespeare may have seen a performing ape somewhere, for he mentions tricks like playing dead or riding a horse and certain characteristic behavior like the baring of teeth. Old maids were said to lead troops of apes in hell. Apes were sometimes called "jackanapes." The ape was sometimes a symbol of well intentioned but incompetent parenting, for it was said to love its offspring dearly and to embrace them so hard at times that it accidentally squeezed them to death. Edward Topsell called them "much given to imitation and derision, . . . wicked crafts, deceipts, impostures, and flatteries."
Baboon	*2H4* II.iv.245 *AYLI* II.v.25 *MWW* II.ii.7–8 *Oth* I.iii.311	Lowly; sometimes called "dog-ape." A "baboon's blood" is one of the disgusting elements of the witches' brew in *Macbeth* (IV.i.37). According to Topsell, "They are evill manered and natured, wherfor also they are picturd to signifie wrath, they are so unapeasable."
Badger	*TN* II.v.102	The badger could also be called a brock or a gray. It dug dens and was a fierce fighter. Topsell noted that it rolled onto its back to fight.
Bat	*MND* II.ii.4 *Temp* I.ii.342 *Temp* V.i.91 *Ham* III.iv.191 *Mac* III.ii.40–43 *Mac* IV.i.15	Frightening, symbolic of night. Sometimes called "reremice."
Bear	*Mac* III.iv.100–101 *MWW* I.i.274–86 *CE* III.ii.155 *3H6* II.i.15–17 *3H6* II.ii.13 *TA* IV.i.96 *1H4* I.ii.73–74 *MND* II.ii.94–95 *John* II.i.249 *T&C* I.ii.20–21 *Lear* II.iii.7–8 *WT* II.iii.186–88	Fierce, ill-tempered. The bear was the emblem of Richard Neville, Earl of Warwick, who featured so prominently as a kingmaker in the Wars of the Roses (*2H6* V.i.144–53, 203, 208–10, V.ii.; *3H6* V.vii.10). Bears were known to be especially aggressive in defense of their cubs. Bearbaiting was a popular sport in which a bear was tied to a stake and beset by packs of dogs. Topsell wrote, "Great is the fiercenes of a beare. . . . a shee beare is more couragious then a male."

Mammal	Citations	Notes
Boar	*TS* I.ii.201 *TA* IV.ii.138 *Tim* V.i.165–66 *2H4* II.ii.145 *Cym* II.v.16 *MND* II.ii.31 *Lear* III.vii.60 *V&A* 1105	Fierce; one of the most dangerous animals to hunt because of its effective use of its long tusks; the emblem of Richard III (*R3* III.ii.11, 28–29, 33, 72–73, 81, IV.v.2, V.ii.7–11, V.iii.157).
Camel	*T&C* I.ii.255–56 *T&C* II.i.54 *Cor* II.i.254–56 *Ham* III.ii.385–86	This is, at least in Shakespeare's usage, a domestic animal, a beast of burden. Topsell noted that it could go for three to four days without water.
Cony	*3H6* I.iv.62 *TS* IV.i.39 *TS* V.i.97 *AYLI* III.ii.338–39 *MWW* I.i.119 *Cor* IV.v.222–23	Rabbit; "cony-catching" was slang for tricking fools. William Harrison thought the warrens of England too numerous to count, and noted that conies were prized both for their meat and for their fur; black rabbit fur, he said, was more desirable than gray.
Dolphin	*1H6* I.iv.107 *1H6* I.vi.12 *2H6* IV.vii.30 *MND* II.i.150 *AW* II.iii.26 *A&C* V.ii.88–90	Lively; associated with mermaids and with the French Dauphin, whose title sounded similar. Stories of dolphins helping shipwrecked sailors, including the mythological Arion, were well known. The dolphin was also supposed to help sailors by wrapping itself around their anchors to help the anchors catch fast in the ocean bottom. The combination of dolphin and anchor, then, was a symbol of care—particularly a ruler's care—for humanity.
Dormouse	*TN* III.ii.19–20	A small, squirrel-like animal.
Elephant	*JC* II.i.205 *T&C* I.ii.20–21 *T&C* II.iii.2, 105–6	Seldom mentioned in Shakespeare, and without any consistent symbolic significance. It is represented as slow, susceptible to pitfall traps, and (mistakenly) as unable to bow or kneel. Topsell called it a "great and ample demonstration of the power and wisdome of almighty God," for it was "like a living Mountain in quantity & outward appearance," yet "serviceable and tractable."
Ferret	*JC* I.ii.186	Topsell noted that ferrets, like mice, could squeeze into extremely tiny holes. He said that the ferret's eyes were "small, but fiery, like red hot yron, and therefore she seeth most clearly in the darke: Her voice is a whyning cry."

The fitch or polecat, from Edward Topsell's *Historie of Foure-Footed Beastes*. Reproduced from the Collections of the Library of Congress.

Mammal	Citations	Notes
Fitchew	*Lear* IV.vi.122 *T&C* V.i.61–64 *Oth* IV.i.145	A wild, ferretlike creature, a polecat. It preyed on poultry and was therefore despised. It also had a strong smell.
Fox	*2H6* III.i.55, 253–59 *3H6* IV.vii.25 *2GV* IV.iv.92 *MND* V.i.230 *1H4* III.iii.119–20 *1H4* V.ii.9–11 *T&C* V.iv.11 *Lear* III.iv.92 *Cor* IV.ii.18	Clever, stealthy, deceptive, and not particularly brave. It was hunted because it frequently stole domestic fowl. Like the rooster, which was widely known as "Chanticleer," the fox had a nickname: Reynard.
Hare	*TN* III.iv.389–90 *3H6* II.v.130 *1H4* I.ii.78 *John* II.i.137–38 *Cym* IV.iv.36–37	Timid, melancholy. The hare was one of the forms that witches were believed to take when they changed into animals. Many people sustained a medieval belief that the hare was hermaphroditic or could change sex from year to year. It was also noted by hunters of the hare, as they butchered their kills, that the hare could conceive a second or even a third litter before the first was born, and a female hare's belly might yield fetuses in two or three stages of development. The hare was also associated with madness, for during the spring rut, it capers and appears careless of its safety—hence the phrase, famously adapted by Lewis Carroll, "mad as a March hare."

Mammal	Citations	Notes
Hedgehog	*R3* I.ii.102 *TA* II.iii.101 *MND* II.ii.10 *Temp* I.ii.328 *Temp* II.ii.8–14 *Mac* IV.i.2	Foul; sometimes called "hedge-pig" or "urchin." Claude Paradin, in his book of emblems, shows a picture of a hedgehog with bits of food stuck to its spines and relates a belief that the animal collected sustenance on the spines to carry back to its den. It was thus, to Paradin at least, a symbol of diligence. Topsell notes that parts of the hedgehog could be used in various medicines.
Hyen	*AYLI* IV.i.151–52	Laughing hyena.
Leopard	*1H6* I.v.31 *R2* I.i.174–75 *Temp* IV.i.261 *MND* II.ii.31 *AYLI* II.vii.148–52 *Tim* IV.iii.339–42	Spotted, with a tuft of longer hair at the bottom of its mouth; sometimes called "pard."
Leviathan	*2GV* III.ii.79–80 *MND* II.i.174 *H5* III.iii.26	A large marine animal, probably a whale.
Lion	*1H6* I.v.28, 29 *3H6* II.ii.11 *TA* IV.ii.138 *TS* I.ii.199 *2GV* II.i.29 *Lear* III.iv.93 *R2* II.i.173 *R2* V.i.34–35 *MND* I.ii.65–83 *H5* III.vii.147–48 *JC* I.iii.20–22 *JC* II.i.206 *AYLI* IV.iii.113–17 *T&C* I.ii.20–21 *Cym* V.iii.38–39 *Temp* II.i.319–20	The lion had tremendous symbolic significance, partly because it was thought to be the king of beasts, the pinnacle of animal creation, and partly because it was one of the symbols of England itself. Lions were brave, loud, proud, and deadly, which made them highly admirable in Renaissance eyes. Thus they appeared often not only in the royal coat of arms, but also in heraldry in general. The lion could be hunted and caught, but only with great difficulty, and it was valiant to the point of death. It also showed a royal demeanor in other ways, scorning carrion and, supposedly, refusing to harm human kings out of professional courtesy. A lion was banned from the baptismal revels for James I's oldest son, Henry, on the grounds that its appearance would frighten the ladies.
Marmoset	*Temp* II.ii.169–74	Today, a specific kind of clawed monkey of South or Central America; in the Renaissance, any small monkey.
Mole	*3H6* II.v.14 *Cor* V.iii.30 *Per* I.i.101–3 *WT* IV.iv.840–41 *Temp* IV.i.194	A small, sightless, burrowing mammal that leaves evidence of its presence by casting up small mounds, or molehills, at the entrances to its tunnels.

Mammal	Citations	Notes
Monkey	*2H4* III.ii.319 *AYLI* IV.i.148–49 *Oth* III.iii.400–401 *Lear* II.iii.7–9 *Temp* III.ii.47	Lewd, silly; tame ones led by a leash and halter around their hips.
Mouse	*LLL* V.ii.19 *2H4* III.ii.163 *Per* III.Cho.6	Small, timid, hunted by cats.
Otter	*1H4* III.iii.134	Obviously an animal that defied Renaissance classification, for Shakespeare describes it here as "neither fish nor flesh." The otter was the aquatic counterpart of the fox, stealing fish rather than fowl, and was widely hunted.

The ounce, according to Topsell. Reproduced from the Collections of the Library of Congress.

Mammal	Citations	Notes
Ounce	*MND* II.ii.30	Lynx or leopard.
Panther	*TA* I.i.495 *TA* II.ii.21	A game animal.
Polecat	*MWW* IV.i.26	A small, brown, strong-smelling predator like a ferret; its name was slang for prostitute or pimp, according to Topsell, because of its "strong stinking savour."
Porcupine	*2H6* III.i.362–63 *T&C* II.i.25	Also spelled "porpentine." It was believed to be able to throw its quills at predators.
Porpoise	*Per* II.i.25–27	Nimble; "half fish, half flesh." On his visit in 1592, Frederick, Duke of Württemberg, was told that their appearance near a boat foretold stormy weather.

Mammal	Citations	Notes
Rabbit	*1H4* II.iv.442	See "Hare," above.
Rat	*R&J* III.i.101–2 *Ham* III.iv.25 *Cor* I.i.164, 251–52 *MM* I.ii.132	A grain-eating pest. Much effort was expended to catch and kill rats or to poison them.
Rhinoceros	*Mac* III.iv.100–101	Fierce; armored.
Squirrel	*R&J* I.iv.68	Emptying nuts.
Tiger	*2GV* III.ii.79 *R&J* V.iii.38–39 *Mac* III.iv.100–101	Fierce.
Weasel	*1H4* II.iii.79–80 *H5* I.ii.169–73 *AYLI* II.v.12 *RL* 307	Capricious, egg-eating, kept by the Romans as mousers. Topsell repeated a belief of English hunters that if they saw a weasel in the morning upon setting out, they would catch no game that day.
Whale	*2H4* IV.iv.40–41 *TC* V.v.22–23 *AW* IV.iii.225–26 *Per* II.i.29–37	Ravenous; helpless when beached.
Wildcat	*TS* I.ii.195 *TS* II.i.270 *MV* II.v.46–47 *MWW* II.ii.25	Nocturnal; also called a "cat-a-mountain."
Wolf	*CE* IV.ii.36 *3H6* II.iv.13 *2H4* IV.v.136–37 *MV* IV.i.128–38 *AYLI* V.ii.108–9 *Lear* III.vi.18	Predatory, savage. There are references to the fable by Aesop about a wolf who fools a flock by dressing in "sheep's clothing" (*1H6* I.iii.55; *2H6* III.i.77). Wolves had been much feared and even hanged as murderers if they killed humans. However, by Shakespeare's time they were extinct in England.

Reptiles

Reptiles were considered an even lowlier form of life than mammals and birds, perhaps because they were literally lower to the ground. Birds and even some insects were capable of flight and thus possessed a power that humans did not; mammals were sometimes superior to humans in strength or armament. However, reptiles were mostly despised and associated with darkness, cold, and poison.

Reptile	Citations	Notes
Adder	*Ham* III.iv.204 *Mac* IV.i.16 *Tim* IV.iii.182 *TA* II.iii.34–35 *JC* II.i.14 *Cym* IV.ii.90 *Temp* II.ii.13–14 *RL* 871–72	Fanged, poisonous, diurnal, forked-tongued, bird-eating snake. The European variety is about three feet long as an adult, with a gray and black body and a bite that is venomous but rarely fatal. It, like the cobra, coral snake, and black mamba, is a kind of viper. William Harrison noted that it cast its old skin in April or May and that its poison could be counteracted with dragonwort or other medicines.
Asp	*Oth* III.iii.447 *A&C* V.ii.243 *A&C* V.ii.350–52	Poisonous snake.

Topsell's illustration of the slowworm or blindworm. Reproduced from the Collections of the Library of Congress.

Reptile	Citations	Notes
Blindworm	*MND* II.ii.11–12 *Mac* IV.i.16	A legless lizard. Harrison says it is poisonous, striped, about a foot long, and commonly found under logs. Topsell says it is blue with some blackish spots at the sides, smooth, scaleless, cloven-tongued, about nine inches long, and a finger-breadth wide, with a tapering tail. He says that the bite is posionous and that the victim of such a bite should pierce the area with a brass bodkin and apply fuller's earth and vinegar.
Chameleon	*2GV* II.iv.26 *3H6* III.ii.191 *Ham* III.ii.93–94	Color-changing. Andrea Alciato's book of emblems repeats the belief that this lizard ate air. Because it can imitate any colors but white or red, says Alciato, it is also a symbol of the flatterer, who can counterfeit anything but true purity or courage.

Reptile	Citations	Notes
Crocodile	*2H6* III.i.226–27 *Ham* V.i.276 *Oth* IV.i.222	Sheds false tears. Myths about its method of reproduction are repeated in *Antony and Cleopatra* (II.vii.27–28, 42). It was a symbol not only of hypocrisy but also of Egypt.
Lizard	*2H6* III.ii.325 *3H6* II.ii.137–38 *Mac* IV.i.17 *T&C* V.i.61–64	Reputed to have a stinger; Edgar calls a lizard a "wall-newt" (*Lear* III.iv.128).
Serpent	*3H6* II.ii.15 *R2* V.iii.57 *MND* II.i.255 *MAAN* V.i.90 *JC* II.i.32–34 *Per* I.i.133–34 *R&J* III.ii.73 *T&C* V.i.93	Dangerous, poisonous, born from eggs, and shedding skin periodically. Synonymous with "snake."
Snake	*LLL* V.i.131–36 *R2* II.i.157 *MND* II.ii.9 *AYLI* IV.iii.69 *R2* III.ii.131	The snake had a powerful presence in myths and legends. Aside from its prominent role in the story of Adam and Eve, it was the monster sent to kill the baby Hercules in his crib and the animal driven from Ireland by Saint Patrick. Another popular tale described how a person took pity on a snake dying of cold and was surprised when the warmed snake, far from grateful, administered a fatal bite. Asked why it would do such a horrid thing, the snake replied that it was only following its nature.
Tortoise	*Temp* I.ii.318	Slow.
Viper	*T&C* III.i.130–31 *Oth* V.ii.284	Poisonous snake.

See also Bees; Birds; Cattle; Deer; Dog; Falconry and Fowling; Farming; Fishing; Food; Horse; Hunting; Hygiene, Sheep.

Archery
See Bow.

Architecture
All over England, the late sixteenth century seemed to be a time of building, rebuilding, remodeling, and adding on (*2H4* I.iii.41–48). In a strip of the country running northward from Dorset to Derbyshire, stone was the preferred material. In the east, where stone was scarce, there were new

brick manor houses. In the Midlands and the counties bordering Wales, timber framing dominated. And in certain areas, especially in Buckinghamshire, Devonshire, Northamptonshire, Lincolnshire, Warwickshire, and Cumberland, houses were built of the unbaked earth called cob or wichert. Across the country, skilled architects, masons (*Ham* V.i.42), and bricklayers traveled from one site to another, setting up kilns and tools and crews of laborers to build mansions (*R&J* III.iii.108), palaces, and substantial but less elaborate homes. And, even in relatively humble cottages (*2H6* IV.ii.123; *AYLI* III.v.107; *MV* I.ii.14), two small but important revolutions were taking place: the addition of brick chimneys and the replacement of lattices and translucent windows by clear glass.

There were also some new developments in the style and arrangement of houses, though these were not as significant as those which would take place later in the seventeenth century. Timber framing had been around for centuries, and though in certain places it grew more exuberant under Elizabeth I and James I, it was more a continuation of an existing style than the importation or development of a new one. Some homes were built in a Gothic style, some with classical elements, others—only a few, and those late in Shakespeare's career—with Italianate touches. A more widespread style, for those who could afford it, was the inclusion of symbolic "devices," such as a motto, a building shape, a decorative window, or a garden design that reinforced a common theme, such as the Holy Trinity or the initials of the owner. Many design changes affected the interior of the house and will be discussed below, but others were visible from the outside, such as the addition of dormer windows or local variations in window type or chimney placement.

Construction Materials and Methods

Timber

A variety of building materials were used in the late sixteenth and early seventeenth centuries, but the standard type of construction, and the one still associated in most people's minds with the period, was a frame of timber infilled with wattle and daub (*Lear* II.ii.67–69) or similar materials. For these buildings, oak was the preferred wood, though sometimes cheaper and less durable woods were used if the cost of oak proved prohibitive. The trunks were halved or quartered and used "green," or unseasoned. As they dried, they sometimes warped or shrank, giving these buildings the haphazard and sometimes slanted look they occasionally bear today. Carpenters (*1H6* V.iii.90; *MAAN* I.i.181; *JC* I.i.7) knew about this potential disadvantage, but green wood was easier to work, and hardened as it dried. Timbers were obtained from carpenters' yards or from growing trees; a skilled carpenter could look at a living oak and tell, from how it bent and where its branches were, for what part of the house it would be most useful.

Bent trunks were particularly useful for cruck-built houses, in which the wall and roof were supported by pairs of massive, naturally angled timbers, charred at the bottoms against rot and driven about a foot into the ground, then fastened together at the top. Later, as the technique developed, a base of wood and stone replaced the practice of driving the crucks into the earth. For better symmetry, the crucks, or blades, were sometimes made of two halves of the same tree. The rest of the roof and a false exterior wall were built on and around two or more pairs of crucks, the roof being supported partly by the crucks and partly by a ridgepole running the length of the house along the top of the roof and lower parallel poles called purlins.

Another method of timber framing was post-and-truss construction, which closely resembles the timber framing of today. Vertical timbers supported either roof trusses or the floor beams of a second story, and so on upward until the house was complete. The roof trusses were triangular arrangements of beams, placed at intervals and joined horizontally by beams that, like their cruck-built house counterparts, were called purlins. Often the upper stories were jettied, which meant that they jutted out and overshadowed the ground floor in front. This became common in most parts of the country that used timber framing and was standard practice in towns, enabling citizens to chat face-to-face from their second- or third-story windows. The upper stories might be further extended by penthouses (*MV* II.vi.1; *MAAN* III.iii.102–3; *LLL* III.i.17), porches (*MWW* I.iv.59) with angled roofs.

When the owners could afford to, they built close-studded houses, with the vertical timbers as little as 6 to 9 inches (15.2 to 22.9 cm) apart. The norm was thin rectangular stripes between the timbers, but some houses were more decorative, with nonstructural timbers added in the infilled spaces to form diamonds, crosses, circles, trefoils, stars, quatrefoils, and other patterns. Frequently parts of the timbers, especially the supports of the jettied second story, were ornately carved.

The spaces between the timbers were filled with wattle and daub. The wattle was an arrangement of willow, hazel, or ash twigs; the daub, a kind of mud made of clay, chopped straw, and perhaps a little animal hair or dung. From the fifteenth to the nineteenth centuries, the wattle was gradually replaced by lath, long flat strips of oak or beech slotted horizontally into grooves in the timbers and sometimes woven through uprights of chestnut or oak, then fixed in place with nails and covered inside and out with daub.

In the case of either wattle or lath, once the stick filling was coated with daub and dried, the daub was painted with plaster (*2H6* IV.ii.131)—white

Close-studded timber-framed house.

for the more prosperous, yellow or dark red for the poorer. The red and yellow plasters were made of earth ochre, and the white, of lime or chalk, with perhaps some chopped straw, hay, animal hair, feathers, manure, or powdered tile. It was usually just painted on, though in some cases it was spread and then decorated with pargeting—raised designs, or incised designs drawn with a stick or fan of sticks. William Harrison adored plaster, "which beside the delectable whiteness of the stuff itself is laid on so even and smoothly as nothing in my judgment can be done with more exactness." As the wood of the house dried, spaces opened between the daub and the timbers, and the holes had to be filled periodically to prevent drafts.

There were some variations on the timber-framed house. The spaces between the timbers were occasionally filled with materials other than wattle or lath and daub. Clay lump, a mixture somewhat like daub but thicker, might be used without wood supports; or flint, chalk, or brick might be set between the timbers. Sometimes wooden weatherboarding (overlapping siding) was nailed over the timbers; this was being used on barns and other farm buildings by 1600, though it was seldom used on houses.

Stone

Several varieties of stone were used for the construction of churches and of finer homes. Usually, it was whatever stone was most plentiful locally; only very rich people imported stone from other areas, and then they used it as an exterior dressing over native materials or locally fired brick. The easiest material to find was rubble, stone that cropped out of the earth without having to be quarried. It was sometimes squared off, but otherwise undressed, and might be laid randomly as the shape of the stones dictated, or arranged in courses (horizontal rows) 2 to 9 inches (5.1 to 22.9 cm) thick. Though stone walls for dividing fields might be simply heaped together without any material to fix the rocks, stone walls for houses were usually joined with mortar made of lime derived from the burning of chalk in special kilns (*MWW* III.iii.76–77; *T&C* V.i.22). The lime was slaked—crumbled and moistened—and mixed with coarse sand. It set more slowly than modern mortar and was somewhat less resistant to weather.

Ashlar, unlike rubble, is cut and smoothed "freestone" (*AYLI* IV.iii.26)—fine-grained and homogeneous stone that can be cut in any direction—whose name was the origin of the term "freemasons." (Stone that could not be cut freely was generally called ragstone.) The stone was quarried by stonecutters (*Lear* II.ii.60) and then shaped on the building site by masons. These craftsmen had to be able to cut stone with a saw or with a mallet and chisel, to shape blocks and set them in level courses with a minimum of mortar (*3H6* V.i.84), to use ashlar as a facing for rubble or brick, to carve stone dressings and perhaps some ornamental pieces, and perhaps to lay out a building site or to work in plaster. Dressings included door and window moldings, tracery (the ribwork on Gothic windows and ceiling vaults), dripstones (moldings designed to divert rain away from a door or window), stringcourses (horizontal rows of stones distinguished from the other stones by shape or size, or set in a brick wall to interrupt the monotony), roof pinnacles, finials, and battlements (the indented trim at the top of a wall, originally used on castles).

Facing blocks could be made of limestone, sandstone, or, less commonly, granite; dressings were usually made only of sandstone or limestone. Limestone (calcium carbonate) varies in hardness, with chalk being one of its purest and softest forms. Once quarried, it is "green," full of water and dissolved minerals, and it remains soft and easy to carve until the water evaporates. It was therefore important to keep the stone moist and full of this "quarry sap" until the masons had shaped it. Sandstone (quartz in combination with various other minerals, such as mica, feldspar, and silica, with the other minerals determining hardness and color) also varied in hardness. Sandstone came in many hues, from reds, browns, yellows, and pinks, to yellows, grays, bluish grays, purples, and greens. Granite, a combination of feldspar, quartz, and mica, was very hard, which made it durable but very hard to work. It might be red, pink, gray, white, or occasionally greenish, and was used unpolished.

Other building stones included cobbles, slate, and flint. Cobbles were rounded, weathered, glacier-carried irregular lumps collected from streamsbeds or fields. They could be used, with a great deal of mortar to fill in the spaces between the round edges, to build walls, and to pave the streets of towns. Slate, a metamorphic rock formed from clay or shale, was used less in walls than in window dressings, floors, and roofs. Flint, a very pure form of silica or quartz, is tremendously hard (*2H4* IV.iv.33; *TN* I.v.284; *R2* V.i.3; *R&J* II.vi.16–17). It occurs in the same places that chalk does, as black, roundish, irregular nodules covered with a white rind from the surrounding chalk. The flints were small, usually 2 to 5 inches (5.1 to 12.7 cm) across at their widest point, and their size and rounded, uneven shape meant that they had to be fixed together with plenty of mortar. If a flint wall were built too high too fast, the entire structure would sag, seep, and collapse, so no more than 12 feet (3.66 m) could be built at once; no more could be added until the mortar had completely dried. Because flint was so hard, it was seldom shaped or cut.

Brick

It was brick, not stone, that eventually replaced the timber-framed, wattle-and-daub building, not only because of the increasing scarcity and price of timber, but also because of the reduced fire danger posed by brick.

However, in Shakespeare's day brick was still too expensive to be used in middle-class homes, let alone cottages. It was used mostly in mansions and in chimneys. For walls, the bricks were set in courses, primarily in one of three patterns or "bonds": English, Flemish, or breaking joint. The English bond had a row of stretchers (bricks placed lengthwise) topped by a row of headers (bricks placed with the ends facing out), alternating courses of stretchers and headers all the way up the wall. The Flemish bond alternated headers and stretchers, too, but did so in the same course. Breaking joint simply meant a pattern in which each brick was offset by half the length of the ones above and below it. Sometimes design elements such as diamonds, checkers, and so on, were incorporated into the brickwork by burning the ends of certain bricks to make them darker. Because of the irregularity of early bricks, all of these patterns were set between thick layers of mortar, usually measuring ½ to 1 inch (1.3 to 2.5 cm) thick. By the end of James I's reign, brick regularity was increasing and mortar-course width decreasing.

For most people, the only bricks in their houses were in the chimneys (*2H6* IV.ii.147; *1H4* Ii.i.20–22; *MWW* IV.ii.50–53, V.v.45–46; *AYLI* IV.i.157–60; *Mac* II.iii.55; *Cym* II.iv.80–82). Prior to the Tudor period, fire ventilation, if there was any, was often through a hole in the roof or through a tube of unfired clay.

Tudor-era brick chimneys, Herefordshire.

Houses built in this way were "smoky cribs" (*2H4* III.i.9) indeed. Brick chimneys, built into new houses and added to old, improved ventilation, reduced the number of chimney fires, and looked splendid. They were often built in clusters and designed as octagonal, hexagonal, round, fluted, or spiraling pillars, with shaped bricks or combinations of colors creating patterns in the sides. Most also had a cap or ring near the top, called the necking, which also could be quite ornamental.

Cob

Cob and similar materials, such as pisé and clay lump, are building materials of earth that, unlike clay, were never fired in a kiln. These materials were all widely used; Sir Walter Raleigh was born in a cob house. Cob was a mixture of chalky clay, chopped straw, gravel, and sand; in Cornwall it was called "clob" and was made of one part shilf (small pieces of slate), two parts mud, and two parts straw. Wichert was a mixture, specific to

Cob house with a thatched roof.

part of Buckinghamshire, composed of the local chalky soil, straw, and water. Both it and cob were trodden by animals or men to blend it fully, then shaped atop a stone plinth (to keep the bottom from becoming wet), layer by layer, in walls 2 to 4 feet (.62 to 1.22 m) thick. Each layer, about a foot tall, was stamped down by a worker atop the wall, then covered with straw and left to dry before the next layer could be added. The process was extremely time-consuming; a two-story house typically took two years to complete.

At the end of construction, the house was roofed and any stray straw ends trimed off. It was then whitewashed (painted with a thin mixture of lime and water) or plastered. In many cases, a mixture called roughcast was used to coat the house. The walls were spread thickly with wet lime and sand, and against this moist backing, a damp combination of lime and gravel was thrown (*MND* III.i.66–68, V.i.131, 161–66).

Pisé, unlike cob or wichert, was a nearly dry mixture of earth and gravel rammed between boards. Clay lump differed from the others in being shaped ahead of time, in molds, rather than on the building itself. The rectangular blocks, air-dried and then assembled on site, offered the advantage that more layers could be built at once without the long drying times required by cob.

Windows

Windows (*2GV* III.i.113; *TS* V.i.54; *R&J* I.i.142; *MAAN* II.iii.2–3; *JC* I.ii.314) are frequently mentioned by Shakespeare, much more frequently than most other parts of houses, for they were of great importance in his time. Up until the sixteenth century, glass was too expensive to be widely used in windows, and until 1579 glass window panes were so valuable that they were considered property, not part of the house, and bequeathable

Diamond-paned casement windows from a timber-framed building.

separately from it. Windows in the homes of peasants, yeomen, and lesser artisans had previously been (and, in some cases, continued to be) mere wooden lattices (*AW* II.iii.215–16) or shutters (*JC* III.ii.259), strips of oiled linen or varnished parchment, or slices of horn or mica. By 1577, Harrison could write that "horn in windows is now quite laid down in every place, so our lattices are also grown in to less use, because glass is come to be so plentiful and within a very little so good cheap." People tended to start by buying one glass window, then adding others as they could afford them. Towns converted to glass first, followed by the rural areas nearby.

The glass for all these windows was usually produced abroad. It was blown in cylinders that were cut lengthwise, flattened, and cut into diamonds or rectangles. Diamond-shaped panes were more common under Elizabeth, but rectangular ones came into fashion under James. These panes were set in lead rims called cames and mounted in frames called casements (*R2* V.ii.14; *MND* III.i.55–57; *MV* II.v.31–34) that were hinged at the sides of window openings. Sometimes, in more expensive homes, there were bay windows (*TN* IV.ii.37) formed by several windows arranged in a curved or bent line.

Roofs and Floors

There were many kinds of roofing materials available in Shakespeare's lifetime, and each had its own strengths and weaknesses. One of the most common, particularly for humbler homes, was thatch (*MAAN* II.i.91–93; *H5* III.v.24; *Temp* V.i.16–17; *Tim* IV.iii.145–46); bundles of straw, sedges, heather, or reeds that were tied to the roof, covered with more tightly bunched thatch and with wet clay, and usually topped by a single course that curved over the peak of the roof or by two that overlapped each other. Of the various kinds of plants used, rye straw was the most durable. The advantages of thatch were its low cost, easy availability, and light weight, the last of which made it possible to save money on the roof timbers. The disadvantages were its susceptibility to fire and its attractiveness to bees, who sometimes built hives in the straw. It could also be susceptible to moisture and rot if not pitched steeply enough to let water drain off quickly.

Heavier materials included baked clay tiles, overlapped and torched (mortared from below); "stone slates" made not of slate at all but of limestone or sandstone; real slate; and lead. All these materials required large, sturdy roof beams to accommodate their weight, but they had advantages that compensated for this extra expense. Lead (*R3* III.vii.54; *Cor* II.i.213–16), for example, was the only material so waterproof that it could be applied to flat roofs; its enormous cost, however, meant that it was used primarily for churches. Stone slates were made by keeping chunks of stone wet until a hard frost split each piece into thin tiles. Then the tiles were trimmed, pierced at the top with a slater's hammer, and hung with oak pegs, iron nails, or sheep bones from battens nailed to the rafters. Stone slate roofs had to be steeply pitched, and they weighed 1 ton (.9 metric ton) per 100 square feet (9.3 m²). True slate was more fissile (splittable) than either limestone or sandstone, which meant it could be made thinner, and thus lighter, than lead or stone slates. It was also nonporous, quick-drying, and resistant to frost and smoke.

The roof might have several different visible features besides the material of which it was made. There were chimney stacks and, on mansions, per-haps a stair-top cupola, a small windowed "lanthorn" (*R&J* V.iii.84) as a decoration, or a small banqueting house from which to enjoy the views of the countryside. Finials or other stone ornaments might be present, as might a weathervane or "weathercock" (*MAAN* III.i.66, III.iii.129; *MWW* III.ii.16; *2GV* II.i.137; *LLL* IV.i.97). On a church roof, of course, there would be a steeple (*1H4* III.i.32; *Lear* III.ii.3; *Per* II.i.36; *2GV* II.i.137), which was usually the town's most obvious landmark.

Floors were typically made of brick, clay tile, wood, or flagstones (*AW* II.i.33). Few floors, except in the very poorest homes, were of dirt. A few floors were made of burnt gypsum (plaster of paris). Floor coverings, when they were present at all, consisted either of fresh rushes and herbs strewn about (*2H4* V.v; *R&J* I.iv.36; *RL* 318; *Cym* II.ii.13) or of rushes or straw woven into mats. Turkish carpets as floor coverings did exist, and became increasingly popular in the seventeenth century, but this use of carpets was still very rare and limited to the extreme upper class.

Interiors

The inside of the house (*LLL* I.i.108; *TS* II.i.359–61; *MM* II.i.238–40), the number of outbuildings it had, and the purpose to which they were put, depended entirely on the family's income. Peasants' houses might have just one room, with no chimney, one story, a thatched roof and clay walls, and a central open fire or simple hearth (*Cor* IV.v.27). The only outbuilding would be a privy.

One step up from this misery was the two-room house, with the hearth usually offset to create two rooms of different sizes, with the fireplace back forming one wall of the smaller room. In the two-room house, one of the rooms, generally the larger, was used as the living area and kitchen (*MM* II.ii.85), while the other room was a bedroom (*TS* Ind.ii.set; *R3* I.ii.111). The front door (*R&J* IV.i.44; *Oth* I.i.93; *RL* 306) might be divided hor-izontally so that the top could remain open and the bottom hatched, or closed (*John* V.ii.138; *Per* IV.ii.33–34). The door was provided with a bolt or bolts to keep it shut against intruders (*Lear* II.iv.173–74); interior doors, if they needed to be made fast, were provided with locks (*Ham* V.ii.313) instead of bolts.

These humble homes were open to the roof, with no attic, garret (*2H6*

Four-centered arch with wood door banded and studded in iron, on a
brick building with stone dressings.

I.iii.193), or second story. As people rose into the middle class, however,
they wanted a bit more space, and they got it by adding on more rooms,
building a ceiling over the main hall, and moving their beds upstairs and
out of the principal room. In the country, a middle-class farmhouse
(*MWW* II.iii.83) might have a lower floor with a hall, a small lobby, a
kitchen, a pantry (*R&J* I.iii.101–2), and a buttery (*TN* I.iii.67–68). The
buttery had nothing to do with butter; its name came from the butts, or
casks, in which alcoholic beverages were stored, and it served as the liquor
pantry. A postern (*2GV* V.i.9; *MM* IV.ii.91) or back door might lead from
the kitchen to the area where the outbuildings, privies, and dunghills were
located.

A staircase, sometimes spiral, sometimes straight, sometimes dogleg, and
sometimes built at right angles around an open stairwell, led to the second
story. Upstairs, the master's room was located at the top of the staircase,
with children's and servants' rooms beyond it and no corridors; this ensured that inferior members of the family would stay where they were
supposed to at night. Some of these upstairs rooms, though not necessarily
all, had fireplaces that fed into the main chimney or chimneys; other rooms
remained unheated.

Outbuildings might include a brewhouse (*MWW* III.iii.9), a stable (*John*

V.ii.140), a dairy, a slaughterhouse, a barn, and perhaps some separate housing for servants. More extensive farms might also have a bakehouse, a pastryhouse, a laundry, and a larder. Conrad Heresbach's ideal farm contained a fireplace for smoking herring, bacon, and beef; a latticed window to let the bailiff spy on his subordinates; a grain loft ; a fruit loft; and "a vault with three roomes, one serving for Butter and Milke, the other for Beere and Wine, the third for to keepe Flesh in." One particular style of country house, the Wealden house, had a central hall (*R&J* IV.iv.set; *Ham* V.ii.200) with a second story above it, two-story miniature "wings" on either side, with jettied upper stories, deep eaves (*MM* III.ii.175–76) over the central section, and a hipped (sloped inward at the short sides as well as lengthwise) roof.

Middle-class town houses were arranged according to similar principles, with a kitchen, brewhouse, storage rooms, and parlor downstairs, and bedchambers upstairs. However, they were generally narrower and taller than farmhouses, having two, three, or four floors rather than one or two. They might also consist of a shop downstairs (*R&J* V.i.55–56; *LLL* III.i.17–18), where the family plied its trade, and living quarters above. There might be a garden or a courtyard behind the house. Some of these town houses could be quite large, with multiple rear buildings; nearly all were timber framed.

The houses of the rich might have dozens of rooms. The children shared a nursery (*Cym* I.i.58–59), and each adult member of the family had a bedchamber (*2GV* III.i.114–16; *TS* III.ii.112; *R3* I.i.12; *R&J* III.iv.33; *MAAN* III.iii.86–87; *T&C* IV.ii.36; *A&C* IV.iv.35; *Cym* II.iv.68–72; *H8* III.ii.77–78), with perhaps a tiring chamber, or dressing room, and a closet (*Ham* III.iv.set; *Mac* V.i.5–8; *2H6* II.iv.24; *TA* III.ii.82; *R&J* IV.ii.33–35; *John* IV.ii.267; *H5* V.ii.200; *JC* III.ii.130; *Lear* III.iii.11), a small room for writing letters, conducting private conversations, or housing scientific collections, books, papers, and works of art. There might also be a tiny room in which the occupant could use a closestool, a chair with a chamberpot under an opening in the seat. To the ordinary kitchen and buttery there might be added multiple pantries, a pastry (*R&J* IV.iv.2) for the cooking of confections, a distilling house, a smokehouse, and a bakehouse for the production of bread. Large country manors (*AW* III.ii.9; *3H6* V.ii.24), with massive amounts of grain to store, might have granaries raised on stone piers. Then there was a study (serving the same functions as a closet—see *TA* V.ii.5; *R&J* III.iii.76; *JC* II.i.7–8), a chapel (*Ham* IV.i.36–37, IV.ii.9), a gate house, a chamber of estate with an adjoining privy chamber (*H8* I.iv.99–100), and a long gallery (*Per* II.ii.57–58; *H8* V.i.set) over the main hall, containing little furniture and used for exercise, ladies' needlework, and children's games.

The hall, which at the beginning of the sixteenth century was the place in which family and servants dined together, was by the end of the century

A Jost Amman illustration from *Panoplia* shows the steps involved in timber framing. The carpenter in the foreground wields an axe to shape a log that rests on a sawhorse. Behind him and to the left, another worker shapes a mortise with a pick, while a third carpenter drills a hole, presumably for a peg. Like framers today, the carpenters are building a wall on the ground before erecting it in the building behind them, where two other laborers trim a beam with a saw. Reproduced from the Collections of the Library of Congress.

losing its original function. In its old, medieval use, it housed the family and special guests at a table on a dais raised about 6 inches (15.2 cm) above the rest of the floor. In the lower area, servants sat at several tables, arranged by department. A screen, often highly decorated, separated one end of the room and turned it into a service corridor. As the seventeenth century began, however, families had grown weary of dining en masse and had begun retreating to a private dining chamber (*2GV* IV.iv.8), leaving the servants to consume their meals in the hall. The hall was still used by everyone at Christmas, and feasts, celebrations, and performances were held there as well (*MND* III.i.55–57), but it was no longer the venue for every meal.

The largest houses, such as the palaces of the royalty and nobility, had multiple courtyards and quadrangles (including the "basse cour," or lower courtyard, of *R2* III.iii.175, 179, 181). They might have moats, which the physician Andrew Boorde urged the owners to keep clean of kitchen scraps; orchards; ornamental gardens; bowling alleys; archery butts; lobbies (waiting rooms for visitors—see *2H6* IV.i.61; *Ham* IV.iii.37–38), and deer parks (*3H6* V.ii.24; *R2* III.i.23; *LLL* I.i.206–7, 238, I.ii.set, II.i.set, III.i.set, IV.i.set, IV.ii.set, IV.iii.set, V.i.set, V.ii. set), for, as Boorde put it, "a parke repleted with dere & conyes is a necessarye and a pleasaunt thyng to be anexed to a mansyon."

Inside, the walls were plastered or covered with a combination of wainscot (*AYLI* III.iii.85–87) and tapestry. The rooms were lighter than they had been in the Middle Ages, since there was less need for nobles to have fortified houses, and more windows, including bay windows, and clerestories (*TN* IV.ii.38), or upper window sections, could be added. The ceilings (*Cym* II.iv.87–88) might be carved, gilded, or made of molded or incised plaster.

Other Shakespearean Terms

Shakespeare mentions a few architectural terms that do not fall into any of the above categories. He uses the term "cell" to denote a monastic or quasi-monastic room, bare of most conveniences or furnishings (*R&J* III.ii.141, III.iii.set; *Temp* I.ii.20). He mentions a cornerstone (*Cor* V.iv.2), the stone laid at one corner of a building's foundation, and "cubiculo" (*TN* III.ii.51), a term that means "little chamber." The temples of *Coriolanus* (IV.vi.86) and other Greek and Roman plays can be imagined to resemble the surviving ruins of such temples, or the columned neoclassical buildings found in various parts of Europe and America. The "lodge" (*MWW* I.i.106–7; *MAAN* II.i.208) is a hunting lodge, a noble's house located near a good site for pursuing deer, rabbits, boar, or other prey. It would not necessarily be a very rustic place; Elizabeth's and James's hunting lodges were often more like palaces than like rural retreats. A "grange" (*Oth* I.i.103; *MM* III.i.265, IV.i.set; *WT* IV.iv.306), on the other hand, implied a respectable, even large, but very isolated house. *See also* Brick; Furniture; Garden; Household Objects; Lighting.

Armor

Ancient Armor

Shakespeare's plays are set in times ranging from his own late Renaissance back to the days of the Trojan War, so it seems appropriate to begin a discussion of armor with that worn in ancient Greece. Greek infantrymen (hoplites) wore bronze armor composed of two principal pieces (in addition to shields and helmets, discussed separately in this book): form-fitting greaves that covered the shins and the sides of the calves, and a breastplate called a muscle-cuirass because it followed and accentuated the shape of the male chest and abdomen. Roman armor was similar. The muscle-cuirass survived as a symbol of high rank; ordinary soldiers wore a cuirass of overlapping scales (the *lorica squamata*) or iron bands (the *lorica segmenta*).

The warriors shown wear Corinthian helmets with crests of varying design and height, muscle-cuirasses, and greaves. They carry large, decorated shields, spears, and short swords. Lysippides Painter, Greek. 6th century *The Bateman Amphora (Wine Jar)*, c. 530–520 B.C.E. Black-figure terracotta, H. 49.50 cm. © The Cleveland Museum of Art, 2001, The A. W. Ellenberger, Sr., Endowment Fund, 1927.433.

Chain Mail

In the Middle Ages—for example, during the eleventh through fourteenth centuries—the standard armor was chain mail, each suit of which was made of thousands of tiny linked iron or steel rings. Wire was hammered or drawn, wrapped round and round a rod, cut, and pushed through a tapered tube so that each ring's ends overlapped slightly. Then

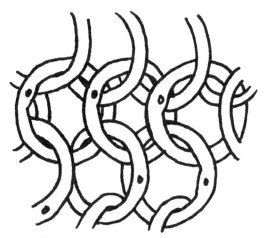

Chain mail: a close-up view. Each ring is linked
with its neighbors and sealed with a tiny rivet.

each ring was flattened at the ends, linked with four adjacent rings, and riveted or welded shut.

Chain mail was worn over a padded garment called an aketon or gambeson and was covered with a long, belted, sleeveless tunic called a surcoat that, like the helmet, shield, lance, pennon, and horse trappings, was emblazoned with identifying heraldic devices. The chief piece of mail, looking like a long shirt, was called the hauberk, and by itself it might contain 250,000 rings. The hauberk had long sleeves ending in mail mittens, with slits at the wrists so that the hands could be removed from the mittens. A suit of chain mail might also include a set of "hose" or leggings and a mail coif (which covered the top and sides of the head like a monk's hood) or aventail (which hung from the sides and back of the helmet, covering the chin, neck, and shoulders).

Chain mail was flexible, but it had many disadvantages. It was labor-intensive to make and, as a result, extremely expensive. Medieval illustrations, including the Bayeux Tapestry, show dead men being stripped of their valuable mail. It was also prone to rust, for the tiny links scratched each other and were exposed to sweat and rain. The surcoat protected the mail from the elements to some extent, but the mesh still needed frequent cleanings by being rolled in a barrel with sand and vinegar. Extensive rust had to be buffed off with a piece of pumice. Most seriously, chain mail was of little use against the formidable longbow and crossbow.

Plate Mail

As a result, beginning in the fourteenth century, knights began increasingly to wear plate mail armor made of forged and hammered plates of

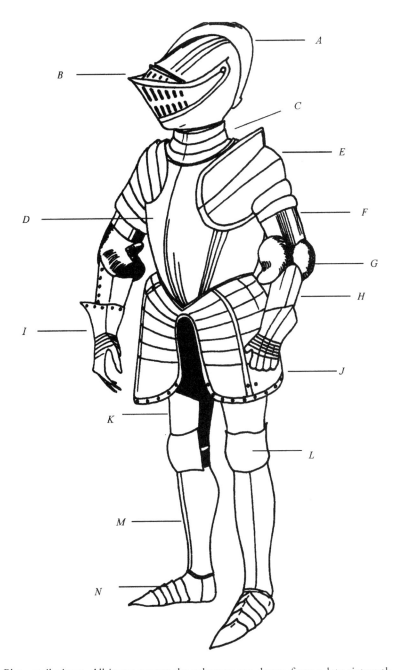

Plate mail pieces. All items except the sabatons are drawn from a late sixteenth-century suit of plate. (A) Comb; (B) Visor with ventilation holes; (C) Gorget; (D) Breastplate; (E) Pauldron; (F) Rerebrace; (G) Elbow cop; (H) Vambrace; (I) Gauntlet; (J) Fauld; (K) Cuisse; (L) Knee cop; (M) Greaves; (N) Sabatons.

steel. This was the type of armor worn in Shakespeare's day. Chain mail was not entirely superseded for some purposes. Small amounts were incorporated into suits of plate—for example in the armpits and groin, which were difficult to cover with plate mail. Mail shirts were also worn by some, including infantrymen and harquebusiers (or arquebusiers), as late as the early seventeenth century.

A knight dressing for combat or the joust began by putting on undergarments, including a fustian doublet, worsted hose padded with "bulwerkis" at the knees, and leather shoes. He then put on metal shoes called sabatons or sollerets. These were followed by greaves and knee cops. Above these he wore cuisses or thigh guards (the "cushes" of *1H4* IV.i.104). Taces and tasses (or tassets), forming a kind of metal skirt called a fauld, protected the hips and, when the rider was seated, the groin. In the late sixteenth and early seventeenth centuries, these pieces were being replaced by a jointed, knee-to-hip piece called a "lobster-tail" cuisse.

The throat was covered by a wide metal collar called a gorget (*T&C* I.iii.174–75), and the torso by breast and back plates (*2H6* III.ii.232–34), the distant descendants of the ancient Greek cuirass. The arms were covered with three different pieces: the rerebrace for the upper arm, the elbow cop for the elbow, and the vambrace (*T&C* I.iii.296–97) for the forearm. The joint between breastplate and rerebrace, a highly vulnerable point, was reinforced with an additional upper plate, the pauldron, that covered the shoulder joint. In jousting suits, the left pauldron had an upward curve to ward lance blows away from the face; it grew quite large and was known as a grandguard (*TNK* III.vi.58). Each hand was encased in a leather or cloth glove or gauntlet (*3H6* IV.viii.74 s.d.; *2H4* I.i.146; *Lear* IV.vi.90; *John* III.i.156) that had a plate-mail covering along the back of the fingers and hand with a flared tube around the wrist. Finally, the knight put on his sword belt and perhaps attached his helm or his shield by means of a chain to keep it from being lost in battle.

The pieces of plate were made somewhat adjustable by sliding rivets (*T&C* V.vi.29; *A&C* IV.iv.1), and they were attached to each other by means of buckles (*A&C* I.i.7–8; *R3* V.iii.212; *TNK* III.vi.54–86), leather thongs or laces (the "points" of *2H4* II.iv.134), or metal pins and staples on the insides of the plates. Putting on armor was a time-consuming process, requiring the full attention of an apprentice knight called a squire (*A&C* IV.iv.11–15), and unarming was equally difficult, made more so when armor had been dented or damaged (*T&C* I.i.1, III.i.147–48).

Plate mail varied in style and composition. Late fifteenth-century armor followed a "Gothic" pattern full of angles, while that of the early sixteenth-century was often in the "Maximilian" style, with thin parallel ridges that, like the corrugations in cardboard, enhanced strength and reduced weight. Later sixteenth-century armor often imitated the puffed-and-slashed appearance of civilian clothing, or the pointed waistlines of doublets. Some

Tilting suit of plate mail (composed) for the mounted joust, South Germany, sixteenth century, made of steel with leather straps and brass rivets. Note the heavier plates and lack of ventilation holes on the left side of the armor, all intended to absorb a lance blow safely. Chain mail covers the groin. A flower-shaped roundel on the right side affixes a bracket designed to brace the end of the lance. *Tilting Suit (composed)*. South Germany. 16th century. Steel, leather straps, brass rivets. © The Cleveland Museum of Art, 2001, Gift of Mr. and Mrs. John L. Severance, 1916.1511.

extremely wealthy men had armor made to match their clothes, with the design of their hose, for example, being echoed in the etching or gilding of their armor. The most ornate suits of plate belonged to the category known as parade armor, intended neither for combat nor for the joust but purely for show. Such, no doubt, is the "armor all of gold" that "was a king's" in *Antony and Cleopatra* (IV.viii.26–27). Furthermore, although it was uncommon, there was also armor for women. Elizabeth I addressed the troops at Tilbury in 1588 wearing a steel corselet (a kind of breastplate and backplate like a cuirass, favored by pikemen and mentioned in *Cor* V.iv.20), and Shakespeare gives Margaret of Anjou armor in *3 Henry VI* (III.iii.230, IV.i.105).

Armor for Man and Horse with Völs-Colonna Arms. North Italy, c. 1575. © The Cleveland Museum of Art, 2001, John L. Severance Fund, 1964.88.

The purpose for which the armor was intended also affected its form. Armor for the mounted joust was noticeably lopsided, since riders rode at each other along opposite sides of a long, low wall, held their lances on the right, and typically struck their opponents on the left side of the face or torso. This method of approach affected almost every aspect of the suit of armor. Jousting plate had no ventilation holes on the left side of the helmet, to reduce the chance of a splinter penetrating the visor. As noted above, the left pauldron was significantly larger than the right, and sometimes tilters wore extra pieces, such as a bracket behind the neck to keep the helmet from being struck off the head, or a round plate over the right armpit, called a lance rest, rondel, or roundel, for bracing the end of the lance. Armor for the field, or for foot combat, was much more symmetrical and might have a gauntlet pin to lock the sword hand around the hilt of the weapon. The variations in form and use of plate mail induced some to invest in garnitures, suits that could be altered for different uses by adding or subtracting pieces.

The knight, who was by preference and definition a mounted warrior, had undoubtedly spent a great deal of time and money acquiring, nurturing, and training his horse, and the animal was one of his principal assets in the field. He would therefore no more think of riding into battle on an unarmored horse than a driver today would willingly operate a car without brakes, doors, and seat belts. There was no satisfactory way to armor a horse's legs without inhibiting its ability to gallop, but large plates called the peytral, crupper, crinet, and chanfron covered its chest, hindquarters, neck, and head, respectively. Horses so reinforced are the "barbèd steeds" of *Richard II* (III.iii.116) and *Richard III* (I.i.10). The horse's armor, called its bard, was in turn covered with a caparison of silk, velvet, or worsted, decorated to match its rider's coat of arms.

Plate Mail Manufacture

A suit of plate began as a lump of iron, preferably from southern Germany or northern Italy, but often from within England. Innsbruck iron was especially desirable; known as "Isebrook" in England, it surfaces in a sword at the end of *Othello* (V.ii.253). The iron was separated from the ore, melted into a "bloom" with a charcoal fire, and left in the furnace to absorb more carbon and turn into steel (*3H6* I.i.58). Steel could be made even harder by heating it and then quenching it in water. Quenching also made the steel brittle, however, so it was generally heated again to temper it. The steel was formed into bars or billets, which were then sold to the armorer (*2H6* I.iii.ch., II.iii.ch.; *H5* II.Cho.3; *T&C* I.ii.6).

The armorer (or sometimes the steel manufacturer) hammered the billets flat. The early stages of this hammering were often performed by huge water-driven tilt hammers, but the later, more precise flattening was done by hand. Some pieces had to be thicker than others; the breastplate, for example, was thicker than the backplate, since most blows, and all blows in the mounted joust, were delivered to the front of the body. Then the plates—up to 200 of them for a single suit of armor—were cut and shaped, using the shop's forge, vises, chisels, pincers, tongs, winches, shears, grindstones, files, and rivet closer. The armorer also kept tools for tending the fire, such as a bellows and a poker, and a water trough for quick cooling of heated plates. There were also several varieties and sizes of hammers and anvils. One anvil was used to shape helmets, for example, another to raise a ridge or comb along the helmet's center, another for visors, another for cuirasses, and so on.

The next step was to test and guarantee the strength of the armor. A knight paying a large sum of money for a suit of plate wanted to be certain that it would withstand a crossbow bolt or sword blow—or, later, a musket ball. Accordingly, the armorer would strike the suit with a sword or fire a musket at it, leaving the resulting dent as a proof (*R3* V.iii.220) of soundness. The armor was then tried on, the fit corrected, and the surface polished (*H5* IV.Cho.11–14). Rivets, buckled straps, or staple-and-hook fasteners were attached, and the insides of the plates were padded for comfort and scratch prevention. Rust was a problem with plate as it had been with chain mail, and all armor had to be carefully stored and cleaned to prevent corrosion (*2H6* I.iii.194; *MM* I.ii.170–72).

In many cases, the armor was also decorated in some way. Edges might be serrated or decorated with wire braid. A seldom-used technique, because of the hardness of the steel, was engraving, in which a sharp tool called a burin was used to carve a design into the plate. More common was etching, in which the plates were painted with wax or varnish and then dipped in acid, the unprotected areas being eaten partially away. There were two ways to accomplish this: waxing the entire piece and scratching away the area to be etched, or painting a design with the wax and perhaps filling background areas with small dots. Either way, the resist material was buffed away after etching, and sometimes the etched surfaces were darkened to create a "black-and-white" contrast between etched and polished areas.

Another decorative technique was embossing, in which a design was hammered into the armor from inside each plate. This could have practical applications as well, with part of the embossing being designed to house an otherwise uncomfortable strap or buckle. Some armor was gilded by means of gold leaf applied to varnish, painting with a mixture of varnish and gold dust, or heating an applied solution of mercury and gold. "Damascening" was an inlay of gold or silver. The steel could also be given a bluish color by heating to more than 590 degrees Fahrenheit and quenched immediately. The blue color could then be selectively removed with acid or vinegar. Bluing, as well as "russeting" (chemical browning), provided some protection against rust. Some of these techniques may have been used on the hypothetical "good armor" of *Much Ado About Nothing* (II.iii.16) or the French lords' armor of *Henry V* (III.vii.1–10, 71–75), including the Lord Constable's, which is decorated with stars.

Other Types of Armor

Not all soldiers in Shakespeare's day wore complete suits of plate mail. In some cases, the expense of such armor was prohibitive. More frequently, as in the case of infantrymen and archers, plate mail was simply too cumbersome. Plate was hot (*2H4* IV.v.29–30), stiff, and heavy; two suits of field plate and one suit of jousting plate from 1590 weigh 55.5, 79, and 103 pounds, respectively. It was a notable, even heroic, feat for a knight to vault into his saddle or even to dance while armed (*H5* V.ii.140–41; *Per* II.iii.96–97, 100 s.d.). The only thing that made an armed knight maneuverable at all was his horse.

Most soldiers wore isolated pieces of armor, such as a breastplate, tassets, and helmet; a shirt of chain mail; armor of padded leather or linen; or a shirt lined with small overlapping plates of metal. This last item, called a brigandine, might have thousands of individual plates, and may be what Cassio means when he boasts, "That thrust had been mine enemy indeed / But that my coat is better than thou know'st" (*Oth* V.i.24–25). Pikemen tended to wear a half-armor called a corselet (*Cor* V.iv.18–21), consisting of a backplate, breastplate, and tassets.

It was the common soldier, lightly armed and horseless, who put an end to plate mail. Armed increasingly with a gun rather than a bow or crossbow, he could penetrate plate that could withstand an attack by sword or pike. His gun was also increasingly accurate and deadly as the years passed, and at last the inconvenience of plate armor was too great in comparison to its defensive value. Armor continued to be a mark of rank or status off the battlefield, but Charles II was the last English king to own and wear a complete suit of plate. *See also* Army; Helmet; Shield; Weapons.

Army

The English army, particularly the Elizabethan army, was not especially strong. It was poorly mustered, paid, and supplied. In many cases, its leaders were inexperienced amateurs; in other cases, they were corrupt or absent from the field. Recruitment was haphazard, and the recruits sometimes extremely unsavory. Though its tactics were in the process of evolving, particularly in the matter of long-distance weapons, it was still very similar to the army of the late Middle Ages portrayed in Shakespeare's history plays.

Personnel

Armies, in Shakespeare's day, were composed of a varying number of regiments that were in turn divided into companies. The army was led by a commander, called a colonel general, (*1H6* IV.ii.2; *JC* IV.iii.123; *AW* IV.i.84) who delegated his duties to several lesser officers. The cavalry was led by a captain general of the horse, who was in charge of the cavalry's marches, encampment, muster rolls, equipment, and battle maneuvers. His subordinate officers included captains (*AW* IV.iii.299) and color-bearers. The cavalry (*1H6* IV.ii.43), which had been the backbone of the army in the Middle Ages, was by Shakespeare's time much diminished in importance. Some portion of the army was still composed of knights on horseback, armed with lances for mass charges, but increasingly knights were being given firearms and being replaced—mainly because of the high cost of breeding, feeding, and training horses—with infantrymen. Their regiments tended to be smaller than infantry regiments, and they were divided into companies of 50 to 200 men, each company specializing in the use of one weapon: lance, pistol, or harquebus.

A second division of the army was the artillery. This was headed by an officer called the master of ordnance or master of artillery, who in theory was supported by a lieutenant, clerks, a master gunner (*1H6* I.iv.ch.), a gunner and gunner's mate for each of his artillery pieces, and assorted craftsmen to keep the cannon and the wagons that hauled them in good working order. Pulling the cannon from place to place took a monumental effort. The larger pieces required several horses or oxen for transport, and additional animals were needed to pull wagons full of ammunition, powder, tools, cotton "match" or fuses, and chemicals. The logistics of training, supplies, and the distribution of munitions to the infantry were handled by the lieutenant, while the master of ordnance (*TS* I.ii.202–5), in addition to his other duties, supervised a company of pioneers and another company of soldiers to protect them.

The pioneers (*Oth* III.iii.343) were the army's most despised soldiers. It was they who dug trenches (*Cor* I.iv.29 s.d.; *1H6* I.v.33) and burrowed under the walls of besieged cities and fortresses. This hard manual labor earned them little respect, though they were in continual danger and were absolutely essential to the proper conduct of a siege. They were so demoralized that they often deserted, and military experts advised paying them nightly to encourage them and motivate them to remain for another day. Some commanders appointed guards to ensure that they did not flee during the night. The pioneers worked under the direction of the "enginers," experts in demolition, and in the "engines"—the machines of war (*T&C* II.iii.7–9; *Ham* III.iv.207–10).

The core of the army was the infantry, headed by the colonel general, who was sometimes seconded by a lieutenant general but more often by

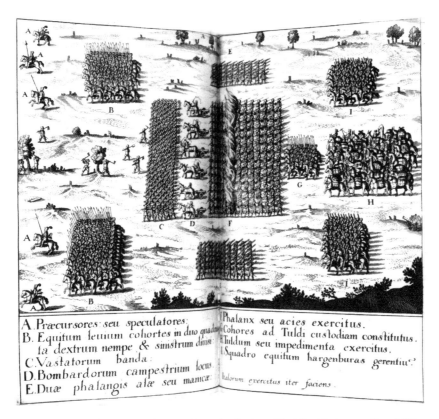

An illustration from an early encyclopedia, Robert Fludd's *Utriusque Cosmi Historia*, shows an army on the move. (The picture appears indented because the book, printed in 1624, is too brittle to open fully.) The parts of the army are labeled on the drawing and identified below in Latin. In English, the groups are: (A) scouts, (B) two companies of light cavalry, (C) engineers with shovels, (D) artillery, (E) two wings of musketeers, (F) a large group of pikemen with ensigns carrying flags, (G) a small group of horsemen, apparently serving as a guard of honor, (H) the baggage train, and (I) mounted harquebusiers. Reproduced from the Collections of the Library of Congress.

the sergeant major general of the army. The sergeant major general was perhaps the single most important person in the Renaissance army. He was likely, as were an increasing number of officers, to be a career soldier, and it was essential that he be competent. He was in charge of marching, encampment, battle position, the appointment of watches (*1H6* II.i.ch.), the muster master's accounts, and the muster rolls with their accompanying inventory of weapons. He also determined the watchword, or password, whenever a watch was set at night.

Below the colonel general ranked the colonels, each of whom commanded a regiment (*AW* II.i.44, IV.i.71). The colonels were too often appointed because they had political influence. A competent colonel, when one could be found, levied troops, divided them into companies, appointed captains (often political favorites and personal friends), and received the funds for his regiment and disbursed them among the captains. He could also name a lieutenant who served as his second in command (*Temp* III.ii.15–16), a regimental sergeant major, a chief harbinger (who advanced before the army to secure lodgings or to prepare the campsite), a drummer, and an ensign to carry his personal standard. He or the sergeant major general was in charge of making sure that the men were adequately equipped with weapons, armor, powder, match, lead, and food. The most important duty of the colonel, in some people's eyes, and the only one he could be consistently relied upon to perform, was leading his troops into battle. The regimental sergeant major performed much the same duties as the sergeant major general, but at the regimental level. In order to do the work of organizing and equipping his men, he had up to four corporals of the field. The lieutenant or lieutenants acted as the colonel's deputies, doing whatever portion of his work he delegated to them.

Each regiment was divided into companies of about 150 to 200 men. Unlike cavalry companies, they did not specialize as a unit in one particular type of weapon. A Lancashire company in 1584 contained about 250 men, of whom one-third used firearms, one-sixth bows, one-sixth halberds, and one-third pikes. (Eventually the bows, much to the dismay of those nostalgic for Agincourt, were replaced throughout the army by firearms.) Each company was commanded by a captain (*2H4* II.iv.140–53; *H5* III.ii.ch.). In theory, the captain trained the men to handle their arms, inspected their baggage for excess, ran them through marching and wrestling exercises, had them jump in their armor to increase their physical fitness, and drilled them on changing formation, stopping suddenly, and "retiring in order." In practice, the army captain was notorious for corruption, theft, gambling, consorting with prostitutes, and committing crimes up to and including murder. In other words, Falstaff actually was fairly typical of the worst of the species (*1H4* II.iv, IV.ii). It was an insult to be likened to a captain.

Lesser company officers included the lieutenants (*MAAN* II.i.184; *H5* II.i.2; *1H4* IV.ii.24–25), who disciplined the men, supervised the noncommissioned officers, posted the guard, and made rounds during the night to see that the watch was vigilant. Each company also had a sergeant, whose duties resembled the lieutenant's, and corporals (*2H4* II.iv.156; *H5* II.i.1; *1H4* IV.ii.24–25), who headed squads (*1H6* IV.ii.23) of twenty to twenty-five men. The corporals trained their men in hand-to-hand combat and marksmanship, appointed scouts (*1H6* IV.iii.1, IV.ii.43; *3H6* V.i.19), and meted out punishments to troublemakers. Ensigns carried the huge battle flags, accompanied by two or three assistants, one or two drummers, and a guard. Stationed either at the front or in the middle of their units, they were essential to morale and helped to keep the troops together during battle, but they had few duties. Much to his dismay, it is this office of ensign or "ancient" (*JC* V.iii.3–4; *2H4* II.iv.ch.; *H5* II.i.3, III.v.i.12), rather than the more responsible position of lieutenant, that Iago is given by Othello (*Oth* I.i.29–30).

In addition to all of these officers, there were chaplains, surgeons (who wore baldrics across the chest and shoulder to indicate that they were noncombatants), drummers, fifers, and trumpeters (*H5* IV.ii.62) in the army; and a small secondary army of wheelwrights, carpenters, coopers, smiths, sutlers (quartermasters—see *H5* II.i.110–11), wives, and prostitutes followed the camp. There were wagons full of baggage pulled by animals and handlers to lead the animals.

And then, of course, there were the ordinary soldiers. Unfortunately, Shakespeare is not always very precise in his use of ranks, and the matter is complicated by the existence of sergeants (*1H6* II.i.ch; *Mac* I.ii.3) and lieutenants at every level of the hierarchy. However, he skillfully portrays the ordinary soldier in all his pride (*2H6* I.i.184–85), bravery, and violence (*AYLI* II.vii.148–52). His soldiers are crude, argumentative creatures, yet it is with regret that we hear of them dying,

> some swearing, some crying for
> a surgeon, some upon their wives
>   left poor behind
> them, some upon the debts they
>   owe, some upon their
> children rawly left. I am afeard
>   there are few die well
> that die in a battle. (*H5* IV.i.138–
>   42)

A fifer and a drummer, from *Panoplia*, illustrated by Jost Amman, 1568. A 1562 guide for militia captains noted that such men "be often tymes sent on messaiges" to call parleys (*Cor* I.iv.12 s.d.) and carry ransoms. They needed to know how to give various kinds of signals with their instruments, including those "to marshe, aproche, assault, all aro[m], a retreate and many others." Reproduced from the Collections of the Library of Congress.

It is hard not to sympathize with men, many of them recruited by force, few of them with any kind of prior training, who were plucked from their civilian lives and asked to risk their lives.

Of non-English forces, Shakespeare says little. He mentions the kerns (light infantry—*2H6* III.i.310, 361, 367, IV.ix.27; *R2* II.i.156; *Mac* V.vii.17–18) and gallowglasses (heavy infantry—*2H6* IV.ix.26; *Mac* I.ii.12–13) of Ireland; the former fought bare-legged (*H5* III.vii.54–55), which made them seem unusual to the hose-wearing English. He also uses a few terms used by the ancient Romans, writing of legions (usually 4,200 soldiers—see *JC* IV.iii.212, V.ii.1–2; *A&C* III.vii.58–59, III.xiii.22), centuries (usually 100 men—see *Cor* I.vii.3) and centurions, the commanders of the centuries (*Cor* IV.iii.43–44). There is also a reference in *Coriolanus* to "th' right-hand file" (II.i.23) as the better sort of people; this may be an allusion to the custom of assigning two centurions to each company, with the first centurion appointed having the honor of commanding the right hand.

Recruiting, Outfitting, and Payment

The levying of troops (*1H4* III.iii.214, IV.ii.12–48; *2H4* II.i.188; *1H6* IV.iii.9–11, IV.iv.29–33) and their treatment thereafter was a national scandal for most of the sixteenth century, and legislation never seemed to do much good. The problems began with the justices of the peace and petty constables, who were entrusted with the preliminary selection of recruits. They, of course, rounded up every vagrant and prisoner of whom they wished to be rid and presented these to the local captain, who made his selection. The draftees had little choice in the matter; if they were between sixteen and sixty years old, they were eligible for military service unless they were cripples, clergy, peers, invalids, members of Parliament, servants of members of Parliament, privy councillors, or justices of the peace. Men who did not wish to serve therefore tried to evade the system through bribery, malingering, sudden urgent travel on business, a pretense of being employed as a servant to some notable man, or the substitution of their own servants or apprentices for themselves. In order to counter these stratagems, captains sometimes sealed off churches during Easter services and impressed men directly from the congregation. This was offensive but legal as long as the men were not bound to fight overseas; impressing men for foreign wars was technically illegal but frequently done anyway.

The scene in which Falstaff recruits his men from the dregs of the county is probably all too accurate (*2H4* III.ii). Little was done to improve the caliber of impressed men (*3H6* II.v.64; *T&C* II.i.97–98; *A&C* III.vii.34–36); in fact, orders were specifically given to impress prisoners. The men thus recruited were often paupers and had little in the way of clothing or supplies; these were Shakespeare's besonians (*2H4* V.iii.117), soldiers who needed everything. Their needs were met poorly; they got a little "press money" (*Lear* IV.vi.87), which was supposed to pay for their basic clothing and transport to the embarkation point; but once in the army, they found that the captains liked to keep supply money for themselves. The soldiers were thus ragged, hungry, sick, and tired (*H5* III.v.56–57, IV.Cho.26).

Their pay was low—4d to 6d a day for ordinary soldiers in 1562—and when it arrived, it was delayed or appropriated by the captains. Until 1586, captains paid their troops directly; the Privy Council's attempt to reform the system transferred payment to the muster masters, so captains simply turned their attention to intimidating these officers. Dead men, known in slang as "shadows," "faggots," or "deadheads," were kept on the rolls so that the captains could continue to collect their pay (*1H4* V.iii.36), with the result that many companies were undermanned. Small wonder that so many soldiers relied on pillage (*1H6* II.i.78–81; *H5* I.ii.195, III.iii.24–27) to make ends meet.

Matters were no better when the army was disbanded (*2H6* V.i.45–47). Soldiers were given 5s each to help them return to the place where they had been recruited, but this was of little help when many were scarred or maimed and unable to make a living. Few were blind to the consequences of military service:

> What would you have me do? Go to the wars,
> would you? Where a man may serve seven years for
> the loss of a leg, and have not enough money in the
> end to buy him a wooden one? (*Per* IV.vi.174–77)

Returned soldiers, with or without wooden limbs, turned in droves to begging or to crime.

Training and Tactics

Despite the number of officers assigned to supervise training, the drilling of soldiers remained rather basic and rather divorced from the actual conditions of war. There was a great deal of practice—some of it at Mile End, a field near London—at forming up in squares (*A&C* III.xi.40), ranks (*JC* II.ii.20), and files. Sometimes the soldiers practiced "doubling of files" (*AW* IV.iii.275–76) or similar maneuvers, in which the ranks or files were re-formed with half or twice as many soldiers in each line. At other times, they practiced holding their pikes in various positions or went through the numerous and difficult steps of firing a musket. Marching typically took place in columns three men abreast, while battle formations usually consisted of a square of pikemen ten men wide and ten men deep, with musketeers either on the flanks or scattered in front of the pikes. The squadrons (*JC* II.ii.20) were usually arranged in three groups: the forward (*R3* V.iii.294) or vanguard, the main battle (*H5* IV.Cho.9) or midward, and the rearward (*MAAN* IV.i.125) or rearguard. Tactics, for the most part, were derived from the study of Roman battles (*H5* III.ii.73–74), though the increasing importance of cannon made the study of mathematics essential for a well-trained officer. Iago scorns this knowledge of angles and trajectories; this is one of the reasons that Cassio, not he, is made Othello's lieutenant (*Oth* I.i.15–24).

Troops were organized into ranks (left to right) and files (front to back). This division is the source of the term "rank and file" to mean ordinary personnel. The diagram below shows one common maneuver practiced in drill, doubling ranks to the right:

Initial Position

Ranks

A	A	A	A	A	A	A	A	A	A
B	B	B	B	B	B	B	B	B	B
C	C	C	C	C	C	C	C	C	C
D	D	D	D	D	D	D	D	D	D
E	E	E	E	E	E	E	E	E	E
F	F	F	F	F	F	F	F	F	F
G	G	G	G	G	G	G	G	G	G
H	H	H	H	H	H	H	H	H	H
I	I	I	I	I	I	I	I	I	I
J	J	J	J	J	J	J	J	J	J

F I L E S (label to the left spanning rows D–F)

At the command, "To the right, double your ranks!" the soldiers in the even-numbered files would step up and to their right, filling in the spaces in the odd-numbered ranks:

```
A B A B A B A B A B A B A B A B A B A B
C D C D C D C D C D C D C D C D C D C D
E F E F E F E F E F E F E F E F E F E F
G H G H G H G H G H G H G H G H G H G H
I J I J I J I J I J I J I J I J I J I J
```

The command "To the left, double your ranks!" would look the same, except that the men in the rear rows would slide to the left instead of the the right as they moved forward. The command "To the left (or right), double your files!" operated exactly the same way, but in reverse. Incidentally, we now speak of the "ranks" of an army to mean all its personnel, but in Shakespeare's day, the proper term was the "files" of an army (*Cym* V.iii.30).

Real war was of course quite different from drill and theory. A pitched battle often began with scouts surveying possible lines of attack or defense. If they were lucky, they would not walk into an ambush or, as Shakespeare puts it, an "ambuscado" (*R&J* I.iv.84). They would return to the general with their news, and he would decide, in consultation with his senior officers, where to form his lines. There was nothing particularly stealthy about any of this. Armies traveled with a huge amount of baggage (*H5* IV.iv.75–78, IV.vii.1–10), and their tents and fires would have been visible to any competent scout from the other side. Last-minute repairs were made to armor and weapons, supper was cooked, horses were fed and watered, and the camp became silent and still except for the movements of the sentinels (*H5* IV.Cho.4–16). In the morning—for battles almost never took place at night—the men armed (*H5* III.vii.91, 157–60) and formed up in ranks and files.

The opposing armies lined up on opposite sides of the chosen battlefield, each trying to secure an advantage by occupying the higher ground (*John* II.i.295–99), placing the sun in the enemy's eyes (*LLL* IV.iii.367), or placing the wind at its own back (*TA* IV.ii.133). There might be parleys (face-to-face negotiations—see *JC* V.i.21) and messages sent back and forth while the masses of soldiers waited for the battle to begin (*H5* IV.ii.42–53). Then, with a trumpet call and a suitable war cry (*1H6* II.i.39 s.d., 78 s.d.)—private war cries in honor of a noble family rather than the crown, God, or St. George had been banned after the Wars of the Roses—one army or both charged. Arrows or bullets flew through the air; the cavalry plunged into the fray with lances leveled, then switched to swords or maces. The pikemen braced their weapons at an angle, presenting the enemy with a wall of spear points, while the halberdiers swung their axe-tipped poles, hacking at anything within reach. The musketeers and harquebusiers laboriously aimed their weapons and lit their powder, moving away in a practiced formation as soon as they had fired so that others could take their place while they reloaded. Sometimes an entire line of marksmen would fire and retreat simultaneously; sometimes the men would parade in a circle, firing as they reached the front of the circle and reloading as they marched around its back.

Eventually, one army's line might break, or things might become so confused that parts of the same army might find themselves attacking each other (*AW* III.vi.48–50). A general retreat might follow (*AW* IV.iii.294–95), seldom in an orderly fashion, and the victorious army pursued. It searched the battlefield, slaying most of the lesser soldiers, and searching for knights or officers who could be taken prisoner and held for ransom (*1H6* I.iv.23–34, III.iii.72; *1H4* I.iii.76–122; *H5* III.v.60, IV.iii.121–23; *LLL* I.ii.62; *TA* III.i.156, 172). A gentleman's agreement governed this practice. The capturing army was expected to treat its prisoners well and to ask an amount that would not bankrupt their families; in return, the prisoners were expected not to attempt an escape unless the agreement was breached by extortion, blackmail, threats of violence, or orders to do something dishonorable. If the battle served to end the war, its close might be marked by a marriage linking the two sides or by an exchange of hostages, usually people of noble birth sent to live with the enemy as living emblems of good faith.

Almost all of the elements of siege warfare are in this woodcut from the early sixteenth century. The infantry, mostly pikemen and a few halberdiers, surrounds the ensigns (ancients) with the battle flags. Artillery assaults the walls of the town from several angles, and the cavalry, with lances, prepares to make a charge. In the foreground are the besieging army's tents (*H5* III.vii.128–29; *JC* V.iii.10; *Oth* I.iii.85; *R3* V.iii.7), and at middle right, an artilleryman repairs a cannon behind a board shielding him from the town's artillery and arrow fire. Round shot lies next to almost all of the cannons. Hans Burgkmair, German, 1473–1531. *The Storming of Nantes*, 1512–1515. Woodcut, 23.2 × 19.7 cm. © The Cleveland Museum of Art, 2001, Dudley P. Allen Fund, 1960.33.

Not all battles, however, were fought between two armies in the field. Often, they took the form of a siege (*1H6* I.iv.103–I.v; *John* II.i.54; *H5* I.ii.152, III.Cho.25–27, III.ii.55–139), with an army encamped around a town or fortress, just out of the range of guns and bows. Since cities relied on the farms around them for their food supply, they could be starved out if the army could wait that long. Sometimes it could not; desertion, disease, and the onset of winter (*H5* III.iii.55–56) could lead to its dispersal before the town yielded, so it often tried to force the town to surrender more quickly. Crucial to this strategy was the making of one or more breaches (*H5* III.ii.109–10, III.vi.72), or holes, in the town's fortifications. There were two principal ways of effecting this. One was to hammer the town walls with artillery fire: sometimes with multiple batteries of guns pointed at a single point, sometimes with cross fire attempting to breach the walls in several places at once. Variations on the artillery fire included ballistas, gigantic crossbows designed to attack defending soldiers rather than walls; catapults, which flung boulders or other objects against the fortifications; and battering rams (*A&C* III.ii.30–31; *RL* 464; *T&C* I.iii.206), which were iron-headed logs suspended from ropes and swung by shielded soldiers against a gate or wall.

The second method was to dig "mines" (*AW* I.i.121–22; *H5* III.ii.59–65), or tunnels shored up with timbers, under the town walls. When the general gave the signal, the timbers would be set alight or the tunnel collapsed with explosives, and the foundation of the walls would give way. For the town's defenders, there were only two ways of combating miners. They could attack the workers as they dug—not always possible due to defensive shields or the lay of the land—or they could dig a countermine, a second tunnel under the attackers', which would collapse the enemy tunnel and kill the pioneers before they reached the town walls. Occasionally, the pioneers attempted to pick away directly at the town walls or to fill in the moat or ditch around a fortress, but this could be even more dangerous than digging a tunnel.

If there was no time to dig and no good vantage point from which to fire cannon, an attacking army could attempt the most dangerous procedure of all. This was to run directly up to the foot of the town's walls, lean scaling ladders (*1H6* II.i; *H5* III.i.1 s.d.; *Cor* I.iv.22) against the walls, and attempt to swarm up and over the walls before the defenders could organize. The defenders, in this case, had a tremendous advantage, for they could send rocks, arrows, or boiling water or oil raining down on the attackers, and sometimes tipped the ladders over so that the attackers fell to their deaths.

When a breach had been made, the attackers rushed in over the rubble of the walls, hoping not to become trapped in any internal chambers within the walls, for in this case they could be shot at leisure by defenders firing through small holes in the walls or ceilings. They might face "barricadoes" (*AW* I.i.116; *WT* I.ii.204), hastily erected walls of timber, barrels, furniture, and other items, and they would have to storm these or circumvent them. When the town was more or less under control, it might be burned (*LLL* I.i.145) or looted; the order for general pillage was "Havoc!" (*Cor* III.i.274). Generally, it was up to the commander to decide how much mercy to accord a town that had not surrendered voluntarily. *See also* Artillery; Firearms; Flags; Knight; Navy; Weapons.

Art

One of the privileges of membership in the upper or upper-middle class was the ownership of art (*TS* Ind.i.47, Ind.ii.49–60), particularly art that reflected or flattered oneself. Accordingly, anyone who could afford to do so hired an artist to paint his portrait. These "picture-painters" (*Lear* II.ii.60; *Tim* V.i.ch.; *R&J* I.ii.40–41; *LLL* V.ii.641) thought of themselves as craftsmen rather than artists in the modern sense. Working on wooden panels or on cloth (the forerunner of the modern canvas), the painter made a few quick sketches (*AW* I.i.96–98) and painted the details in at a later date, sometimes using a screen with a few wires or cords that divided what

The painter, by Jost Amman, from *Panoplia*.

he saw into square or rectangular sections. The painted cloths were more likely than the formal portraits to depict classical or biblical themes (*MAAN* III.iii.133–34); they were for everyday use, while family portraits and expensive works from overseas were jealously guarded by their owners and even veiled in cloths to keep them safe from dust (*TN* I.v.231–32). Paintings were also used among aristocrats as tools of courtship, or at least of the arrangement of marriages. Young people whose political and financial interests suggested a marital alliance, but who lived far from each other, would exchange portraits (full-size or miniatures) as a means of determining whether they disgusted each other. Several instances of the portrait as love token appear in Shakespeare (*TNK* IV.ii.1 s.d.; *2GV* IV.ii.120–21, IV.iv.87, 115, 117, 184–205; *MV* III.ii.115–29), and Henry VIII chose one of his wives, Anne of Cleves, in this fashion; he regretted it the moment he saw her in person, declaring she looked nothing like her picture and instead resembled a "Flanders mare."

Sometimes works of art, like the painted cloths, purported to convey some sort of moral. Sometimes they were more humorous in intent. The "picture of We Three" (*TN* II.iii.17) is in this vein, being a famous representation of two asses—the person looking at the painting is supposed to be the third.

Sculpting, too, was a craft rather than an art. The demand for church sculpture had diminished as a result of the Reformation, which favored less ornamentation in places of worship. However, the nobility still required carved stone

The sculptor, by Jost Amman, from *Panoplia*.

and woodwork for their palaces, and the prosperous needed to be memorialized in stone on their tombs. Statuary was also in evidence on the outsides of churches, for even the Reformers seldom dared meddle with the facades of cathedrals, contenting themselves instead with destroying rood lofts, altars, fonts, and images of saints inside the buildings. Nonetheless, most of Shakespeare's references to statues appear in classical contexts (*JC* I.ii.283–84, I.iii.145–46, III.ii.188).

Artillery

Gunpowder (*2H4* IV.iv.48; *1H4* V.iv.120; *R&J* II.vi.10–11), composed of varying percentages of saltpeter (potassium nitrate, *1H4* I.iii.59), sulfur, and charcoal, was introduced to Europe by the thirteenth century. Cannons (*Oth* III.iv.133–36; *3H6* V.ii.44; *H5* III.Cho.25–27, 32–34, III.i.10–11; *MWW* III.ii.29–30; *Mac* I.ii.36–38; *R&J* V.i.64–65; *Ham* IV.i.42–44; *H8* V.iv.11–13) at first fired arrows, later lead shot, and over the centuries they became somewhat more accurate and somewhat less likely to explode in the midst of their operators.

Deciphering which kind of cannon Shakespeare meant at any given moment can be tricky. Even determining that he means cannon at all can be difficult, for "gun" may apply to a fowling piece (*MND* III.ii.20–24) or to a cannon (*LLL* III.i.62–65); and "bullet" may be a cannonball (*TN* I.v.93), the ammunition for a pistol, or simply a metaphor for something swift and deadly (*2H4* IV.iii.33; *H5* IV.iii.105–7). A reference to the recoil of a "gun" (*2H6* III.ii.330–31) could thus apply either to firearms or to artillery.

When cannons are mentioned by name, they are either artillery generally or specific large pieces of ordnance that threw 60-pound iron balls, but there were other types of artillery. These included the 40-pound basilisk (*H5* V.ii.17; *1H4* II.iii.53), a "demi-cannon" (*TS* IV.iii.89) with a bore of 6½ inches, the 17½-pound culverin (*1H4* II.iii.53), the tiny 2½-pound sling (*Ham* III.i.58), and the "mortarpiece" (*H8* V.iv.45), identified by various authorities as a squat, wide-mouthed cannon or a short launcher for a 2-inch-wide grenade. Occasionally, Shakespeare mentions an individual part of the cannon, for example, the wheeled "carriages" (*H5* III.Cho.26) that enabled the cannon to be dragged into position, or the "chambers" (*H5* III.Cho.34 s.d.) that facilitated rapid firing. The chambers were removable sections of the cannon that could be preloaded and wedged into alignment with the barrel of the gun by means of a large iron peg. Each chamber was filled with a load of powder, a wad, and a cannonball. When it was time to fire the gun, the chamber was dropped into the breech (the loading area at the rear of the gun), fixed in place, and lit at the "touchhole," a narrow channel that ran into the powder chamber. After the gun had been fired, the spent chamber was removed and another inserted. Most cannon, however, were muzzle-loaded. *See also* Army; Firearms; Weapons.

Astrology

Astrology is one of the topics that seems to invite much conjecture about what Shakespeare really believed, probably because it is hard for postindustrial readers to accept that such a brilliant playwright could really have held what are now thoroughly discredited views. Surely a man of such obvious insight and intellect ought to have seen that the astrologers of his day were a pack of charlatans. Surely he used astrological metaphors and foreshadowing only because they were helpful devices, easily comprehended by his more gullible audiences.

Yet disbelief in astrology was, in Shakespeare's day, a fringe position. That astrology was in the beginning of its decline is perhaps true, and it was condemned by a few, including the theologian John Calvin. But even noted scientists and academics, among them the physician Paracelsus and the astronomers Johannes Kepler, Tycho Brahe, and Erasmus Rheinhold, espoused at least a partial belief in the power of the stars to affect human lives. In an age when astronomy, astrology, alchemy, physics, folklore, superstition, medicine, magic, and religion were imperfectly distinguished from each other and all trying to interpret the same phenomena, the same man might condemn judicial astrology—the branch that used the stars to predict political events—yet be perfectly willing to accept the effects of the stars on his own character, or at least the humors or fluids in his body, and so have horoscopes cast for his newborn children.

John Calvin, for example, scoffed at the idea that hundreds of men slain in the same battle all had planetary clues to their simultaneous demise, or that the stars even determined personality, but he conceded that they might influence the weather or disease. The English author George Carleton, responding in 1623 to a 1603 defense of judicial astrology, called the entire field a "delusion" of the learned or "a more simple and grosse kinde of insinuation" on the ignorant. In his opinion, it was heretical and illogical to believe in astrology or to consult an astrologer. Yet he does not rule out any possibility of stellar influence—"For that influence which is apparant in the Moone and Sunne may bee gathered in other Planets"—only a predictable cause-and-effect relationship between planetary and stellar positions and events, and he accepts the existence of divine revelation and familiar spirits as sources of knowledge of the future. Many educated people seem to have accepted a moderate view: that the stars could affect the humors or influence events in a certain direction, but that they allowed for the possibility of free will, in the same way that a person with high blood pressure today might be told he is at greater risk for a heart attack, without being absolutely assured that he *will* die of a heart attack on such-and-such a date.

What did Shakespeare believe? Those who argue that he was in the skeptics' camp base their claims primarily on two passages in the plays, Cassius's assertion to Brutus that destiny lies "not in our stars, / But in ourselves" (*JC* I.ii.140–41) and Edmund's diatribe against astrology in *King Lear*:

> . . . we make guilty of our disasters the sun, the moon, and stars; as if we were villains on necessity; fools by heavenly compulsion; knaves, thieves, and treachers by spherical predominance; drunkards, liars, and adulterers by an enforced obedience of planetary influence; and all that we are evil in, by a divine thrusting on. An admirable evasion of whoremaster man, to lay his goatish disposition on the charge of a star. My father compounded with my mother under the Dragon's Tail, and my nativity was under Ursa Major, so that it follows I am rough and lecherous. Fut! I should have been that I am, had the maidenliest star in the firmament twinkled on my bastardizing. (I.ii.123–36)

Both of these speakers, however, are unsympathetic characters. Cassius's disregard of the stars is consistent with his disregard for law and sovereignty; it is all part of his fatal contempt for the natural order. Edmund, too, gets his comeuppance for being, if not necessarily "rough and lecherous," then certainly tough and treacherous. His ill-omened nativity proves true in the long run.

Balanced against these two instances of anti-astrological reasoning, we have a host of references to planets and stars as guides to character and behavior, tragedies blamed on malevolent stars, and prophecies that inevitably come true. While all of this can be explained away as a set of convenient poetic and suspense-building devices, all evidence appears to reside on the side of Shakespeare's being "a sectary astronomical" (*Lear* I.ii.153–54). He would have been in good company. Henry VIII believed in astrology for its value in tracking planetary movements and making medical diagnoses, and Elizabeth I had an interest in it as well, patronizing the noted astrologer John Dee. Even if Shakespeare privately disagreed with astrology, it would have been unwise to reject one of the queen's pet theories.

John Dee and the other English astrologers of the day—some of them reputable astronomers or consultants to the nobility; others, adventurers and swindlers—engaged in a variety of activities and used a variety of techniques and instruments to reach their conclusions. Practitioners of judicial astrology tried to predict invasions, wars, dangers to the throne, and so forth; it was a dangerous business, particularly when it involved predicting the possible death of a monarch, but it offered a unique chance to influence the course of political and spiritual affairs. Astrologers to both the

An astronomer at work. From *Panoplia*, illustrated by Jost Amman. Reproduced from the Collections of the Library of Congress.

rich and the poor also helped their clients with "elections," that is, choosing a propitious day for some activity, such as starting a business venture or getting married. One of the most common reasons to hire an astrologer was to cast a "geniture" or "nativity," a schematic map of the heavens at the moment of the client's birth. It was this arrangement of the stars and planets that, it was believed, affected the client's character, health, and destiny throughout life.

It was not an easy matter. Astrologers used almanacs and other more or less reliable reference works, measuring tools like astrolabes and armillary spheres, and a square or rectangular layout of the twelve "houses" of the zodiac, beginning with Aries and continuing counterclockwise through the rest of the zodiacal constellations. Each house was believed to be influenced by one of the planets and to be connected to one of the four prime elements; each was also believed to have a strong influence over a different part of the body. It is this property of the zodiac that is debated by Sir Andrew and Sir Toby in *Twelfth Night*; they disagree over whether Taurus governs the "sides and heart" or "legs and thighs" (I.iii.132–36). Actually, the signs ran approximately straight down the body, with Aries governing the head and Pisces the feet; Taurus, being the second sign, was thought to influence the neck, so both characters are mistaken.

Name	Symbol	Representation	Elemental Quality	Ruling Planet
Aries	♈	Ram	fire*	Mars
Taurus	♉	Bull	earth	Venus
Gemini	♊	Twins	air	Mercury
Cancer	♋	Crab	water	Moon
Leo	♌	Lion	fire*	Sun
Virgo	♍	Virgin	earth	Mercury
Libra	♎	Scales	air	Venus
Scorpio	♏	Scorpion	water	Mars
Sagittarius	♐	Archer	fire*	Jupiter
Capricorn	♑	Goat	earth	Saturn
Aquarius	♒	Water Bearer	air	Saturn
Pisces	♓	Fish	water	Jupiter

*The fiery Trigon of *2H4* II.iv.271.

Each house represented 30 degrees of the sky as it appeared to pass around the earth along the plane of the ecliptic. Not all astrologers agreed as to where the houses began and ended. Each astrologer filled out the geniture form according to his own formulas for determining the houses, using the center box and the edges of the paper for notes about the subject's name, exact time of birth, place of birth, and destiny according to the position of stars and planets.

The most important aspect of the geniture was the ascendant, or horoscope. This was the house of the zodiac, and the degree of arc within that house, that was just appearing over the horizon at the place and time of the subject's birth. (When a person was actually born was a matter of much dispute, with some arguing for the moment of conception, some for the emergence from the womb, some for the complete impossibility of determining such a thing precisely.) This house automatically became the first house on the geniture chart, occupying the nine-o'clock position, and the other signs of the zodiac, with more or less complexity according

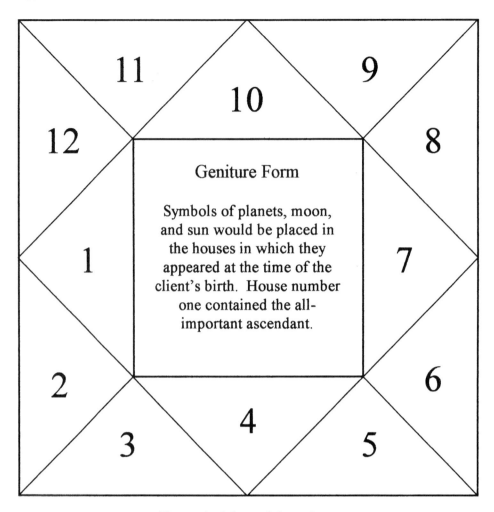

Geniture Form

Symbols of planets, moon, and sun would be placed in the houses in which they appeared at the time of the client's birth. House number one contained the all-important ascendant.

The standard shape of the geniture.

to the individual astrologer, continued through the other houses. Each house governed a different aspect of the client's life.

House	Aspect of life
1	birth
2	wealth
3	brothers and sisters
4	parents
5	children
6	sickness
7	marriage
8	death

House	Aspect of life
9	religion
10	rulership; honors
11	good spirit; fortune
12	evil spirit; sorrows

The astrologer then plotted the position at the moment of birth of the sun, the moon, the head and tail of "the dragon" (the ascending and descending nodes of the moon's orbit), and the five known nonterrestrial planets: Mercury, Venus, Mars, Jupiter, and Saturn. Up until this point, the casting of a geniture was mostly a matter of mathematics and astronomy. Now it became a matter of art, geometry, analogy, and guesswork. Each planet had its own characteristics, which could be magnified or minimized by its geometrical relationship to other planets, or by its position within a house or constellation.

	Influences	Gender	Metal	Body Part	Symbol
Moon	moisture, tides, theft, plant life, lunacy, women, weakness, voyages, plebeians	F	silver	brain	☽
Sun	rank and rulership	M	gold	heart	☉
Mercury	sciences, arts, intellect; friendly to Saturn, Jupiter, and Venus	M, but can be F when surrounded by F elements	mercury	lungs	☿
Venus	air, water; friendly to all other planets except Saturn	F	copper	kidneys	♀
Mars	dishonesty, theft, violence, murder; friendly only to Venus; evil influence in ascendant, less so if in conjunction with Venus; conjunction with Venus a favorable time for a wedding	M	iron	gallbladder	♂
Jupiter	ceremony, religion	M	tin	liver	♃

	Influences	Gender	Metal	Body Part	Symbol
Saturn	old men, melancholy, scholarship, poetry, troublesomeness, madness, hindrances to thought and action, occasionally justice, holiness; hostile to Venus and Mars; influence can be moderated by Venus or Jupiter	M	lead	spleen	♄

Appearances of planets within certain houses or signs had many possible meanings, some of which were quite well known. Saturn, for example, was especially malevolent in the twelfth house. Each planet also had certain signs that it "ruled"—Aries and Scorpio, for example, were ruled by Mars; Cancer by the moon; Gemini, by Mercury; Capricorn by Saturn. The ruling planet of a person's ascendant was given particular weight in determining his or her character. Sometimes the symbolism was used for humorous purposes: the marriage or dalliance of an old man and a young woman was said to be "Saturn in Virgo."

The planets' relationships to each other also affected astrological predictions. Planets were naturally friendly or hostile to each other, and when located at regular intervals from each other, they could become more or less so. Planets were said to be in opposition when they were 180 degrees apart, and in conjunction when they were in the same direction. Other significant configurations included trine, 120 degrees apart; quadrature, 90 degrees; and sextile, 60 degrees. Sextile and trine were considered positive; quadrature and opposition, negative; and conjunction the most important of all, whether for good or evil. The rarer the conjunction, the more important, with the Saturn-Jupiter conjunction, occurring about every twenty years, the most significant of all. The location of a conjunction in a sign of the zodiac, or in the geniture of a person (or nation or city, based on the time and date of founding) determined much of its meaning, but conjunctions in general were often assumed to herald great change or unusual weather. This aspect of astrology, too, was well enough known to elicit some sly humor; one seventeenth-century astrologer described his wedding night, according to his and his bride's dominant planets, as the first conjunction of Saturn and Mercury.

Astrology in Shakespeare

The attribution of events to planetary influence is found often in Shakespeare's works. There are "planets of mishap" (*1H6* I.i.22), "adverse planets," (*1H6* I.i.54), an "ill planet" (*WT* II.i.105) that must be allowed to pass until action is taken, and even a "bawdy planet, that will strike / Where 'tis predominant" (*WT* I.ii.201–2). The planets rule (*2H6* IV.iv.16), strike men down (*TA* II.iv.14), and outwit mere humans with their grand designs (*Oth* II.iii.180). We see the influence of Mars (*1H6* I.ii.1–4), of Venus and Saturn (*TA* II.iii.30–31), and of Saturn and Mercury in genitures—the influence of Saturn making for a gloomy constitution (*MAAN* I.iii.11), that of Mercury shaping Autolycus the thief (*WT* IV.iii.25). Shakespeare even makes reference to the well-known enmity of the planets Saturn and Venus, as well as to their association with old men and young women, respectively: "Saturn and Venus this year in conjunction! / What says th' almanac to that?" (*2H4* II.iv.269–70).

Stars, like planets, are frequently blamed for the terrible state of things. They are "malignant and ill-boding" (*1H6* IV.v.6), "louring" (*2H6* III.i.206), "thwarting" (*3H6* IV.vi.22), rebellious and bad (*1H6* I.i.4–5), frowning (*Per* I.iv.107), "inauspicious" (*R&J* V.iii.111), and unlucky (*WT* III.ii.96–97). The most famous of these references is undoubedly that to Romeo and Juliet as "star-crossed lovers" (Pro.6). Conversely, when things are going well, the stars often get the credit (*TA* IV.ii.32–33). Beatrice, in *Much Ado About Nothing*, explains her jesting nature by referring to the skies at her nativity: "there was a star danced, and under that I was born" (II.i.323). Prospero, too, places faith in the stars. He refers to the practice of choosing an astrologically propitious time to begin an important enterprise when he explains the timing of his move against his foes:

> I find my zenith doth depend upon
> A most auspicious star, whose influence
> If now I court not, but omit, my fortunes
> Will ever after droop. (*Temp* I.ii.181–84)

Another attribution of character to the heavens is an example of how freely some terms were used. The sun and the moon, for example, were often referred to as "planets," and planets were often referred to as "stars." In *All's Well That Ends Well* (I.i.191–99), Helena and Parolles discuss whether Parolles was born under "the charitable star" of Mars, and whether Mars was "retrograde" at the time, which would have given his geniture an entirely different meaning.

That Shakespeare and his audiences were familiar with astrology is also obvious from his references to individual astrological signs. There are mentions of Virgo, Taurus, and Aries (*TA* IV.iii.65, 70, 72); to Cancer as the beginning of summer (*T&C* II.iii.196–97); and to the slowly revolving cycle of the zodiac's constellations as equivalent to one year (*LLL* V.ii.795,

MM I.ii.170–72). There is even an exchange that refers to the "zodiacal man" of the almanacs (*TN* I.iii.132–36), in which Andrew and Toby debate the astrological influences over various parts of the body. Almanacs, widely consulted as weather guides and prognostications, included standard reference pages, much as an appointment book today might include a perpetual calendar, a list of national holidays, and a guide to time zones or international currency. The zodiacal man was this sort of standard reference, a picture of a naked man with symbols to indicate the parts of the body ruled by various astrological signs.

Especially useful for Shakespeare's histories and tragedies was the belief that temporary celestial phenomena had earthly significance. Eclipses, comets, meteors, false suns, and the like were the bread and butter of judicial astrologers, who attempted to foresee the fates of nations and rulers. Comets were associated with the deaths of rulers, changes in government, war, pestilence, and invasions (*1H6* I.i.2, III.ii.31); the mathematician Leonard Digges said they were meant to "signifie corruption of the ayre. They ar signes of earthquakes, of warres, chaunging of kyngdomes, great dearth of corne, yea a common death of man and beast." Eclipses had similar meanings (*Lear* I.ii.139–44). Ptolemy, whose theories were accorded great weight, associated the colors formed around eclipses with different planetary influences and believed that the duration of the eclipse determined the length of its effects. A three-hour lunar eclipse would cast its shadow over the next three months; a three-hour solar eclipse would affect the earth for three years. *See also* Alchemy; Astronomy; Magic.

Astronomy

In 1603, near the time that Elizabeth I died and Shakespeare was writing *Othello*, a knight named Sir Christopher Heydon published a defense of astrology, to which he appended what a critic called "a Chronologicall Index of Astronomers (meaning thereby Astrologers)." Heydon, like many of his contemporaries, hardly distinguished between the two, for the study of the movements of the stars and planets and the study of their possible earthly influence borrowed from each other and were often pursued by the same people. Notable men remembered today for their contributions to astronomy, including Tycho Brahe and Johannes Kepler, were practitioners of astrology as well, and the two disciplines used the same instruments—armillary spheres (three-dimensional models of the known arrangement of stars and planets), astrolabes, sextants, quadrants, and globes. (Shakespeare's writing career ended just as the telescope was coming into use among scientists but before it had permeated the popular imagination.)

Shakespeare lived during a time of widespread interest in the stars and solar system. Among the learned, a revolution was taking place. The old Ptolemaic understanding of the universe, with a fixed, motionless earth at its center, was under siege. Almost twenty years before Shakespeare's birth, the dying Nicholas Copernicus published *De revolutionibus orbium coelestium* (On the Revolutions of the Celestial Spheres), in which he advanced the theory that the planets, including the earth, revolved around the sun. In 1610, just before Shakespeare's retirement, Galileo published his *Siderius Nuncius* (Starry Messenger), announcing his discovery of four moons around Jupiter. Bracketed between these remarkable events was a host of observations, theories, and discoveries that revolutionized humanity's understanding of the skies: supernovas in 1572 and 1604, the latter brighter than Jupiter; a 1577 comet as bright as Venus with a 22-degree tail (compared to the full moon overhead, which occupies only half a degree of arc) that led to much animated discussion about the distance of comets from the earth; noteworthy comets in 1582 and 1607; William Gilbert's *De Magnete* of 1600, in which he postulated that the earth itself was a giant lodestone or magnet; a total solar eclipse that would have appeared near-total in England, in October 1605; and Kepler's 1609 study of Mars, *De Motibus Stellae Martis*, in which he outlined his historic formulas for planetary motion. Astronomers across Europe were adopting Copernicus, first for his improved mathematical tables (which were acceptable even to those who defended a geocentric solar system), and later for his reordering of the solar system.

It was a monumental change in thought, and it did not happen overnight. Even to the end of Shakespeare's life, there were prominent scientists who disagreed with Copernicus, and there were others who accepted only a partial reorganization: a fixed earth in a Copernican arrangement of planets; an earth orbited by the moon and sun, with all other planets orbiting the sun; or only Venus and Mercury revolving around the sun, with the sun and all other planets orbiting the earth. The controversy was a compelling one in the scientific community, but it did not mean much to the rest of English society. Discussion was confined for thirty-three years to those who had read Copernicus in Latin, and there are only a few scattered references to the theory in English until a partial translation in 1576 by Thomas Digges. Even then, if we are to judge by Shakespeare's works, people continued to think about the universe in conventional ways. Ulysses' speech is sometimes taken to be a profession of Shakespeare's affinity for the Copernican system:

> The heavens themselves, the planets, and this center
> Observe degree, priority, and place,
> Insisture, course, proportion, season, form,
> Office, and custom, in all line of order.
> And therefore is the glorious planet Sol
> In noble eminence enthroned and sphered
> Amidst the other. (*T&C* I.iii.85–91)

But this passage is ambiguous at best; "this center" could just as easily be the earth as the sun, and the sun is described as "Amidst the other" planets, which could mean at the center of all their orbits or in its traditional Aristotelian/Ptolemaic position between Venus and Mars.

When Shakespeare mentions heavenly bodies, he does so as a poet and an ordinary man, not as a scientist steeped in controversial new theories, but even common people were aware of the basic symbolism and motions of sun, moon, planets, and stars. The sun (*R&J* III.ii.25; *TN* V.i.270) was symbolic of light, daytime, kingship, and masculinity. The moon, for its mutable shape and its subordination to the masculine sun (*Tim* IV.iii.68–70, in which the moon's light is renewed by borrowing from the sun), and perhaps also for the correspondence between its cycle and the menstrual cycle (though Shakespeare does not mention this), was associated with women. Cleopatra, disavowing womanly weakness and fickleness, does so by likening such faults to the feminine moon:

> My resolution's placed, and I have nothing
> Of woman in me: now from head to foot
> I am marble-constant: now the fleeting moon
> No planet is of mine. (*A&C* V.ii.238–41)

Folk beliefs about the moon's effects were given equal weight with its actual gravitational ones. To the ordinary sailor or farmer, the idea that the moon brought insanity (*Oth* V.ii.109–11) or increased plant growth (*T&C* III.ii.175) seemed just as obvious as its light, its regular cycle by which months could be measured (*MND* I.i.2–4, 8–11; *WT* I.ii.1; *MND* III.i.52–53), and its influence over the tides (*1H4* I.ii.25–39). It was an old, reliable friend, the pits and gouges on its surface translated by the imaginative mind into the Man in the Moon (*Temp* II.i.253, II.ii.139), banished there with his dog for gathering wood on a Sunday.

The moon was also generally understood to be the celestial body closest to the earth. In the traditional ordering of the planets, the earth sat at the center, surrounded sometimes by spheres of water, air, and fire. The moon's sphere was next, followed by those of Mercury, Venus, the sun, Mars, Jupiter, Saturn, and the stars. These spheres were considered to be literal, solid objects. The Renaissance mind, like the classical mind upon which it was based, abhorred the notion of a lot of wasted space. There were, therefore, no vacuums and no void. Each heavenly body had its own sphere, and they were nested one inside the other; when these spheres rubbed against one another, they made a kind of celestial music not normally audible to humans (*John* V.ii.53; *1H4* V.iv.63; *A&C* IV.xv.9–10, *TN* III.i.112; *H8* IV.ii.80; *Per* V.i.232).

The planets, which were of intense interest to both astrologer and astronomer, appear in Shakespeare's writings chiefly in their astrological context. As purely physical bodies, they rarely occur. There is a reference to "wand'ring stars" (*Ham* V.i.256), probably meant to apply to the planets, which were known for their regular deviations from the fixed order of constellations; "star" is commonly used to mean "planet" in Shakespeare's works. Similarly, he mentions the "eastern star"—Venus, so called because it was often visible in the early morning near the sun—(*A&C* V.ii.308)—and makes a specific reference to Venus's brightness (*MND* III.ii.60–61).

The stars, too, get short shrift except in an astrological context. They occasionally appear metaphorically—compared, for example, to Juliet's eyes (*R&J* II.ii.15–22). The few glimpses that we get of stars outside an astrological or eyes-of-the-beloved state, however, are quite useful. They reveal a world in which the nighttime sky, undimmed by electric light, its vast expanses and periodic movements eminently familiar, lay above the viewer in all its grand, threatening glory. The apparent movement of the stars can be seen in the likening of a disgraced political favorite to a star hastening "from that full meridian of my glory / . . . to my setting" (*H8* III.ii.225–28). References to certain well-known stars by their colloquial names make it clear that the average person knew at least a few of the features of the nighttime sky. Polaris is "the Northern Star, / Of whose true-fixed and resting quality / There is no fellow in the firmament" (*JC* III.i.60–62); the Pleiades are simply "the seven stars" (*2H4* II.iv.189–90; *1H4* I.ii.14–15; *Lear* I.v.35). The constellation Ursa Major (Latin for "Great Bear"), known today as the Big Dipper, was then "Charles' wain [cart]" (*1H4* II.i.2), and was so familiar a sight that the people told time by its rising and setting. The Latin name of Ursa Minor must also have been common knowledge, for Shakespeare calls it "the burning Bear" and makes reference to Polaris as one of its stars (*Oth* II.i.13–15).

The nighttime sky was so well known, in fact, that the disruption of its orderly cycles by unusual celestial events, coupled with ignorance about the origins and meanings of those events, made Shakespeare's contemporaries highly uneasy. People watched the sky with the jumpy intensity of Wall Street analysts watching economic indicators; a bad omen could cause public confidence to plummet. "Meteors" (*John* V.ii.53; *JC* II.i.44–45; *1H4* V.i.15–21; *MWW* II.ii.273–75; *V&A* 815), which could be any form of disturbance, including shooting stars and comets, almost always portended evil. (For more about their supposed significance, *see* Astrology, above.) Shakespeare mentions at least three types of phenomena: comets (*JC* II.ii.30; *1H4* III.ii.47; *1H6* I.i.2; *Per* V.i.89), eclipses of sun and moon (*Oth* V.ii.99–101; *A&C* III.xiii.153–54; *S* 35; *S* 60), and parhelia or sun dogs (*3H6* II.i.25–32), an optical illusion in which the real sun, at low altitude, is flanked by two mock suns and often crested with a reverse rainbow—an illusion caused by refraction of the sun's light through hexagonal ice crystals. After a time, as the angle of the sun changes, the false suns blend back into a single image, just as Shakespeare describes.

All of these phenomena, treated as straightforward omens of doom or destiny in Shakespeare's works, were of great scientific interest to the astronomers of the day. Comets in particular were controversial, since they appeared to cross between the supposedly solid planetary spheres. There was also vigorous discussion about the composition of comets. Aristotle, whose scientific theories were still highly influential, believed them to be burning fires. The alchemist Paracelsus called them "newly begotten stars, not produced at the first creation, but freshly exhibited by God. Such were the star of Christ and others like it." A new theory advanced at this time, equally wrong but quite inventive, was that comets were lenses, and their tails the refracted light of the sun or Venus. *See also* Astrology.

Baptism

Of all the sacraments of the Roman Catholic Church, the only two retained by the Anglican Church were baptism (*Oth* II.iii.340) and Communion. Baptism was thus an exceedingly important ritual that almost every English person experienced. The christening (*TA* IV.ii.70) was usually arranged by the father or another of the baby's relatives, since the mother was still exhausted from the delivery and not, according to custom, allowed to appear in public. All that was religiously required was that the minister say, "I baptize thee," but socially much more was involved.

The first requirement was that the ceremony be held when the congregation was present, so it was customary to hold the christening on the first Sunday after the child's birthday. This was not always possible, however; the most common reasons for delay were the child's health and delays in the arrival of godparents (*MV* IV.i.397–99; *H8* V.v.1 s.d., V.iii.161–62; *LLL* I.i.93; *R3* I.i.48). Speed was of the essence, for many believed that the child was damned if it died without being received into the church. There was, as with many other aspects of the ritual, controversy about what happened to unbaptized babies. Anabaptists, of whom there were still a few in England, believed in adult baptism and felt a child was not condemned for having failed to undergo a procedure it could not understand and to which it could not consent. Other religious nonconformists objected to parts of the Anglican ritual and refused to have their children baptized; at least some of these people were forced by law to bring their children to the font. Children born out of wedlock were also less likely to be baptized than children born within a marriage. Whatever people thought about the fate of infants who died unchristened, they seldom denied them the final worldly comforts in their power, and these babies were often buried in consecrated ground.

On the day of the ceremony, the infant was dressed in a long garment called a mantle (*H8* V.v.1 s.d.) and carried to the church by the midwife, who often received a small present for performing this duty. It was borne on a cushion, often highly decorative, to the part of the church that held the font (*MV* IV.i.397–99) or basin. The font, a permanent structure, was perceived as more conformist; the basin, more Puritan. The minister laid a linen chrisom cloth on the baby's face and read the liturgy noting the child's passage into the church, promise of salvation, and deliverance from original sin (*H5* I.ii.31–32). Exactly how much sin was washed away and how much of a chance of salvation was offered by baptism was another source of religious controversy.

Next, the child was dipped into the water of the font or sprinkled with water from the basin. The Reformation had eliminated the Catholic ritual of hallowing the font, but the water itself remained an important part of the ritual. The priest made the sign of the cross over the child (yet another source of controversy, for some thought this smacked of Catholicism), recognized its godparents, and gave it its name (*R&J* II.ii.50–51), saying the name followed by the formula, "I baptize thee in the name of the Father, and of the Son, and of the Holy Ghost." A feast followed (*H8* V.iv.8–10), and friends of the family brought the baby presents (*H8* V.v.1 s.d.) that were examined and compared by all the guests. Typical gifts included shirts, cups, porringers, cradles, and especially spoons (*H8* V.iii.161–62, V.iv.38). *See also* Pregnancy and Childbirth; Religion.

Basilisk

The mythical basilisk's exact form was unknown because its gaze was said to kill observers instantly, but authors tended to agree that it was monstrous in its lack of a mother. Some said it was the product of a yolkless egg, laid by a rooster and hatched by a serpent. The alchemist Paracelsus, unusual in his departure from the rooster-serpent hybrid, thought it might be a calf born of a bull rather than a cow. However, it was generally assumed to have the head and wings of a rooster and the tail of a snake, with a triple comb on its forehead. In England, though not necessarily elsewhere, the basilisk and the cockatrice were synonymous (*H5* V.ii.17; *Cym* II.iv.107–8; *2H6* III.ii.52, 324; *3H6* III.ii.187; *WT* I.ii.389; as cockatrice, *RL* 540, *TN* III.iv.200–1; *R&J* III.ii.47). Because of its killing connotations, the basilisk gave its name to a type of cannon. *See also* Artillery.

Bastardy

Illegitimate births were certainly discouraged during Shakespeare's lifetime, both by men who wished to avoid individual responsibility for their maintenance and also by the public at large, which wished to avoid communal responsibility for their support. The ideal was marriage first, children after, fathered by the husband and no other man. If an illegitimate birth was unavoidable, the hope was that the mother-to-be would name the father of her child and confess her guilt publicly in church, and that the father-to-be confess responsibility and agree to marry the woman, or at least to pay for the child's upbringing. Neither model was followed all of the time.

Part of the difficulty lay in Renaissance courting customs. There were two distinct phases to the creation of a marriage: a marriage contract or betrothal and a church wedding. The two steps might be far removed from one another in time, and the first one did not require the presence of a minister. Generally speaking, a betrothal could be held to be valid if the man had said, in the present tense, that he took the woman for his wife.

Promises to marry in the future were less sound; the gift of a ring argued for the validity of the union. From the betrothal on, the parties were held to be joined to one another. However, declarations made in the absence of witnesses—for example, late at night, as an inducement to physical intimacy—were hard to enforce. All too often, a man promised marriage in order to gain access to a woman's body. Having attained that goal, he might decide that he preferred the single life. If the woman became pregnant, he could disavow both her and the child, and hope that no one could prove he had been really betrothed to her. Shakespeare offers an illustration of such a case in *Measure for Measure*:

> . . . Mistress Kate Keepdown was
> with child by him in the duke's time; he promised her
> marriage; his child is a year and a quarter old, come
> Philip and Jacob [May 1]; I have kept it myself, and see how
> he goes about to abuse me. (III.ii.200–4)

All the classic elements are present in this brief passage: the fraudulent promise of marriage, the unintended pregnancy, the negligence of the father in supporting his child.

This situation, in which a woman believed herself to be married but could not prove it, was a common cause of illegitimacy. Sometimes, the cause of her child's apparent bastardy was not abandonment by the father but a delay in the completion of the marriage or the death of the father before the church marriage. In any case, the mother was unlikely to receive much sympathy from the community, particularly if she were poor or a servant. Envisioning another mouth to be fed by the parish poor rates, the community would often ensure that she was fired from her post, whipped, shamed, or even imprisoned. If she refused to name the father, who could also be whipped if he were a servant, she would be hounded to confess his name, even by the midwife during the delivery of the baby. The shame and difficulties of raising a child out of wedlock were too much for some mothers, who fled the area where they lived, gave birth in the homes of strangers or in guest houses that specialized in delivering unwed mothers, and moved to places where they were unknown, sometimes abandoning or killing their infants along the way. Baptismal records indicate that perhaps 4 percent of births were illegitimate in the years around 1600, but it is likely that a good many illegitimate children did not survive to be baptized.

If a bastard lived, it was more likely to be poor than a child born in wedlock. Even if its father acknowledged it, it had no automatic right to inherit any of his estate. Similarly, royal bastards could not inherit the throne, and rumors of the supposed illegitimacy of a rival claimant to the crown were often started or employed by the ambitious (*R3* III.v.75, 86–94). Even Elizabeth I was, for much of her youth, officially illegitimate.

Like her half sister Mary I, she was declared a bastard and allowed to succeed to the throne only because it was stipulated in Henry VIII's will. Like Henry, fathers could and did make voluntary bequests to their bastards. It was also not unknown for a father to be fond of his illegitimate children and to do a great deal to help them; certainly there is no implied shame in the exclamation of an older man to a younger one, in *Love's Labour's Lost*, "O, and the heavens were so pleased that thou wert but my bastard, what a joyful father wouldest thou make me!" (V.i.72–74).

Shakespeare's attitude toward illegitimacy seems mixed. He recognizes the sense of betrayal that a married man might feel in discovering that "his" children were actually fathered by another man; when the Duke of York is prepared to sacrifice his traitorous son Aumerle, the duchess repeatedly insists not that her son is innocent of treason, but that he is the legitimate offspring of the duke. Only a belief in his bastardy, she believes, could account for the duke's lack of paternal loyalty (*R2* V.ii.88–109). In several of the plays, there is an implication that bastardy is, if not shameful, at least embarrassing (*MAAN* V.iv.43–51; *Lear* I.i.14–16; *A&C* I.ii.37–38). Certainly the mock confession of Juliet in *Measure for Measure* (II.iii) follows the ideal pattern of profound shame and repentance on the part of the woman, whose fault is supposedly greater than her lover's. Shakespeare also invents a couple of diabolical bastard characters, Edmund in *King Lear* and Don John in *Much Ado About Nothing*. Edmund's impassioned speech in defense of bastards (I.ii.2–22), and his scorn for the astrological circumstances of his birth, prove to be deeply ironic. Yet the bastard of *King John* is an honorable man whose virtues are in evidence from the very first scene of the play, and there is a touching solidarity between illegitimate children in *Troilus and Cressida* (V.vii.14–20). Ultimately, Shakespeare seems not to blame the bastard as much as the weak woman who bore it, and to judge each character as an individual. *See also* Children; Marriage.

Beard

By Shakespeare's day, the clean-shaven faces of the Middle Ages and the early Renaissance had gone out of style in England. Henry VIII had brought facial hair back into fashion, and the beard was an essential sign of manliness. To grow one is a blessing (*TN* III.i.45–46; *AYLI* III.ii.207–8; *H5* III.Cho.22–24), to lack one, or to lack a flourishing one, is to be less of a man (*LLL* V.ii.822–26; *TS* III.ii.174; *2H4* I.ii.25–26; *MAAN* V.i.191). It is the essential characteristic of the masculine visage, so that "in his beard" means "to his face" (H5 III.ii.72).

The existence of the beard was assumed; the shaping of it was left to individual preference. There were plenty of choices; a 1583 listing includes the French beard, the new beard, the old beard, the court beard, the bravado beard, and so on; Motto in Lyly's *Midas* (1591) asks, "How, sir, will you be trimmed? Will you have your beard like a spade or a bodkin? A penthouse on your upper lip, or an alley on your chin? . . . Your Mustachios sharpe at the ends like shoemakers' awles, or hanging downe to your mouth like Goates' flakes?" The barber was not solely a beardshaper, for he also pulled rotten teeth (*MM* V.i.322) and performed medicinal bleeding, but in Shakespeare the principal functions of the barber are the shaving and trimming of beards (*2H4* I.ii.25–26; *MAAN* III.ii.41–44; *TNK* I.ii.52–55; *MND* V.i.24–27).

Soldiers often wore a beard shaped like the spade on a playing card, which widened as it left the chin and then swooped back into a sharp point. Clergymen might wear the cathedral beard, long, wider at the bottom, and either squared off or round. The fashionable favored the marquisette, a very short beard, or the pique devant, a shortish beard that came to a point. Other popular styles included the forked beard, which came to two points, the square-cut, the round or bush beard, and the

A sampling of sixteenth- and early seventeenth-century beards. In most cases, a particular style of beard could vary in length or in whether it was connected to the hair by side whiskers. A. The pique devant. B. Forked beard. C. Spade beard. D. Marquisette. E. Square-cut beard. F. Cathedral beard.

fantail, limited to the upper class because of the care it required—it stuck out for three inches or so in a fan shape, and had to be stiffened with scented wax in the daytime and preserved in a bag at night.

The early seventeenth century brought a gradual reduction in the size of beards and the popularization of inverted mustaches and sharply pointed "stiletto" beards. Shakespeare rarely mentions the shape of beards, preferring to make the beard a symbol of masculinity rather than a comment on fashion, but he does drop a reference here and there to a "beard of formal cut" (*AYLI* II.vii.154) or "a great round beard like / a glover's paring knife" (*MWW* I.iv.19–20). *See also* Clothing; Hair.

Bees

Bees (*1H6* I.v.23; *2H6* IV.i.109; *TA* V.i.14–15; *JC* V.i.34–37; *Temp* V.i.88–89) were almost alone among the insects in being cultivated by humans. They produced honey for food, cosmetics, medicines, and mead; filled their hives with beeswax; and pollinated crops. They even served as weather forecasters, for it was said that if the bees stayed in their hive or close to home, rain would soon follow.

In order to harvest the honey and wax, farmers built bee hives and houses. The bee house was a wooden structure, open to the warmest side, located far enough from the brewhouse and kitchen that the bees would not be disturbed by smoke, and provided with a shelf for the hives. The additional height afforded by this shelf kept the hives safer from damp and from pests like mice and moths.

The honey and wax were harvested after no more than three years, for older hives were said to yield worse honey. The farmer first allowed the bees to colonize a new hive by placing the old hive on its side and another hive atop it with the entrances facing. William Lawson, who endorsed this method, warned his readers not to allow the entrances to touch directly, but to separate them a bit with sticks, lest the bees seal the two hives together. The farmer then drove the bees from the old hive with smoke or water and carried the empty hive to a closed room so that the bees could not harass him. The combs were broken up and placed over a clay or wood vessel. Lawson admitted that wood vessels would leak at first, but he preferred them because they tended to be more durable. After two to three days of draining, the honey was skimmed and the combs pressed to yield more honey.

The comb, fully pressed, was converted into wax. Conrad Heresbach, in *The Whole Art and Trade of Husbandry* (1614), gave detailed instructions:

> The drosse that remaineth after the pressing, after that you have diligently washed it in sweet water, must be put in a brasse Caldron, and putting a

little water thereto, melted upon the fire, which when you have done, you must straine the waxe through a Sive, or such like thing made of Straw, or Rushes: and after seeth it againe, and powring it into some vessell with water, from whence you may easily take it, make it up in cakes, or what fashion you like.

The soft, pliable wax that resulted was used for candles and letter seals (*2H6* IV.ii.81–83).

Considering the assiduity with which bees were housed and tended, there were a number of important misunderstandings about their habits. Chief among these were the sex of the queen bee and the role played by drones. Shakespeare, like most people of his time, knew that bees had a highly organized social system, but he misses a perfect opportunity to flatter Elizabeth I by giving them not a queen but a king. In this he is merely following the experts of his day, who all ascribed leadership of the hive to a king. Elizabeth or no Elizabeth, it was simply inconceivable that such an organized and hierarchical insect would have a female as its leader (*2H6* III.ii.125–27).

> They have a king, and officers of sorts,
> Where some like magistrates correct at home,
> Others like merchants venture trade abroad,
> Others like soldiers armèd in their stings
> Make boot upon the summer's velvet buds,
> Which pillage they with merry march bring home
> To the tent-royal of their emperor—
> Who, busied in his majesty, surveys
> The singing masons building roofs of gold,
> The civil citizens kneading up the honey,
> The poor mechanic porters crowding in
> Their heavy burdens at his narrow gate,
> The sad-eyed justice, with his surly hum,
> Delivering o'er to executioners pale
> The lazy yawning drone. (*H5* I.ii.190–204)

"The lazy yawning drone" presented another problem to Renaissance naturalists and agriculturalists, who very rarely suspected the truth, which was that the drone was involved in reproduction. Almost to a man, they deduced that the drone was a shiftless rogue, a thief, a gelded bee, an unnatural bee, or something of the kind. Lawson called drones "an idle kind of Bees and wastfull," while Heresbach found them "unperfect." Edward Topsell concurred, complaining that they were cowardly "theeves" who "bestow no paines in gathering the Hony, nor labour it throughly to have it perfectly wrought." Shakespeare, following the consensus, uses them as emblems of the idler and the robber (*MV* II.v.47; *Per* II.Cho.18–19, II.i.50).

Very little of the literature on bees explains how they actually made wax and honey. It seems to have been a complete mystery. Obviously, people could see that flowers did not contain honey or wax, and Topsell, as quoted above, knew that some sort of labor on the bees' part was required to create honey. Yet writers seem to have been content to leave the process alone. Shakespeare, no exception to the rule, makes no guesses as to the means of chemical alteration and leaves manufacture out of the equation entirely. His "humblebees" (*LLL* III.i.84, 88, 94; *MND* III.i.168, V.i.10–17; *AW* IV.v.6–7; *T&C* V.x.41–44) carry honey and wax, ready-made, to the hive (*2H4* IV.v.74–77; *MND* V.i.10–17; *AW* I.ii.65–66).

Bell

In the Renaissance world, so quiet compared to our own, one of the most familiar sounds to villagers and townsfolk was the bell of the parish church. How it was rung, when, and how many times conveyed valuable information. Most important to the daily rhythms of life, it marked the passage of time, summoning parishioners to morning and evening prayers (*2H4* IV.ii.4–7); the curfew bell (*MM* IV.ii.76), originally rung in the Middle Ages as a signal to extinguish fires, continued into Shakespeare's day as an evening bell. Apparently bells were rung at midnight, too, in some places, for Shakespeare mentions "the midnight bell" in *John* III.ii.47* and *A&C* III.xiii.185. While there were bells in some households (*Mac* II.i.31–32), the bell was primarily associated with the church (*AYLI* II.vii.113), as in the First Fisherman's tale in *Pericles* of monsters "who never leave gaping till they / swallowed the whole parish, church, steeple, bells, / and all" (*Per* II.i.35–37). Bells were rung in church not only to begin the service but as part of it, particularly in the old Catholic rites such as the Mass (*H8* III.ii.296) and excommunication (*John* III.ii.22).

Bells rung out of the normal sequence betokened joy or sorrow. They were rung for festivals, weddings, royal visits, and the monarch's coronation day. They rang at the death of the old king (or queen) and the accession of the new (*2H4* III.ii.185–87, IV.v.111–12); York commands that his invasion be greeted by such a universal peal in *2H6* V.i.3. Bells might also be rung to sound an alarm, as in *Oth* II.iii.159, and they rang to announce a death in the community, with different numbers of strokes for the death of a child, a woman, or a man, to assist the listeners in guessing who might have passed away. This death knell (*Mac* II.ii.3–4, IV.iii.170; *2H4* I.i.101–3) was followed by the lych bell, a handbell rung near the bier during the funeral procession, and the funeral bell at church. All this ringing was hot and sweaty work for the ringers, who stood below

---

The Complete Signet Classic Shakespeare combines two scenes in *King John*, so that the "midnight bell" appears in many other editions of the play at III.iii.37.

the bells, pulling on ropes to swing them back and forth. It was customary, therefore, to leave a consideration for the ringers in one's will, in the form of money or refreshment.

Larger churches might have multiple bells in various sizes. A skillful set of bell ringers might then be able to play simple tunes, though this was extremely tricky. Getting a bell to ring at precisely the right time required learning to let the bell "rest" at a certain point in its swing, and the speed of each bell depended on its size. Churches yearning to possess a "ring" of five or six bells for musical patterns might buy them all at once, add a few new bells to their pre-Reformation ones, or melt down old bells and recast them as a lighter, more numerous group.

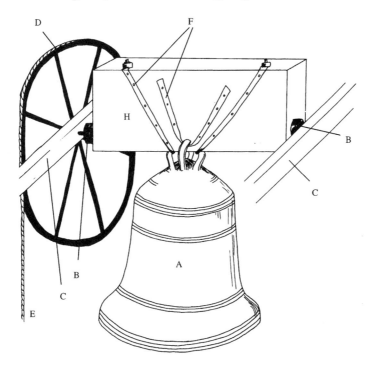

A standard bell-mounting assembly. (A) Bell; (B) Gudgeons; (C) Bell tower framing; (D) Wheel; (E) Rope; (F) Straps; (G) Cannons; (H) Headstock.

Some churches actually reduced their number of bells. A 1552 inventory of the church in the small village of Hapton, Norfolk, lists three bells, the heaviest weighing 600 pounds (271.8 kg), worth a total of £115s. That was a lot of money, and some churches treated their bells (and their roof lead) as sources of emergency funds, to be sold in time of need. Even in the best of circumstances, bells could be a drain on the parish resources. Their weight and motion put a great deal of strain on the belfry, and had to be constructed carefully. Their parts periodically wore out and had to be replaced, lubricated, or moved to account for wear. They might crack and need to be recast. And there was always the danger that they might work loose and fall on someone.

Great care was therefore paid to the casting and hanging of bells. They were cast by braziers (brass smiths), using hard clay inner and outer molds separated by a layer of soft loam shaped with wire and a molding template called a strickle. If an inscription was required, it was affixed to this soft layer, using wax letters that would melt away when the molten bronze was poured into the mold. Large loops called cannons were cast on the top of the bell, on the outside; these would be used to attach the bell to the beam above it, called a headstock. On the inside was a loop or staple to which the iron clapper would be attached with either a leather band or an iron ring and a wooden board (*MAAN* III.ii.11–12; *John* III.ii.47–49; *MND* V.i.362–63). The clappers wore out faster than the bells and were periodically "quartered," or rotated, so that a different face would strike the bell. The fact that they were not considered an integral part of the bell is reflected by the Hapton inventory, which lists the church's three clappers separately and gives them a total value of 2 shillings.

When the bell was finished, it was attached to the headstock with iron bands, which were run through the cannons and then nailed or bolted to the sides or top of the headstock. Axles called gudgeons ran along the headstock, either inserted through a lengthwise hole drilled into the beam or placed in a gouged-out channel in the bottom. These gudgeons fit into bearings in the framing of the bell tower and, on one side, into a wheel with a rope used to swing the bell.

Birds

Birds were a source of both joy and frustration. Their song was much appreciated (*LLL* I.i.103; *R2* I.iii.287; *R&J* II.ii.22), and small birds were often kept as pets (*TA* III.i.84–86; *MAAN* I.iii.32; *R&J* II.ii.178–84; *Lear* V.iii.9). The family shown in the Children entry, for example, owns both a goldfinch, whose perch is pictured in the lower left of the portrait, and a parrot. They were also eaten in great profusion and variety—even sparrows, gulls, and swans were dressed for the table. Yet it was common knowledge that they destroyed crops—a partially incorrect perception, for they ate harmful pests as well as seeds and fruit—and much effort was devoted to keeping them away from crops with scarecrows and children too small to perform any other useful work.

Birds were caught using birdlime, a sticky material made from holly bark that was smeared on branches. When they landed, their feet were trapped in the lime, and people could collect them easily (*2H6* I.iii.90–91, II.iv.54,

III.iii.16; *3H6* V.vi.13–17; *2GV* III.ii.68; *MAAN* III.i.104; *AW* III.v.23–24). Sometimes they were netted instead (*V&A* 67; *Mac* IV.i.34).

Birds were believed to be powerful omens. Different birds had different symbolic meanings, and the departure of a superior bird or the arrival of a foreboding one was a dire sign (*JC* V.i.79–87). Birds were even believed to be able to reveal the identity of murderers (*Per* IV.iii.21–23).

Bird	Citations	Notes
Barbary hen	*2H4* II.iv.100–101	An African fowl, perhaps a guinea hen, that has ruffled feathers.
Bunting	*AW* II.v.6–7	A finch with a thick, short bill; considered an inelegant, ordinary sort of bird.
Buzzard	*R3* I.i.133	Like all carrion eaters, the lowest of the low.
Chewet	*1H4* V.i.29	Another name for the chough or red-legged crow; a chattering, noisy bird.
Chough	*TNK* I.i.20 *Mac* III.iv.125 *Lear* IV.vi.13	A red-legged crow; linked in all these examples with other loud birds.
Cormorant	*LLL* I.i.4 *T&C* II.ii.6	A bird that dives and catches fish, swallowing them whole. Its name is used as an adjective meaning "ravenous." Visitors to England in 1610 saw tame cormorants who fished in the river near Thetford, catching and regurgitating whole fish for their masters.
Crow	*CE* III.i.80–84 *2H6* V.ii.11 *3H6* V.vi.45 *MND* II.i.97 *H5* IV.ii.51–53 *T&C* IV.ii.8–9 *R&J* I.v.50–51 *AW* IV.iii.291 *Mac* III.ii.50–51	A bird that, perhaps because of its black plumage, its harsh voice, or its tendency to scavenge, was considered a bad omen, usually of death. It haunted gibbets, battlefields full of corpses, and the carcasses of diseased livestock, so it was no wonder that it developed dismal connotations. One of the most oblique and yet vivid references to the crow is in *Henry V*, where one character predicts of an-

Bird	Citations	Notes
		other that "he'll yield the crow a pudding / one of these days" (II.i.88–89). The characterization makes more sense once "pudding" is understood as the Renaissance equivalent of "sausage." Thus, the character in question will fill the intestines of a crow—after he is hanged for his crimes. England was said, in 1606, to have more crows than any other land in Christendom.
Cuckoo	*LLL* V.ii.885, 896–98, 904–6 *AW* I.iii.64 *MV* V.i.112 *1H4* V.i.60–66 *MWW* II.i.121–22 *Lear* I.iv.216–17 *A&C* II.vi.28 *TNK* I.i.19–22	The cuckoo's chief claim to fame in the works of Shakespeare is its habit of laying its eggs in other birds' nests, leaving unsuspecting adoptive parents to do the work of raising its chicks. It thus embodied the great masculine fear of an adulterous wife passing off another's man's offspring as one's own, and gave rise to the term "cuckolded," which meant being duped in this fashion or, more generally, having an unfaithful wife whose liaisons did not produce children. Every man, apparently, no matter how much he trusted his wife, secretly feared himself to be a cuckold and feared the song of "The plain-song cuckoo gray, / Whose note full many a man doth mark, / And dares not answer nay" (*MND* III.i.130–32). Folklore invented various reasons for the cuckoo's appearance around the middle of April and an abrupt change in its song to a more staccato rhythm around June (*1H4* III.ii.75–76). By late summer or early fall the cuckoos were gone for the year.

Bird	Citations	Notes
Daw	*MAAN* II.iii.249 *Oth* I.i.61–62 *LLL* V.ii.902 *TN* III.iv.36–37	The jackdaw, a black-and-gray bird related to, and slightly smaller than, the crow. It had much the same reputation as the crow, being a scavenger and a bird of ill omen.
Divedapper	*V&A* 86–87	A type of small grebe, also called a dabchick or didapper, noted for its ducking and diving behavior.
Dove	*R&J* I.v.50–51 *R&J* II.i.10 *MND* II.i.232 *MWW* II.i.78–79 *WT* IV.iv.154–55 *1H6* II.ii.30 *LLL* IV.iii.209 *TS* II.i.207–8 *2H4* III.ii.163 *A&C* III.xiii.196–97 *V&A* 153, 366	Associated less with peace than with gentleness, the goddess Venus (whose chariot was drawn by doves), and love. The turtledove, often simply called a "turtle," as in the title of the poem *The Phoenix and the Turtle*, was noted for its fidelity to its mate. Doves were encouraged to nest in specially built houses by some farmers, who fed the birds in winter and then caught and ate them periodically for most of the year.
Duck	*1H4* II.ii.103–4 *Temp* II.ii.128–29 *A&C* III.x.19–20	Rarely a symbol of anything. It is a good swimmer, not particularly courageous, and fond of its mate. The mallard is mentioned specifically in *Antony and Cleopatra*.
Eagle	*2H6* III.i.248 *Cor* III.i.139 *R2* III.iii.67–68 *1H4* IV.i.98 *R3* I.iii.263, 269 *TA* IV.iv.83 *LLL* IV.iii.223, 331 *R&J* III.v.221–23 *H5* I.ii.169–73 *Cym* III.iii.21 *TNK* II.i.91–92 *V&A* 55–58	In the Renaissance mind, which arranged all things in hierarchies, the eagle was the king of birds. It soared and nested high; it was physically large and powerful; its vision was acute. It could look directly at the sun, and so had almost magical abilities.

Bird	Citations	Notes
Falcon	*3H6* I.iv.41 *R2* I.iii.61–62 *TS* IV.i.179–85 *Mac* II.iv.12–13	Whereas scavengers were at the bottom of the hierarchy of birds, raptors were at the top. The falcon was no exception. It was valued for its speed, its grace, and its usefulness as a hunter. There were specialized terms for these birds kept for the sport of falconry, which are discussed in the Falconry and Fowling entry.
Finch	*MND* III.i.129 *T&C* V.i.37	An inferior bird in Renaissance eyes, emblematic, when any symbolism was applied to it at all, of something small and insignificant.
Guinea hen	*Oth* I.iii.310	See "Barbary hen" above.
Gull	*Tim* II.i.31 *TN* III.ii.67	Can mean either the seabird or a dupe.
Halcyon	*Lear* II.ii.80–81	Kingfisher. Its name came from the myth of Ceyx and Alcyone (Halcyone), who supposedly were changed into birds by the gods. The birds were then said to nest on the sea itself in especially calm weather. The bird's association with weather was adapted into a folk practice of suspending a dead specimen by the bill to act as a weathervane.
Hawk	*1H6* II.iv.11 *TS* Ind.ii.43 *TS* IV.i.182 *TS* IV.ii.39 *TS* V.ii.72 *MAAN* III.i.35–36 *T&C* III.ii.41–42	The hawk is usually mentioned in the context of falconry. A "haggard" was a hawk too wild to train as a hunter.
Jay	*TS* IV.iii.174 *Temp* II.ii.171 *WT* IV.iii.9–10	A clever but noisy and aggressive bird, associated in Autolycus's song with summer (*WT*).
Kite	*2H6* III.i.249 *2H6* III.ii.191 *2H6* V.ii.11	A scavenging bird, and thus lowly and despicable, a bird of ill omen. It is sometimes called

Bird	Citations	Notes
	R3 I.i.133 *Mac* III.iv.73 *Lear* I.iv.264 *WT* II.iii.185 *T&C* V.i.62	a puttock. It has a forked tail. It was known to scavenge not only for food but also for small items of linen left to dry on hedges, which it stole to augment its nest.
Lapwing	*CE* IV.ii.27 *MAAN* III.i.24–25 *MM* I.iv.32 *Ham* V.ii.188–89	The peewit, a bird whose running on the ground to divert predators from its nest was considered comical. It was even thought to run about when newly hatched, carrying half its shell on its head.
Lark	*TS* Ind.ii.44 *TA* II.iii.149 *TA* III.i.158 *R&J* III.v.2, 6, 21–22, 27–32 *MND* III.i.129 *MND* IV.i.95 *T&C* IV.ii.8–9 *AW* II.v.6–7 *Lear* IV.vi.58 *Cym* III.vi.93 *WT* IV.iii.9–10 *V&A* 853–54	A symbol of morning, when its song is heard. Larks were captured by being frightened or distracted with red cloth and mirrors by one person while another netted them. The lark's song is lovely and warbling, but its eyes are notoriously ugly; hence the belief that it somehow got the toad's eyes by mistake.
Magpie	*3H6* V.vi.48 *TNK* I.i.19–22 *Mac* III.iv.125	A bird of bad omen at a birth or a marriage, known for its chattering voice and often associated in Shakespeare's works with other unsavory birds such as choughs. Sometimes it is called a pie or a maggot-pie.
Martlet	*MV* II.ix.27–28 *Mac* I.vi.3–10	The martin, a swallow that is blue-black on top and white underneath. It builds hanging nests, often on buildings. In heraldry it was represented as missing its legs and was associated with fourth sons, who were as landless as the bird was legless.
Nightingale	*TS* Ind.ii.36 *2GV* III.i.179	A bird valued for its song, which it sang at night, supposedly

Bird	Citations	Notes
	2GV V.iv.5 *R&J* III.v.2–6 *TNK* III.iv.25–26 *TNK* V.iii.123–28 *TN* III.iv.36–37 *A&C* IV.viii.18 *RL* 1080	while leaning against a thorn to keep itself awake. It was a symbol of chastity because of its associations with the myth of Philomela, though according to the myth, it was the faithful sister Procne, not the desperate and ravished Philomela, who was changed into a nightingale by the gods. The mournful sweetness of the song was supposed to arise from Procne's murder of her only son to punish her husband for raping her sister. The nightingale supposedly returned to England on April 3 of each year (old calendar). It was believed to sing *only* at night, though this was false.
Osprey	*TNK* I.i.138–39 *Cor* IV.vii.33–35	The osprey, like most birds of prey, was admired for its skill at hunting. Ospreys ate fish, which they caught so apparently easily that they were said to exert a kind of hypnotic control over their prey, which rolled over, belly up, at the ospreys' approach. Some believed the osprey had one foot taloned like a raptor and one foot webbed like a goose.
Ostrich	*2H6* IV.x.29 *1H4* IV.i.97 *A&C* III.xiii.196–97	Sometimes appears as "estridge."
Ousel	*2H4* III.ii.8 *MND* III.i.124–25	A blackbird; sometimes appears as "woosel."
Owl	*CE* II.ii.191 *1H6* IV.ii.15 *JC* I.iii.26–28 *2H6* III.ii.327 *T&C* II.i.91 *3H6* II.vi.55–58 *Cym* III.vi.93 *Mac* II.ii.3–4	Unlike most birds of prey, the owl was unquestionably an evil bird, probably because it hunted at night. All things associated with the night and darkness were negative to the Renaissance mind. The screech owl in particular was an omen of death,

Bird	Citations	Notes
	R3 IV.iv.507 *TA* II.iii.97 *LLL* IV.i.141 *LLL* V.ii.885, 913–14, 921–22 *V&A* 531	and could put any ill person "In remembrance of a shroud" (*MND* V.i.377). Shakespeare extends this belief into metaphor, using "screech owl" as a term for a person who brings bad news (*T&C* V.x.16–17). Elsewhere, the owl is noted as a slow flyer, a nocturnal creature, and an eater of mice. Another myth, that the owl was originally "a baker's daughter" who objected to, and substantially diminished a gift of bread to, Jesus, is referred to in *Hamlet* (IV.v.42–43).
Paraquito	*1H4* II.iii.85	Parakeet.
Parrot	*1H4* II.iv.100–101 *2H4* II.iv.265 *MAAN* I.i.135 *MV* III.v.46–47 *Oth* II.iii.277	Parrots were sometimes kept as pets and were noted for their ability to imitate words and do tricks. Shakespeare speaks in *Troilus and Cressida* of one being rewarded for its performance with an almond (V.ii.191–92).
Partridge	*2H6* III.ii.191	Appears as a kite's prey.
Peacock	*CE* IV.iii.79 *1H6* III.iii.6–7 *T&C* III.iii.251–52 *Temp* IV.i.74 *Ham* III.ii.288	A symbol of pride. Sometimes appears in variant spellings, for example as "pajock."
Pelican	*R2* II.i.126 *Lear* III.iv.74 *Ham* IV.v.147–48	Thought to bite its own breast to feed its young with its blood, the pelican was a symbol of parental sacrifice and filial ingratitude.
Pigeon	*TA* IV.iv.44 *Ham* II.ii.583 *LLL* V.i.71–72 *TA* IV.iii.78 s.d., 88, 92–111	Pigeons seldom appear as symbols of human faults or virtues, and are given no human characteristics except timidity. They are simply birds—small, eating peas, stuffing the mouths of their chicks, nuzzling their mates, and being eaten in turn by humans.

Bird	Citations	Notes
Popinjay	*1H4* I.iii.49	As a bird, a parrot; as a person, a fop or affected fool. It is sometimes rendered as "popin-gay."
Raven	*2H6* III.i.76 *3H6* V.vi.47 *TA* II.iii.97, 149, 153–54 *LLL* IV.iii.85 *John* IV.iii.152–53 *MAAN* II.iii.81–83 *Mac* I.v.38–40 *WT* II.iii.185 *TNK* I.i.19–22 *Oth* IV.i.20–22 *Ham* III.ii.258	The raven, being black, a carrion eater, and harsh-voiced, could hardly have had positive connotations in Shakespeare's day. Its presence was an omen of death, and was especially foreboding when glimpsed near a house in which a birth had taken place or in which someone was seriously ill. The raven is an especially long-lived bird.
Robin	*2GV* II.i.21–22 *Cym* IV.ii.224–27	Mentioned for its song; also appears as "ruddock." A nineteenth-century compilation of folklore lists various dire consequences believed to be caused by the harming of a robin, including the tendency of the local cows to give red milk afterward.
Rook	*LLL* V.ii.902 *Mac* III.iv.125	A crowlike bird with many of the same connotations.
Seamew	*Temp* II.ii.169–74	Seagull; appears in some editions as "scamels" in this passage.
Sparrow	*MND* III.i.129 *John* I.i.231 *AYLI* II.iii.44 *T&C* II.i.71–73 *T&C* III.ii.31–32 *MM* III.ii.175–76 *Lear* I.iv.216–17 *Ham* V.ii.222	Usually appears as something small and insignificant, but sometimes with references to its actual behavior, such as its frantic fear when caught, its nests in house eaves or hedges, and its inadvertent raising of cuckoo chicks. When kept as pets, sparrows were likely to be named "Philip" or "Phip" from the short chirping sound they made.
Starling	*1H4* I.iii.222–23	A small, dark brown or greenish-black bird.

Bird	Citations	Notes
Swallow	*R3* V.ii.23 *TA* II.ii.24 *TA* IV.ii.173 *2H4* IV.iii.32 *Tim* III.vi.29–30 *WT* IV.iv.118–19	Mentioned for its swift flight and its migratory behavior, which caused it to leave England in winter and return in April. There is also a reference to its nesting behavior in *Antony and Cleopatra* (IV.xii.3–4). Swallows flying low were said to portend rain. A medieval "cure" for blindness was to blind a swallow chick and watch the parent to see where she flew; the stone she lit on was supposed to have healing powers for the sightless. At the same time that it was acceptable to mutilate the young, however, the swallow was considered a sacred bird—the building of its nest near or on one's house was a special blessing, and the destruction of such nests was sure to bring down a curse of some kind.
Swan	*1H6* V.iii.56 *TA* IV.ii.102 *3H6* I.iv.19–21 *MWW* V.v.6–8 *T&C* I.i.60 *Oth* V.ii.247–48 *Cym* III.iv.140 *MV* III.ii.43–45 *R&J* I.ii.89	Swans were not purely ornamental birds in Shakespeare's time; they were also eaten at feasts. Yet they were appreciated for their white plumage, which to the Renaissance mind made them virtuous. There are references in Shakespeare's works to the softness of the cygnet's down, to the belief that swans died singing, and to Jupiter's disguising himself as a swan to seduce Leda (who bore four children in eggs, including Helen of Troy). The secretary of Frederick, Duke of Württemberg, in England in 1592, noted that there were many swans in the Thames but that it was forbidden to injure them because their feathers were reserved for use at Elizabeth's court.

Bird	Citations	Notes

Thrush	*MND* III.i.126
	MV I.ii.59
	WT IV.iii.9–10
		Mentioned for its song, especially in the summer; sometimes appears as "throstle." The missel thrush was noted for its willingness to sing even during storms. An 1875 approximation of its song went thus:
		    Knee deep, knee deep, knee deep,
		    Cherry du, cherry du, cherry du, cherry:
		    White hat, white hat;
		    Pretty Joey, pretty Joey, pretty Joey.
		Nineteenth-century superstitions held that the thrush shed its old legs periodically and got new ones, and that it was deaf.

Vulture	*TA* V.ii.31 *Mac* IV.iii.74 *MWW* I.iii.84 *2H4* V.iii.144 *V&A* 551	Like all carrion eaters, despicable.
Wagtail	*Lear* II.ii.69	A pipit-like bird with a long tail that it jerks up and down while running or after landing. To Shakespeare its behavior resembled the frequent bowing of obsequious men.
Woodcock	*3H6* I.iv.61 *TS* I.ii.159 *MAAN* V.i.156–57 *LLL* IV.iii.79 *TN* II.v.81 *AW* IV.i.94 *Ham* V.ii.308 *WT* IV.iii.35–36	A bird that could easily be trapped in a snare ("springe" or "gin"), hence anyone stupid or easily fooled.
Wren	*2H6* III.ii.42 *R3* I.iii.70 *MND* III.i.127 *Lear* IV.vi.111–13 *Cym* IV.ii.304–5 *TNK* V.iii.2–3 *TN* III.ii.64 *Mac* IV.ii.9–11	Small and timid.

See also Animals; Falconry and Fowling.

The woodcock, from Konrad Gesner's *Icones Avium Omnium*. Reproduced from the Collections of the Library of Congress.

Bleeding

One of the most common surgical prodecures in Europe for 1,500 years, bleeding (or phlebotomy) was primarily the legacy of one man, the second-century physician Galen, who vociferously championed its practice. Its popularity arose from a basic misunderstanding of the circulatory system, also propagated by Galen, that overlooked the cyclical path of blood in the body in favor of a kind of slow, tidal progress affected by the demands of various organs and the changes wrought in the blood by their activities. Practitioners, mistaken about the amount of blood in the body and what happened to the blood once it was produced, believed that a surfeit or "plethora" of blood could easily accumulate in the body, or even turn rotten, posing grave risk to the patient. Women of childbearing age were presumed to be at less risk; their menses, loss of blood in childbirth, and presumed loss of blood during conception and lactation were thought to confer upon them substantial immunity to "diseases of plethora," and there was much concern, therefore, when a woman's menstrual cycle was unexpectedly disrupted.

For patients without a menstrual safety net, practitioners deemed it useful to let off a little of the surplus blood from time to time, particularly in the spring (when blood production was assumed to be at its height), when diseases of plethora were evident, or to prevent such disease in those naturally susceptible. Since blood was considered a hot humor, bleeding was a common treatment for "hot" illnesses, such as fever (*2H4* IV.i.54–57; *LLL* IV.iii.94–95). Shakespeare also uses it as a potential cure for aggressiveness or pride (*R2* I.i.153–57; *T&C* II.iii.212–14), and, indeed, humoral imbalances were thought to distemper the mind as well as the body.

However, it was not sufficient merely to make an incision and let blood flow into a basin. The physician, if there was one, and the barber-surgeon who actually performed the operation had to know a great deal about the patient, the illness, the celestial conditions, and even the weather before determining when, where, and whether to bleed. The most important variable was the patient himself. Was he old or young? The young were thought to have more blood; the old, less—hence Lady Macbeth's perplexity that "the old man" Duncan ". . . had so much blood in him" (*Mac* V.i.42). Old people, therefore, were to have less blood removed than vigorous young adults (children under fourteen, as a rule, were not bled at all). Was he being bled for the first time? Then one should take less than usual, and work up to the standard amount in subsequent treatments. Was he dark-skinned, large-veined, or of a sanguine temperament? Then more should be taken. Was his pulse strong or weak to begin with, and how did he react to being bled? Galen recommended taking a little less than two pints (850 ml) from a typical patient, but advised that the session end when the patient fainted, the blood flow changed, or the quality of the pulse altered. Even Galen was aware of possible complications in the procedure; gangrene from the tourniquet and actual bleeding to death were two of the most severe.

The nature of the patient's disease was also crucial, particularly in choosing the vein to open. The temple or head was best for headaches and for diseases governed by the constellation Aries. The veins of the feet were best for diseases ruled by Pisces. The third finger of the left hand was indicated for ailments of the spleen; the elbow, for the eyes, ribs, lungs, diaphragm, spleen, liver, or stomach; the hams or ankles for the hips, bladder, and uterus; and either elbow or ankle for the kidneys. Sufferers from gout should be bled at the elbows, and epileptics at the legs. Diseases supposedly mitigated by bleeding—often really symptoms, rather than true diseases—ranged from simple fevers and coughs to arthritis, apoplexy, speech loss, tremor, and madness. Practitioners sometimes disagreed about which vein worked best for which body part, but most agreed on the upper body, especially the elbow or temple, for diseases of the upper body, and the legs or feet for diseases of the lower abdomen, pelvic region, and lower extremities. Almost all agreed that if only one side of the body was afflicted, the bleeding must take place on that side. Some argued further that the side of the body must also be determined by the time of year.

Timing was held to be as crucial as vein selection to a successful outcome. Particular attention was paid to the position of the sun, moon, and "lord of the ascendant" (*see* Astrology), for these controlled chronic disease, acute disease, and the fate of the patient, respectively. Bleeding could not take place when any of these bodies was in the disease's governing sign, during certain parts of the zodiacal year, near the change of the moon, during the dog days of late summer, or at any time when the weather was hot. Young people were best bled in the moon's first quarter, middle-aged men as it reached full, and the old as it waned. Such guidelines were doubtless in Richard II's mind when he advised, "Let's purge this choler without letting blood. . . . Our doctors say this is no time to bleed" (*R2* I.i.153–57). Certainly the rules for the timing of phlebotomy were standard fare in the immensely popular almanacs, and no doubt many people adhered to them, but they could be broken in severe cases.

These beliefs prevailed for all of Shakespeare's life. Therefore, when a character says, "God make incision in thee!" (*AYLI* III.ii.70), it is not a wish for harm to befall the person addressed, but for the heavens to perform healing surgery on him. Not until 1628 did William Harvey demonstrate the circulation of blood, and even then bleeding would remain a popular surgical treatment for at least another 250 years. *See also* Disease and Injury; Humors; Medical Practitioners.

Books

Books (*R&J* I.v.112; *T&C* IV.v.238; *1H6* V.i.22; *TA* IV.i.25; *AYLI* III.i.16) were certainly nothing new when Shakespeare began his literary career; they had been around, in one form or another, for thousands of years. Even printed books, made in large quantities on a press with movable type, had been around for more than a century, and the methods of their production were to remain unchanged in some particulars for another three or four centuries. Some details of readers' habits mentioned in Shakespeare—reading in bed (*Cym* II.ii.3–7), folding down a page corner to mark one's place (*Cym* II.ii.44–46; *JC* IV.iii.270–71), lending a book (*MWW* I.i.193–94), reading aloud to children (*TA* IV.i.12–14), filling a library or study with favorite volumes (*TS* III.i.81; *TA* IV.i.34; *Temp* I.ii.166–67), or reading in a quiet spot outdoors (*MAAN* II.iii.2–3)—are as familiar today as they were four centuries ago. Yet books were not nearly as numerous then as they are today, and in some ways they still bore traces of their manuscript origins.

Paper

Perhaps the most obvious difference between book manufacturing today and in the Renaissance is that then everything was done by hand, one piece at a time. Paper (*LLL* IV.ii.26; *TN* III.ii.45; *2H4* V.iv.10; *H5* II.ii.74), for example, was shaped one sheet at a time and pressed mostly dry in small batches. The paper pulp or "stuff" was made of washed, rotted, chopped, pounded, and simmered linen rags. When the tub of cooking stuff had reached just the right consistency, the papermaker used a wood-and-wire frame, often augmented with a wire watermark, to scoop

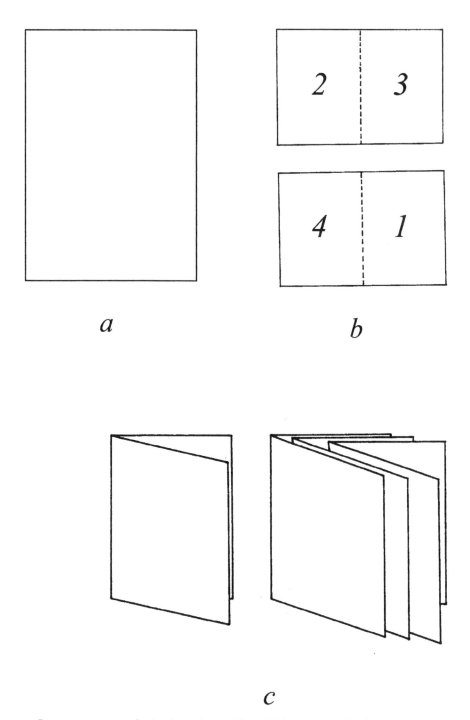

a   *b*

c

Page arrangements for books and pamphlets: (a) broadsheet; (b) folio back and front, showing the inner and outer formes; (c) a folio in twos and a folio in sixes; (d) inner and outer formes of a quarto; (e) a folded quarto, ready to be sewn and trimmed at the top edge; (f) inner and outer formes of an octavo sheet.

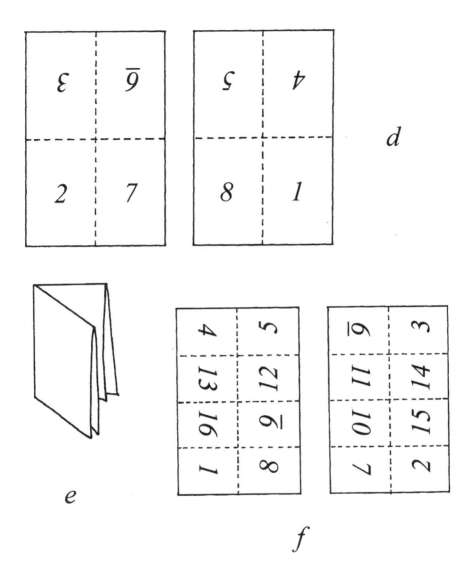

up, shake side-to-side, and drain a small portion of it. The drained sheet was turned out onto a felt pad, and several layers of these pads and sheets were pressed to remove the bulk of the water, using a mechancial press with two flat plates and a long screw to drive the plates together. Then the layers were unstacked and the paper sheets restacked and pressed again. Finally, the damp sheets were allowed to dry fully.

The size of the paper depended on the size of the mold. By the end of the sixteenth century, there were six supposedly standard sizes, ranging from imperial (75 × 50 cm / 29" × 19¾") down through royal, demy, crown, and foolscap to the tiniest, pot (32 × 38 cm / 12½" × 15"). Sometimes there was a double watermark—one to indicate the manufacturer and the other to indicate the size of the sheet. For example, a crown was used to signify crown-sized paper, a tankard for pot, a jester's hat for foolscap. In reality, these standard sizes might vary according to the frames used by the individual papermaker. Most paper was made on the Continent and imported, though there were some English papermakers (*2H6* IV.vii.38), like Sir John Spilman, who was granted a patent to manufacture white paper, including stationery for Elizabeth I, in 1589.

Paper for books, pamphlets, and broadsides could be folded in different ways to produce different publication sizes. A full sheet of paper, called a broadsheet (abbreviated as 1°), might be used, printed on one side only, as a public notice. Printed on both sides, it might serve as two pages of a very large-format book such as an atlas. The same sheet, folded in half once, yielded four folio (2°) pages, with pages 2 and 3 on one side and pages 4 and 1 on the other (*LLL* I.ii.180–81).

Pages 2 and 3, because they were on the inside of the folded sheet, were called the *inner forme*. Pages 1 and 4 were the *outer forme* (and, no matter how many pages a signature had, the side that contained the first and last pages of the signature was always the outer forme). Only one forme, or sheet side, could be printed at a time. Many books were printed in sizes smaller than the folio. A quarto (4°) sheet was folded twice, to yield eight pages. An octavo (8ᵛᵒ) was folded three times, and a sextodecimo (16ᵐᵒ) four times. Each of these folded sheets was usually considered to be a *signature*, one of the units of page sequences that were later sewn into the binding. (In some cases, the signature had multiple pages; a *folio in twos* was a book in which each sequential signature had only one folio sheet, while a *folio in sixes* had page sequences composed of three nested folio sheets.)

Ink

The ink (*LLL* IV.ii.27; *2H4* IV.i.50) applied to paper was not water-based, as were the inks used for pens and woodblocks, but oil-based, since oil-based inks stuck to the metal type without beading. These inks might be made with superior ingredients for lasting blackness and minimal bleeding—Gutenberg's Bible used lead, copper, and titanium to achieve the desired effects—or with cheap, inferior substitutes like lampblack. Once the thick, pasty ink was prepared, it was placed in a tray or on a block near the press to be applied to the type.

Type

Each individual type character was engraved on a steel punch, which was used to stamp a form, or matrix, from a softer metal. The matrix was then placed at the bottom of a wooden mold, designed so that its height and depth were consistent with others of its font or style, so that the press would strike all the characters with the same force and each line of type would be a uniform height on the page. The width of the mold could

industriam

Whines

eſt religionis

This Was an Apple

horſe

diſcretió

historia & amor

Type faces (and their texts in parentheses). From top: civilité (industriam); Wynkyn de Worde's great primer
(Whines); roman (est religionis); gross bastarda (This Was
an Apple); textura (horse); rotunda (discretion); italic
(historia et amor). Note the use of the long *s* in civilité,
roman, textura, and rotunda; the ligature of *s* and *t* in
civilité and the near-ligature of the same two letters in
italic; the ampersand for *et* (which means "and") in italic;
and the tittle standing for a dropped *n* in rotunda.

be varied to accommodate the difference in width between letters like *m* and *i*.

Next the typefounder—usually an employee of one of the three big typefounding houses located in Antwerp, Frankfurt, and Paris—poured a molten alloy into the mold. This alloy, containing about 75 percent lead, 12 percent tin, 12 percent antimony, and 1 percent copper, was developed by Gutenberg and remains in use, with minor changes, to this day. Its advantages included a low melting point, quick cooling, durability, and consistent volume at a wide range of temperatures. Considering the fact that each letter had to be cast individually and all its rough edges smoothed by hand, the process was remarkably quick. A trained typefounder could cast about 4,000 characters per day.

Printers needed as many characters as they could afford. Because printed books tried to re-create the experience of the manuscript book, in which every stroke of the pen required time and expensive vellum, printed text used many of the same shortcuts as the medieval manuscripts. Abbreviations, such as *y* for *th*, & for "and" (derived from "et," the Latin word for "and"), or a tilde for a dropped *m* or *n* (as in mã or Jonathã) were common. Other letters, such as *ct, fi, ff*, and *ae* were often linked or squashed together, and this required an additional piece of type for each such "ligature." The letter *s* sometimes appeared as we see it today, particularly at the ends of words, but it frequently appeared as *f*, a character known as the "long s." A printer thus needed a host of characters not found on today's keyboards, up to 300 in all including numerals and punctuation marks, and he (or she—there were some women in the trade) needed multiples of every character. An entire sheet—usually four to thirty-two text pages—or e's and j's and t's and so on were required for every tray of type that went into the press.

There were two ways to print the two sides of a sheet of paper. The first was *seriatim*, in sequence, with page 1 being composed first, then page 2, and so on. The problem was that, in the case of a quarto book, page 1 could not be printed until page 8 was also completed, and all the type from pages 1 through 6 lay idle once set, waiting for the completion of page 7 so that the inner forme could be printed. Print shops had a staggering number of type pieces available, but not so many that they could afford to compose large sections of a book at a time. Most therefore chose to compose pages by casting off, or estimating the number of words per page, and then composing pages 2, 3, 6, and 7, which were printed while pages 1, 4, 5, and 8 were being composed.

The compositor had to be skilled in order to guess how many words to allot to each page in advance. He began a page by arranging the type line by line in a thin tray called a composing stick, justifying for even margins on the left and right sides of the page by contracting words, altering spelling, and adding spaces. These lines were placed in a shallow tray called a galley, and the sheet as a whole was given a letter on its first page to help the binders put the signatures in alphabetical order. A few pages of each signature were also numbered to help keep them in order during folding, and to the bottom of each page the compositor added the first word appearing on the next page. This catchword assured the folders and cutters of the pages that they were assembling the pages in the proper order. In some cases, especially for the Bible and classical works, annotation might be added to the margins or "margent" (*R&J* I.iii.86; *Ham* V.ii.158). Such "glosses" could elucidate the text or merely confuse the reader further; to "gloze" could therefore mean to provide an explanation or to obfuscate the meaning with specious reasoning (*T&C* II.ii.165). The whole type block was moved to a flat table called an imposing stone with all the other pages of its forme. Pictures, titles, or framing lines were added, and all of these elements were wedged into an iron chase with blocks of wood.

The type thus arranged came in two principal styles. The more old-fashioned of the two, "black letter," mimicked the hand-lettering of medieval manuscripts. It came in five fonts: textura, fere-humanistica, rotunda, bastarda, and an informal mock cursive called "french letter" (later, civilité). In England, textura became known as the English black letter or great primer type; the other black-letter fonts were quickly superseded by this one. Black-letter, however, was doomed to be superseded by lighter "roman" fonts, which were easier to read and were thought to be more appropriate for classical works. Here, too, there was an informal, mock-cursive font, called italic, which was its own typeface, used to print entire books, for quite some time before being incorporated into roman typefaces for titles and emphases. After 1500, black-letter was decidedly a minority type style, except in specific regions; in Germany, it flourished until the mid-twentieth century.

Printing

The composed type, of whatever style and size, was now inked. Two ink balls, about 6 inches (15.2 cm) in diameter and held by wooden handles, were rolled and rotated on the ink block or tray and rolled together to ensure a smooth and even coat. Then they were rolled again on the type block. This work was easier than running the press and might be done by an apprentice, or by a skilled pressman as a break from harder labor. Simultaneously, another printer arranged a paper sheet, moistened to help the ink adhere, on a double-hinged frame. When this frame was open and ready for a new sheet of paper, the layer farthest from the press held a parchment frame called a frisket, with as many rectangular holes in it as there were pages on the forme. The frisket kept the margins of the paper ink-free. The paper itself was fixed to the middle layer, called the tympan, by being pressed over two pins. Then the frisket was folded onto the tympan and again onto the inked type block. The whole assembly was then rolled into the press (*MWW* II.i.74–77), where the pressman cranked down the platen and released it. The sheet was removed, proofread, and set aside to dry until it came time to imprint the other side. (Discovery of a mistake did not always mean the resetting of the type block; such work was often too time-consuming. Instead, a page of errata was added to the end of the book.) The next sheet was now affixed to the tympan while the inker rolled the ink balls together or re-inked them; the balls were re-inked every one to three impressions, depending on the density of the type.

It took about four hours to run one forme of a 1,000-copy edition (1,000 to 1,500 copies was a standard print run); then the sheet, still

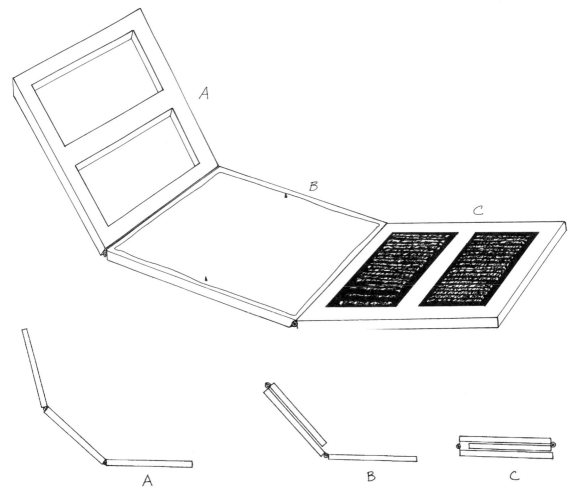

Simplified diagrams of the paper and type block setup. The top figure shows the frisket (A), tympan with a sheet of paper affixed to the pins (B), and type block (C). The bottom figure shows the open assembly (A); the frisket folded onto the tympan (B); and then again onto the type block (C) before being impressed.

Printers setting type, inking the blocks, and printing pages. The composi-
tors work in the background, while an assistant inks the type and the
master removes a freshly printed page. Soon a new sheet of paper will be
affixed using the two small pins. From *Panoplia*, illustrated by Jost Amman. Reproduced from the Collections of the Library of Congress.

somewhat moist, was "perfected," or printed on the other side. A forty-
eight-page folio or ninety-six-page quarto took about twelve days to print
at this rate, assuming that only one press was in use. Many printers, however, had more than one press so that they could work on multiple jobs
or on multiple sheets of the same book. At the end of the printing of one
forme, the printers washed all the type and stored it in the proper parts of
each type case. When the workday was over, the ink balls were disassembled, the stuffing thoroughly washed, and the covers soaked in urine.

Authors, Booksellers, and Printers

An author who wanted to see his work published (or an acquaintance who chose to publish another's work, with or without his consent) almost always had to go to London. The only presses located outside of the capital were those at the universities and those clandestinely publishing works considered to be heretical or seditious (*TN* I.v.226). There were twenty to thirty printers in London at any one time during Shakespeare's life, some with multiple presses; in May 1583, there were two who owned as many as five presses.

Not all authors went straight to a publisher. Some sold their work to booksellers, who in turn contracted with a printer for publication. By far the largest concentration of bookstalls was in St. Paul's Churchyard in London, where apprentices cried their wares—"Buy some new book, sir!"—and volunteered to search for a book to suit the client's taste, standing below the colorful signs that marked their employers' shops: the Brazen Serpent, the Green Dragon, the Hand and Star, the Tiger's Head, the White Greyhound. Some customers preferred to browse for themselves, perusing the extra copies of title pages that were posted as advertisements. This practice explains why Renaissance book titles often tended to be dozens of words long; the first page had to serve as both title and what today would be the dust-jacket copy (*2H4* I.i.60–61; *Per* II.iii.3–4). The cost of books can be judged from a 1598 Stationers' Company ordinance setting the price of pictureless books at 1d per ½ to 2 sheets, depending on typeface. Keeping in mind that a sheet yielded eight quarto pages, this meant that a book like one of the early quartos of Shakespeare that predated the publication of the First Folio might sell for about 6d. Readers in the provinces could buy these London-printed books at town booksellers (of which there were at least a few) or from traveling salesmen and peddlers at fairs and markets who stood on stools to cry their wares.

To supplement their limited income, authors liked to seek a patron for their work (*Tim* I.i.; *TS* I.ii.154). A patron might provide a gift of money in exchange for the pleasure of seeing his or her name in print, although authors complained frequently that such gifts were never substantial enough. More important, a patron served as a "brand-name" recommendation for the book, assuring the reader that some aristocrat or clergyman or scholar approved of the work. This use of the patron's good name to sell books was sometimes audaciously used by authors who were not personally acquainted with their patrons, and explains why some dedications to patrons were so cautious and fawning. Even if the patron in question responded to the flattery of the dedication with a monetary present, the author's income was hardly generous. Translator Richard Robinson, for example, made only £40 in publication fees and £20 from the sale of author's copies from twelve books published over a period of fifteen years.

He received occasional sums from patrons, varying from a few pounds to 2 shillings, but hardly enough to make him wealthy or even comfortable. Authors seldom made substantial sums from their works.

The books, complete with dedication (S 82), apologetic address to the reader, contents, title page, errata, illustrations (if any), and perhaps an index, prologue, or appendix (*Oth* II.i.257–58; *T&C* I.iii.343; *TS* IV.iv.104), were sold unbound (*R&J* I.iii.87–88, III.ii.83–84). Some booksellers bound the pages themselves; some did not, but could direct the customer to a nearby bookbinder. The customer chose the sort of cover he liked—parchment, calfskin, and sheepskin were the most common materials—and the book was collated, folded, and sewn to a strip of cords or thongs. Sturdy endpapers were pasted to the front and back pages, and the three unsewn sides of the book were trimmed; in the case of quartos, sextodecimos, and other small books, this was when the folded edges of the pages were cut. Boards were then pasted to the endpapers and the leather binding pasted to the boards. Hot iron stamps could be used to print letters onto the leather, and for an extra fee this tooling could be gilded. Some books were sold already bound, including school texts, the Bible, the Prayer Book (*R3* III.vii.46, IV.iii.14; *MV* II.ii.187), and law books (*MV* IV.i.156); some were given particularly ornate bindings, complete with jeweled covers or metal clasps (*R&J* I.iii.91–92; *1H4* I.iii.186; *TN* I.iv.13–14). An octavo could be bound for a few pennies, a Shakespeare First Folio for perhaps 4s.

Not all printers specialized in books or printed books exclusively. Only 4,370 books were published between 1580 and 1603, an average of 180 a year from 1590 to 1603, and with twenty to thirty printers in business, there was not enough book-printing work to go around. Some printers, therefore, produced lottery tickets, announcements, event programs, music, and other items as well as books and pamphlets (*1H6* III.i.2).

The governing body of the printers was the Stationers' Company; its authority was limited to London but, as we have seen, almost all presses were located there. Authors could pay a nominal fee to the Company to have a copyright entered, and until 1586 the Company did most of the censoring and licensing of published works. Between 1557 and 1588, however, this licensing duty shifted gradually to a board of twelve deputies of the Archbishop of Canterbury. The Company remained an important body, however. It arbitrated disputes between printers, appointed pairs (and, after 1586, trios) of inspectors to locate and shut down unauthorized printers, and supervised apprenticeships. It heard complaints of copyright violations, print runs exceeding the legitimate number of copies, and bookstalls open on Sundays or feast days.

A common complaint was that a rival printer was issuing copies of patented works—items such as the ABC and Little Catechism, proclamations, dictionaries, and the Bible, which were granted by royal fiat to the presses of one printer alone (*TS* IV.iv.93). Plagiarism was a serious problem. In the case of the ABC and Little Catechism, for which John Day held the patent, an unauthorized printer named Roger Ward issued 10,000 copies of the stolen work, going so far as to copy Day's name and mark. Though warned to stop his activity, he persisted, and his house was searched, his property seized, his three presses destroyed, and his type mangled. He kept at it, and his next operation, hidden in a tailor's shop and some henhouses, and the one after that, located in a tanner's house, were also found and destroyed.

Types of Books

London's presses, authorized and illicit, produced a wide variety of reading material. The largest single category, comprising about 40 percent of the titles published, was religious literature: the Bible (at least 100 editions during Elizabeth I's reign), the New Testament (at least thirty editions during the same period), sermons, prayer books, theological arguments, catechisms, and descriptions of the deaths of martyrs and heretics. Almanacs, prognostications, and calendars were also popular. There were hundreds of almanacs (*A&C* I.ii.149–50; *WT* IV.iv.792–93; *CE* I.ii.41; *MND* III.i.52–54; *2H4* II.iv.269–70) published during the sixteenth century, and they tended to follow more or less the same pattern. They contained a calendar, fast days, saints' days, a leap year chart, the phases of the moon, the dates of holidays that might fall on different days each year (like Easter), the best times to bleed and purge, weather predictions, horoscopes, predictions for places and rulers, a diagram of the zodiacal man, and the best times for planting crops or castrating livestock. General predictions for the coming year contained a standard assortment of calamities, diseases, eclipses, comets, and natural disasters.

Literature, in the form of poetry, plays, romances, and classical literature was also popular. Most of the books mentioned by name (though not necessarily by publisher's title) in Shakespeare's works are literary or quasi-literary: the "Book of Riddles" (*MWW* I.i.191–92), "the 'Hundred Merry Tales' " (*MAAN* II.i.125), and the "Book of Songs and Sonnets" (*MWW* I.i.188–89), which was actually the *Miscellany* published by Richard Tottel (at the sign of the Hand and Star, mentioned above). The poetry of Chaucer was particularly popular.

Nonfiction works, other than religious publications and almanacs, included histories (such as Raphael Holinshed's *Chronicles*, a project so large that it was shared by five publishers), law books, medical texts, travel accounts such as Richard Hakluyt's *Voyages*, grammars, descriptions of notable trials, cookbooks, and guides to beekeeping, silk production, hunting, riding, farming, sailing, mathematics, economics, proper behavior (*AYLI* V.iv.90–91), and science. *See also* Education; Letters; Literacy; Writing.

Bow

The sword was the weapon of prestige in Renaissance Europe but, in England at least, the weapon all men knew how to use was the bow. They were, in fact, required by statute to practice the bow between the ages of seven and sixty. This is not to say that they all knew how to use it well; those arguing for the replacement of bows by muskets in the English army, near the end of the sixteenth century and at the beginning of the seventeenth, complained about archers who shot without fully drawing back the bowstring, or who shot without aiming properly, or who became too fatigued to use their all-important arm and back muscles to the fullest. In *King Lear* there is also a complaint about such an amateur who "handles his bow like a / crow-keeper" (IV.vi.87–88), and an injunction for the incompetent to draw his arm back so that the distance between shaft and string was a full yard at its widest point. An adequate "draw" is also a subject of discussion in *Titus Andronicus*, when Marcus gives a demonstration of his skills (IV.iii.2–3, 53).

The Longbow and Its Arrows

The great longbow victory at Agincourt in the days of Henry V was a distant memory, and Shakespeare's audience must have grown nostalgic when they heard his eulogy for a great archer of the best old-fashioned sort:

> 'A drew a good bow, and dead! 'A shot a fine shoot.
> John a Gaunt loved him well and betted much money on his head. Dead!
> 'A would have clapped i' th' clout at twelve score, and carried you a fore-
> hand shaft a fourteen and fourteen and a half, that it would have done a
> man's heart good to see. (*2H4* III.ii.45–51)

This man, in other words, could hit the white center (*TS* V.ii.188) of a target or clout at twelve times twenty yards, and shoot a heavy forehand arrow up to 280 or 290 yards. Archery is a common source of metaphor in Shakespeare's works; any desired goal can be a butt (a mark or target), and love in particular is likened to the arrow's flight because of the association of Cupid and the bow (*3H6* I.iv.29; *MAAN* I.i.38, II.i.238–39; *R&J* I.i.209–11; *H5* I.ii.186; *Oth* V.ii.267; *Per* I.i.163–65).

The English longbow (*MND* I.i.9–10; *Lear* I.i.143; *LLL* IV.i.116–40; *AYLI* IV.iii.4) was a formidable weapon, with a six-foot shaft of yew or elm; yew (*R2* III.ii.116–17) was the stronger and more expensive wood, but the making of cheaper elm bows was required by law, to make the weapon accessible to all for the sake of national defense. The string (*MAAN* III.ii.10; *MND* I.ii.109) was of hemp, flax, or silk. Archers, being ordinary fellows mustered in time of war, needed little in the way of special equipment. They were instructed to use a bracer—a laced tube of leather,

Longbowmen flanking a halberdier, from a broadside.

metal, or some other sturdy material—around the left forearm to protect arm and shirtsleeve against the string, and to wear a glove made of leather and lined with scarlet, a kind of fabric, on the right hand. They also needed, if they wished to take good care of their bows, wax for polishing the wood, wool for wrapping them, and leather or wood bow cases (*1H4* II.iv.249–50) for storing them.

Archers in the army stood as many as six deep, with the ranks in back firing higher into the air to pass over their companions' heads and onto the enemy's troops. Practiced longbowmen could fire six arrows per minute, compared with the musketeers' top rate of one shot per minute and a half by about 1600. However, the bow was also used for hunting (*LLL* IV.i.24), and there were different arrows (*H5* I.ii.207–8; *2H4* IV.iii.32; *LLL* V.ii.262; *Ham* IV.vii.21–24) for different purposes.

Standard longbow arrows were a yard long, but arrows came in different sizes and with different points. Sharp arrows included the broadhead, which, with its wide slashing edges, was best against big game; the forkhead, with a double point, which was used for small game; and the bodkin, which had a stiff, straight point for piercing armor in war. Blunt arrows included the birdbolt (*MAAN* I.i.40; *TN* I.v.93), used to shoot birds and mammals so small that piercing arrows would have ripped them apart, and the target head. The steles or shafts of the arrows could be made of almost any kind of wood; goose feathers were glued to the butt or back end of the stele to stabilize the arrow during flight. The heavier the arrow, the stiffer the feathers needed to be, and so feathers for fletching heavy arrows tended to be taken from older geese. Unfletched arrows were called "butt-shafts" (*LLL* I.ii.171–72; *R&J* II.iv.17). Whatever the fletching, the arrow was notched on the butt end so that it could be rested on the drawn bowstring.

Crossbows

The crossbow (*3H6* III.i.1 s.d.; *H5* IV.viii.93) operated on the same principle as the longbow—a taut string and a curved piece of wood being used to propel a sharpened object a great distance—but the resemblance ended there. For one thing, the longbow had only a shaft and string; the crossbow had several important parts. It had a bow of ash or yew that was crossed (hence the name) at a right angle on top of the front end of a piece called a tiller or stock. Later versions had a bow of a composite material, made of glued wood, horn, and sinew wrapped in parchment, and still later versions had a stock and bow of steel.

Another difference was that the crossbow's bow was much stiffer than the longbow and re-quired one or more special ad-aptations to draw it. One of these was a stirrup. The crossbowman could place the front end of the stock on the ground, insert one or both feet into a stirrup, and pull up on the string with all his might. The stirrup was often paired with a windlass, a device consisting of several pulleys and a crank that were used to draw the string backward. This windlass-and-stirrup combination could be

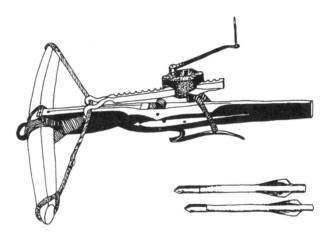

German crossbow fitted with a possibly French cranequin, both from the late fifteenth century, and quarrels.

used only by infantrymen, for a rider had no place to brace his feet in order to draw the bow. An easier device, one that could be operated by a man on horseback, was the cranequin, which used a rack, a cranked iron drum, and a pair of hooks that gripped the string and pulled it back. In either case, the string, once pulled tight, was kept in place by a notched nut or "sticking-place" (*Mac* I.vii.60) until the crossbowman was ready to fire.

The typical missile fired by a crossbow was a short, arrowlike projectile with a wooden or leather shaft and a quadrangular iron head. It was called a "quarrel," from the Latin *quadrellus*, "little square." The quarrel had no nock, or notch, in the end to affix it to the bowstring, but sometimes the butt end was reinforced with bone or horn. Because of its high velocity, it could not be fletched with feathers, but had to be stabilized with wood, leather, or brass. Quarrels were carried in quivers of wood or leather hung from bandoliers or belts.

Some crossbows fired specialized bolts. There was a large type of quarrel with a crescent-shaped head nearly a foot wide that was used for cutting ships' rigging. An enormous type of crossbow called a ballista was used in siege warfare to fling gigantic arrows at defenders. And a small, lightweight crossbow called a stonebow (*TN* II.v.44) or pellet crossbow was used in hunting. Spannable by hand, it had a pouch made of crossed strings, meant to hold a pebble or a metal or clay bullet, instead of a single bowstring. Hunting remained the primary use of the crossbow long after it had been superseded in warfare by the musket. *See also* Firearms; Weapons.

Brass

Brass (*T&C* I.iii.64; S 65), an alloy of copper and zinc, was one of the hardest metals known in Shakespeare's day. He uses it as a symbol of something enduring (*H8* IV.ii.45; *MM* V.i.11; S 64). He rarely identifies an object as made of brass, though he does mention a military trumpet (*T&C* I.iii.256–57) and a cannon (*H5* III.i.11). The copper used in brass was mostly imported, although there was some mining of it in Cornwall and Wales. Zinc and copper alike could be found in Britain's highlands. Workers in brass were known as braziers (*H8* V.iv.39).

Brick

Brick buildings were a brand-new concept in Shakespeare's England and were still fairly rare. He never mentions a brick house in all his works. However, he does mention a brick chimney (*2H6* IV.ii.147–48), a brick wall (*WT* IV.iv.794) of indeterminate use, and brick walls around gardens (*MM* IV.i.28–33; *2H6* IV.x.7–8). Jack Cade's father is a bricklayer (*2H6* IV.ii.43, 144), and perhaps Shakespeare had seen a brick kiln, a brick-lined tunnel in which bricks were fired. One Essex example from the period was 12 feet long and 16 feet wide. For large projects with access to a good supply of clay (*R2* I.i.179; *Lear* I.iv.306), the bricks might be fired on-site, but wherever they were fired, they were made of clay that had been picked clean of stones and trodden by barefoot workers, mixed with sand to keep it from sticking, then pressed into wooden molds sprinkled with sand, dried for at least two weeks, and then fired in a kiln for about 48 hours. The color of the bricks varied with the composition of the local clay, and initially the width, depth, and height of bricks varied from region to region. Eventually, width and length were standardized, though depth remained inconsistent until the twentieth century.

Tiles for floors and roofs were made in much the same way, though more care was taken in the selection and preparation of the clay, and tiles were baked harder than bricks. They were fired along with bricks in the same kilns, the bricks being arranged to shield the more delicate tiles from the fiercest heat. Sometimes floor tiles were made in two colors by stamping a design in red clay and filling it with a lighter color or by spreading the lighter clay on the design block just before stamping the tile. *See also* Architecture.

Bridges

Bridges (*1H6* I.iv.67; *MAAN* I.i.309; *H5* III.vi.2–4, 11–13, 64, 89–95, 172; *Lear* III.iv.56) were built much as they had been in Roman days— of stone, in a sequence of arches topped by a cobbled pavement. The one at Stratford-on-Avon had fourteen arches and had been built in the fifteenth century; London Bridge (*1H6* III.i.23) was longer and older. It had already had several incarnations, and would have more between Shakespeare's day and ours, but the one that stood at the same time as the old Globe Theatre had been built in 1209. The cartographer Abraham Ortelius called it "a faire stone bridge of twenty piles, very goodly arched. Upon this bridge are houses so built on ech side, that it seemeth almost to be a continual street, not a bridge." Ships sailed under the stone arches while overhead, people passed under a set of spikes upon which traitors' heads and parboiled body parts hung as a perpetual warning against treason.

Few bridges were built in England in Shakespeare's lifetime, though many were repaired. Potholes developed in the pavement and had to be filled with new stone, and sometimes entire arches were damaged; both ends of the Stratford bridge were broken by a flood in 1588 and had to be rebuilt. Repairs of this kind were typically undertaken by the corporate town in which the bridge was located or, if the bridge lay outside a town, by the county government.

Business

What we think of as a modern economy did not exist in the Renaissance, when business was conducted almost entirely as it had been in the Middle Ages. There were no banks and no stock market. There was little credit. There was no insurance, so a business loss could mean bankruptcy and devastation. Worst of all, those who fell into debt were liable to arrest, and once arrested, they were seldom able to become solvent.

Merchants and Tradesmen

Most artisans were also shopkeepers, for there was little wholesaling of goods. The craftsman who made a pair of gloves or a suit of armor sold it from his shop or his market stall. Nevertheless, there were some middlemen, or "chapmen" (*LLL* II.i.16; *T&C* IV.i.75–76), whose only job was to buy and sell the handiwork of others. Brokers (*2H6* I.ii.100–101; *3H6* III.iii.63) bought and sold commodities like grain and cattle on a grand scale, and merchants (*2H4* II.iv.63–66; *R&J* II.iv.151; *MV* IV.i.23; *Tim* I.i.ch.) sent ships to Italy, Spain, Africa, or the Levant to bring back rich cargoes of spices, ivory, gold, cloth, and wine. A lot or shipment of some substance was called a "commodity" (*TN* III.i.45–46) and could be purchased with a "bill" (*2H6* IV.vii.128) or promissory note.

On a smaller scale, grocers retailed items like the merchants' spices, and peddlers traveled to fairs and markets, selling trinkets like mirrors, ribbons, ballads, and cheap jewelry (*2H6* IV.ii.47–48; *TS* Ind.ii.19; *LLL* V.ii.318–

A peddler, from *Panoplia*, illustrated by Jost Amman. He carries a standard array of wares, including knives, cheap jewelry, gloves, and a mirror. Reproduced from the Collections of the Library of Congress.

19; *WT* IV.iv.181–228, 600–603). Shakespeare tends to dwell on the makers rather than the sellers of goods, but he does mention costermongers (*2H4* I.ii.171), who sold fruit, especially apples; orange-wives, who sold oranges (*Cor* II.i.73); fosset-sellers (*Cor* II.i.74), who sold keg taps; and oyster-wenches (*R2* I.iv.31), who cried their wares in the streets. He also says a little about their tactics, for he accuses tradesmen of habitual lying (*WT* IV.iv.725–26), insists that they denigrate items in order to get a better price when buying wares, and indicates through the character Costard that haggling was an important aspect of the marketing experience (*LLL* III.i.135–41).

If buyers sought to emphasize the defects in their purchases, so as to get a better price, sellers sought to do the opposite. Wandering through the streets with a basket or wagon, or stationed near their stalls on market days, they sang the virtues of their merchandise. Booksellers' apprentices accosted passing gentlemen with encouragement to "buy some new book," victuallers called out that they had hot pippin pies, and the oyster-women, according to an early seventeenth-century ballad, asked at the tops of their lungs whether their customers wanted

> Anye muscles lilly white!
> Herrings, sprats or place,
>   or cockles for delight.
> Any welflet oysters!

Sellers of bed-mats and brooms and colliers hauling coal filled the streets as well, and the Thames was crowded with watermen happy to ferry passengers to the playhouses across the river in Southwark. The pander in *Pericles* is thus one voice among many when he tries to generate interest in his latest girl; he reports that "I have cried her almost to the number of her / hairs; I have drawn her picture with my voice" (IV.ii.95–96). Merchants had other skills as well. They might show their least attractive goods first, so that they could bring out some that were slightly better; the contrast sometimes induced the customer to buy the more expensive products (*T&C* I.iii.358–61). When a price was agreed upon, the customer handed over money or barter goods. For larger transactions, a handshake might seal the deal (*H5* V.ii.132), and a deposit, called "earnest" (*H5* V.i.65; *CE* II.ii.24; *Per* IV.ii.45), might be given as a sign of good faith. Not all deals went well, however; "bought and sold" (*CE* III.i.72; *1H6* IV.iv.13; *R3* V.iii.306) was slang for cheated, betrayed, or deceived.

Billing and accounting were low-tech but performed in a way that most people today could understand. When goods had been deliverd or a service performed, especially in complicated transactions like the sewing of a complete suit of clothes or the provision of food and entertainment at a tavern or inn, it was customary for the seller to write out an itemized bill (*1H4* II.iv.540–44, III.iii.77–89), also called the "reckoning" (*1H4* II.iv.103) or "score" (*1H4* V.iii.31; *2H6* IV.ii.73–74). Merchants kept books in which they wrote credits and debits; when sums owed to them were paid, they crossed off the item (*Cym* III.iii.26) and often kept some sort of note as further proof that the debt was canceled. There were no calculators, but tradesmen, unlike aristocrats, tended to be well schooled in practical mathematics either with pen and paper or with counters, small tokens that stood for ones, tens, hundreds, and thousands (*Cym* V.iv.139–40). The owners of small shops performed this duty themselves; substantial landowners and merchants had stewards or clerks (*2H6* IV.ii.85–92) to handle their accounting (*TNK* V.ii.57–59; *H5* I.Pro.17) and perhaps audited the books occasionally (*Tim* II.ii.162–64).

Cash and Credit

Most transactions were conducted on a cash basis, but there was some credit (*MV* I.i.177–85; *MM* I.i.39–40; *1H4* I.ii.54–55) available even in the absence of banks. Wealthy individuals, including some women and many merchants and goldsmiths, would lend money if given some sort of collateral and a promise to pay interest (*AW* I.i.149–51). Usury (*R&J* III.iii.123–24; *MAAN* II.i.183; *Lear* III.ii.90; *Tim* II.ii.98) had an extremely bad name in the Renaissance, though it was to become essential to the conduct of commerce in later centuries. Contrary to Shakespeare's implication in the *Merchant of Venice*, it was not only Jews who lent money at interest; kings and queens, including Henry VIII and Elizabeth I, permitted foreign nobles and rulers to borrow from them.

If one needed money quickly and could not secure a loan, pawning valuable possessions was the preferred route (*MWW* II.i.94–95; *2GV* I.iii.47, II.iv.91; *2H4* II.i.140–42; *2H6* V.i.113; *3H6* IV.ii.9). Even nobles did this on occasion. The pawnbroker's symbol was three gold balls, taken from the arms of Lombardy; Lombard moneylenders had replaced the ousted Jews of England in the fourteenth century after the English realized that someone had to be around to supply emergency cash.

Some merchants would extend credit to good clients. Cloth and clothing retailers, for example, so often had customers who owed huge sums that credit seems to have been a routine part of their business. It is all the more telling, then, that Falstaff cannot secure credit for twenty-two yards of satin (*2H4* I.ii); even the tailors and silk merchants will have nothing to do with him. Many a man, like Falstaff, got so deeply in debt to his tailors, and the other purveyors of his lavish lifestyle (*MV* I.i.122–60), that he hardly knew how to extricate himself; he grew to dread the bills (*2H4* V.i.19–20; *MAAN* III.iii.174–75) delivered by the various tradesmen who supplied him.

For the tradesmen it was almost as bad, for if their clients defaulted, there was little they could do. The best advice was that given by Pistol to his tavern-hostess wife: "The word is 'Pitch and pay' [Cash only]. Trust none: / For oaths are straws, men's faiths are wafer-cakes" (*H5* II.iii.49–50). Failing that, businessmen were to write down in their books (*Lear* III.iv.96) every sum owed them, secure the creditor's signature and seal on important documents (*MV* IV.i.139), and, if possible, confiscate goods in lieu of cash. Shakespeare writes of horses being seized to pay debts (*MWW* V.v.115–16) and of land being mortgaged at interest for the same purpose (*Tim* I.ii.202–3). Sometimes, merchants digsuised moneylending as a purchase of worthless goods, such as the "commodity of brown paper and old ginger" of *Measure for Measure* (IV.iii.5), charging an exorbitant rate that was really the repayment of the loan.

If all else failed, merchants could pay a bailiff to arrest (*CE* IV.i.1–11, 69, 77, 103–9; *Tim* I.i.94–99; *2H4* II.i) the bankrupt (*2H4* Epil.11–12; *MV* III.i.315–20, or "bankrout"—*R2* IV.i.263–66; *MV* III.i.315–20; S 67) customer for debt. The debtor would be placed in jail, and freed when he managed to repay his debts (*CE* IV.iv.108–20), but for most men, being in jail meant being out of work. Combined with the high fees extorted from prisoners by jailers, this meant that it was hard, if not impossible, to become solvent again. Many a man begged people passing by the jails for a scrap of food or a spare coin; many a man arrested for debt spent the rest of his life in jail and died there. For this reason, creditors (*Cym* V.iv.138) used arrest as a last resort, sometimes waiting until the debtor was dead and arresting his corpse at the graveside. The arrest of Antiochus in *The Comedy of Errors* is thus much swifter than it would have been in real life. A real tradesman would first have tried, if his resources permitted, negotiation (*2H4* Epilogue.14–16; *Cym* V.iv.18–21) and confiscation. The more likely course is that taken in *Timon of Athens*, a play that is mostly about a man in debt. Here there are attempts to recover loans, the day-to-day fielding of bills, the desperate pleas of the debtor for more money or more time, the horror of being dunned in tones of contempt and suspicion, whereas at one time there had been nothing but respect and graciousness (II.i, II.ii).

Candles

See Lighting.

Carnation

A pale pink; used in Shakespeare's time to signify a European flesh tone. (*LLL* III.i.144; *H5* II.iii.33).

Castle

Castles (*2H6* I.iv.36, 38; *TA* III.i.169; *R2* II.iii.159–60, III.ii.170) were introduced into England with William the Conqueror, who solidified his hold on the countryside by building earth mounds with wooden fortresses on top, surrounded by sharpened-stake fences called palisades (*1H4* II.iii.51) and sometimes by ditches or moats. Once the Norman conquest was reasonably secure, the nobles began to make their castles more permanent, replacing wooden rectangular fortresses on artifically constructed "mottes," or mounds, with rectangular and later circular stone shell-keeps on natural hills or islands. The keep (or "donjon," hence the word "dungeon"—see *R3* I.ii.111; *JC* I.iii.94) was a single large structure that rose three to four stories, dominating the surrounding curtain wall and reachable only by means of a drawbridge (*R3* III.v.15), with perhaps another ring of fortifications, another ditch, and another drawbridge beyond the first. Inside the almost windowless keep, rooms for the lord of the castle and his family rose story by story within the thick stone shell.

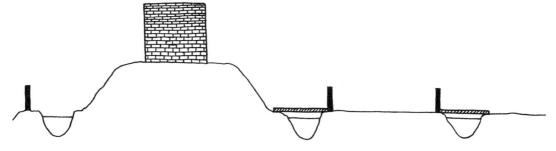

Cross-section of a motte-and-bailey fortification, showing square keep, curtain walls, water-filled ditches, and bridges over ditches. The artificial mound on which the keep stands is the motte; the area within the walls is the bailey. The keep has been rendered in a stonework pattern for the sake of clarity, but it would actually, if built on a motte rather than a natural hill, have been constructed of timber.

As time went on, the castle changed in design. Gradually, the space within the "bailey" or outer wall was absorbed by an assortment of buildings, some housing the lord and his servants, others devoted to storage, stabling, workshops, armories, and so on. The massive stone walls of the keep were seen as, at least in part, a waste of good space, and more and more chambers on the upper floors were built into hollow spaces in the walls. These "mural chambers" made the most of space, but they weakened the structural integrity of the walls. Eventually, the whole notion of the keep was abandoned, though the assemblage of shorter buildings in the bailey remained. England was building keepless castles from about 1170 until about 1485, though the old-fashioned rectangular keep survived in new construction until about 1250.

Even the new keepless castles had weaknesses, however, and several innovations were introduced to remove them. Round or D-shaped towers (*R&J* IV.i.78; *S* 64; *TNK* V.i.55) were installed at strategic points around the curtain walls, with arrows slits in the walls to protect defending archers

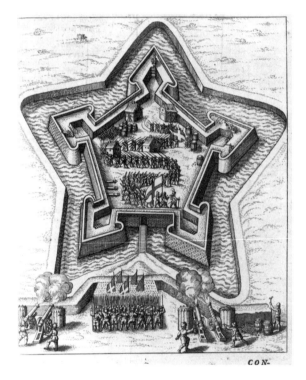

The new style in castles, a star-shaped fortress with angle bastions, is shown on the first page of the section on military science of Robert Fludd's *Utriusque Cosmi Historia* (1624). Note the presence outside the fortress of cannon and a "square" of pikemen with ensign-bearers in their center. Inside the castle, a troop of men with firearms marches, led by a commander, a drummer, and an ensign or "ancient" with a huge flag. Reproduced from the Collections of the Library of Congress.

from enemy fire, and crenellations or battlements (indented stone trim, the raised portions of which were called merlons) on the tops of walls and towers for the same purpose. Battlements (*Mac* I.ii.22–23, I.v.40; *R2* III.iii.51; *John* II.i.374; *Ham* V.ii.272) were seen as such a significant strategic advantage that, in the fourteenth century, nobles needed a royal license to crenellate the towers of their homes. The entry gates now had portcullises (*R2* I.iii.167), cross-hatched gates that could be lowered on both sides of an emeny. The soldiers, trapped between the portcullises, could be shot at leisure through murder holes that overlooked this fortified entrance, or barbican. In 1591, Claude Paradin's book of emblems, *Heroicall Devises*, showed a portcullis with the chains that raised or lowered it and the motto *Securitas altera*, "another (or second) security." With a crown between the chains, it was a favorite symbol of Henry VIII, appearing on his coinage.

Further improvements were found to be necessary as the centuries passed. Round towers had been an improvement over square ones, because missiles tended to bounce off curves and shatter corners. But round towers allowed for blind spots at which the attackers could mine the walls with gunpowder. Therefore, pointed or polygonal towers were introduced to do away with the blind spots. By this time, however, the castle was hopelessly old-fashioned in an England that had been quite peaceful under the Tudors and seldom in serious danger of foreign invasion. A fear of the French led Henry VIII to build a series of coastal fortifications and signal beacons, with most of the bastions being built with round towers and multiple levels of guns. Nobles, however, were no longer building fortified castles. Instead, they were building lavish mansions with huge windows and pastoral grounds. Castles now incorporated towers and walls into one harmonious, symmetrical structure dotted with courtyards, and were designed less for defense than for a good view. By 1606, the first English translation of Abraham Ortelius's atlas could claim of the English people, "They build no castles, yea those which their auncestors have built in former ages, and now are decaied, ruinous and radie to fall, they care not for the reedifying and upholding of them."

Cattle

Cattle were some of the most important animals on England's farms. The "poor men's cattle" (*TA* V.i.132) were among their greatest assets, and a man bragging of wealth might well note the size of his herd:

> Then, at my farm
> I have a hundred milch-kine to the pail,
> Six score fat oxen standing in my stalls. (*TS* II.i.349–51)

Cattle had multiple purposes. The large, horned, black-haired oxen (*1H6* I.v.31; *2H6* V.i.27; *LLL* V.ii.248–56; *AYLI* I.i.9–10; *1H4* V.i.14; *TS* III.ii.231), for example, had lumpy backs that could be fitted with a yoke which was secured with ropes or oxbows (U-shaped collars—*AYLI* III.iii.78). The yoked oxen, in pairs, were hitched to a plow, cart, wagon, or harrow, to prepare ground and haul goods (*T&C* II.i.106–7; *MND* II.i.93). A standard ox team was composed of four or six animals. Oxen were cheaper to feed than horses and better plowers of heavy soil, but they were slower and less nimble on uneven ground. The oxen were kept at work for about ten years, then fattened and eaten (*2H6* IV.iii.3).

Some cattle were kept purely to be bred, eaten, and sold for beef. Each farm or village kept a breeding bull (*3H6* II.v.126; *1H4* IV.i.102; *2H4* II.ii.157; *TA* V.i.31–32); the rest of the males were castrated and became bullocks (*2H4* III.ii.40; *MAAN* II.i.188–89) or steers (*2H4* IV.ii.103–4). Female cows were heifers (*2H6* III.ii.188; *2H4* II.ii.156) until they had borne a calf (*2H6* III.i.210–12; *LLL* V.ii.248–56; *1H4* II.iv.262–63; *MAAN* III.iii.69–71). The calves were weaned at fifty days old and turned out into a sheltered bit of pasture; the cows were milked until November, when sparse winter fare caused their milk to dry up.

Most were sold or killed in November, since the stored fodder would not supply the needs of all the farm's cattle, but a few were saved, tended throughout the winter, and inspected in January. If at that point they were in a weakened state, they were dosed with verjuice, and their tongues were rubbed with salt. The naturalist Edward Topsell recommended feeding them cabbage leaves pulverized in vinegar, followed by chaff and bran, to fatten them. As soon as the new grass was well sprouted in April, they were turned out into the fields, often under the care of a village herdsman, who collected them in the morning and returned them to individual farms in the evening.

Many cattle, male and female, had horns (*MAAN* II.i.21–22); the tips were covered with wooden balls to prevent injury to animals or farm workers. A cow might also be called a "neat," a term applied equally to "the steer, the heifer, and the calf" (*WT* I.ii.124). By the same token, the herdsman who cared for them was called a neatherd (*Cym* I.i.149; *WT* IV.iv.327). *See also* Animals; Farming.

Children

Childhood was not easy in the Renaissance. In the first place, it was hard to survive. Haphazard medical care, inadequate nutrition in some cases, and poor hygiene combined to make deaths from illness extremely common. Combined with birth defects (*MND* V.i.408–13; *John* II.ii.43–47) and injuries, the result was huge infant mortality (*2H6* III.ii.392–93); 2 percent of all babies died by the end of their first day of life, and 5 percent total died within one week, 8 to 9 percent within a month, and 12 to 13 percent within their first year. Moreover, the mortality rate for adults, though never as high as that for infants, was higher than today, with the result that there were more orphans (*2H6* V.i.187; *RL* 905). Despite all the forces working against children's survival, however, a high birth rate—five or six children per family being about average—made England's a young population, in which 30 percent were under fifteen years old and only 10 percent over sixty.

Parental love, though strong (*R2* III.ii.8–9), was often expressed as a supposedly necessary heavy hand in the discipline department. Beating was the approved form of chastisement, either with the hand or with a rod (*MWW* V.i.24–26; *T&C* III.ii.121–22; *MM* I.iii.23–32; *Lear* I.iv.173–75; *R2* II.iii.102–4). Children were given very little time before assuming adult responsibilities. Between the ages of five and ten, most were employed in some capacity in the fields or workshop or, if the family could afford it, sent to school to labor over their Latin for ten or eleven hours a day. Toys were rare, and children's literature virtually nonexistent; children were entertained not by picture books but by songs and their mothers' and nurses' tales of bugbears (*TS* I.ii.209), fairies, and fierce foreign enemies (*1H6* II.iii.17). In upper-class families, children were particularly formal with their parents (*R&J* I.iii.5–6). In part this was because all children were supposed to be respectful, even subservient, to the adults around them; in part it was because upper-class children were raised to a greater or lesser extent by the servants; in part it was no doubt their awareness that their parents, to some extent, considered them extensions of the family honor and wealth. This meant that parents had to think about arranged marriages with other prominent families, the grooming of an heir, and the provision for younger sons. Aristocratic children had little say in their own destiny.

Baron Cobham and his family. The children's ages, from left to right, are two, one, six, five and five (twins), and four. The two younger boys, on the left, have not been breeched. Their skirts, and the hanging sleeves on the back of the two-year-old's bodice, are visible. Reproduced by permission of the Marquess of Bath, Longleat House, Warminster, Wiltshire, Great Britain.

Yet this implies, perhaps, too much severity. Not all Renaissance parents were tyrants. A minority who objected to flogging and thought that a stern word or shake of the head should be a sufficient check to a well-trained child. Surviving letters are full of weighty advice, but also of the day-today questions and answers of all correspondence, and frequently of love as well. One of Sir Henry Sidney's letters to his younger son, Robert, whom he called Robin, ends:

> I love thee, boy, well. . . . God bless you, my sweet child, in this world forever, as I in this world find myself happy in my children. From Ludlow Castle this 28th of October, 1578. To my very loving son, Robert Sidney, give these. Your very loving father.

Mothers, too, offered plenty of affection, though sometimes their grown-up children found them a little too affectionate. Sir Francis Bacon's mother was forever convinced that his innocence was being imposed upon, even after he was fully grown, and she perpetually worried about the behavior, diet, schedule, medical treatment, and domestic arrangements of her other adult son, Anthony.

In some respects, however, childhood was virtually indistinguishable from childhood today. Parents and other adults spoke to very young children in baby talk (*John* II.i.160–63). They hugged and played with them (*V&A* 362) and considered their "barnes"—bairns, a northern word for children—their greatest treasures (*AW* I.iii.25–26). Children, as they grew up, aspired to be like adults for part of the time (*WT* I.ii.155–57), and for the rest of the time contented themselves with outdoor activities such as chasing butterflies (*Cor* IV.vi.95) or spinning tops. Shakespeare also mentions snowballs (*Per* IV.vi.144–45), a fact that certainly implies that someone, most likely children, made and threw them, just as they do today. Special objects were bought for children by those who could afford them—coral teething rattles, child-sized tables and chairs, and pets.

One noticeable difference between the children of 400 years ago and today is how they were dressed. As babies, they were at first swaddled, or bound with linen bands. Later, the arms were released from this constrictive wrapping, and then, at a few months old—more or less depending on class—they were into long, trailing garments. As soon as they could walk, they were put into skirts. This was, for both boys and girls, a miniature version of adult female dress, sometimes with laces or "hanging sleeves" trailing down the back so that the children could be restrained by this built-in leash if necessary. The costume for boys and girls at this age was so similar that some portraits of male aristocrats were for centuries misidentified as portraits of girls. At about age six, boys were "breeched," or given a miniature version of adult male costume. *See also* Clothing; Education; Inheritance; Toys.

Church
See Religion.

Clocks and Watches

Most of the clocks known to common people in the sixteenth century were large, public clocks with bells that struck the hours. This is the kind of clock by which many of Shakespeare's characters tell the time (*1H4* V.iv.146; *MWW* V.v.1–2). Sometimes clocks of this kind had automata, mechanical figures of people, that appeared and moved when the hour was struck; such are the "Jack" and "minute-jacks" of *Richard III* (IV.ii.113) and *Timon of Athens* (III.vi.98). Small household clocks were rare except in the homes of the rich, and watches (*TN* II.v.58–59; *R3* V.iii.63; *2H4* III.i.17) that could be carried on the person were rarer still.

Unlike the sundial and hourglass, which were purely visual, clocks usually struck the hour on a bell, hence their name, which came either from the Dutch *klok* or French *cloche*, meaning bell. The clock was not yet a regular, ticking device but a noisy, uneven, often inaccurate (*LLL* III.i.191) machine that was said to "jar" rather than to tick or tock. It had no minute hand, only one to show the hour. There were no pendulum clocks; instead, most clocks were run by

A clockmaker, from *Panoplia*, illustrated by Jost Amman, 1568. Reproduced from the Collections of the Library of Congress.

a weight suspended on a cord that was wrapped around a cylinder. The cord unwound at a rate controlled by a device called an escapement. This type of clock was a fairly simple mechanism that could be made by a blacksmith, but many clocks—or at least their styles—were imported from France or Holland. (The confusion of things Dutch and German, common at the time, may be why Shakespeare refers to "a German clock" in *LLL* III.i.189.) Some Flemish clockmakers were present in England from the late sixteenth century, which is about the time that a domestic clockmaking in-

Two late sixteenth-century clocks: a drum clock and a weight-driven vertical clock with a bell.

dustry was established. The Clockmakers' Company was not founded until 1631; in the meantime, clockmakers were usually either blacksmiths or goldmsiths.

There were two principal styles of household clocks. One was a vertical arrangement, much like the familiar fancy mantel clock. It had the mechanism for the hands in the top part and the mechanism for the bell in the bottom, and might, in rare cases, have an alarm as well. The second was shaped like a drum or round box, with the dial on top. Drum clocks did not always have a bell, but when they did, it was usually located between the movement mechanism and the dial. *See also* Time.

Cloth

See Fabric.

Clothing

It was often said that the people of England, especially in the middle and upper classes, paid far too much attention to their clothing or, more specifically, to fashion and its capricious changes. Certainly foreign visitors noted that the English were well dressed. They marveled that even the common people wore gloves and that the women, whom they were surprised to see moving freely about London, were finely, even gaudily, arrayed. Jacob Rathgreb, private secretary to Frederick, Duke of Württemberg, wrote in 1592 that the citizens of London were "magnificently apparelled." Looking at the portraits of the age, modern observers must concur, while remembering that ordinary working people dressed far more simply than those who could afford to hire artists.

Women's Clothing

An upper-class woman began to get dressed, with her maid's assistance, by putting on a smock (*MWW* III.v.87; *A&C* I.ii.169; *LLL* V.ii.480, 903; *R&J* II.iv.108; *Oth* V.ii.273) that had been warmed by the fire. The smock was 30 to 40 inches (76 to 102 cm) long, with long sleeves and a vertical slit at the front of the neckline. It had a small collar and often embroidery around the yoke (or "square"), hem, and cuff (or "sleevehand"—see *WT* IV.iv.208–11). If the wearer could afford it, the sleeve ends were trimmed with lace as well.

After the smock, the woman put on her petticoat (*Oth* IV.iii.77–78; *3H6* V.v.23; *2H4* II.ii.80; *AYLI* I.iii.15; *TNK* V.ii.83), which was sometimes just an underskirt, sometimes an entire dress in itself with a separate bodice and skirt. The bodice was be stiffened by strips of wood or whalebone, called busks, inserted into casings, and the bodice and skirt laced together at the waist with ties called points. Social critic Phillip Stubbes, who was generally shocked by the expense and extravagant decoration of clothes, noted that the petticoat, which was rarely seen, was nevertheless made of a fine material like taffeta or scarlet, and might even have a silk fringe at the bottom. Stockings went on next, made of, in Stubbes's words, "silke gearnsey, worsted, crewell, or at least of as fyne yarn, thread, or cloth as is possible to be had cunningly knit," along with garters to hold them up (*The Anatomie of Abuses*). The stockings were of one color except at the ankles, which had a decorative inset called a "clock" that began at the ankle and tapered to a point somewhere along the outside of the calf.

Shoes were usually made of velvet or leather. Though shoes might be quite plain among the peasantry, with hobnailed soles and plain leather uppers, the shoes of fine ladies were slippers with low soles or pantofles with cork soles "which beare them up a finger or two from the ground," according to Stubbes. He noted that the pantofles were technically over-shoes but quite unsuitable for outdoor use, being made of fine, colored leather, sometimes embroidered in silk and trimmed in gold and silver. The pantofles were awkward to walk in, and ladies had to practice gliding smoothly in them and learning to dance without tripping or falling.

After her hair was dressed and bejeweled and her face washed, the lady strapped on a farthingale (*2GV* II.vii.42–56, IV.iv.38; *MWW* III.iii.60–62), or hoop skirt. From the 1560s to the 1580s, this was likely to be the bell-shaped Spanish farthingale, which reached its maximum width in the 1580s. In the 1590s, it was replaced by the French or wheel farthingale, which began at the top with an oval, roughly horizontal platform, somewhat lower in the front than in the back, creating a shelf 8 to 48 inches (20 to 122 cm) wide. It then dropped to the floor in a more or less straight line. A cheaper, less fashionable substitute was the bum-roll, a nearly circular roll of padded fabric that curled around the waist and tied in front with tapes or ribbons.

Over the farthingale or bum-roll came a kirtle (a skirt—see *2H4* II.iv.280) made of silk, velvet, taffeta, satin, or scarlet, and a bodice instead of or in addition to the petticoat bodice. From the 1590s, it became

Woman in French farthingale, c. 1590–1600. From the *Roxburghe Ballads.* Reproduced from the Collections of the Library of Congress.

fashionable to wear a bodice and kirtle of different patterns. Matching the bodice were sleeves, separate from it and tied on with laces at the bodice's armholes (*LLL* V.ii.455–59; *T&C* V.ii.59–94), the joint between the two disguised by shoulder projections called wings. The sleeves might be relatively tight, with slashes through which the fabric of the smock could be pulled in small bunches, or, as in the 1580s and 1590s, hugely padded "trunk sleeves" that tapered along the lower arm to a width little greater than that of the wrist. The neckline of the bodice might be high, with a standing collar, or low, with the area between neckline and chin filled by jewelry, the decorated yoke of the smock, or a partlet (*WT* II.iii.75), a detachable yoke that might match the sleeves or be transparent so as to reveal the smock edge. The Jacobeans wore an elongated bodice, more tubular than triangular, with a sharply pointed bottom; a shorter hem that revealed the feet; larger shoulder wings; large tabs along the base of the bodice; and a kirtle with a flounce that covered the tilted farthingale top.

It was customary for the bodice to fasten at either the side or the front, and laces were considered the most feminine and appropriate form of fastening. It took a while to tighten them properly, working from the bottom up, and it took nearly as long to loosen them—hence the commands, when Shakespeare's female characters are upset and need to breathe freely, to cut the laces (*R3* IV.i.33; *A&C* I.iii.72; *WT* III.ii.170). Buttons were more masculine fastenings, and bodices shaped like men's doublets, complete with a row of buttons, were the sartorial scandal of the age. Phillip Stubbes was appalled at these doublets and even jerkins,

> buttoned up the brest, and made with wings, welt and pinions on the shoulder points, as mans apparel is, for all the world, & though this be a kinde of attire appropriate onely to man, yet they blush not to wear it.

The bodice might be augmented by a more feminine form of adornment instead. This was the stomacher (*WT* IV.iv.225), a decorated panel that could be fastened to the front of the bodice.

In addition to the bodice and skirt (*TNK* II.i.184–87), a woman might wear a gown (*Oth* IV.iii.77; *2H6* I.iii.87–88; *2GV* IV.iv.161; *2H4* II.i.159). The loose variety (*1H4* III.iii.3–4; *TS* IV.iii.133–36) could be worn open, but was usually worn fastened from the neck to the waist. It fit loosely around the torso and had either short sleeves ending below the shoulders, hanging sleeves that departed from the arms partway down and fell in long, thin tubes or strips to the floor, or no sleeves at all; the loose gown ordered for Kate in *The Taming of the Shrew*, uncharacteristically, has slashed trunk sleeves (IV.iii.89–91, 140), though perhaps the tailor has brought both a bodice and a gown, or even a whole outfit, to show to Petruchio. The closed gown fit snugly to the waist and then fell loosely to the floor; it might have short or long sleeves. It might be a very rich garment, as is that of the Duchess of Milan in *Much Ado About Nothing*:

. . . cloth o' gold and cuts [slashes], and laced with silver, set with pearls, down sleeves, side-sleeves, and skirts, round underborne with a bluish tinsel. (III.iv.19–21)

The down sleeves were fitted undersleeves; the side-sleeves, hanging over-sleeves open from the shoulder. Stubbes noted that the materials of the gown were similar to those used for the kirtle and pointed out that the gown also usually had "gardes" or lapels faced in velvet and sometimes trimmed with lace.

Three fans. Left to right: a white feather fan owned by Queen Elizabeth I, c. 1592, the handle of gold with gemstones; a red and black feather fan with a gold, red, and black handle and a crown to signify royal rank, owned by James I's wife, Queen Anne, c. 1605–10; and a white folding fan owned by Princess Elizabeth, James I's daughter, in 1603.

After the petticoat and gown were in place, the woman pinned or tied a ruff around her neck; usually matching ruffs were pinned to the ends of her sleeves. From the 1590s, she might also wear a decorative gauze apron. Another round of jewels followed, including strings of pearls, a girdle, and clusters of gems to be pinned or sewn onto the ruff and gown. Last, the lady amassed her accessories for the day—at least the ones that an attending servant would not carry for her: comfit (candy) box, mask, fan (*Oth* IV.ii.9; *LLL* IV.i.147; *MWW* II.ii.10–12; *A&C* II.ii.205), handkerchief (*Oth* III.iii.431–32, 289–319, III.iv.23–101; *Cor* II.i.266–68—sometimes referred to as a "napkin," as in *LC* 15–17), gloves, pomander, mirror, nosegay, tasseled silk scarf (*Cor* II.i.267), or perhaps a jewel or portrait miniature suspended from a ribbon. Ribbons might also be used as trimmings, tied into pretty bows and pinned or sewn onto various parts of the clothing (*LLL* III.i.144–48; *MWW* IV.vi.41–42; *WT* IV.iv.204–5; *TNK* III.v.28–30). Small wonder that, according to Stubbes, "when they have all these goodly robes uppon them, women seeme to be the smallest part of themselves." One version of the popular ballad "Greensleeves" provides a catalog of the sorts of finery with which upper-class women were adorned: "kerchers to thy head," fine petticoats, jewels, a white silk smock, a gold girdle, a purse, crimson silk stockings, white pumps, a green gown with satin sleeves, and gold-fringed garters.

Ordinary women—farmers' wives, servants, and tradeswomen—wore much the same pieces, but with far fewer jewels and "gewgawes," and of far inferior materials. The kirtles or gowns in this walk of life were not made of taffeta or scarlet, but of some inexpensive variety of wool. A picture of the three successive wives of a yeoman who died in 1586 shows all three garbed in skirt, bodice, sleeves, partlet, open gown, and shallow ruff so narrow that only the edge, not the pleated top, can be seen. None wears a farthingale.

Man's embroidered shirt, c. 1588.

Men's Clothing

The two essential pieces of a man's clothing were the doublet and hose (*AYLI* III.ii.196–97, 221; IV.i.200). Worn over an embroidered, cuffed, and collared shirt (*Tim* IV.iii.224; *MWW* III.v.87; *LLL* V.ii.696, 702, 707–10; *2H4* II.ii.16–22; *R&J* II.iv.108; *1H4* III.iii.72–75, IV.ii.42–45) that was practically indistinguishable from a woman's smock, the doublet (*2H6* II.i.150, IV.vii.52; *TS* Ind.ii.9; *2H4* V.v.83; *MAAN* III.ii.35; *MV* I.ii.72) might be sleeved or sleeveless and was often decoratively slashed. The sleeves (*LLL* V.ii.322; *MND* III.ii.29–30; *T&C* IV.iv.70) were tied to the body of the doublet and covered by wings. Between shirt and doublet a man might wear, on cold days, a knitted or quilted vest called a waistcoat for warmth.

Over the doublet he might also wear a jerkin (*TS* III.ii.43; *1H4* II.iv.70; *Temp* IV.i.235–38), a sleeved or sleeveless jacket that was at times hard to distinguish from the doublet itself (*2GV* II.iv.18–20). Like the doublet, it was closed with hooks and eyes, laces, or buttons (*MWW* III.ii.65; *Lear*

III.iv.108, V.iii.311; *R&J* II.iv.24). Fashionable jerkins were made of expensive material and sometimes perfumed; the common man's garment was made of coarser fabric or of an oiled oxhide called buff. The buff or leather jerkin (*1H4* I.ii.43–46; *2H4* II.ii.170; *T&C* III.iii.264–65) was a lower-class garment and eventually became associated with sheriff's officers. Working men might also wear, instead of the jerkin, a knee-length, belted tunic called a coat (*2H4* III.ii.295; *MAAN* III.ii.6–7; *R&J* I.iv.64; *H5* IV.Cho.26; *Oth* I.i.50).

A rich man's manner of dressing in the morning was much like a rich woman's. He set aside his nightshirt (in which he slept) or nightgown (a dressing gown or casual indoor garment, not actually worn to bed—see *Mac* II.ii.69–70) and his nightcap or "biggen" (*2H4* IV.v.26). Assisted by a servant, he put on his warmed shirt and a separate collar of some kind, possibly a ruff, possibly a stiffened and propped standing collar called a rebato, possibly a falling band, a wide strip of fabric, unruffled, worn open at the throat with its tying strings dangling. After the waistcoat, doublet, and jerkin, a man put on his drawers— a linen undergarment that extended from the waist to somewhere above the knees—and hose (*2H6* IV.vii.52; *LLL* IV.iii.55). The hose were divided into upper hose, also called breeches, and lower hose, also called netherstocks or netherstockings. The upper

Boys' pinked leather jerkin, c. 1560.

hose were joined to the doublet with laces called points (*1H4* II.iv.215–16; *A&C* III.xiii.157; *2H4* I.i.53; *WT* IV.iv.205) that might be tied above, but were usually tied below, the skirt of the doublet. Netherstocks were then attached to the bottom of the upper hose either by points or with tied or buckled garters.

Upper hose varied from immense, balloon-like, knee-length affairs to tiny puffs of fabric. Trunk hose, which Phillip Stubbes called "french-hose," varied in length and were the most common form of upper hose. In their standard form, they were made in at least two layers, with the lower layer forming a kind of bag around each leg, jutting full from the waist and coming back to the leg somewhere along the thigh. The upper layer was split into vertical panes that ran the length of the hose and al-

Men's clothing, c. 1584: a tall hat with a metal band and ostrich
plumes, a propped falling band, striped doublet, gold chains,
sleeved cloak, trunk hose, sword belt and hangers, brocade canions,
stockings, and tasseled garters.

lowed the lower layer to peek through. (For an illustration of trunk hose,
see the drawing of James I in the Jewelry entry.) The length of fashionable
trunk hose rose and fell throughout the Shakespearean period, becoming
a mere token roll of padding in the 1580s (*H8* I.iii.30–31). In their shorter
versions, trunk hose were worn with canions: tight-fitting, knee-length
breeches.

Canions, however, were not called breeches. The word "breeches" (*2H6* I.iii.148; *3H6* V.v.24; *Oth* II.iii.91–93) was applied to long, loose pants that, like trunk hose, varied considerably. Galligaskins (*TN* I.v.23–26) or, in Phillip Stubbes's words, "Gally-hosen," fell to the knee with open seams along the outside of the leg, fastened in three or four places and exposing the stockings beneath. Venetians fell just below the knee. The fashionable might distinguish between particular cuts and lengths, but to most people, baggy breeches gathered at the knee were known collectively as "slops" (*MAAN* III.ii.34; *2H4* I.ii.29–30; *R&J* II.iv.46). Working men might wear any of these types of upper hose, or they might instead wear trousers; trousers did not, however, become fashionable for the upper classes for another 200 years. The difference between fashionable and serviceable breeches is outlined in detail in Robert Greene's *A Quip for an Upstart Courtier* (1592). The courtier wears paned breeches of velvet, Spanish satin, and "the cheefest Neapolitane stuffe," decorated with gold braid and pearl. The countryman who debates with him wears "a plaine payre of Cloth breeches, without eyther welt or garde, straight to the thigh, of white kersie, without a sloppe, the neatherstocke of the same, sewed to above the knee, and onely seamed with a little coventrie blew."

The gradual adoption of breeches coincided with the disappearance of the codpiece (*2GV* II.vii.42–56; *LLL* III.i.183; *MAAN* III.iii.135–37; *Lear* III.ii.27; *MM* III.ii.116), a piece of fabric and padding worn over the genitals and designed to jut out between the folds and panes of the upper hose. When trunk hose were short, the codpiece might be especially prominent, giving the man the appearance of a permanent and highly decorative erection. It was an old-fashioned ornament by the turn of the sixteenth century, but Shakespeare found it irresistible as a symbol of manhood, just as he found the placket (the slit in a petticoat—*WT* IV.iv.613; *LLL* III.i.183; *T&C* II.ii.20; *Lear* III.iv.96) an irresistible symbol of womanhood.

Over his feet and the lower part of his legs, a man wore stockings (*TS* IV.i.42–44; *2H4* II.ii.16–18; *TN* I.iii.130; *Lear* II.ii.17; *H8* I.iii.30), or "netherstocks" (*1H4* II.iv.117; *Lear* II.iv.10), which were sometimes tied to the upper hose with points but were usually fastened to the leg by garters (*2GV* II.i.74–75, 79–82; *H5* I.i.46–47; *Oth* V.i.83; *Lear* II.iii.7–10). Garters were usually tied just above or just below the knee, but in some cases, a long garter might be wound both above and below the knee, or "cross-gartered" (*TN* II.v.148–50). Garters might be made of very fine material; a man's garters, particularly, were designed to be seen, and might be decorated with fringe, jewels, or trimmings; humbler folk simply used "caddisses," or worsted tapes (*WT* IV.iv.207; *1H4* II.iv.70–72).

The hose were made of knitted or bias-cut material; Italian silk was the most prized and costly, but cloth and worsted were also common. The best stockings could cost as much as 40s per pair, though most cost much less, and measures were taken to economize where possible. Accordingly, stockings were dyed rather than replaced when their color fell out of fashion, and they were protected with boot hose (*TS* III.ii.66), a thick over-stocking, when the wearer was wearing boots for riding. Sometimes the breeches and netherstockings were combined in a waist-to-foot unit called "round hose" (*MV* I.ii.73). Lucetta, garbing Julia as a boy in *The Two Gentlemen of Verona*, decides on round hose for her breeches:

LUCETTA   What fashion, madam, shall I make your breeches?

JULIA   That fits as well as, "Tell me, good my lord,
What compass will you wear your farthingale?"
Why, ev'n what fashion thou best likes, Lucetta.

LUCETTA   You must needs have them with a codpiece, madam.

JULIA   Out, out, Lucetta! That will be ill-favored.

LUCETTA   A round hose, madam, now's not worth a pin,
Unless you have a codpiece to stick pins on. (II.vii.49–56)

Round hose, because they were fitted all the way down, left a man perhaps too conscious of what might be revealed, and eager to conceal or augment the genitals with a codpiece. The reference to pins may have to do with the habit of tailors, who were said to use their codpieces as pincushions while they worked, or perhaps with folk beliefs about fertility, for in the early eighteenth century women visitors to the Tower of London stuck pins in one of Henry VIII's old codpieces for good luck in conceiving.

Once the stockings were on, a man put on shoes. These might be sideless slippers (*Temp* II.i.280–81; *TS* IV.i.142), which were usually worn for comfort indoors; pumps, which covered the whole foot and were often decorated with ribbons, pinking, trims, or embroidery (*R&J* II.iv.63–67, III.i.29–30; *MND* IV.ii.34–36); shoes, which rose to the ankle; pantofles, which were cork-soled overshoes that could be worn indoors or out; or boots, which usually rose to the calf or knee and were worn for outdoor work and riding (*2GV* V.ii.6–7; *TS* IV.i.133; *2H4* V.i.56; *R2* V.ii.77; *1H4* III.i.67–68; *MWW* IV.v.94–96). Working people seldom wore the fancy slippers and pumps of the upper classes. They stuck to boots and hobnailed or "clouted" shoes (*2H6* IV.ii.184; *Cym* IV.ii.23–15). Shoes were followed by a hat, rapier, dagger, gloves, and a handkerchief (*H5* III.ii.48–49; *AW* V.iii.320–21; *AYLI* IV.iii.92; *Cym* I.iii.6–7; also called a napkin, as in *TA* III.i.140, 146; *JC* III.ii.134; *Mac* II.iii.6). A scarf was another possible accessory. It was usually worn by military men, in which case it was draped over the shoulder (*MAAN* II.i.184; *AW* II.iii.205–6, IV.iii.146, 327–28), but any man might tie a scarf around his arm as a love token from an admirer.

He might also don a cloak (*2H6* II.i.108–9, 114; *TS* I.i.207; *2GV* III.i.130–36; *2H4* I.ii.29–30; *H5* IV.i.24) or other outer garment. Spanish cloaks were hooded and short; Dutch cloaks were hoodless and wide-sleeved, though the sleeves were not used but allowed to dangle; French cloaks were worn over one shoulder only, fastened imperfectly by laces to keep them from falling off. The cassock was widely worn by middle-class men, especially for travel. It was a loose garment with wide sleeves and a standing collar. It was a practical piece of clothing, unlike the mandilion, which was worn purely for fashion's sake. The mandilion was a jacket that, like the cassock, had a standing collar. Like the cassock, it had sleeves, but these sleeves were not functional; they were decorative hanging sleeves. The mandilion had open side seams and an unbuttoned front from chest to hip, meaning that it bestowed only minimal warmth. Sometimes it was worn sideways, or "collywestonward," with the sleeves hanging not at the sides but at the back and front, making it even less useful.

Loose gowns (*MAAN* IV.ii.1 s.d., 85–86; *2H6* II.i.110–11, 114; *TN* II.v.45–46; *MWW* III.i.33) were often lined with fur (*MM* III.ii.8–11; *Lear* IV.vi.165). The type of fur and the length of the gown varied according to the wearer's status. Short gowns, extending no lower than the calf, could be worn by almost anyone, but ankle-length gowns, with long hanging sleeves open at the elbow to allow the arms to emerge, were restricted to scholars, lawyers (*MV* III.iv.50–51), judges, physicians, government officials, and men over sixty. A loose, smocklike gown called a gaberdine is associated by Shakespeare with Jews and with Caliban (*MV* I.iii.109; *Temp* II.ii.38–39).

Class, Occupation, and Nationality

Some mention has already been made of the distinctions between upper and lower class costume. For the most part, this disparity was caused by differences in wealth. It was also, less effectively, enshrined in the law. Sumptuary laws, or laws restricting the wearing of certain kinds of clothes, had long been enacted in the hope of reinforcing class distinctions. The laws on the books near the turn of the seventeenth century split society into nine classes, from the top rank, barons and above, to the lowest, non-wage-earning servants. The group making £100–200 per year, for example, could use velvet for sleeveless jerkins, doublets, coifs, partlets, and purses, but could not have outerwear of satin, damask, silk, or taffeta. Those making £5–20 could have doublets and jackets of no imported fabric except camlet, a ribbed fabric. Everyone except children under seven and certain exempt classes had to wear a "statute cap" of wool, until the statute in question was repealed in 1597.

In practice, the sumptuary laws were haphazardly followed. The ability to pay the tailor's bill was far more important in most cases than the income per annum or the blurry line between yeoman and gentleman. General condemnation, however, was likely to follow upon the gentleman who dressed too raggedly or upon the servant who aspired to dress like his master. Petruchio's wedding costume, for example, appalls his in-laws (*TS* III.ii.43–48), and it is equally horrifying to contemplate a servant dressed in "A silken doublet, a velvet hose, a scarlet cloak, and a copatain [fashionable conical hat]" (*TS* V.i.64–65). There was a general expectation, rarely enforced under the law, that people of the upper, middle, and lower classes would be recognizable by their clothing, so that etiquette could be satisfied in casual encounters and the proper respect or authority demonstrated.

Apprentices, beadles, and servants often wore blue (*TS* IV.i.82–83; *2H4* V.iv.19–20), and blue's association with their ranks made it an unfashionable color for the upper class. Apprentices might also wear white, blue-white, or mulberry-colored breeches and stockings. Menservants were dressed in a uniform or livery (*2H6* IV.ii.74–76, V.ii.47; *R3* I.i.80; *2H4* V.v.12–13; *R&J* II.ii.8, III.i.58; *Per* III.iv.9) of blue, russet, tawny, or gray, with the badge of their household stitched onto the left sleeve (*Temp* V.i.267; *RL* 1054), but maidservants wore no livery. Color was also important to jesters, or fools, because their habitual uniform was a "motley" or "parti-coloured"—both terms meaning multicolored—garment (*LLL* V.ii.764; *H8* Pro.16; *Lear* I.iv.148) and a fool's cap, also called a "cock's comb" or "coxcomb" (*H5* V.i.43; *MWW* V.v.141; *Lear* I.iv.96; *TS*

The different dress of courtier and countryman, an illustration appearing on the title page of *A Quip for an Upstart Courtier*, taken in this case from the *Roxburghe Ballads*. The courtier's doublet is undone, in a style common from the 1590s. Reproduced from the Collections of the Library of Congress.

II.i.223). On the other end of the scale of respectability, judges had their own distinctive uniform: a long gown, girdle, hood, coif, and mantle (*RL* 170; *JC* III.ii170, 187) lined with silk in summer and fur in winter.

Laborers wore a tunic buttoned to the waist and open to the knee, a jacket or coat, and some kind of simple legwear, be it stockings, breeches, trunk hose, or trouserlike leggings. Countrywomen wore gowns or bodices with skirts, aprons, kerchiefs (*JC* II.i.315), and smocks. The apron (*2H6* II.iii.77; *Per* IV.vi.61; *A&C* V.ii.210) was a common garment for working men and women alike. Cooks wore them, as did artisans, waiters at table, brewers, butchers, masons, blacksmiths, farriers, and shoemakers. Sometimes these aprons were made of white cloth, sometimes of leather, depending on the trade. Leather garments were more common in some occupations than in others; Shakespeare gives the name Pilch (*Per* II.i.12), a word for a leather outer garment, to a fisherman, implying that fishermen wore such clothing while they worked, perhaps because leather was more waterproof than cloth.

Shakespeare seems to have been uncertain of the clothes worn by foreigners, or at least disinclined to include details of foreign costume in his plays. He mentions Greek clothing from time to time (S 53) but without specifying what he means, and he gives the noble lovers of *Love's Labor's Lost* Muscovite attire, but describes it merely as "shapeless gear" (V.ii.304). He is on firmer ground with Roman costume, for he knows that the Roman wore togas (*Cor* II.iii.117) and that candidates for political office wore a special kind of toga (*Cor* II.i.235–37, II.iii.41 s.d.), though he knows only that it indicated humility and never mentions its proper name, *toga candida*, or "white toga," from which the word "candidate" is derived.

Sellers of Clothing

Clothing was extremely expensive, since every piece, and every scrap of material, had to be made entirely by hand. A suit of fine clothes could, and did, lead to bankruptcy, and men of fashion were perpetually and proverbially in debt to their tailors (*AYLI* V.iv.46–47). The tailors (*1H4* III.i.256; *2H4* III.ii.153; *MWW* III.iii.31–33; *AW* II.v.17–20; *A&C* I.ii.164; *TNK* IV.i.108–9; *MND* ch.; *TS* IV.iii.ch.), on the other hand, were constantly overworked, haphazardly paid, habitually abused (*Oth* II.iii.91–93), and given conflicting orders by their clients (*Lear* III.ii.84; *TS* III.vii. 87–165). Accused of padding his bills and stealing the scraps of fabric brought to him by the client (*Mac* II.iii.13–15), the tailor could be a harried man. His tools were the needle, the shears (*John* IV.ii.196), the yard measure (*R&J* I.ii.39–40), and the "goose," or pressing iron (*Mac* II.iii.15); his method was to accept the customer's fabric, note any instructions concerning the garment to be made, make recommendations as to the style, take the customer's measurements (at least in the case of ladies) from existing clothes rather than from the body, and hope that, in the end, the garment would be found acceptable and the customer solvent. The styles he made spread slowly throughout the country. A courtier would make an appearance, often in the aisles of St. Paul's in the morning, in a new doublet of his own or his tailor's design, and report of it would move from the rival tailors gathered to observe the dandies, to the tailors' customers, to relatives in the country eager to know the London fashions. Some styles were demonstrated on fashion dolls that could be carried from France or elsewhere to England, allowing a local tailor to copy a garment without an expensive, full-size model.

A tailor, from *Panoplia*, illustrated by Jost Amman. Scraps of cloth such as those visible on the floor were one of the tailor's perquisites. Reproduced from the Collections of the Library of Congress.

The tailor was not, however, the only merchant or craftsman to whom a gentleman could be deeply in debt. The making of a full suit of clothes required supplies from many shopkeepers. Woolens came from a draper, who sold such materials as kersey, serge, and bays (baize). Linens came from a linen-draper. ("Draper" was a generic term for a seller of something; male alehouse keepers were called ale-drapers.) Haberdashers sold hats and other accessories (*H8* V.iv.45–46). Milliners, whose name came from their original occupation—importers from Milan—dealt in accessories, too. They sold bracelets and other minor pieces of jewelry, fans, garters, wigs, gloves, ruffs, cuffs, shirts, ready-made waistcoats, perfume (*1H4* I.iii.35), and powder. Mercers (*MM* IV.iii.10–11) sold expensive imported fabrics, including satin, sarcenet, taffeta, velvet, and cloth of gold. Their London shops were concentrated mainly in Cheapside. Add to these the sundry starchers, feather sellers, cobblers (who made shoes—see *JC* I.i.11–28; *R&J* I.ii.39–40), attire makers (hairdressers), and seamstresses (who made linen clothes such as ruffs, falling bands, and nightcaps), and it was possible to be so beholden to so many tradesmen for a bride's trousseau that a family might have to sell part of its land to pay the bills. *See also* Doublet; Fabric; Gloves; Hair; Hat; Inkle; Jewelry; Pomander; Ruff; Tawdry Lace.

Coronation

English monarchs were (and still are) crowned in Westminster Abbey (*2H6* I.i.37–38). The king or queen entered the Abbey, was acclaimed by the assembled crowd, swore to govern according to the law and to defend the church (*R2* IV.i.203–14), then sat while the Archbishop of Canterbury presided over the service. A canopy was held over the coronation chair by four Knights of the Garter. Underneath this canopy the king or queen was anointed with holy oil (called "balm" in Shakespeare's works—*3H6* III.i.17; *R2* III.ii.55), poured from a gold ampulla shaped like an eagle into a gilded spoon dating from the twelfth century. The ampulla used for Elizabeth I, James I, and all the previous rulers from Henry IV (*R2* IV.i.319) on, was destroyed during the Commonwealth and replaced with a larger version after the Restoration. The original ampulla was said to have been given to St. Thomas à Becket by the Virgin Mary and was used in order to shore up Henry IV's shaky claim to the throne.

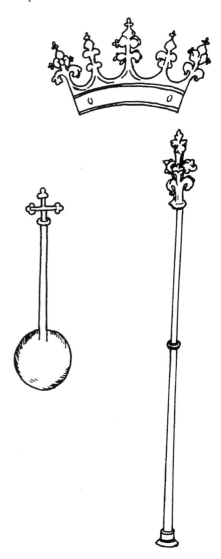

The coronation regalia included spurs symbolic of chivalry that were held before queens regnant and buckled onto the feet of kings. The king- or queen-to-be was also draped in a long robe. Shakespeare describes a coronation robe as an "intertissued robe of gold and pearl" (*H5* IV.i.262), while Richard III's gown was of purple velvet and ermine. An unsheathed sword, made especially for each coronation, was held or worn by the monarch and then carried before him or her. An orb or "ball" (*H5* IV.i.260; *Mac* IV.i.121) topped with a cross, symbolizing the global rule of Christianity, was placed in the monarch's right hand and then placed on the altar. After the orb was withdrawn, the monarch was handed a scepter (*1H6* IV.i.192, V.iii.118; *2H6* I.i.243, V.i.9–11, 98, 102; *3H6* I.iv.17, III.i.16; *R2* I.i.118, II.i.294, III.iii.79, IV.i.109, 204; *MV* IV.i.189–92; *Mac* IV.i.121), and then the archbishop placed the crown (*2H4* IV.v.; *H5* II.Cho.10; *A&C* V.ii.280; *Ham* V.ii.275–76) on his or her head. A general cry of "God save the King (or Queen)" was followed by artillery salutes, trumpet flourishes, and celebrations. Alms were given, presents were made to the new ruler, amnesties were declared, and symbolic pageants illustrated the virtues and sovereignty of the new monarch.

Coronation (*1H6* I.i.169, IV.i.1; *R3* III.i.62, 173, III.iii.2, 15, III.vii.241; *3H6* II.vi.86–87, 95) did not always take place immediately after the death of the previous monarch. Celebrations of the proper magnitude took time to plan, and in many cases the new ruler was too young to be crowned.

The orb, scepter, and crown of Richard II, after a painting in Westminster Abbey.

The orb, scepter, and crown of Edward IV, after a manuscript illumination at Lambeth Palace. The enclosed crown of red cloth and gold has alternating rubies and black stones, probably diamonds, which were often represented in paintings as black. The rubies are those set in the small fleurs-de-lis and in the band beneath the large fleurs-de-lis. The scepter's bottom is not shown in the original illumination, so it has been drawn without any sort of pommel or elaborate base.

Henry VI, for example, was only nine months old when his father, Henry V, died in 1422 (*3H6* I.i.112). He was finally crowned king of England at Westminster in 1429 and king of France in Paris in 1431 (*2H6* I.i.70–72). The crowning of a queen consort could take place at any time after her marriage to the king (*2H6* I.i.70–72; *R3* IV.i.31–32); Anne Boleyn's (*H8* IV.i.14–18) was held when she was visibly pregnant with the future Elizabeth I, to emphasize God's favor in making her more fertile than her predecessor. Catherine of Aragon and Richard III's Queen Anne, on the other hand, were crowned at the same time as their husbands.

Cosmetics

Elizabethan and Jacobean cosmetics served, as cosmetics always have, to alter the natural appearance in accordance with the dictates of fashion. In that time, the ideal was a very pale, glossy skin, red cheeks and lips, and fine eyebrows. Accordingly, the skin of the face was washed with various substances, such as urine, boiled lemon rind, the water left after boiling beans, or a mixture of rose water and wine, to whiten it. One such wash for pale skin required at least thirteen hours of beating by hand and included eggs, burnt alum, powdered "white Sugar candy," borax, water from under a mill wheel, and white poppy seeds, strained through linen. Sometimes, after being washed, the face was glazed with egg white to give it a smooth texture.

The face could also be painted white with compounds made of white lead or powdered borax. The cheeks were reddened with ochre or mercuric sulfide; the lips with a mixture of cochineal, gum arabic, egg white, and fig milk. Elizabeth I certainly took this route as she aged, and courtiers and authors went out of their way to avoid criticizing her for it. The women (and a few men) who followed her example were, however, ridiculed by many. Phillip Stubbes, in his *Anatomie of Abuses* (1583), lambastes women who "colour their faces with certain oyles, liquors, unguents and waters." Shakespeare certainly uses "painting" as an insult, citing it as evidence of deceit or foolishness (*2GV* II.i.58–62; *LLL* IV.iii.256–70; *MAAN* III.ii.52–53; *A&C* I.ii.20). Hamlet takes women to task for this vice:

I have heard of your paintings well enough.
God hath given you one face, and you make yourselves
another. (*Ham* III.i.143–45)

Worse still, he characterizes painting as the kind of cheap deception practiced by whores (*MM* IV.ii.37–40; *Cym* III.iv.49–50).

Eyebrows were plucked, and sometimes hairlines also, to broaden the forehead. The expanse of white face was set off further by the addition, late in the sixteenth century and throughout the seventeenth, of small black velvet or taffeta patches. The origin of the patches is not known. There is some evidence that they evolved from a common remedy for toothache. Another theory is that they were intended to cover pimples or scars, the interpretation that Shakespeare himself prefers (*AW* IV.v.94–97). What is certain is that they became popular primarily because they created a contrast between skin and patch, setting off the whiteness of the face.

A civet cat, from Edward Topsell's *Historie of Foure-Footed Beastes*. The cat's "uncleanly flux," in Shakespeare's words, was an important ingredient in perfume. Reproduced from the Collections of the Library of Congress.

Perfume owed its popularity in large part to the poor hygiene of the time, when clothes were difficult to wash, people were disinclined to wash, and waste matter was thrown carelessly into the streets. They were made of such ingredients as herbs, flowers (especially roses—*MND* I.i.76; S 54), civet, musk, and ambergris. Civet (*MAAN* III.ii.47; *Lear* III.iv.104, IV.vi.130–31; *AYLI* III.ii.61–62) was a strong-smelling, yellowish liquid found in a pouch near the sexual organs of the African civet cat, hence Shakespeare's characterization of the substance as "the very uncleanly flux of a cat" (*AYLI* III.ii.66). Musk (*MWW* II.ii.64) came from a sac in the abdomen of the male musk deer, and ambergris from whales. People perfumed gloves, fans, rooms, and jewelry (*1H4* I.iii.35–40; *MAAN* I.iii.55–56, III.iv.60–61; *WT* IV.iv.221–24), using the pleasant smells to drive away less pleasant odors (*TNK* III.i.86). *See also* Clothing; Hair; Jewelry; Pomander.

Court

The English court (*2H6* I.ii.25; *3H6* I.i.210), according to William Harrison's *The Description of England*, "one of the most renowned and magnificent courts that are to be found in Europe," had no fixed location. Its center was always wherever the monarch—Elizabeth I from 1558 to 1603, James I from 1603 to 1625—resided (*1H6* II.v.105). With Elizabeth in particular, the court might find itself in a dazzling variety of places, for she owned dozens of palaces and for many years went on annual progresses through the kingdom, staying at the homes of noblemen. In the London area alone, Elizabeth owned Whitehall, the Tower, Greenwich, St. James's, Somerset House, the Charterhouse, and Durham Place, though monarchs seldom resided in the Tower except for the night prior to coronation, and Durham Place was usually reserved for ambassadors (*1H6* V.i.) and other distinguished guests. When she was in town, which was most likely in the winter and when Parliament was in session, Elizabeth usually lived at Whitehall, a haphazard collection of buildings bordered on one side by the Thames and on another by St. James's Park, with the road from London to Westminster running through the middle. When she was not in town, she might be found at Richmond, Hampton Court, Oatlands, Hatfield, Woodstock, Nonsuch, or another of her estates. James I was fond of many of these places, though he preferred the hunting at Theobalds, a palace he had acquired from Robert Cecil, Lord Burghley, in a trade.

Wherever the court stayed, it needed plenty of room, for it was composed of hundreds of people, all of whom had to be fed, clothed, housed, and entertained. There was a department devoted to the outdoors, staffed by gardeners, grooms, and such, and headed by the master of the horse and his assistant, the chief avenor, who together supervised the extensive stables. The master of the horse, like the heads of the other departments, had several tiers of servants below him, extending downward past upper administrators like the chief avenor to serjeants, clerks, yeomen, grooms, pages, and, humblest of all, children.

The downstairs servants—those of the kitchen, bakehouse, pantry, cellar, buttery, pitcher-house, spicery, chandlery, wafery, confectionery, ewery, laundry, larder, boiling-house, accatry (where purchases were made), poultry, scalding-house, pastry, scullery, almonry (from which charity was distributed to the poor), wood-yard—were under the dominion of the lord steward. His immediate subordinates were the treasurer, the comptroller of the household, the cofferer or purveyor (who was responsible for acquiring the huge quantities of supplies that the court devoured), and an assortment of clerks. Also under the lord steward's authority were the porters, marshals, sewers, and surveyors of the hall.

The third department dealt with upstairs service, for example, the dressing and undressing of royals. This was headed by the lord chamberlain, who was in charge of entertainment, the queen's wardrobe and jewels, the royal chapel, the royal barge, the care of beds and bedchambers, and the outer and privy chambers. His staff included the serjeant at arms, the guard, the gentlemen pensioners who were Elizabeth's personal escort, the master of revels (who planned pageants and masques), physicians, musicians, an astronomer, and the monarch's personal attendants. In Elizabeth's case, these were her white-clad ladies-in-waiting, young women of noble birth who had been sent, much as Valentine is sent to the duke of Milan (*2GV* II.iv.75–80), to find favor, fortune, and polish at the court. These maids of honor were her companions, her servants, and her entertainers. As she desired, they read aloud, danced, sang, or played musical instruments for her delight; Harrison mentions their skill on the lute and cittern specifically.

The higher offices came with good salaries, better perquisites, and sometimes great power. The three department heads, for example, were members of the Privy Council, and the lord chamberlain controlled access to the monarch, a privilege that cannot be too highly estimated. Prominent offices within the royal household were therefore eagerly sought. The lucky recipient of such a post was informed of his good fortune, according to E. K. Chambers in *Shakespeare's England*, "by the delivery of a white staff, which became the symbol of his office, and which at the funeral of the sovereign he solemnly broke over his head before the bier." Shakespeare makes a reference to this practice, though in the context of withdrawal from a post rather than the death of the king; he states that Richard II's lord steward, "the Earl of Worcester / Hath broken his staff, resigned his stewardship" (*R2* II.ii.58–59).

In each department, there were purely ceremonial offices that granted the holders social status and an income but entailed little or no work. The titles of lord high steward, lord great chamberlain, and chief butler of England fell into this category. In other cases, an office might require real work and plenty of it—so much of it, in fact, that a noble holding the post wished to be free of the tedium so that he could flirt, hunt, flatter the monarch, or tend to his own estates. In this event, the noble hired a subordinate who performed the duties of the office.

The court was crowded not only with its legions of employees but with others as well. Actors and other performers came at the request of the monarch or royal functionaries. Heralds confirmed and proclaimed rank and status. Foreign ambassadors and royal suitors—first to Elizabeth, then to the children of James I—came to be recognized and to conduct their business. Above all, courtiers (*2H6* IV.iv.36; *AYLI* IV.i.12) swirled around the queen or king, flattering, amusing, and trying to secure the seemingly infinite privileges—offices, lands, titles, gifts, trade monopolies, and so forth—that being a royal favorite could secure. The influence possessed by those with the ruler's ear was significant; hence Shallow's claim that "A friend i' / th' court is better than a penny in the purse" (*2H4* V.i.31–32). The "friend" himself might see things the other way around, for he could sell his influence to those with suits (petitions) and thus make money from his proximity to the throne (*R&J* I.iv.77–78). Small wonder that Ferdinand of Navarre's courtiers (*LLL* I.i.), little as they like his plan of study and celibacy, are willing to accede; few defied a king.

In order to gain such proximity, courtiers went to great lengths to call attention to themselves. They dressed well and expensively; they cultivated fine manners (*Ham* V.i.82–83) and personal honor; they endeavored to dance, hunt, talk, fight, and love with grace and flair. In *As You Like It*, behavior, not rank, is the evidence of court connections:

> I have trod a measure; I have
> flattered a lady; I have been politic with my friend,
> smooth with mine enemy; I have undone three
> tailors; I have had four quarrels, and like to have
> fought one. (V.iv.44–48)

In *The Winter's Tale*, likewise, the courtier's residence in the lofty environs of the court is demonstrated by his "gait," his perfumed "court-odor," and his "court-contempt" for lesser mortals (IV.iv.735–37). Some, like Harrison, admired the courtier with his fine clothes and his knowledge of many languages; others found him exaggerated and ridiculous.

Courtship

Marriage began with courtship and, as is true today, not all courtships were successful. It was the role of the man to do the wooing and the role of the woman to wait to be wooed and hope that an acceptable man would approach her. For both parties, the choice of a partner was critically important, for husband and wife were a financial team, each depending on the other for certain strengths. Furthermore, there was no such thing as divorce in the modern sense. Although a couple could separate if they disagreed, such a separation was rare even in cases of extreme cruelty.

The Choice of a Spouse

A man, when considering the choice of a wife, would certainly notice appearance and usually preferred an attractive woman. However, appearance was far from the only consideration; temperament mattered as well. The ideal woman, according to the writers of the day, was neither an idiot nor exceptionally learned, low-voiced and reticent rather than shrill and garrulous, not pretty enough to be flattered and wooed by other men, industrious, thrifty, obedient, loving, and, above all, chaste. Age was also a factor. It was best if the two were reasonably similar in age and neither too old nor too young, though aristocratic families sometimes betrothed their children as young as seven and waited until they were older to secure their consent and finalize the match. The legal age of consent was twelve for girls and fourteen for boys; anyone younger than this needed parental consent before contracting a valid marriage or betrothal. Juliet, at thirteen, is thus quite capable of entering into a legal marriage with Romeo (*R&J* I.ii.6–13).

Men also considered, though it seems unfeeling to modern lovers, women's prospects for dowry and inheritance. The dowry (*1H6* V.i.20, 44; *TS* I.i.120–23, I.ii.60–95, 183, II.i.120–27, IV.v.63–66; *AW* II.iii.144–45, III.vii.35; *Lear* I.i.44, 191–257; *MWW* I.i.221–22) was a daughter's share of her father's estate, delivered with her at the time of her marriage according to an oral or written marriage contract (*Lear* V.iii.230; *WT* IV.iv.393). When she was betrothed (*H5* II.i.20; *2GV* II.iv.179–82; *TS* IV.iv. 49–50, 56–59), her father would agree to a dowry of a given size, paid in cash, goods, land, jewelry, livestock, or a combination of these. In return, the prospective husband promised to grant his wife a jointure—a widow's inheritance—if he should predecease her. The size of the dowry, more than any other qualification, determined the number of marriage proposals a woman was likely to receive. A woman was even more attractive if she came with property of her own, perhaps inherited from a previous husband, for in this case no negotiations would be necessary. If she married, all her property passed immediately into her husband's control, and he could do with it as he liked. Still better was a woman who was likely to be her father's only heir, for then there would be a dowry right away and the promise of more later. This may seem like a grisly sort of calculation, but everyone made it, for it was the Renaissance's only equivalent to a retirement plan. The importance of the dowry made it a common form of charity to bequeath money to be used for poor girls' dowries.

In return, women scrutinized the men who offered to marry them. They, too, looked at physical attributes, personality, and relative age. Women also looked at the financial bottom line; their friends or parents asked, if they did not already know, how much prospective suitors made each year, how much they were likely to make in the future, whether they had a profitable trade, and whether they expected to inherit anything one day. Among the nobility, courtship was likely to be more like a business deal than a romance, for aristocrats were anxious to keep titles and family fortunes consolidated. A nobleman's daughter had a nominal right of veto if she truly detested a prospective husband, but her parents could legally beat her until she agreed to their choice. The same was true of sons.

Few parents resorted to such tactics, however, partly because they wanted their children to make reasonably happy marriages, partly because the culture ingrained obedience in the children, and partly because the marriage was not considered valid in the eyes of the church unless both parties entered it willingly (*1H6* V.v.62–65; *MWW* V.v.224–29; *2GV* IV.iii.31–32). Nevertheless, the reaction of Juliet's parents to her refusal to marry Paris, which seems so extreme to modern readers and audiences, is characteristic of upper-class parents in Shakespeare's day (*R&J* III.v.117–205). It is Juliet's reaction that would have seemed so inexplicable to anyone who did not know of her clandestine marriage to Romeo. Likewise, a Renaissance audience would have been inclined to side against Bertram in *All's Well That Ends Well*, for though he would veto Helena as a wife, he has relinquished the right of veto by going through with the marriage ceremony (*AW* II.iii.272–73). However, Hermia's case in *A Midsummer Night's Dream*, which balances a well-known love against parental authority (I.i.39–179), would have led even a Renaissance audience to sympathize mainly with the daughter. If the child's choice was made clear, and the forced marriage was not consented to, then the parent had no legal or moral right to compel the union.

Forms of Courtship

Once a prospective partner had been selected, the process of courtship began. A partner's receptiveness might first be sounded by an intermediary, who would sing the praises of the wooer, carry gifts, and advise in favor of the match. The use of an intermediary was not confined to men; this was one of the few ways in which women could make the first move. It was essential, however, that the go-between first obtain explicit consent from the party he or she represented, for serious misunderstandings could arise if one side considered the arrangements binding and the other did not. Courtship was often accompanied with gifts (*WT* IV.iv.350–55; *MND* I.i.28–35; *MWW* II.ii.61–65) of money, clothing, gloves (*TNK* III.v.46), jewelry, or household items; pairs of knives were a popular token of esteem, as were rings. Sometimes gifts were given to the woman's parents or to the intermediary as well to indicate honorable intent and to secure the family's favor. In exchange, a woman might offer gifts of her own, perhaps a set of napkins or a handkerchief that she had embroidered. These may have served the dual purpose of being personalized and displaying the woman's domestic talents. Other popular gifts included bracelets made of the giver's hair (*MND* I.i.33) or a picture of the giver, perhaps a portrait miniature; Benedick selects a request for her picture as the best way to assure Beatrice that he loves her (*MAAN* II.iii.257).

Gifts, called "favors" (*LLL* V.ii.776; *LC* 36–37, 204–5), served multiple purposes. They demonstrated thoughtfulness and commitment. Especially when they were items meant to be worn or used daily, they encouraged the recipient to think fondly of the giver. They could also serve as a means of proving reciprocal affection on the part of the recipient, because the acceptance of the gift was as important a gesture as the giving of it. Furthermore, the use or wearing of the gift was a visible display of continuing affection. Accordingly, a man might wear a scarf, ribbon, glove, or hand-kerchief given him by his beloved in some visible location—over the heart (*LLL* V.ii.710–12), in the hat (*Lear* III.iv.85), pinned to the sleeve—that advertised its identity as a love gift. The exchange of gifts, when the validity of a marriage contract was in doubt, could serve as valuable evidence of mutual consent. When one of playwright Thomas Heywood's characters enters into a betrothal, he brings his lover, Luce, gifts of a ring and twenty angels; after they agree to marry and her father consents, he gives her more money to buy a new smock, a new bed, and various dishes and household items.

A man could offer more signs of his love, however, than gifts. If he were an assiduous lover, he would compose verses in honor of his lady (*H5* V.ii.135–38; *MAAN* V.ii.4–5, 25–41, V.iv.85–92), serenade her or hire musicians to do so on his behalf (*MND* I.i.30–31), and dance with her if the opportunity presented itself (*H5* V.ii.135–38). He could write love letters and find some suitably discreet servant to deliver them; if he were lucky, she would respond in kind, for women, too, wrote love letters (*MAAN* II.iii.131–44; *MWW* II.ii.61–65). He could address her with en-dearments such as "sweeting" (*1H6* III.iii.21) or "chuck" (*Oth* III.iv.49) and, in Berowne's words, "love, write, sigh, pray, sue, [and] groan" (*LLL* III.i.203). The seriousness of his affection was supposed to be visible in his obvious physical suffering. The lover must have no appetite, sleep poorly or not at all, be pale (*MAAN* I.i.240–44), sigh (*MAAN* III.ii.25) and groan (*TN* I.v.253–54) frequently or utter mournful exclamations of despair, pay special attention to his attire (*MAAN* III.ii.38–53) or abso-lutely no attention to it (*AYLI* III.ii.371–79), and be in a perpetual mel-ancholy (*MAAN* III.ii.51, 55–56; *AYLI* IV.i.10–15), sitting about brooding with crossed arms.

If the first stages of courtship were successful, the couple might proceed to an expression of their love through some form of physical intimacy, such as kissing, fondling, or even sexual intercourse (*AW* IV.ii.54–55; *Lear* III.iv.85–88). It was not uncommon for intercourse to take place after a betrothal, or in the understanding that a betrothal had occurred; however, this could be a dangerous intimacy for the woman, who might not have sufficient proof to force a full marriage if she should become pregnant. Even if the man were willing to marry her, there was a certain amount of shame inherent in having yielded before the full ceremony; Juliet, in *Meas-ure for Measure*, suffers (albeit to an unusually extreme degree) from the legal gap between betrothal and marriage (I.ii.148–56). There was some tolerance in the community for sexual activity in this interim, but none for unchastity before a betrothal (*WT* I.ii.276–78).

Kissing, which was part of English etiquette at wassailing, the greeting of guests in one's home, and the completion of a dance, seems to have had a dual life. It could be entirely casual and polite, or it could be a gesture of deep intimacy. This may seem to be an obvious state of affairs, until we realize that visitors from other parts of Europe found this duality shocking, for in some parts of the Continent it was only intimate (*H5* V.ii.253–83), never casual. Shakespeare tends to use the kiss in the intimate sense, between husbands and wives (*R2* V.i.95–100; *R&J* III.v.42; *TS* III.ii.176–78, V.i.141–46, V.ii.182) and between courting couples who have reached an understanding (*MAAN* V.ii.50–54; *John* II.i.534–35; *MV* III.ii.138; *H5* V.ii.358; *2GV* II.ii.6–7; *TS* III.ii.122, IV.ii.27; *Oth* I.iii.157–58; *TNK* V.ii.6). The kiss Paris offers Juliet is of this latter type (*R&J* IV.i.43); the audience realizes how inappropriate his assumption is, but he of course does not. Occasionally the kiss is divorced from its sexual context and converted into a courtly greeting or a familial farewell (*2GV* II.iii.25–28; *R3* II.i.21), but most often it is connected to an intimate bond between man and woman, even when that bond is parodied by a forced kiss between two severed heads (*2H6* IV.vii.131–32, 137–38). *See also* Marriage; Wedding.

Crime

Crimes were divided into misdemeanors, or minor crimes, and felonies (*2H6* III.i.129, 132, IV.ii.68), which were more serious. Misdemeanors included such offenses as selling underweight bread or adulterated beer, disturbing the peace, vagrancy, and being drunk or obscene in public. More serious offenses included battery (*MM* II.i.175–76; *Ham* V.i.103; *TN* IV.i.35–37), forgery, counterfeiting, murder (*2H4* V.iv.15–17; *2H6* III.i.128; *3H6* III.ii.182), witchcraft, rape, treason (*1H6* II.iv.83–97), poaching game, sodomy, embezzlement of records or of amounts over £2, and various types of theft. The emphasis placed on the sanctity of personal property is reflected in the number of times that Shakespeare mentions theft and the sheer variety of names by which it is known. There was burglary, which involved an invasion of the home (*MAAN* IV.ii.51); robbery, which was theft by force (*H5* IV.i.150–53; *2H6* V.i.185; *R2* V.iii.9–10); and theft, or stealing, or pilling, which simply meant that the property had been taken by someone other than the owner (*LLL* IV.iii.333; *AW* IV.iii.254–57; *WT* IV.iii.23–24; *Tim* IV.i.10–12; *MWW* I.iii.28–29), with or without force. Thieves (*MM* II.i.22–23; *Lear* III.vii.24; *A&C* II.vi.96; *3H6* V.vi.12; *R2* III.ii.36–46) who robbed travelers were highwaymen (*1H4* I.ii; *AYLI* II.iii.31–33). Those who stole at sea were pirates. Cozeners (*MWW* IV.v.74–76; *Lear* IV.vi.163) were thieves who stole by gaining the victim's confidence and then tricking him out of his goods. Thieves who stole from the clothing or body of a person by stealth rather than force were pickpockets (*1H4* III.iii.56–109, 163–76), pickpurses (*AYLI* III.iv.22–23; *LLL* IV.iii.206; *WT* IV.iv.612–15), or cutpurses (*Ham* III.iv.100; *TNK* II.i.270; *H5* V.i.87), depending on how they accomplished their task; John Stow wrote of an alehouse keeper who trained boy thieves by challenging them to noiselessly steal counters out of two bags that were hung with bells. Of course, every good cutpurse knew that the best picking were in "throngs" (*Lear* III.ii.89) that had assembled for fairs, processions, or hangings, for in such a noisy and crowded setting, hardly anyone would notice a jingle or a bump. Alehouses and taverns, because the people they contained were often drunk, were also prime settings for picking pockets (*MWW* I.i.120–21).

In an age in which people owned few personal possessions, the loss of a napkin, a smock, a tool, or a cooking pot was serious indeed, the loss of a horse or cow still greater, and theft was taken very seriously. It was often a hanging offense. Nevertheless, Shakespeare seems to have a grudging affection for his thieves, particularly if they are spectacularly competent, like Autolycus (*WT* ch.), or spectacularly incompetent, like Falstaff (*1H4* ch.). He is drawn to their slang—their use of "purchase" as a synonym for ill-gotten gains (*H5* III.ii.42), "bung" for pickpocket (*2H4* II.iv.129), and "prig" for thief (*WT* IV.iii.102)—and to their unconventional ethical system (*Tim* IV.iii; *2GV* IV.i, V.iii), in which the highest offense of all is to "peach" (*1H4* II.ii.44), or inform on a colleague.

Execution was the most severe punishment for criminals who were caught, but even the comparatively minor punishments would seem harsh to many people today. The very mildest took the form of public humiliation and immobilization. For "scolding" women or cheating alehouse keepers, this might take the form of a ducking in the local pond or river. Minor crimes such as gambling, scolding, fighting, vagrancy, drunkenness, and minor theft resulted in one or more exposures in the stocks (*2GV* IV.iv.30; *AW* IV.iii.103, 248–49; *Lear* II.ii.130, II.iii.7–10, 85; *WT* IV.iii.22; *Cor* V.iii.159–60) or pillory (*2GV* IV.iv.32). Both were devices that held the offender helplessly in such a posture that she could not fight back if taunted, pelted, or struck by the crowd. The difference was in the part of the body confined. The stocks held the offender by the legs or heels; the term of one's stay was usually about six hours. The pillory, on the other hand, held the neck and often the wrists as well.

Offenses that were too grave to be punished by mere humiliation, but not serious enough to merit execution, resulted in sentences of physical pain or disfigurement. Often, one of these penalties would be substituted for execution if the prisoner pleaded "benefit of clergy." Benefit of clergy was a proof of literacy that mitigated the severity of punishment for some offenses, and a maiming of some kind in place of execution served as notice to any other jurisdiction that the "stigmatic" (*2H6* V.i.215) prisoner had used up his one chance of rehabilitation.

Whipping was a common punishment (*TS* I.i.131–32; *AW* IV.iii.189–92, 238–39; *MM* II.i.252, V.i.524–25; *Per* II.i.92–97; *Cor* IV.vi.48; *A&C* III.xiii.99–101, IV.i.2–3). This was usually done "at the cart's tail" or "cart-arse," meaning that the offender, often a bawd, prostitute, adulterer, or vagrant, was tied to the back of a cart and paraded through town to some highly conspicuous location, often the site of the weekly market, and whipped by the beadle. Since men and women alike were stripped to the waist for this procedure, it was a popular public spectacle. Branding (*TNK* II.i.259) on the hand (*2H6* IV.ii.64), cheek, forehead, or shoulder was another common penalty. Sometimes part of the face was cut; one punishment inflicted on whores and pimps was the clipping of the ears or the slitting of the nose. A list of the penalties for various crimes reads today like a catalog of cruelty. Vagabonds could be whipped at the cart's tail and then burned through the ear with an inch-wide iron. Sheep smugglers' hands were cut off. Spreaders of sedition could have one or both ears severed. Perjurers (*MAAN* IV.ii.43) were branded in the forehead with the letter *P* and deprived of their goods; in a curious addition, their trees were uprooted, depriving them of their arboreal posterity. Whores, in addition to being carted, ducked, and whipped, were made to do penance in public places, dressed only in sheets. A man who fought in the churchyard had to be absolved before he could enter the church again, a fairly mild penalty, but if he used a weapon, he was excommunicated and had one of his ears cut off. A second offense would result in the loss of the other ear, and a third offense required the branding of an *F*, for fray-maker, on his cheek. *See also* Execution; Law.

Crown

The crown (*2H6* IV.viii.68; *3H6* II.v.57–60; *1H4* I.ii.132; *H5* IV.viii.57; *Oth* II.iii.91–93) is one of Shakespeare's most frequently mentioned coins, with good reason. For much of the sixteenth and early seventeenth centuries, it was available in both gold and silver versions. As a coin of less value than the pound, it was more likely to be familiar to the bulk of the audience, and it came in a smaller version, the half crown, whose design echoed that of its larger cousin (though this half crown coin is not mentioned in Shakespeare's works). Most significantly, from a dramatist's perspective, it was almost an international denomination, issued in similar weight and metal by France as the *écu*, by England as the crown, and by the Holy Roman Empire as the *kroon*.

The *écu à la couronne* had, by Shakespeare's time, been the standard unit of French currency for two centuries. Its salient features were a crowned shield adorned with three fleurs-de-lis on the obverse and a cross or quatrefoil design with a fleur-de-lis at each point on the reverse. Its dominance makes this a natural coin for Shakespeare to mention, especially in plays dealing with the Hundred Years' War or French diplomacy (*H5* IV.iv.39–50; *LLL* II.i.129–65; *R2* IV.i.16; *AW* III.vii.35; *John* II.i.590). Furthermore, the name of the coin offered plenty of opportunities for

An écu à la couronne or French crown of 1515–47. Obverse inscription: FRANCISCVS DEI GRATIA FRANCORVUM REX. Reverse: XPS VINCIT XPS REGNAT XPS IMPERAT. Actual size is 26 mm in diameter. © 2002 The American Numismatic Society. All rights reserved.

puns. A crown could be a coin, an emblem of royalty, or the top of the head; "French" could be a simple reference to things from France or to one thing in particular, the French disease, later known as syphilis (*H5* IV.i.225–29; *MM* I.ii.53; *AW* II.ii.21–23), which, among its other effects, made men bald.

Occasionally Shakespeare overestimates the antiquity and distribution of the crown. References to it in *Timon of Athens* (III.iv.29–30), *Pericles* (IV.ii.114), and *A Midsummer Night's Dream* (I.ii.93) are clearly anachronistic. However, the crown was designed to be easily recognized and traded abroad, so it is not odd that it should turn up in Padua (*TS* V.ii.70–74, 115, 130) or the invented landscape of *As You Like It* (I.i.2–3, II.iii.38–41).

In England, the crown was introduced in 1526 and given a value of 5s, comparable to the French crown's value of 4s 6d. The English gold crown was worth 5s and the half-crown 2s 6d, a quarter and an eighth of a pound, respectively; these values remained constant until 1611, during the reign of James I, when a rise in the value of gold relative to that of silver resulted in an awkward revaluation of gold coinage, and their values were raised to 5s 6d and 2s 9d.

The English crown was introduced by Henry VIII and continued by his son, Edward VI. No crowns or half crowns were issued under Edward's half sister Mary I, but the denominations were revived under Elizabeth I, who issued gold crowns and half crowns throughout her reign, silver crowns from 1583 to 1603, and silver half-crowns from 1601 to 1602. Both silver and gold showed a bust of the queen with the standard proclamations of sovereignty; the reverse of the gold coins bore the legend

English silver crown of Elizabeth I, 1601. Actual size is 42 mm in diameter. © 2002 The American Numismatic Society. All rights reserved.

SCVTVM FIDEI PROTEGET EAM (The shield of faith will protect her). The silver coins bore on the reverse the royal arms quartered by a "long cross," a thin cross that extended beyond the boundaries of the shield and into the outer rim of the coin, interrupting the letters of the legend and splitting in two at each tip, so that each point of the cross bore what looked like a pair of leaves. The legend thus quadruply pierced read POSVI DEVM ADIVTOREM MEVM (Behold, I have made God mine helper.)

James I issued the same denominations with several stylistic changes. His own portrait replaced Elizabeth's, obviously, and I R (for *Iacobus Rex*) replaced his predecessor's E R (*Elizabeth Regina*) to the sides of the crowned shield. Since he was James VI of Scotland as well, Scotland was

English gold crown of James I, 1604–5. Actual size is 21 mm in diameter. © 2002 The American Numismatic Society. All rights reserved.

now added to the list of countries ruled, and the royal arms on the reverses of the coins now featured the quartered arms of England and France in the upper left and lower right quadrants of the shield, the arms of Scotland in the upper right quadrant, and the Irish harp in the lower left. The reverse legend on the gold crown and half crown read TVEATVR VNITA DEVS (May God protected united things), a hopeful message for a united Britain. The silver crown and half crown showed James on a caparisoned horse on the obverse, with the royal arms (this time without either the long cross or a crown) on the reverse, accompanied by the legend EXVRGAT DEVS DISSIPENTVR INIMICI (Let God arise and let his enemies be scattered).

Further evidence of the union of Scotland and England under one crown was offered in 1604, when James's coins began to bear the term MAG BRIT (*Magna Britannia*, Great Britain) instead of ANG SCO (England and Scotland) on their obverses; the gold half crowns and "thistle crowns" (so called because they had a crowned rose for the Tudors on one side and a crowned thistle for the Scots on the other) continued to bear the legend TVEATVR VNITA DEVS, and the silver crown bore a new saying with the same substance, QVAE DEVS CONIVNXIT NEMO SEPARET (What God hath joined together, let no man put asunder). *See also* Money.

Crusadoes

Crusadoes (*Oth* III.iv.26) were Portugal's cruzados, gold coins minted from the products of mines in Senegal and Guinea. First issued in the fifteenth century, the cruzado played an important part in Lisbon's trade with India and Antwerp; Portuguese shipowners brought African gold to Lisbon, where it was minted and used to buy European silver for trade with India, where silver was in demand. The cruzado bore a crowned shield of arms on the obverse and a cross (hence the name) on the reverse. *See also* Money.

Dance

In the *Anatomie of Abuses* (1583), Phillip Stubbes deplored the emphasis placed on "the horrible vice of pestiferous dauncing" in social life. Dancing, he wrote, "as it is used (or rather abused) in these daies, is an introduction to whordom, a preparative to wantonnes, a provocative to uncleanes, & an introite to al kind of lewdenes." Stubbes, who also disliked music, football, hunting, fancy clothes, and Christmas revels, particularly objected to dancing schools, the touching of dance partners, and the ceremonial kiss at the end of the dance (*H8* I.iv.95–97). He considered these as nothing less than endangerment of the immortal soul: "Every leap or skip in dance, is a leap toward hel." His opinion, however, was decidedly in the minority, for dancing was one of the most popular Renaissance recreations, enjoyed by both sexes and all social classes. It was equally a part of the entertainment at a wealthy man's banquet (*Tim* I.ii.145 s.d.) and at a pastoral sheep-shearing festival (*WT* IV.iv.153–55). Shakespeare appears to share the popular attitude rather than Stubbes's, for while there is many a merry dance in his plays, references to dancing as a sin, akin to drinking or swearing, are hard to find (*2H4* IV.v.124–26).

The etiquette of dance could be quite complicated. Ladies as well as gentlemen could invite a partner to dance with them; the invited person was obligated to accept, and to return the favor when his or her next turn to dance arrived. A lady asking a gentleman to dance would approach him, curtsy, and look directly at him to avoid any confusion about whom she was inviting. He was to rise, and she was to curtsy again and look away to give him a discreet moment, free from embarrassment or any implication that the two were engaged in a romantic conversation, in which to remove his gloves. If the dance were a lively one, such as a galliard, he might also choose to remove his sword and cloak. Women who did not wish to dance at all were supposed to remain veiled to avoid having to refuse a partner; men had no such escape.

Slow Dances: The Pavan and the Measure

Several types of dances were known in the late sixteenth and early seventeenth centuries, including the basse danse, the tourdin or tordion, the passepied, the tarnatella, and the almaine. The pavan or pavane, a courtly, ceremonial dance, was familiar to many. The basic dance consisted of advancing for eight measures with two single steps and two double steps, then retreating for eight measures with two singles and two doubles; the foot one began on depended on whether one was moving forward or back. The lady typically stood on the right; the gentleman, on the left. Variations included a long version, a short version that included sideways steps, a processional in which the couples moved forward only, and a set dance, with couples facing each other. A move called a conversion called for the lady to move forward while her partner stepped backward, still holding her hand, so that each walked a semicircular path.

The pavan was a strutting, graceful, dignified dance that allowed the man to flourish his cape in a manner suggesting the fanning of a peacock's tail. It was, in short, too grave to survive unaltered in merry England, and more spirited versions were accordingly invented. These included a Spanish variation with "fleurets" or skips, which flourished around 1600, and a similar Italian *passamezzo* pavan, whose name came from the phrase *passo e mezzo,* "a step and a half." The reference to this dance in *Twelfth Night* (V.i.198–99) may be a pun on the number eight, for the eight measures of the music, or may be meant to suggest a slow and staggering drunkard's walk, with an allusion to the slow, careful movements of the pavan.

In James I's court, the pavan fell out of favor altogether, though throughout Europe the music associated with the dance continued to be used for ceremonies, processions, pageants, and the transit of well-born brides to church. As a dance, however, even the *passamezzo* pavan was gone by 1636.

Another stately dance was the measure. The term was sometimes used to mean any slow and dignified dance (*LLL* V.ii.186, 188; *R2* I.iii.289–90; *Per* II.iii.103–5; *R&J* I.iv.10; *AYLI* V.iv.193; *H5* V.ii.135–38). An example from 1570 consisted of a double step forward, four singles back, two singles to the side, a double forward, and a retreat. "Measure," of course, could also refer to a passage of music, an amount of something, poetic rhythm, or the act of quantifying, and Shakespeare plays with an almost palpable glee on all these meanings. The measure as a distinct dance disappeared during the reign of Charles I.

Working-Class Dances

Peasant dances included the hay (*LLL* V.i.149–50—the term could also be applied to an interweaving figure found within several dances), the bergomask (*MND* V.i.352–53), and the roundel (*MND* II.ii.1—a choral dance in a ring). Another kind of "country footing" (*Temp* IV.i.138) was the Morris dance, typically performed by working people but often patronized by the rich and even by royalty. The Morris dance (*TNK* III.v.105–7), so called because it was thought to be Moorish or "Morisco" (*2H6* III.i.365–66) in origin, was usually performed by a small set of men—often six, but any number from two to ten could be found—wearing bells at their elbows and knees and dressed in outlandish costumes. Sometimes one of them was dressed as a dragon; more commonly, a dancer wore a mock horse or "hobbyhorse" (*Ham* III.ii.136–38; *MAAN* III.ii.68–69; *TNK* V.ii.50–51) around his waist with a caraprison hanging to the ground to make it seem that he was mounted. Another dancer served as a "Bavian" or fool (*TNK* III.v.ch., 33–37, 130–31). Characters from the legends of Robin Hood, including Robin, Marian, and Friar Tuck, were also common, with a boy in a dress impersonating Marian. The Morris was associated chiefly with Whitsuntide (six weeks after Easter—*H5* II.iv.25) and May Day (*TNK* II.ii.36–41, III.v.28–30), when it was danced to welcome summer, but it made appearances at other festivals, including Shrovetide, Christmas, and Twelfth Night. A bean-planting version sent the dancers through the fields, making holes with sticks into which the bean seeds were dropped.

Morris dancer and musician, from the *Roxburghe Ballads*. The woodcut was taken from a book called *Kemps Nine Daies Wonder* (1600), an account by comedian William Kemp of a famous wager he made. He bet that he could morris-dance from London to Norwich and set out on the first Monday in Lent, 1600, accompanied by taborer Thomas Sly. Reproduced from the Collections of the Library of Congress.

Faster Dances

A courtly dance with variations in several tempos was the branle, a dance whose name came from a French word meaning "to swing back and forth." It was so called because the steps glided first to the left, then to the right. It was danced in a circle or line with the dancers holding hands or fingers. In order of increasing gaiety and decreasing age of the typical participants, the variations were the *branle double*, the *branle gay*, and the *branle de Bourgogne*. In Italian, the branle was called brando; in English, a braule or brawl (*LLL* III.i.8–9).

Toward the end of the sixteenth century, there was a tendency away from dances set in 2/4 or 4/4 time and toward dances in triple time, "a good tripping measure" (*TN* V.i.37–38). Jigs (*LLL* III.i.12; *TN* I.iii.124; *MAAN* II.i.69; *TNK* V.ii.48–49) were popular even at court. The danse des canaries or canary (*LLL* III.i.12; *AW* II.i.75–78) was a lively courtship dance, with a couple dancing together through the hall, separating, and taking turns advancing toward each other and retreating, skipping and stamping with heel and toe. It required agility and much practice, and could be dressed up with fancier movements such as pirouettes and capers; capers (*2H4* I.ii.193; *TN* I.iii.116; 135–36; *MWW* III.ii.62–63) were leaps with footwork in midair. The courante or coranto (*H5* III.v.33; *AW* II.iii.43–44; *TN* I.iii.123–24) was a fast dance in which the participants half-hopped, half-ran, through the hall in a zigzag pattern.

The *capriole*, or caper, from Thoinot Arbeau's *Orchésographie*, 1588.

The volta (*H5* III.v.32–33; *T&C* IV.ix.86) went through a period of brief but intense popularity near the end of the sixteenth century, with even Queen Elizabeth performing its athletic figures. It was danced in triple time and involved what was then a unique degree of physical contact between dance partners. Man and woman stayed in constant, intimate contact, the woman placing her right hand on the man's neck or shoulder and using her left hand to keep her skirts from flying up during the volta's series of leaps and turns. The man, meanwhile, assisted her in jumping and kept her from falling down out of dizziness by placing his left hand on her hip, his left thigh against her right thigh, and his right hand on the bottom point of her busk (the triangular stiffening-board at the front of a woman's bodice). The busk handhold was ostensibly to help one's partner gain extra height in the leaping part of the dance.

The steps of the volta were fairly simple: a hop on the left foot with a quarter turn, a long step without hopping on the right foot while executing a second quarter turn, a high leap that resulted in a third quarter turn, and a rest in place, preferably in a graceful posture. Sometimes, to alleviate dizziness and fatigue, a couple might rest for several measures while others took their turns. Thoinot Arbeau, in his 1588 *Orchésographie*, noted that a lady spun around for a while in this way would

> feel (no matter what good countenance she makes) her head whirling, full of vertigo or giddiness, and you will perhaps be much the same: I leave to ye to judge whether it be a proper thing for a young girl to make large steps and wide movements of the legs: and whether in this volte her honour and well-being are not risked and involved.

Perhaps because it seemed so immodest, or because its physical demands were too severe, the volta soon fell out of favor.

The galliard (*TN* I.iii.115, 127), however, survived for much longer. Originally danced at court after the pavan, it was retained after the stately pavan was dropped from the rotation. It often used the same music as the pavan but played in a livelier tempo. The galliard was distinctive for several reasons. It was unique among the dances of the time in that the man danced with his hat in his hand rather than on his head. It also had a dramatic or pantomimic element that diminished over time and that included a promenading circuit of the room, a series of increasingly athletic performances by the man for the approval of his partner, and a series of coy advances and retreats. Even after the pantomime disappeared, the jubilant, energetic character of the galliard remained.

Its most fundamental set of steps had six movments. It began with a grue or *grève*, a kind of thrusting kick. Four of these *grèves* were performed in a row, followed by a *saut majeur* and a fifth *grève*. The *saut majeur* was a high jump; perhaps Shakespeare means "jumpers" when he refers to his herdsmen-dancers as "saltiers" in *The Winter's Tale* (IV.iv.329). The five *grèves* gave the sequence its name—*les cinq pas* or "the five steps"—which Shakespeare called the "sink-a-pace" or "cinquepace" (*TN* I.iii.25; *MAAN* II.i.69–75). This basic set of steps alternated with far more energetic passages, in which the male partner, or sometimes a solo male dancer, demonstrated his skill and power by incorporating the *pied croisé* (crossed foot), stamping of toes and heels, high and low kicks, a backward kick called a *ruade*, a sideways kick called the *ru de vache* (cow kick), the high jump, a jump with footwork in the air (caper or capriole), and even a jump with two full rotations and a graceful landing. The demands of the dance were so exhilarating that the 56-year-old Elizabeth I danced six or seven galliards each morning as a form of calisthenics. The galliard ended with a mutual salute called a *congé* (*AW* IV.iii.88). *See also* Music.

Death

Several elements were usually present at a deathbed. If the dying man or woman was lucky, there would be friends and family gathered, tending to last-minute issues of comfort, hearing final requests and commands, and making assurances of love and promises to meet in the hereafter. At such a time, the dying person might make a new will or revise an old one (*2H6* II.iii.75–78; *R2* III.ii.145–50; *RL* 1198), perhaps with instructions as to the form of the funeral (*H8* IV.ii.167–72). There might be a physician present to expound upon the likelihood of recovery, but most people, accustomed to plague, smallpox, typhus, tuberculosis, and a variety of vaguely named diseases, had a good idea of what would ensue if the patient showed signs of delirium or nervous twitching (*H5* II.iii.12–26). When the breathing became imperceptible and the skin cold, it was time to make an assessment of life or death; often a feather or piece of glass was held to the patient's nose and mouth to see if there were signs of breath. In Catholic times, it would have been of utmost importance to have a priest present to administer the sacrament of extreme unction, but in Protestant times it was also likely for a parson to be present to offer spiritual comfort. One other element signaled the passage from life into death. This was the tolling of the death knell (*MAAN* V.ii.76–82; *Mac* IV.iii.170–72), a series of peals of the bell on the parish church. Nine peals were customary for a man, six for a woman, and three for a child; this was sufficient to alert the community to the imminent demise of one its members and usually enough, combined with local gossip, to identify the decedent.

Once death had been established, the preparation of the body followed a mixture of custom and the wishes of the deceased. Sometimes the wish of the deceased was to be left completely alone for a period of days or even weeks, in the fear of being buried alive. This was rare, but not unheard of; in one case, a man was revived from a coma when the coffin was accidentally dropped during his funeral procession. More commonly, preparation of the body was immediate and the burial nearly so, taking place within anywhere from a few hours to three days. Usually someone was paid to wash the body and lay it out decently (*T&C* II.iii.30–32), wrapped in a white length of linen called a shroud (*LLL* V.ii.480; *MND* V.i.377; *R&J* IV.i.85; *TN* II.iv.55; *WT* IV.iv.460; *Ham* IV.v.36) or winding-sheet (*3H6* II.v.114). The winding-sheet might be smeared with wax, gum, or a similar substance, in which case it was called a cerecloth (*MV* II.vii.51), from the Latin *cera*, "wax." If the body was to rest overnight before burial, watchers might be paid to attend it by candlelight. This "wake" or watching was falling out of favor during Shakespeare's lifetime and was generally abandoned in the south and east, though it survived for longer in the north.

In the case of aristocrats, whose funerals might draw notables from across the country, and whose burial trappings had to be approved by the College of Arms, the preparations could take quite a while; it thus became necessary to embalm (*H8* IV.ii.170) the corpse by removing and burying the bowels (*1H4* V.iv.107) and filling the abdominal cavity with spices or sawdust. Sometimes this was done quite skillfully; at other times the job was performed so badly that it had to be reattempted, or the corpse quickly and quietly buried and an image borne in its place at the formal funeral. Despite the occasional failures of embalming, its association with the upper classes made it increasingly popular in the ambitious middle class. Embalmed or not, the typical corpse was dressed in a smock or shirt and laid in the shroud, which was tied closed at the feet and at the top of the head, with flowers tucked into the front where the edges met. Other rituals might be performed, varying from place to place and corpse to corpse. In some cases, the deceased was given a treasured possession to wear or hold; in others, salt was put into the shroud as a protection against evil or against the swelling of the body. Some families, optimistically, put a coin in the mouth as a fee for St. Peter.

At times another step might be added to the period between the death and the funeral. In cases where the cause of death was uncertain—an important consideration in a society that buried suicides with less honor and ceremony—a coroner, Shakespeare's "crowner" (*TN* I.v.133–35; *Ham* V.i.1–25), held an inquest to determine the cause of death. In cases of accidental death, suicide, or homicide, the body was watched until the coroner could inspect it. This was one of the few instances in which the "wake" continued in southern and eastern England after the turn of the seventeenth century.

Preparation was slightly different in the case of very young infants or stillborn babies. In the latter case, midwives were simply advised to bury the body someplace where it would not be scavenged by animals. In the former, an infant who had been baptized but whose mother had not been churched was buried in the chrysom cloth used at baptism. Sometimes, dead infants whose mothers had died in childbirth were buried in their mothers' arms.

The body was then placed in a coffin (*R2* V.vi.30; *JC* III.ii.107; *R3* I.ii.38; *TA* I.i.70 s.d., 35, 150 s.d.). This was made of wood in most cases (*1H6* I.i.18; *TN* II.iv.52), and for paupers' funerals was rented. The pauper's shrouded body was placed in the coffin until interment, then dumped into the grave and the coffin saved for the use of the next pauper to die. Middle-class families could afford a wood coffin for each member of the family, and members of the upper classes often opted for a lead coffin (*1H6* I.i.64) instead of or in addition to the wooden one; they wanted their bodies to be preserved as well as possible. The difference in cost was significant. At one funeral in the late 1570s, the wood coffin cost only 15s, but the lead coffin inside it cost more than £5 and was given an inscription for an additional cost of more than £2. Some coffins were even simpler and cheaper than the wooden one at this funeral; a 1618 example cost only 5s.

Funeral and Interment

When the body was ready, the guests—often 50 to 150 of them, sometimes a great many more—assembled at the home where the body was laid out in its coffin. Cakes were usually eaten at this time, occasionally with the coffin serving as the table. If the deceased had been a member of a trade guild, his fellow guild members were expected to turn out for the funeral and, in many cases, to offer a sum of money to help support his widow. The procession consisted of the clergyman, clerk, mourners, friends, guests, coffin bearers, pallbearers (who supported the drapery over the coffin as one might carry a bridal train), and almoners, who were poor men or women, walking in pairs and often equal in number to the number of years lived by the deceased. The almoners were given clothes and sometimes money in exchange for walking in the procession; the coffin bearers, too, were usually hired from among the poor. The chief mourner was someone closely related to the deceased and was usually a woman when the decedent was also a woman. The mourners were identified by their black hooded gowns (*3H6* II.i.161; *LLL* V.ii.832), and within the group of mourners, distinctions of rank were made by the amount of fabric used in the mourning clothes.

At heraldic funerals (funerals for people who were entitled to coats of arms), there might be a framework called a hearse (*JC* III.ii.165; *R3* I.ii.2; *1H6* I.i.104; *TNK* I.v.1 s.d.; *2H4* IV.v.113) that covered the coffin and was topped by a hearse cloth. The size and decoration of this cloth, like the mourners' clothes, were dictated by rank. So were the number and kind of flags, painted with the decedent's arms, that were hung around the inside of the church, and use of swords and arms in both temporary and permanent monuments (*Ham* IV.v.212–16). Some people attempted to evade the heralds' restrictions and to appropriate more honors than were their due by burying their dead at night, by torchlight. In time, like embalming, this practice became fashionable, and many people of middling birth and people who had no intention of deceiving the heralds adopted the practice. Some of the more elaborate funeral trappings were available to members of the middle class as well as to the rich. Trade guilds, for example, owned gorgeous palls—cloths like hearse cloths that lay over the coffin and sometimes extended ahead of and behind the coffin to be carried by mourners or attendants. These palls, like the crimson velvet and yellow silk specimen owned by London's Saddlers' Company, could be rented by families for the funerals of guild members. For women who died while still virgins, the coffin might be decorated with garlands of lilies (*Ham* V.i.232–33). In some cases, particularly those of Oxford and Cambridge scholars, the pall or church draperies might be pinned with hundreds of small sheets of paper bearing verses composed by friends, relatives, or hired poets.

Women bearing a maiden's coffin, from the *Roxburghe Ballads*. Reproduced from the Collections of the Library of Congress.

The guests and mourners, singing doleful songs (*TNK* I.v.1–10, II.v.15, III.vi.249; *2GV* III.i.241; *Ham* V.i.235–38; *R&J* IV.v.88), walked in a procession (*R3* I.ii.1–33; *R&J* IV.i.109–12) to the church. In Catholic times, the priest had rung a handbell as he walked, and this practice, despite the opposition of Anglican leaders, was still sometimes carried out. Another conflict between the old ways and the new manifested itself in the ringing of the bell or bells of the parish church (*3H6* II.v.117; *TNK* III.ii.20; *R&J* IV.v.86; S 71). The Anglican authorities insisted on a single peal at the time of death, another before interment, and a third after it, but many parishes retained the old practice of ringing for hours, even for the whole day. At the church, which was draped with as much black cloth as the family could afford to buy or rent, a sermon was read (*JC* III.i.228–30), reminding the hearers of the fragility and brevity of mortal life and the importance of living for what came afterward. Then the parson named the virtues of the deceased, sometimes entirely fabricated, sometimes embellished, sometimes so true and heartfelt that the sermon had to be interrupted while the minister himself wept.

The body was then buried (*R&J* II.iii.83; *WT* IV.iv.459–61; *2GV* IV.ii.107, 113; *TA* I.i.348–49, IV.ii.164) either in the churchyard or in the church itself. Interment in the church cost more, but carried some promise of eternal remembrance. The churchyard, by contrast did not, for tombstones were rare, and only immediate family and the gravedigger (*Ham* V.i.ch.) remembered who was buried where for very long. Thus the command in *Henry V* to "lay these bones in an unworthy urn, / Tombless, with no remembrance over them" (I.ii.228–29), is consistent with contemporary practice, the "urn" in question being the grave itself, the final container. Between inadequate marking of graves and overcrowding, it was common for gravediggers to find, as does the one in *Hamlet* V.i, the bones of a decomposed corpse in the hole intended for a new one. In this case, the bones were simply heaped up and removed to a charnel house (*R&J* IV.i.81–83; *Mac* III.iv.71) for storage. The grave (*2H6* IV.x.83; *3H6* I.iii.27–28; *2GV* IV.iii.22; *R&J* IV.i.84; *Cym* IV.ii.398–400; *R3* IV.i.94; *R2* III.iii.153–56) dug was about 6 feet (1.9 m) deep and usually faced east-west, with the head at the western end so that the body faced the dawn. The grave's length was about "two paces" (*1H4* V.iv.89–90, 98). The body or coffin was laid into the grave, earth shoveled on, and flowers (*Cym* IV.ii.283–85; *TN* II.iv.59–60; *R&J* V.iii.282) or sprigs of rosemary tossed on top. The body was committed to the earth with the words "earth to earth, ashes to ashes, dust to dust, in sure and certain hope of resurrection to eternal life."

The geography of the graveyard was important for more reasons than the avoidance of old graves; the north side of the church, for example, was reserved for those who had died in un-Christian circumstances, such as possible suicides or unbaptized infants. The interior of the church, too, had a language of position. The farther toward the chancel (the railed or screened end of the church where the service was conducted), the more expensive the burial plot. Those with great wealth might choose to be buried not in the church, but in the private chapel of a favorite home or in a family tomb (*LLL* I.i.2; *2H4* V.ii.123–24; *R&J* III.v.55–56; *MV* II.vii.69) or sepulcher (*3H6* I.i.236; *2GV* IV.ii.117; *S* 68) consisting of an above-ground building and underground storage space for the bodies of generations of relatives.

Bodies buried inside the church usually merited a memorial of some kind (*MAAN* V.ii.76–82). This was often a carved stone plaque set into the wall or floor, but might in the case of very notable people include a statue of the deceased. These statues usually showed the deceased at rest as in a coffin, hands neatly folded, body fully dressed; such memorials, like the stone plaques, can still be seen in churches all over England. Plaques and statues alike featured the name of the deceased, the dates of birth and death, perhaps a description of the person's accomplishments and status within the community, often a statement of religious faith, and sometimes a direct address to the viewer, phrased as a plea for remembrance, a piece of advice, or even a joke. Collectively, these inscritpions made up the epitaph (*MAAN* V.i.283, V.iii.3–10; *H5* I.ii.233; *1H4* V.iv.99; *Tim* V.i.185, V.iii.5–6, V.iv.67–73; *AW* I.ii.49–50, II.iii.138–42; S 81). Some were humorous. One, for example, mounted on the grave of a person not quite rich enough to be buried inside the chancel, criticized the selling of choice spots to the wealthy:

> Here I lie at the chancel door,
> Here I lie because I'm poor:
> The further in, the more you pay:
> Here lie I as warm as they.

Some offered encomiums upon the deceased's virtue; that for Susanna Shakespeare Hall, William's daughter, testified to her compassion and wit:

> Witty above her sex, but that's not all,
> Wise to Salvation was good Mistress Hall:
> Something of Shakespeare was in that [the wit], but this [the virtue]
> Wholly of Him with whom she's now in bliss.
> Then, passenger, hast ne'er a tear
> To weep with her that wept with all?
> That wept, yet set herself to cheer
> Them up with comforts cordial,
> Her love shall live, her mercy spread,
> When thou hast ne'er a tear to shed.

Some epitaphs were briefer, consisting merely of a Latin phrase offering hopes of remembrance or peace for the departed. Some were ominous or pleading; Shakespeare's is both:

> Good friend for Jesus sake forbear
> To dig the dust enclosed here:
> Blest be the man that spares these stones,
> And curst be he that moves my bones.

Since Shakespeare was buried inside the church, he had less to fear in this regard than those buried in the churchyard, but his fears were not wholly unfounded. From time to time, even the stone plaques inside the church were intruded upon to make room for new ones. Shakespeare's admonition has been heeded, however; his memorial still stands, and his bones have not been moved, as some have desired over the centuries, to the Poets' Corner in Westminster Abbey.

Shakespeare makes only brief references to non-Christian burials. He clearly knew that the ancients burned rather than buried their dead, for he mentions cremation in connection with funerals in ancient Greece and Rome (*JC* III.ii.254; *TNK* I.i.43–42). Yet in *Titus Andronicus,* he for some reason retreats to the familiar, burying Titus's sons in a coffin and a family tomb, and consigning only the Scythian queen's son to flames (I.i.70–156).

"Drinking" and Mourning

After the burial, it was customary to hold a "drinking"—a small feast usually held in the churchyard, occasionally in the church itself. Beer was the most popular beverage for this purpose, though wine or mead might be substituted. Bread, cakes, biscuits, buns, or "cakebread," a confection of butter, sugar, currants, spices, and rosewater, were the usual comestibles. Sometimes the drinking was followed by a more extensive meal at the home of the deceased. This custom, so deeply ingrained that it was performed even in time of plague, is what is meant by the instructions to "stay [for] dinner" in *Romeo and Juliet* (IV.v.146). As a way of spreading respect and remembrance for the deceased, alms were also distributed to the poor. Cash or penny loaves of bread were given to anywhere from 50 to 200 paupers, causing one cleric to complain in 1589 that "the dead do give more than those that are alive."

It was considered appropriate for close relatives to continue to mourn for some time after the death and funeral (*R&J* III.v.71–80). One way that they demonstrated their continuing affection for the deceased was by wearing black (*R2* V.i.49, V.vi.47–48; *RL* 1585), often for a period of one year (*LLL* V.ii.805–6) in the case of widows or other members of the immediate family. These "mourning weeds" (*3H6* III.iii.229, IV.i.104; *TA* I.i.70)—"weeds" was simply another word for clothes—might be fashionable clothing that simply happened to be black and less elaborately adorned or, for widows, an almost nunlike habit.

Funeral Costs

The cost of burying a loved one could be extremely high; in the case of the poor, it often amounted to 12 to 20 percent of the deceased's total estate. In some cases, for example, the funerals of debtors, the cost of the death and burial exceeded the resources of the family. Such importance was ascribed to a "decent burial," however, that families often ignored the wishes of the deceased to be buried without pomp or expense. Paupers' funerals were paid for by the local parish, including a drinking afterward, and debtors' funerals were supposed to be paid for before the creditors could claim anything from the estate. Even prisoners and those executed for their crimes were usually given a funeral of sorts; debtors who died in prison were buried at the prison's expense, and executed felons were buried in whatever churchyard was nearest to the jail.

Numerous people had to be paid whenever someone died. The woman who washed and dressed the corpse had to be paid, as did the watchers (if any), who were given food, beer, candles, and perfume each night; the last item was intended to counteract the increasingly rank aroma of the corpse. Those who rang the death knell were likewise fed and paid, as was the coroner if his services were required. The pallbearers, torchbearers for night burials, almoners, clerk, gravedigger, and priest each got a sum for his work, and sometimes there was a fee to register the death as well. Then there were expenses for the coffin, the flowers, the embalming, the burial plot, the alms, and the food and drink before and after the funeral. Fees varied by place and year, but typical sums might include a few pence each for the gravedigger, watchers, and ringers; a few shillings for the coroner, the priest who presided at the burial, and the surgeon who disemboweled the corpse for embalming; a shilling for the clerk; about 10s for a funeral sermon; between about 6s 8d and 10s for the burial plot, depending on location; and £5 or so for the embalming. *See also* Inheritance.

Deer

One of the animals mentioned most frequently in Shakespeare's works, the deer was a favorite prey of aristocratic hunters. Only the upper classes could hunt deer, and to increase their pleasure in the sport, they kept their deer fenced in behind pales (*V&A* 229–40) in special parks whose shape was often designed to herd the deer toward waiting hunters. The secretary of Frederick, Duke of Württemberg, noted that Windsor Castle had up to sixty deer parks designed so that "the animals can be driven out of one inclosure into another, and so on; all which inclosures are encompassed by fences." The deer's role as quarry ensured that its behavior in all circumstances was well documented. Its tracks, sign, and spoor were the subjects of intense study; the droppings, for example, varied according to the animal's sex and age and according to the time of year. The deer was timid, hiding when wounded or when feeding its young; the hart, or adult male red deer, was said to be so fearful (*1H6* IV.ii.46–54) that only a special "bone" (actually a piece of gristle) within its heart kept it from dying of terror at the slightest provocation. However, the males went horn-mad (*CE* III.i.72) in rutting season, battling each other and searching for females with obsessive determination.

England had three types of deer: red, fallow, and roe. The red deer was considered the loftiest prey. Males had different names depending on their age; a one-year old male was a calf, becoming a bullock at two, a brocket at three, a staggard at four, a stag (*TNK* III.v.152; *MWW* V.v.12) at five, and a hart of ten (for the ten tines it now bore on its antlers) at six (*TA* I.i.494; *JC* III.i.204). (William Harrison, in *The Description of England*, gives these stages as calf, brocket, spade, stag, great stag, and hart.) Until it was six it was, along with other inferior deer, a "rascal," unworthy to be hunted (*2H4* II.iv.41; *AYLI* III.iii.55). The female had no such hierarchy based on age and was simply called a hind (*R3* II.iv.50; *MND* II.i.232) as soon as she was full-grown.

The hunting season varied but was usually in the spring and summer, called the "time of grease" because the deer were putting on weight and growing their antlers in preparation for the mid-September to mid-November rut. George Turberville, in *The Noble Art of Venerie or Hunting*, first printed in Elizabeth's reign and reissued in James's, noted a peculiarity of the hart's feeding during rut that Shakespeare also mentions (*MWW* V.v.12–15). "During the time of their Rut," Turberville writes, "they live with small sustenance, for they feed only of such things as they see before them, and rather regard the tracke of the Hinde [female red deer]. Their chiefe meat is the red Mushrome or Todestoole, which helpeth well to make them pisse their grease."

The fallow deer, from Konrad Gesner's *Icones Animalium Quadrupedam*. Reproduced from the Collections of the Library of Congress.

Fallow deer were less hunted and less admired than red deer, though they actually produced more (and, some thought, better) venison per pound. They went into rut about two weeks later than the red deer. A male fallow deer was a fawn its first year, a pricket its second (*LLL* IV.ii.12, 22, 49–60), a sorrel its third, a sore its fourth (*LLL* IV.ii.12, 22, 49–62), a buck of the first head its fifth (*LLL* IV.ii.10), and a buck its sixth; like the red deer, it was not considered a worthwhile quarry until it was at least six years old. The female was called a doe; a misunderstanding based on this word takes place in *Love's Labor's Lost*, when one character says *haud credo* (Latin for "I don't believe it") and another believes he has said "old gray doe" (IV.ii.11–12). This would make more sense in reference to the fallow deer than the red, for the fallow deer's color was white, black, speck-led white and black, or sandy with a black streak down the middle of the back. In the *Historie of Foure-Footed Beastes*, the naturalist Edward Topsell claimed, inaccurately, that the animal was so timid because its blood lacked a clotting factor. The red deer's antlers were thin and pointed, but the fallow deer's main antler was relatively thin at the base, rose and sprouted two points, then became much wider and flatter like the antler of a moose, with additional points growing from this broader area.

The roebuck.

The roe deer (*TS* Ind.ii.48) could be hunted year-round, but it was a smaller and therefore inferior prey. It, too, had names for each year of its development and became huntable not in its sixth year but in its fifth, when it was called a roebuck. The roebuck's habit of pair bonding, so unlike the red and fallow deer's promiscuous coupling, made the roe deer a symbol of chastity in the Middle Ages.

Deer were in the odd position of being semi-domestic and semi-wild animals. They were kept in parks, looked after by gamekeepers, fed with cows' milk if orphaned, and fretted over by landowners concerned with the triple ravages of dogs, poachers, and disease. Yet they were not herded in the same way that sheep or cattle were, stabled, and subjected to human touch, for the idea was to keep them wild enough that they would run away when hunted. The parks created an odd environment in which the deer sometimes behaved in ways contrary to their behavior in the wild. For example, in the parks, but not in the wild, the dominant deer during the season of rut was killed by the other males after the season was over and he was at his weakest. *See also* Animals; Hunting.

Demon

There was widespread belief in the existence of devils. These demons were thought to work mischief in the world, to stir up disbelief in God, and to possess the bodies of their unfortunate victims. Those believed to be possessed betrayed their condition through fits, treasonous statements, convulsions, personality and facial changes, speaking unknown languages, clairvoyance, superhuman strength, disgust for church objects and Scripture, and an inability to say the Lord's Prayer. One woman, Katherine Wright, "foamed at mouth, gnashed with her teeth, cried and scritched, catched & snatched at those stood by her." A musician's apprentice supposedly had a mouse-sized lump that moved from place to place on his body, though one observer said it was just his hand, and the boy later admitted that he had been shamming. In Shakespeare, a supposed case of possession (also a sham) is supposedly "proven" by the afflicted person's anxiety at hearing the devil maligned (*TN* III.iv.104–5); such apparent defenses of devils and resentment toward God were commonly presumed to be signs of possession. Such cases often ended with an exorcism and with an accusation against some witch or other who had supposedly summoned the offending spirit. The actual causes of the sufferers' symptoms are unclear. Some of the attacks can be tentatively attributed to Tourette's syndrome, others to out-and-out fraud, and many, probably, to ergotism. This last is a serious and sometimes fatal disease accompanied by hallucinations and caused by spoiled grain, especially rye.

Because of its occasional connection with treason, demonic possession was of great interest to the authorities. Furthermore, the Anglican Church frowned on exorcisms, which smacked either of old-fashioned popery or of radical Puritan zeal. Catholic exorcism had no set form until the seventeenth century, but relics, holy water, sanctified candles, crosses, Masses, noxious potions "such as might have made a horse sicke," and foul smoke were often employed in the ritual. The smoke, created by burning such substances as brimstone, asafetida, galbanum, St. John's wort, rue, and feathers, was so thick that it could blacken the faces of the possessed. Sometimes the victim was bound in a chair or prodded with needles. The clergy laid hands on the sufferer's body, commanding the demon to migrate to some specific part of the body or to reveal its name. When the demon left, it was thought to leave some sign of its departure, like a cracked glass or extinguished candle.

The Puritans tended to exorcise with mass fasting and prayer sessions called "prophesyings." From 1604, ministers were forbidden to hold prophesyings without ecclesiastical permission, which was never given. One of the most prominent Puritan exorcists was John Darrell, a lay preacher who pretended to greater authority; it has been argued convincingly that Feste's charade as a clergyman in *Twelfth Night*, as he visits the supposedly possessed Malvolio, is a direct reference to Darrell's antics (IV.ii).

Archbishop Samuel Harsnett attacked both exorcism and the idea of demonic possession in his *Declaration of Egregious Popish Impostures* (1603), a book that was read by many, including Shakespeare. F. W. Brownlow, in *Shakespeare, Harsnett, and the Devils of Denham*, explains how Harsnett timed the publication of his book, describing a series of Catholic exorcisms that took place in Denham in 1585–86, to serve as an attack on prophesyings and Puritan exorcists as well. Harsnett calls the exorcists the true devils and makes fun of the "devils' " claims through their human hosts. In one case, involving a young woman named Sara Williams, he mocks the ridiculous statements made by her devil, Maho:

> The Exorcist asks *Maho, Saras* devil, what company he had with him, and the devil makes no bones, but tels him in flat termes, *all the devils in hell*. Heere was a goodly fat *otium* [laziness] this meane while in hell! The poore soules there had good leave to play; such a day was never seene since hell was hell. Not a doore-keeper left, but all must goe a maying to poore *Saras* house.

This passage calls to mind the cry, "Hell is empty, / And all the devils are here!" (I.ii.214–15) from *The Tempest*, though Shakespeare did not necessarily cull the image from Harsnett. That Shakespeare did read Harsnett's book is evident, however, from phrases, ideas, and the names of demons that occur in *King Lear*. For example, the *Lear* demons Flibbertigibbet, Mahu, Frateretto, Hoppedance / Hobbididence, Obidicut, and Modo (III.iv.113–17, 141–42, III.vi.6, 30, IV.i.59–63) all have parallels in Harsnett's account of the Denham exorcisms. Hobbididence, for example, was a character in a story made up by Sara Williams, and few of the devils' names occur anywhere else in print before Harsnett's book.

Brownlow does an excellent job of linking *Lear* and the *Declaration*, though he is less convincing when he tries to prove that *Lear* is a veiled attack on Harsnett, for Shakespeare appears to be on Harsnett's side. While spirits of some kind do appear in the plays when conjured by witches, the "possessions" in the plays are both false. Malvolio is told he is possessed as part of a practical joke; Antipholus of Ephesus is thought to be mad or possessed but is really quite sane (*CE* IV.iv.45–56), and Edgar is only "counterfeiting" (*Lear* III.vi.60) his possession as part of a larger charade of madness. While Shakespeare is almost certainly lampooning John Darrell, and probably poking fun at the delusions of the mad (for it was still considered jolly fun to do so), he does not seem to be attacking Harsnett's basic premise, that demonic possession was false and the exorcists frauds or fools.

As for the term "exorcism," Shakespeare uses it rarely, and as the opposite of its modern meaning. In his usage, "exorcisms" (*2H6* I.iv.5) are the summonings of devils, while a "conjurer" (*CE* IV.iv.45, 53–56; *MAAN* II.i.247–48; *2H6* I.ii.76–81, I.iv.16–41) is one who either summons or banishes spirits. Hence there are sentences that sound extremely peculiar to the modern ear, such as "Thou, like an exorcist, hast conjured up / My mortified spirit" (*JC* II.i.323–24). Shakespeare's conjurers "practice and converse with spirits" (*1H6* II.i.25), whether that means raising them, bidding them to perform tasks or answer questions, or sending them back to their native domain.

Another question of terminology concerns Shakespeare's names for these supernatural creatures. In *Henry V*, the "demon" (II.ii.121) is clearly a malevolent being. In *Antony and Cleopatra*, however, the demon seems to be synonymous with Antony's soul, and is just a few lines later called "thy angel" (II.iii.18–21). Shakespeare once uses the term "cacodemon" (*R3* I.iii.143), in a context that makes it clear this is a devil of some kind, and he often refers to devils as coming from hell and working mischief, though by persuasion, tricks, and their own actions, rather than by possessing human bodies. At other times he simply calls raised creatures "spirits," and it is difficult to know whether by this he means demons, fairies, or ghosts (*2H6* I.iv.20; *Temp* II.ii.1–14). His meaning is clearest when he says "the devil" or the name of a specific and well-known malevolent being, such as Beelzebub (*TN* V.i.283; *Mac* II.iii.4). *See also* Magic; Witch.

Disease and Injury

Identifying the medical complaints of patients in Renaissance England can be tricky. Medicine in the late sixteenth and early seventeenth centuries was a mixture of superstition, legend, blind faith in ancient authorities, hit-and-miss treatment, observation, and waiting for nature or God to do something to kill or cure the patient. It was hampered by a poor understanding of the causes of disease and none of the technology or methodology that makes it possible today to identify specific diseases. Therefore, symptoms were treated as individual illnesses. For example, fever, which today we recognize as a symptom of many diseases, was treated as a disease in itself. No wonder that any one type of treatment, when applied to all fevers of whatever origin, usually failed to work.

Retroactive diagnosis is also complicated by other problems. Some diseases that existed in the Renaissance have simply disappeared, perhaps because they mutated into more benign forms or perhaps because they killed their hosts so quickly or spread so ineffectively that they became extinct. Some diseases correspond in name to diseases we know today, but the names were applied with less specificity in the Renaissance. Thus a person who contracted "smallpox" in the sixteenth century may actually have had smallpox or may instead have had measles, rubella, or scarlet fever. A "consumption" might mean tuberculosis (*MAAN* V.iv.95–96; *2H4* I.ii.237–40; *Tim* IV.iii.152–53, 202), a fatal disease that usually first attacked the lungs and could be spread by infected milk or airborne droplets, but it might equally mean any disease that caused the sufferer to waste away. Furthermore, tuberculosis was not called by that name; it was often called phthisis, and when it affected the lymph nodes of the neck, it was called scrofula. Even the term "disease" itself might be used, by Shakespeare at least, to mean illness, "dis-ease" in the sense of physical or psychological discomfort, or anything causing "dis-ease" (*1H6* II.v.44; *2H6* IV.vii.90; *TS* I.ii.80; *2H4* V.i.78–79; *MAAN* I.i.82–86).

Ailments

There were certainly as many types of illnesses and injuries then as now—more, since childhood ailments like measles (*Cor* III.i.78), mumps, chicken pox, and rubella were without vaccines. The only "vaccine" available was for smallpox: milkmaids contracted cowpox, a less virulent disease, which was similar enough to smallpox to confer immunity. However, this relationship was as yet undiscovered and would lurk for another two and a half centuries in the deep, deep shadows of English medical ignorance. In the meantime, people suffered acutely from

> rotten diseases of the south, the guts-gripping raptures, catarrhs, loads o' gravel in the back, lethargies, cold palsies, raw eyes, dirt-rotten livers, wheezing lungs, bladders full of imposthumes, sciaticas, lime kilns i' the palm, incurable bone-ache, and the riveled fee-simple of the tetter, and the like. (*T&C* V.i.19–24)

In other words, they had sexually transmitted diseases, dysentery and other digestive complaints, mucus discharge as during a cold, kidney stones, loss of energy, paralysis, sore eyes, cirrhosis, asthma, bladder abscesses and infections, sciaticas, psoriasis, arthritis or perhaps the bone pain caused by syphilis, and skin rashes such as those caused by eczema, herpes, or ringworm. Such diseases could make life miserable, with few real remedies and with little more than liquor or laudanum to dull the pain.

Some ailments were minor, although what we think of as inconveniences, such as a simple cold (*2H4* III.ii.185–87—also called "rheum" in *T&C* V.iii.104–5; *A&C* III.ii.58; and *MM* III.i.31) or cough ("tisick"— *T&C* V.iii.101) would have been much more serious impairments without modern medicines for the ease of symptoms. Toothache (*MAAN* III.ii.20–26, V.i.35–36; *Oth* III.iii.411–12; *Cym* V.iv.142–43) was crippling in its agony. People suffered headaches (*Oth* III.iii.283–86; *John* IV.i.41–49), heartburn (*MAAN* II.i.4; *1H4* III.iii.55), and cramps (*AW* IV.iii.296; *Temp* I.ii.327–28) with little to relieve the pain and discomfort.

Even a simple-sounding condition like "ague," meaning chills and fever (*Mac* V.v.4; *H8* I.i.4; *T&C* III.iii.232; *Lear* IV.vi.105; *Temp* II.ii.66) could be life-threatening. Ague made one "pale and faint" (*V&A* 739), shaky (*Cor* I.iv.38), and "lean" (*JC* III.ii.113), giving us some idea of the intended appearance of Sir Andrew Aguecheek in *Twelfth Night*. Some agues, such as the "burning ague" and "ague with spots," may actually have been typhus, an often fatal disease characterized by fever and tiny hemorrhages that look like flea bites. Skin conditions such as blisters (*Tim* V.i.132; *R&J* I.iv.74–76), boils (*T&C* II.i.1–6; *Cor* I.iv.31; *Lear* II.iv.220–22), corns (*R&J* I.v.18–22; *Lear* III.ii.33), kibes or chilblains (*Lear* I.v.9; *Temp* II.i.280–81; *Ham* V.i.141; *MWW* I.iii.31), and sunburn (*MAAN* II.i.307) would have been excruciating at times and might, in some cases, have betokened a more serious disease. Spots of one kind or another, boils, and lumps were symptoms of several potentially fatal illnesses.

Similarly, fever, which today is rarely a frightening symptom unless the body temperature is very high, was then taken very seriously. Fevers accompanied many of the potentially fatal illnesses for which there was no cure but time and luck. Smallpox, for example, began with a high fever, back and limb pain, headaches, and sometimes convulsions. Within two to five days, the characteristic rash developed. Death might follow, particularly if the rash became confluent, meaning that the patient's flesh began to slough off in large pieces on the outside while the virus destroyed the liver, lungs, intestines, and other organs within. There was a 25 to 30 percent mortality rate, and even if the patient survived, the illness left a legacy of round, disfiguring scars (*LLL* V.ii.45), possible blindness, and possible male impotence. It was terrifying, and made more so by the common misidentification of measles as smallpox, making smallpox seem even more widespread and unpredictable. Its most famous victim in the Tudor era was Queen Elizabeth herself, who nearly died of it in 1562. Fever might also herald influenza, one of the era's biggest killers, which broke out in several epidemics and a few pandemics during the sixteenth century. Scarlet fever was another killer, as was typhus, mentioned above, which often struck in crowded, dirty places like jails (*2H4* V.v.35) and army camps.

It was thus quite natural for fever to cause great apprehension and to be considered a serious illness in itself, capable of weakening, disabling, and killing (*JC* I.ii.119–28; *MM* IV.iii.70–72, V.i.151–52; *V&A* 739; *2H4* I.i.140–45). It was at once deadly and mysterious, responding to treatment at one time and stubbornly refusing to break at another. How maddening it must have been for Renaissance physicians to see fever fall into certain predictable patterns, but never knowing why any patient followed the pattern she did, or prescribing half a dozen medications and therapies at once, and never knowing which of them worked, or if any of them did, or why. Physicians, unable to determine the cause of fever, concentrated instead on looking for patterns that might give a hint as to the outcome. A quotidian fever spiked every day, a tertian every three days; these were terms that must have been in common but not universal usage outside the medical profession, for Mistress Quickly misuses them (*H5* II.i.120).

The diseases that killed the most people were seldom the ones most feared. Tuberculosis, influenza, and dysentery ("flux" or "bloody flux") were the era's great murderers, but they never captured the popular imagination, perhaps because they were so commonplace. The diseases that really frightened were those that went into hiding for a while, then erupted without warning, killed swiftly, and disappeared. Plague, discussed in a separate entry in this book, fell into that category, as did the sweating sickness, which struck repeatedly between 1485 and 1551, killing several notable people. It began with a high fever and profuse sweating; coma and death ensued in a day or two. Epidemics began and ended within a few days, and it was probably this swift and deadly passage that ended the disease, which likely killed its hosts too quickly to sustain its own survival. For whatever reason, the disease was gone by the second half of the sixteenth century, and the organism responsible has never been identified. However, the fear it caused lingered, and later fevers were often mistakenly categorized as sweating sickness.

Diseases that disfigured the body or damaged the mind, such as "pox" (syphilis), were also frightening. Many diseases affected the nervous system or caused convulsions, but they were poorly understood even by physicians, and Shakespeare uses them without much concern for accuracy. His characters suffer "Hysterica passio" (*Lear* II.iv.55–57), fits (*2H4* IV.iv.110), apoplexy (*2H4* I.ii.109–18, IV.iv.130; *Ham* III.iv.74), and epilepsy or "the falling-sickness" (*Lear* II.ii.83; *JC* I.ii.250–52; *Oth* IV.i.51–56) with similar sets of symptoms—fainting or near-fainting and some kind of facial symptom, such as grimacing, foaming at the mouth, and changes of color (*2H4* IV.v.6). Leprosy, though it had mostly disappeared from Europe by the fifteenth century, remained a byword for filthy, maiming disease (*2H6* III.ii.75; *Tim* IV.i.28–32, IV.iii.361–64; *TNK* IV.iii.46;

A&C III.x.11), and "lazars" or lepers were synonymous with outcasts (*H5* I.i.15; *T&C* II.iii.30–32).

Life could be made miserable, or even ended, by any of the other ailments for which there were few effective palliations and even fewer cures. Diphtheria attacked mostly children, beginning with a sore and swollen throat and ending with the gradual closing of the throat and eventual strangulation. Deafness (*JC* I.ii.213), palsy (*2H6* IV.vii.94; *T&C* I.iii.174), gout (*TNK* V.i.112, V.iv.8; *AYLI* III.ii.319–22; *T&C* I.ii.28; *Cym* V.iv.5; *2H4* I.ii.234; *RL* 855–56), and cataracts, called the pin and web (*Lear* III.iv.114–15; *WT* I.ii.290–91), affected the old. Gout, which inflamed the joints and filled the blood with uric acid, was especially painful. People suffered from jaundice (*T&C* I.iii.2; *MV* I.i.81–86), colic (*Cor* II.i.77), the nerve pain of sciatica (*Tim* IV.i.23–25), the discomfort of edema—fluid retention caused by any number of ailments and known then as "dropsy" (*1H4* II.iv.456; *Temp* IV.i.230; *AW* II.iii.129), and the frustration of skin inflammations and varicose veins.

Injuries, too, were common. People worked physically and with few safeguards; while there were no car accidents, there were plenty of fractious horses, wayward carts, sharp farm and shop tools, drunken and mischievous coworkers, duelists, and, of course, wars. The wounds (*2H6* III.i.286) that resulted often became lethally infected. Any discussion of infection is, however, once again complicated by semantics. When Shakespeare uses the word "infection" (*Per* IV.vi.173; *2H6* III.ii.287; *Cor* III.i.309), he means "contagious disease," not festering. When he means what we think of as "infected," he says "cank'red" (*1H4* I.iii.135), "festered" (*1H6* III.i.193–94), or "affected by gangrene" (*Cor* III.i.305–6). He was not, for the most part, concerned with medical specificity, and he is likely to refer to an open wound simply as a sore or an ulcer (*T&C* I.i.55; *Ham* IV.vii.123), without reference to its stage of infection; similarly, swellings and abscesses are variously called cankers, fistulas (*AW* I.i.35), or imposthumes (*V&A* 743). An additional complication of terminology is that "canker" (*1H6* II.iv.68, 71; *2H6* I.ii.18) could mean either a gangrenous infection or the abnormal growth known today as cancer.

Causes

Thanks to hindsight and four centuries of medical research, the causes of illness in Shakespearean England are well understood. Poor hygiene allowed bacteria and viruses to move freely between food, bodies, clothes, and waste, and also contributed to the spread of disease-carrying vermin such as rats, fleas, and lice. Malnutrition provided microbes with hosts too weak to resist them, particularly among the poor, who were routinely short of protein and vitamins. Poor nutrition also compromised the health of the rich, who had too much protein and thus suffered from gout and other digestive complaints, such as chronic constipation. Contaminated food could lead to illnesses such as ergotism, caused by mold-tainted rye bread, which could produce hallucinations, the twitching known as St. Vitus' dance and the gangrenous skin inflammation known as St. Anthony's fire. Iron deficiencies caused anemia, then as now associated with menstruating women, who lose iron along with their menstrual blood. Severe anemia could cause a yellowish pallor, leading to the condition known in Shakespeare's time as "greensickness" (*R&J* III.v.157; *2H4* IV.iii.93; *A&C* III.ii.6; *Per* IV.vi.13).

However, few of these causes were understood at the time. This is not to say that no effort was made to determine the origins of diseases; quite the opposite. Theories were diverse, but most arose from the organizational structure of the ancient Greek physician Galen, who divided the body and its processes into naturals (the four elements, the four humors, the complexion or temperament of the patient based on his humoral balance, the parts of the body, the systems or processes of the body, and the operations of individual organs), nonnaturals (influences through or outside the body, such as diet, air, sleep, rest, exercise, excretion, and emotion), and contranaturals (diseases).

Thinking of disease in this way, Renaissance physicians often sought a "natural" cause for disease—that is, one that arose from an essential imbalance within the body. The humors or fluids within the body, which were constantly being produced, could be thrown out of balance by a failure of the body to eliminate them. Thus, a reduction or stoppage of sweat, urine, feces, or blood was widely supposed to create illness. Catarrh, for example, the overproduction of mucus during a cold or flu, was thought to be the product of a surplus of phlegm, the wet, watery humor. The theory of disease originating in the blood or humors is one that appears frequently in Shakespeare's works (*MAAN* III.ii.26; *2H4* IV.iii.88–125).

Other authorities, including the Swiss alchemist Paracelsus, believed that health was influenced by the movements of stars and planets (*Tim* IV.iii.109). Each sign of the zodiac was believed to have special influence over certain parts of the body and certain diseases. Pisces, for example, because it was a water sign, was thought to increase coughs and infection. Unusual astronomical events, like eclipses and comets, were thought to herald epidemics.

Contagious disease was understood to a surprising extent, given that the microscope had not been invented. As early as 1546, Girolamo Fracastoro published a treatise on contagious illness, which he postulated was spread by touching, air, or tiny particles called "fomites." He correctly identified several diseases, including smallpox, measles, sweating sickness, tuberculosis, syphilis, and leprosy, as contagious. Shakespeare, too, understood the outlines of this concept, for he knew that "men take diseases, one of another" (*2H4* V.i.79). But without microscopes, no one could prove the existence of fomites, and while it seemed clear that something in the air could make people sick, no one was sure of what that "something" was. Perhaps, they reasoned, it was the air itself that was corrupt, particularly if it smelled bad—and air, in Renaissance markets, streets, slaughterhouses, outhouses, and crowds, frequently stank. People tried to avoid places with wet, rotting materials and bad odors; fens and bogs were thought to be especially deadly (*Temp* I.ii.258, II.ii.1–3). Certain kinds of weather were also deemed dangerous. The heat of August's dog days bred all kinds of disease in the air (*H8* V.iv.39–41), as did certain conjunctions of the planets, "foul weather" (*1H4* III.i.67–68), the spring sun (*1H4* IV.i.110–11), the "south fog" or south wind (*Cym* II.iii.132; *Cor* I.iv.30), and the moisture of early morning (*JC* II.i.261–67). Hippocrates blamed imposthumes, consumption, and cough on summer winds.

Treatments

Limited comprehension of the causes of illness made diagnosis difficult and effective treatment nearly impossible. A physician, when consulted, had few tools available to him. He did not take the patient's temperature except by feeling the forehead or chest, and he felt for the pulse (*2H4* II.iv.22–25; *Ham* III.iv.141–42; *Per* V.i.158), but only to assess its strength and regularity rather than to measure its rate. His principal task was to collect the patient's excreta—saliva, stools, and urine (*MWW* II.iii.31, III.i.14; *2H4* I.ii.2–5). Urinalysis was considered an essential skill for a physician, who could hardly send it to a lab for testing as today, but instead assessed its color, clarity, odor, and even taste. Some physicians thought urine an infallible diagnostic tool; others thought it useful within certain limits. Andrew Boorde, for example, claimed he could fool any physician with his own urine, and thought the contents of urine, but not the color, definitive. The wise woman of Hogsdon, in the eponymous play by Thomas Heywood, bases much of her false reputation for cures on her fraudulent analysis of urine. (Sometimes one has to look closely to find references to urinalysis in Shakespeare, since urine is sometimes referred to as "water"; see *TN* III.iv.104–6 and *Mac* V.iii.50–52). Unlike the surgeon, who had lancets and basins to collect blood, tourniquets, tents (wound probes—see *T&C* V.i.10–12), scalpels, and other tools, the physician had little in the way of equipment. Much, if not most, of his information came from simply asking questions and listening to the patient's account of symptoms.

Bleeding and Purging

Once he arrived at a diagnosis, the physician decided on a course of treatment that was based on his guesses about the state of the patient's humors, what he knew about the nature of the disease, and possibly the alignment of the stars in relation to the patient's hour of birth. A common course of action was to rid the body of whatever was poisoning or unbalancing it either by bleeding (discussed in a separate entry) or purging. Bleeding might be done with leeches (*TNK* I.ii.73) but was usually performed by a barber-surgeon, who opened a vein near the affected part of the body with a sharp tool called a lancet. Purging (*Ham* III.ii.311; *Mac* V.iii.50–52, 55) might involve an enema, performed with a tube called a clyster pipe (*Oth* II.i.173–75), to cleanse the bowels or an emetic to empty the stomach. A commonly used purgative was bitter-apple or coloquintida (*Oth* I.iii.344), an orange-sized gourd with a bitter pulp that was pounded and could be made up into pills. Treatments that had the same theoretical basis included "bruising" or squeezing an infected and swollen injury (*H5* III.vi.122–24), inducing heavy sweating as a treatment for joint diseases and syphilis (*T&C* V.x.54–55), and cupping, a minor form of bleeding often performed by the operators of bathhouses, in which a heated cup was slid onto the skin, creating pressure as it cooled and causing small blood vessels to burst.

Bleeding and purging were applied not only as treatments but also as preventive measures. It was common to bleed and purge whenever the earth was thought to be in state of growth, for that growth would of necessity translate into a superfluity of humors in the body. Thus the practice was common in the spring and during signs of the zodiac considered cold or wet, especially if the moon happened to be in Cancer, Scorpio, Pisces, or Gemini. Purging or bleeding in hot weather was discouraged except in emergencies.

Medications

Medicines were abundant, though many were no doubt more useful as placebos than as actual therapies. They fell into two classes, "simples" (*MWW* I.iv.61), which contained one ingredient, and "composita," which blended many. There were also two principal types of ingredients—minerals and plants—which were chosen with as much care by real physicians as by Friar Lawrence in his garden (*R&J* II.iii.8–30), though their application had less to do with science than with poetry, symmetry, and optimism. Shakespeare mentions few medicines by name. He prefers to use general terms such as "potion" (*MND* III.ii.264; *MWW* III.i.96–98), "balm" (*TNK* I.iv.30–31; *T&C* I.i.63), "physic" (*1H6* III.i.148; *MM* IV.vi.7–8; *Cor* III.i.154–55; *2H4* I.i.137–45), "salve" (*3H6* IV.vi.88), or "medicine" (*AYLI* II.vii.59–61; *1H4* II.ii.17–20; *AW* II.i.75–81, I.iii.222–31), without going into details about ingredients. This vagueness may betray an ignorance of medical practice or a simple wish to avoid being wrong on an important detail; in some cases, it is almost certainly because he has ascribed magical or near-magical powers to the medicine, and can hardly be expected to produce a recipe for a potion that can bring a dying king back to life, induce affection, or suspend all apparent signs of life. In a few instances, he lists specific substances—"Carduus Benedictus" or holy thistle for heart palpitations (*MAAN* III.iv.71–73), leek for a "green wound" (*H5* V.i.42), spermaceti for internal injuries (*1H4* I.iii.56–57), and a solution of gold known as *aurum potabile* (*2H4* IV.v.160–62). His mention of gold, Friar Lawrence's reference to the medicinal virtues of "stones" (*R&J* II.iii.16), and Cerimon's use in "physic" of "vegetives, . . . metals, stones" (*Per* III.ii.32–36) testify to the influence of Paracelsus, who strongly advocated the use of rocks and minerals in medicines.

Paracelsus listed dozens of substances that could be made into medicines, often by being burned or reduced in some way, then suspended in oils, unguents, or wine. He recommended gold for leprosy, "oil or spirits of vitriol" for epilepsy, antimony for a host of ailments including leprosy and wounds, magnets for wounds and ulcers, gems to encourage lactation, sulfur for asthma and pleurisy, and coral

> for menstruum and profluvium; poison taken internally; thunderings or rumblings of the stomach; charms, if any be enchanted; obsession, if any be mad; nervousness, if any be timorous; melancholy, for those who appear wise in their own eyes but are foolish.

In some cases, his potions may have had an effect, but not because of their principal mineral ingredient. His concoction for a rumbling stomach included beans, and that for charms, obsession, and nervousness incorporated St. John's wort. Other Paracelsian remedies included silver for brain, spleen, and liver complaints, tin for jaundice and worms, and copper for wounds, worms, and mouth ulcers.

Paracelsian, or alchemical, medicine was, however, the "alternative medicine" of the sixteenth century. It was popular but not officially sanctioned by the strictest medical authorities. Physicians preferred to rely on herbal remedies: rue for poison or infection, verven (verbena) for sexually transmitted diseases, verven and peony seeds together for epilepsy. Plants were often chosen for medicines because they resembled or seemed opposite to the ailment or organ involved. For example, yellow substances, like saffron, yellow broomseed, and radish, were used to induce urination or to treat jaundice, which made the skin yellow. Red substances were often applied in cases involving bleeding or rashes. Plants might also be chosen because they had an astrological connection to the disease or affected part; diseases thought to be governed by the moon were sometimes treated with plants that had crescent-shaped leaves, and plants were sometimes gathered, prepared, or administered at an astrologically propitious time. Other medications were selected for their humoral properties—wet, cold, hot, or dry. A "wet" disease needed to be treated with a "dry" plant. Wormwood, because it was thought to be naturally "hot," was used to treat "cold" agues.

Paracelsus used this approach in choosing mineral medications as well.

He recommended garnets for heart tremors or bloodshot eyes, topaz for jaundice and diseases of the heart (which was ruled astrologically by the yellow sun), and bloodstone for bleeding ulcers, menstrual difficulties, and dysentery. This theory of medication, which constituted wishful thinking more than anything else, extended beyond what a patient ingested to her surroundings. A common treatment for smallpox was the "red cure," in which the patient would be put in a room with red furnishings, dressed in red clothes, given red wine to drink, and so forth.

Physicians frequently applied multiple therapies at once, making it impossible to tell what had worked and why. For example, Gerolamo Cardano, a prominent astrologer, treated the Archbishop of St. Andrews in 1552 for a cough diagnosed by another doctor as tuberculosis. Cardano disagreed with his colleague's opinion, called the disease asthma, and prescribed a regimen of diet, exercise, cold baths, brain purges, and plenty of rest on a new bed of unspun silk rather than the feather bed the archbishop had been using. The treatment worked—but which treatment? In retrospect, it seems probable that the archbishop suffered from allergies and that the new bed did the trick; everything else, including the purging of the brain, was irrelevant. Cardano was not the only practitioner to stumble onto a cure; the physician Andrew Boorde, author of *The First Boke of the Introduction of Knowledge*, recommended several possible remedies for asthma, including the avoidance of almonds, nuts, cheese, and milk, which are foods often associated with allergic reactions.

Most so-called remedies were useless, like theriac, a highly regarded anti-poisoning concoction with dozens of ingredients (including vipers' flesh), none of which did a thing to counteract poison. Boorde, who often had relatively sensible advice in matters of diet and exercise, was as likely as his colleagues to prescribe ineffective treatments. He suggested scratching the skin raw for itches, to let out the corrupt blood; drinking ale for tertian fevers; and rubbing the body with turpentine and brandy, taking treacle and pepper internally, or smelling a quartered fox simmered with herbs, for palsy. For persistent and unwanted erections, he prescribed oil of juniper applied to the genitals; rue, vinegar, and camphor as smelling salts; cold-water immersion; or nettles placed "in the codpeece about the yerde [penis] and stones [testicles]."

Painkillers

Just as there was little that could be done to cure disease, there was little that could be done to alleviate pain. Narcotics were known to physicians; Paracelsus prepared laudanum and experimented with anesthetizing chickens. Even the layman Shakespeare knew of "poppy" (opium—*Oth* III.iii.327) and "mandragora" (mandrake—*Oth* III.iii.327; *A&C* I.v.4). However, these palliatives could not be indulged in continuously, nor could that other time-honored painkiller, liquor. Therefore, there were less effective alternatives, including warm poultices "for . . . aching bones" (*R&J* II.v.64) and "cramp rings" blessed by the king or queen on Good Friday for labor pains. People desperate to feel better may have tried almost anything, including the Italian physician Antonio Beniveni's recipes for toothache—aqua vitae (liquor), henbane, pomegranate, sumac, vinegar, oil of vitriol, and adder's skin in one case, a recipe involving a frog, vinegar, and water in another. Toothache was a source of intense pain, but there was little remedy except to bore out the cavity without anesthesia and fill it with gold or, more commonly, to pull the tooth out. Tooth drawing was done by specialist barbers, working on patients whose senses might be dulled by a little aqua vitae, but nothing more.

Nonpharmaceutical Treatments

Sometimes the care of a patient required surgery or simply a little common sense. People who fainted were to be lifted and wrung "by the nose" (*2H6* III.ii.34). Those with sore body parts could bind them with a piece of cloth (*T&C* V.i.32–33). Those having fits of one kind or another were to be given air, space, and quiet until they recovered (*2H4* IV.iv.114–16, IV.v.6–7; *Oth* IV.i.51–56). An awareness of contagion, if not its mechanism, was reflected in advice to leave areas afflicted by epidemics and the government's desire, particularly in the case of plague, to quarantine the victims of contagious disease (*R&J* V.ii.5–16). Exercise was recommended for general health and the promotion of digestion (*T&C* II.iii.110–12). Cataracts were successfully treated by "couching" them, a procedure in which the lens was pressed down into the vitreous humor.

Broken bones were treated much as they are today; they were set (*2H4* IV.i.220–21) and splinted (*Oth* II.iii.320–21). (Costard's "broken shin," *LLL* III.i.70, is probably just a cut or bruise, just as characters frequently speak of "broken heads" to indicate a bloody cut or bump.) An injured arm might be slung in a scarf (*AYLI* V.i.20; *Cor* I.ix.1 s.d.) or another piece of cloth. Injured or weakened legs—whether the condition was temporary or permanent—were assisted with a walking stick or a crutch (*Cor* I.i.244; *Cym* IV.ii.200; *2H4* I.i.145; *2H6* III.i.189; *3H6* III.ii.35; *R3* II.ii.58). The crutch, like gout and palsy, was a typical symbol of old age (*LLL* IV.iii.242; *Tim* IV.i.10–14; *WT* I.i.42–44; *R&J* I.i.79).

Wounds and sores were rubbed with salves (S 34; *LLL* III.i.72–74), covered with plasters (fabric smeared with medicinal or sticky substances— *Temp* II.i.143–44, filled with cobweb to stop bleeding (*MND* III.i.182– 84), or covered with plantain leaf (*TNK* I.ii.60–61; *LLL* III.i.73–74, 107; *R&J* I.ii.51–52). A kind of plaster made of "flax and whites of eggs" appears to be described in *King Lear* (III.vii.108). More serious wounds were bound with tourniquets to stop the bleeding (*TNK* IV.ii.1–2); Cassio's leg is bound, hastily, with a garter (*Oth* V.i.72–73, 83–84). This would, however, be a temporary measure, until a surgeon could arrive to sew up the wound with linen, silk, or catgut. Andrew Boorde recommended stitches and plasters, often medicated, for large wounds. After twenty hours, he wrote, the plaster should be opened and the wound "mundified" with white wine; the patient should meanwhile be warned against "venerious actes & . . . [consuming] contagious meates and drynkes."

Surgery, because of the risk of infection it entailed, was avoided except in extreme circumstances. Brain inflammations were treated by trepanning, that is, by drilling a small hole in the skull. Tumors or abscesses were sometimes removed. Amputations (*1H4* IV.i.43; *Cor* III.i.295–96; *Per* IV.vi.174–77) were performed whenever an injured limb turned gangrenous. This was more common in war, but could easily happen in peacetime. All it took was a careless swing with a hoe or a scythe to cause a serious injury. Many a cut, stab, crushed limb, or gunshot wound became infected.

Gunshot wounds, because they carried fibers and dirt far into the body, were especially likely to become infected, to such an extent that they were considered poisonous by many medical authorities. Accordingly, until well into the sixteenth century, bullet wounds were cauterized (burned—*Tim* V.i.133), in the belief that this would disable the poison. This practice, as ineffective as it was painful, was generally ended after the researches of the sixteenth-century military surgeon Ambroise Paré, who treated these injuries instead with a mixture of egg yolk, oil of roses, and turpentine.

Other treatments smacked more of magic, superstition, and desperation. Strategies included dunking in cold water (Paracelsus's remedy for St. Vitus's dance); admitting fresh air to the patient's room; shutting fresh air out of the patient's room; strong smells; carrying specific animal parts, such as a stag's heart, near various parts of the body; or ceremoniously "transferring" the disease or pain to an inanimate object and then destroying the object. Paracelsus's approach to this last method of treatment was to cure a wound by dipping the weapon that caused it into a magical salve. Cramp rings were believed to cure epilepsy as well as labor pains, and they were not the only instance in which the monarch's touch was believed to have healing properties. Sufferers from scrofula came routinely to be touched by the king or queen as a cure (*Mac* IV.iii.146–59). *See also* Alchemy; Anatomy and Physiology; Astrology; Bleeding; Humors; Medical Practitioners; Plague; Pox.

Dishes

One of the most extraordinary developments of the sixteenth century, at least to contemporaries, was the increase in personal possessions at all levels of society. William Harrison, author of *The Description of England* found it astounding that nobles now owned perhaps £1,000 to £2,000 worth of plate—dishes of gold or silver—each, and that knights and wealthy merchants frequently owned £500 to £1,000 worth. Just as amazing was the presence of any plate at all in humble homes that had formerly been supplied only with dishes of wood or earthenware. Wooden platters, Harrison wrote, had been ousted in most places by pewter, and wooden spoons by those of silver or tin. Whereas the average, reasonably prosperous farmer had once owned perhaps four pewter dishes, a man of equivalent means might now have a garnish of pewter, a number of miscellaneous pewter vessels in various rooms, a silver saltcellar (*2GV* III.i.355) for the dinner table, a dozen spoons (*John* IV.iii.131; *Temp* II.ii.100), and one or more wine bowls (*LLL* V.ii.920; *JC* IV.iii.155; *Per* II.iii.67; the last example is a standing, or footed, dish). A "garnish" was a set of twelve platters, twelve dishes, and twelve saucers, and was sold by the pound.

Harrison's assessment is borne out by executors' inventories of property. Yeoman Thomas Blampin of Devon (d. 1623), who was not rich enough to have any glass windows, nevertheless owned £3 16s worth of pewter and twenty silver spoons. His contemporary Thomas Spicer had a silver bowl, a dozen silver spoons, a silver-edged cup, a good deal of brassware, and £3 10s worth of pewter, including twenty-five platters, three basins, seven porringers, twelve dishes, twenty-two saucers, a pottle, a quart pot, four pots, two saltcellars, a funnel, and three candlesticks. Yeoman farmer Thomas Gyll of Wardington (d. 1587) had twenty-eight pieces of pewter, "two saltes & A basen, fyve sylver sponnes," six brass pots (*T&C* I.ii.151–52), two brass pans, and two kettles. This equipment was considered necessary, especially if a man planned to marry. Gremio, trying to win the hand of Bianca, brags that his home "Is richly furnished with plate and gold, / Basins and ewers to lave her dainty hands," as well as "Pewter and brass, and all things that belongs / To house or housekeeping" (*TS* II.i.340–41, 348–49). Similarly, the hero of Thomas Heywood's play *The Wise-Woman of Hogsdon* (1633), after contracting marriage with a young woman, gives her money to furnish their new home with "dishes, platters, ladles, candlesticks, etcetera."

The finest and most expensive dishes (*TS* IV.iii.44; *AYLI* III.iii.29–30), most often made of silver, were classified as "plate" (*Tim* III.ii.21; *H8* III.ii.126; *R&J* I.v.8) and were owned chiefly by the gentry. Most people, however, aspired to own at least a little silver, and the first silver item purchased was usually a "salt" or a set of spoons. Some people also owned spoons because these were common christening gifts (*H8* V.iv.38). Taverns, apparently, were also well supplied with plate for the use of their customers (*2H4* II.i.141). "Plate" included not only the plates in a silver service, but also the goblets (*2H4* II.i.86; *AYLI* III.iv.24; *R2* III.iii.149), bowls, cups (*2H6* IV.i.56; *3H6* II.v.51–52; *H5* I.i.20; *JC* IV.iii.158; *MWW* II.ii.73), platters, and other items; it referred not to the form of the dish but to the material of which it was made.

Less expensive than plate, but still potentially quite luxurious, was glass. The best and clearest glass came from Murano, the glassmaking district of Venice. Domestic glass was less expensive, greenish, and more brittle, and many people found it to be uneconomical. Nevertheless, many people loved glass for its novelty and beauty. Shakespeare writes of "glasses" being used at alehouses and taverns, where they were gradually replacing metal tankards (*TS* Ind.i.7; *2H4* II.i.143), and glass plates were often used at rich people's banquets. Those who could not afford a complete set of Venetian plates for the latter purpose could rent them.

If silver or glass could not be had, then pewter was the preferred material. An alloy of brass, tin, and bismuth, or sometimes lead, pewter (also called tin) was used to make almost every kind of tableware, including platters, cups (*1H4* II.iv.47), dishes, bowls, goblets, porringers, candlesticks, and pots. Harrison gives the recipe for pewter as 30 pounds (13.6 kg) of kettle brass to 1,000 pounds (453 kg) of tin to 3 or 4 pounds (1.4 to 1.8 kg) of "tinglass" (bismuth), and adds that the more brass is added, the better the alloy. Brass was another common material for household items such as pots, pans, and kettles. Less prized than metal and glass were ceramic, wood, and leather. Pottery was used for several kinds of dishes but was probably most popular for mugs and pitchers. Wood (*R2* III.iii.149) was used for bowls, spoons, and trenchers (*2H6* IV.i.57; *2GV* IV.iv.9; *LLL* V.ii.478, 465; *TS* IV.i.154; *Cor* IV.v.53; *MAAN* I.i.49; *A&C* III.xiii.116–17)—the last being a platter of any material, typically wood; in the Middle Ages it was often simply a slab of bread that could be eaten after it had finished its service as a plate.

Leather was a peasant's material, used to make the simplest cups and bottles. The cups (*TS* IV.i.154), also called stoups (*TN* II.iii.14, 121; *Ham* V.i.60, V.ii.269, 285; *Oth* II.iii.30), mugs, and cans, were cylinders of leather closed at the bottom and sometimes decorated with metal or mounted in metal frames. A half-pint vessel, the jack (*TS* IV.i.45), was made of a pitcher-shaped tube of leather with a circular bottom, sometimes glazed with pitch inside to make it more watertight, and given a thick leather handle. Its even larger cousin was the bombard (*Temp* II.ii.21–22; *1H4* II.iv.456; *H8* V.iv.80), named for the eponymous short, wide-mouthed cannon, and resembling a jug more than a cup in size. Drinking horns (*Lear* III.vi.74), made of hollowed ox horns, were old-fashioned by Shakespeare's time, but shepherds and other rural workers carried leather bottles (*3H6* II.v.47–48) made by folding a sheet of leather in half, adding panels to the sides, and stitching up the top with a hole left for a wood, horn, or leather cork (*AYLI* III.ii.201–3).

The well-equipped alehouse, tavern, or kitchen had an assortment of vessels. Containers for liquids included the elegant stemmed and footed cup called a goblet, ceramic mugs with handles, cans of various shapes and sizes (*TN* II.iii.6), leather jacks, and even "jills"—gill-sized metal cups (*TS*

IV.i.45). Ceramic or metal pots (*2H6* I.iii.88–89) were usually deep and fairly narrow, but they came in different sizes; Shakespeare mentions pots that held a pint (.47 l—see *1H4* II.iv.402), a quart (.95 l—see *2H6* IV.x.15), or a "pottle"—half a gallon (1.9 l—see *2H4* II.ii.76, V.iii.66; *MWW* II.i.203–4). Alehouses might also possess peg tankards, pottle-sized mugs spiked at one-gill intervals with pegs. Each peg marked the quantity a man was to drink when sharing the tankard with his fellows.

Kitchens might have, in addition to some of these drinking cups, a motley collection of trenchers, jugs, flagons (large bottles—see *Ham* V.i.179), cooking pots, skillets (*Oth* I.iii.267), cleavers, soup bowls called porringers (*TS* IV.iii.64), skewers, sieves (*MAAN* V.i.5; *T&C* II.ii.69–72; *Mac* I.iii.8), pitchers (*R3* II.iv.37; *TS* IV.iv.52), and perhaps a tundish (*MM* III.ii.172), a wide, shallow wooden funnel used to fill tuns or casks with ale. Dining utensils were few. Forks were not in common use yet, and people mostly used knives (*R&J* II.iv.206; *WT* IV.iv.602; *Tim* I.ii.43) and the fingers of their left hands. An exception was made at expensive dessert courses called banquets, where a combination implement had been in use since at least the fifteenth century. It had a spoon at one end for eating jellies and creams and a fork at the other for picking up sweetmeats too sticky to be eaten with the fingers. The sweetmeats themselves, along with fresh and dried fruits, were displayed in footed dishes (*MM* II.i.87–92; *H8* V.v.1 s.d.), often of silver and often sold in sets of four. Banqueting plates for most of the sixteenth and early seventeenth centuries were miniature wooden trenchers, about 5 inches (12.7 cm) in diameter and ⅛ to ¹⁄₁₆ inch (.3 to .16 cm) thick, ornately painted and gilded with, by the 1580s, a motto on one side to be read or sung at the meal's conclusion. Alternatively, the plates might be silver or even edible, made of a stiff sugar jelly or of marzipan. *See also* Household Objects.

Dog

No animal has been more manipulated through selective breeding by humans than the dog. Hundreds of distinct breeds are recognized today. Most of these breeds were unknown in Shakespearean England, either because they came from faraway places or because no one had yet developed them. England had no Boston terriers, no Lhasa apsos, no akitas, no samoyeds, no poodles, and not one dalmatian, let alone a hundred and one. There were fewer than twenty kinds of dogs that were recognized as something like "breeds," and even those of the twenty that sound familiar, such as the mastiff, spaniel, and greyhound, were not necessarily the same in appearance as dogs of those names today. One thing that can be firmly established is that English dogs were admired throughout Europe; the Flemish cartographer Abraham Ortelius, for example, wrote in *Theatrum*

Orbis Terrarum that "There is no place in the world greater and larger dogges, nor better."

To understand the classification of dogs in Shakespeare's day, we need to shift our perceptions of what makes a breed. Today, it is bloodlines and conformity to very specific guidelines about weight, height, color, and shape. Then, it was the purpose to which the dog was put and the method or sense by which it worked. Dogs were classified by whether they hunted, herded, or guarded; by which prey they hunted, if they were hunters; and, more specifically, by which sense they used more in the hunt, sight or smell. Lists of dogs tended to overlap, depending on which criterion was being used to organize the catalog, but most dogs fell into one of the following categories: greyhounds, mastiffs, lymers, hounds, terriers, harriers, spaniels, tumblers, lapdogs, curs, shepherds' dogs, and Iceland dogs.

Greyhounds (*LLL* V.ii.657; *MAAN* V.ii.11–12; *2H4* II.iv.99–100; *H5* III.i.31–32; *MWW* I.i.84–91), of all the dogs listed above, perhaps looked most like their modern namesake. Edward Topsell wrote in *The Historie of Foure-Footed Beastes* that they had large sides, small bellies, "large bodies, little heads, beaked noses, but flat, broad faces above their eies, long necks but great next to their bodies, fiery eies, broad backs, and most generous stomacks, both against al wild beasts & men also." They varied greatly in size and were sometimes smooth-coated, sometimes shaggy. The larger ones could be set to fight bulls, boars, and even lions, while the smaller specimens might chase rabbits

Greyhound, from Konrad Gesner's *Icones Animalium Quadrupedam*. Reproduced from the Collections of the Library of Congress.

(*3H6* II.v.129); Shakespeare also employs them as hunters of deer (*TS* Ind.ii.47–48). Topsell preferred them to all other dogs and believed that they instinctively recognized and disdained any prey unworthy of their talents. Sixteenth-century texts seem to imply that the "gazehound" was a different sort of creature, but the only distinctive characteristic of a gazehound was that it hunted primarily by sight, which is true of greyhounds.

The mastiff (*T&C* I.iii.389–90; *Lear* III.vi.67) was a purely English dog. John Caius' 1570 treatise *De Canibus Anglicis* (*Of English Dogs*), translated in 1576 by Abraham Fleming, served as the standard source of information on the breed for writers like Edward Topsell and William Harrison. Harrison noted that the breed was sometimes called a tiedog or a bandog (*2H6* I.iv.19) because its aggressive tendencies led it to do "hurt abroad" if allowed to roam free. Mastiffs might, for example, hunt and harm or kill sheep (*Cor* II.i.259–60). Topsell's reprint of Caius called it "vaste, huge, stubborne, ougly, and eager." The mastiff was occasionally used by tinkers to haul supplies or by householders to draw water from wells by walking in a wheel, but it was principally a good guard dog and a good fighter. It would attack foxes, badgers, boars, bulls, or lions, and was the breed most commonly used in bear-baiting (*2H6* V.i.146–53, *3H6* II.i.15–17, *H5* III.vii.143–48) and bullbaiting. One or two were thought an equal match for a bull, three for a bear, and four for a lion. Huge spiked collars were sometimes worn by mastiffs to protect their throats, but they often fought without any collar at all. The modern bulldog was probably descended from bull-baiting mastiffs, and it is a mastiff or a proto-bulldog that Shakespeare calls "as true a dog as ever fought at [the bull's] head" (*TA* V.i.102). Fighters were trained by men armed with pikestaffs, clubs, swords, or protective armor, who wrestled with the dogs to increase their skill and aggression (*John* IV.i.115–16). The shape and color of the mastiff varied, but Conrad Heresbach, in *The Whole Art . . . of Husbandry*, thought it should be brown or gray, with a short tail, big feet, and a disinclination to bark without cause.

Bloodhound, from Konrad Gesner's *Icones Animalium Quadrupedam*. Reproduced from the Collections of the Library of Congress.

Lymers, whose name came from a French word for leash (*WT* IV.iv.469), hunted by scent rather than sight. Because of overlapping terminology, it is hard to be absolutely certain, but the lymer seems to have been identical to the bloodhound, which on the Scottish border was called a sluth-hound. Shakespeare shortens the name in order to make a rhyme and calls it a "lym" (*Lear* III.vi.68). The sluth-hound, according to Topsell, was spotted and brown or sandy-colored, whereas the bloodhound was "sometime red, sanded, blacke, white, spotted, . . . but most commonly browne or red." Both were used to track thieves and would, if the wily fugitive crossed a stream, go to the opposite bank and run back and forth along it until they caught the scent again. In size, the lymer was between a common running hound and a mastiff, and because it was quiet, it was used to locate a deer or other prey without disturbing it until the other hounds could be brought into place. This, too, makes it sound like the bloodhound, which Topsell noted "sildome barke[d], except in their hunting chase."

The running-hounds (*1H6* IV.ii.47–52; *TA* I.i.495, II.ii.1 s.d., 11 s.d., 25, II.iii.17, 27, 63, 70; *TS* Ind.i.61, Ind.ii.45–6; *LLL* IV.ii.59, IV.ii.128; *TNK* II.i.103–8) that pursued the quarry after the lymer had found it were a motley bunch. Illustrations show them as flat-faced and heavily muscled in comparison to modern hounds. (Since their principal use was in the hunt, much more information about their behavior there can be found in the Hunting entry). Terriers and harriers were smaller dogs. Shakespeare does not use the term "harrier," though Caius does; in Harrison's account of dogs, which draws heavily on Caius, he writes that the harrier can hunt foxes, hares, deer, badgers, otters, polecats, stoats, weasels, and conies, though it was the chase of the hare that gave the dog its name. A similar dog today in appearance and quarry is the beagle, and Shakespeare does use the term "beagle" on occasion (*TN* II.iii.178; *Tim* IV.iii.176). Topsell, too, uses this name, stating that "Terriors or Beagles" hunt foxes and badgers in their dens, though his reprint of Caius uses the terms "terrier" and "harrier," and says that "we may knowe these kindes of Dogs by their long, large and bagging lips, by their hanging eares." In the Middle Ages, and perhaps also in the Renaissance, harriers were used not only for hare-hunting but for clearing a forest of younger deer so that the larger dogs could be set on the superior prey. The "tumbler" was a clever, "somewhat pricke eared" dog used for hunting conies; Caius stated that it would crouch down so as not to be seen by its prey as it approached and, when successful, would carry its kill back to its master.

Spaniels, whose name came from their Spanish origin, were used to hunt birds, either alone or as a falcon's assistant. They were mostly, as they are today, white with red or red and black spots. They were affectionate dogs, and Shakespeare often refers derisively to their "fawning" (*MND* II.i.203–10; *JC* III.i.43), yet Petruchio is quite fond of his spaniel Troilus and asks for him immediately upon his return home (*TS*

Spaniel, from a late-sixteenth-century portrait.

Water spaniel, from Konrad Gesner's *Icones Animalium Quadrupedam.* Water spaniels were often cut "poodle style." Reproduced from the Collections of the Library of Congress.

IV.i.139). The water spaniel (*2GV* III.i.271) or "finder" had "long, rough, and curled haire," according to Caius, and was "likewise named a dog for the duck, because in that quality he is excellent." Some dogs flushed the birds for a falcon to hunt; others silently indicated the birds' location to a fowler with a net.

The most common kind of lapdog, favored by ladies for companionship (*John* II.i.459–60, *Oth* II.iii.50–51), was called a "spaniel gentle or comforter" by Caius. However, his description of its place of origin, and Topsell's account of its appearance, make it fairly clear that the dog in question is not a spaniel but a Maltese, a small, white, fluffy dog. Caius thinks them a noxious waste of time, "instruments of folly" good only as stomach warmers for the sick. He adds, clearly hoping this will be the outcome, that perhaps the invalid's disease will pass through the skin into the dog and kill the dog instead of the person. Topsell is more tolerant of the Maltese:

> They are of pleasant disposition, and will leape and bite, without pinching, and barke prettily, and some of them are taught to stand upright, holding up their fore legs like hands, other to fetch and carry in their mouths, that which is cast unto them.
>
> There be some wanton women which admit them to their beds, and bring up their young ones in their owne bosomes.

Topsell notes that they are so delicate that they usually have a litter of one, but he also believes that they are made small by being buried up to the neck in the earth or deprived of food, so it is unlikely that he had much experience with their puppies.

Curs (*2H6* III.i.18; *3H6* I.iv.56; *2H4* V.iii.107; *JC* III.i.46) or mongrels, like lapdogs, were sometimes taught to do tricks. Topsell calls such dogs "mimick dogs"; they could perform a variety of stunts, including dancing, begging, spinning with tail in mouth, and stealing caps from members of the audience. Many households had one cur, and one only, more than that being considered extravagant for those too poor to hunt. No doubt Crab, Launce's dog, is a cur (*2GV* II.iii.5–40, II.v.31–33, IV.ii.78–80, IV.iv.1–39). Although the cur received little respect, it was ubiquitous, used not only as a professional performer but also as a watchdog and a "turnspit." The watchdog, according to Topsell, should be "fatter and bigger then the Shepheards Dog, of an elegant, square and strong body, being blacke coloured, and great mouthed, or barking bigly, that so he may more terrifie the theefe," with a large head and ears, "and blacke eies in his head, broade breast, thicke necke, large shoulders, strong legs, a rough haire, short taile, and great nailes: his disposition must not be to fierce, nor yet to familiar, for so he will fawne upon the theife as well as his maisters friend." The black coloring was recommended so that the dog would have the advantage of surprise in the night, "and therefore a spotted, branded, party-coloured Dogge is not approved." The watchdog (*Lear* IV.vi.154–55; *Temp* I.ii.385) was useful not only to householders but also to sailors, who took dogs aboard to guard their cargoes. The turnspit was a smaller dog, able to fit into a wheel like a larger version of the wheels seen today in the cages of pet hamsters, gerbils, and mice. The wheel was attached to the kitchen spit, and, according to Caius, "when any meat is to be roasted, they go into . . . [the] wheel, which they turning round about with the waight of their bodies, so dilligently looke to their businesse, that no drudge nor scullion can do the feate more cunningly."

Sheepdogs were crucial to a wool-producing nation like England. Descriptions of their appearance are woefully inadequate—Harrison, infuriatingly, says that they are "so common that it needeth me not to speak of them"—though their behavior seems remarkably similar to that of well-trained herding dogs today. The shepherd's dog, signaled by the shepherd's voice "or at the wagging and whisteling in his fist, or at his shrill and horse hissing bringeth the wandering weathers and straying sheepe, into the selfe same place where his maisters will and wish is to have them."

A few dogs, despite English pride in native breeds, were imported. Caius described "a new kinde of Dog brought out of France. . . . And they be speckled al over with white and black, which mingled colours incline to a marble blew. . . . These are called French dogs." He also mentioned "Island [Iceland] dogs, curled and rough all over, which by reason of the length of their haire make shew neither of face nor of body. And yet these curs, forsooth, because they are so strange are greatly set by, esteemed, taken up, and many times in the roome of the Spaniell gentle or comforter." Harrison noted that these animals were notable for "their sauciness and quarreling," yet the Iceland dog (*H5* II.i.43–44), despite its temperamental faults, survived for quite some time; in the eighteenth century, Linnaeus described it as having erect ears with hanging tips and long hair everywhere except on the snout.

The English loved their dogs, yet they were often cruel to them as well. Launce's affection for Crab, and Petruchio's for Troilus, are good examples of the master's devotion to his dogs. But Shakespearean references to tender care of dogs are far fewer than references to beatings, drownings, hangings, and other abuses (*MAAN* II.iii.79–80; *MWW* III.v.9–11; *Cor* II.iii.218–19, IV.v.55–56; *Oth* I.iii.330–31; *2GV* IV.iv.21, 24–25). It was, in general, a more violent age than this one, and dogs suffered along with horses, women, children, bears, bulls, cats, and criminals in this respect.

"Dog" was a common insult precisely because dogs were servile and subject to frequent, often arbitrary, punishment. Good owners, according to the standards of the time, might beat their animals, so long as they trained them, fed them adequately, and, in the case of large packs of hounds, kenneled them; George Turberville, in *The Noble Art of Venerie or Hunting*, indicates that a kennel (*MM* III.ii.85; *Lear* I.iv.113) should be 80 paces square with a high wall.

A good owner also provided his dog with medical care, which might include curing illness, docking tails (to create the "curtal" or "bobtail" dogs of *CE* III.ii.147; *MWW* II.i.108; and *Lear* III.vi.69), and treating the coat for fleas. Agriculturalist Leonard Mascall recommended that a flea-bitten dog be washed with cucumber, olive-oil dregs, or a mixture of cumin, hellebore, and water. Hellebore was also mentioned by Caius as a treatment for mad dogs (*MWW* IV.ii.121; *Lear* III.iv.93), though most authorities, after listing a few useless treatments for hydrophobia (such as, in the case of bitten humans, being inundated by nine ocean waves, praying, applying rue plasters, or cupping and hot vegetable poultices), confessed that a mad dog or bite victim was almost certain to die. Fear of mad dogs, however common, was not enough to discourage dog ownership. Large or small, cur or greyhound, brach (bitch, a female dog—see *1H4* III.i.233; *Lear* I.iv.114) or dog, worker or pet, dogs were an integral part of life in Shakespearean England. *See also* Animals; Farming; Hunting.

Doit

A small Dutch coin that circulated illegally in England during the fifteenth century, a doit was equal to one-eighth of a stuiver. It appears in Shake-

Dutch doit, 1555–76. Actual size is 20 mm in diameter. © 2002 The American Numismatic Society. All rights reserved.

speare and was in common English usage during the Renaissance, as an achetype of something small and valueless (*2H6* III.i.112; *Per* IV.ii.51; *Temp* II.ii.28–33; *Cor* I.v.6; *MV* I.iii.137). *See also* Money.

Dollar

In various incarnations, the dollar (*MM* I.ii.50; *Mac* I.ii.59–62; *Temp* II.i.20) was one of the principal coins of Spain and the Netherlands during the late Renaissance. As the leeuwendaalder (lion dollar) of 1575, it was a Dutch coin worth 32 stuivers. Some provinces began producing another version, the rijksdaalder, an imitation of the German reichsthaler, in 1584; Friesland did so, while Holland issued both the leeuwendaalder and the rijksdaalder at the same time, and Utrecht stuck with the leeuwendaalder. Older philippusdaalders, Philip II's European version of the colonial piece of eight, still circulated as well. Some regions, including Haarlem and Middelburg, minted coins simply called daalders. Political confusion in the Netherlands during this period meant that similarly named and sized coins varied widely in actual value and metal fineness. *See also* Money.

Spanish dollar, 1597. Actual size is 41 mm in diameter. © 2002 The American Numismatic Society. All rights reserved.

Doublet

The doublet (*Cor* I.v.5–7; *AYLI* III.ii.196–97, 221; *MWW* III.i.43–44), one of the garments that defined men's dress, was a fitted jacket, sometimes sleeveless, worn over a shirt. If it had sleeves, they usually matched the body of the doublet and might, like the body, be adorned with small slashes designed to let the shirt fabric show. The garment fastened up the front with buttons, hooks and eyes, or laces. Along the waistline, at the bottom, was a nominal "skirt" that might be several inches wide or reduced to a token roll of fabric. As a principal masculine garment, the doublet was adapted by all classes of men and might be made of an expensive fabric such as velvet, satin, or "changeable taffeta" (*TN* II.iv.74), or a humble and serviceable material like white canvas (*1H4* II.iv.75–76).

Doublet fashions seemed to contemporaries to change rapidly (*MAAN* II.iii.15–17). Fabrics and colors were considered carefully, as were bits of metal lace and trim, embroidery that might have symbolic meaning to the wearer or certain observers, slashes, pinking, and eyelets. Variations were devised for the shoulder wings and standing collar, which increased or decreased in size from time to time. Wings, collar, cuffs, and skirt might be trimmed with small tabs called "pickadils." The way the doublet was worn also altered over time; it was worn fully fastened for most of Shakespeare's life, but late in the sixteenth century it began to be worn partially or fully "unbracèd"—that is, unlaced (*JC* II.i.262). The most noticeable development, however, was the advent and eventual disappearance of the "peascod belly."

Pinked and slashed doublet worn by Robert Dudley, Earl of Leicester, c. 1577. Note the peascod belly (by no means the most exaggerated example of its kind); the pickadil trim at the sleeves, shoulders, and waist; the standing collar; and the button closures. The small sleeve ruffs have been shown, but not the open neck ruff that also appears in the portrait.

The front waistline dropped in the second half of the sixteenth century, reaching below the natural waistline by 1575. The doublet was, over the succeeding years, increasingly padded toward the front and bottom so that the man's so-called peascod belly curved out around the middle of his torso, dropped slowly out and down, and then curved sharply back to a point. In order to achieve this shape, the front of the doublet had to be hardened and filled with "bombast," a stuffing made out of whatever material was handy, preferably horsehair, cotton, wool, or flax. By the end of the century, the peascod belly was fading from fashion, and it had of course never been worn by the working classes, who had to be able to bend at the waist easily. Shakespeare refers to the padded and unpadded fashions as great-belly and thin-belly doublets, respectively (*H5* IV.vii.47; *LLL* III.i.18–19). *See also* Clothing.

Drachma

The drachma (*JC* IV.iii.73; *Cor* I.v.5) or drachm, a coin descended from the Greek tetradrachm, certainly had its place in the history of Roman coinage. Some of the earliest surviving Roman coins are didrachms. By the time of Julius Caesar, however, the drachma and its kind were hardly the dominant coins of the Republic, so Caesar's bequest of "seventy-five drachmas" to each citizen seems a little odd and anachronistic. Shakespeare's indirect source, Plutarch, mentioned only a sizable legacy to the citizens of Rome, not a specific type of coinage, and it would have made much more sense to render the bequest in aurei or denarii, which were more standard Republican denominations. Yet Rome was not entirely without drachms in this approximate era. A tetradrachm of 39 B.C.E., only a few years after Caesar's assassination, shows Mark Antony with his new wife, Octavia. Thereafter, the drachma, with its Greek heritage, remained a coin with eastern associations. It was minted in Parthia, on the Asian frontiers of the empire, well into the third century C.E. *See also* Money.

Parthian drachma, issued in the reign of Artabanus IV. Actual size is 19 mm in diameter. © 2002 The American Numismatic Society. All rights reserved.

Dragon

The dragon, a popular beast in heraldry (*Lear* I.i.122) and mythology, might be represented as a four-footed reptile with wings (*1H6* I.i.10; *T&C* V.viii.17), a two-footed reptile with wings (the wyvern), or a large toothed and possibly crested or winged snake. It was widely believed to be fierce and predatory and to live in caves (*R&J* III.ii.74; *John* II.i.68). In his *Etymologies*, Isidore of Seville, a Spanish prelate of the sixth/seventh cen-

Three dragons, from Edward Topsell's *Historie of Serpents*, 1607. Reproduced from the Collections of the Library of Congress.

tury, called it a serpent that lived in India and preyed on elephants; it was poisonous, he claimed, but killed by constriction.

The most famous dragon story, at least in England, was that of St. George (*John* II.i.288, *R3* V.iii.350–51). George was a historical Christian martyr whose story, due to an accident of geography, was probably confused by Crusaders with the Greek myth of Perseus. Like Andromeda, the heroine of the Perseus myth, the princess in the St. George story lived in an area being ravaged by a serpentlike beast. Like Andromeda, she was sentenced by ill fortune to be fed to the monster. George, like Perseus, arrived just as the monster was about to devour her. Here the myths diverge, for St. George did not kill the monster immediately and marry the princess. Instead, according to a thirteenth-century version, he subdued the dragon, leashed it with the princess' girdle, led it back to town, and promised to kill it on the condition that the entire town convert to Christianity.

Another dragon tale, more directly drawn from classical mythology, was that of the golden apples of the Hesperides. These golden apples belonged to Juno and were guarded by goddesses known as the Hesperides, who lived in the far west. The tree upon which the apples grew was encircled by a dragon (*Per* I.i.28–30), which was slain by Hercules during one of the hero's twelve labors. *See also* Mythology.

Drink

Drink, to the Elizabethans and Jacobeans, was a curse and a pleasure, a sin and a necessity. Water was thought—perhaps rightly, given the hygiene of the time—to be unhealthful (*TS* IV.i.138, 142–43). Milk (*2GV* III.i.277, 295; *MND* V.i.337) was a drink for babies and invalids, though some healthy adults drank whey or buttermilk. That left alcohol, which in its various forms served as a social lubricant (*TS* I.ii.277; *TA* IV.iii.85–86; *2H4* IV.ii.63–75, V.iii.64), a proof of manliness (*1H4* II.i.79–81), a cause of misbehavior or incompetence (*TN* I.v.129–35; *Oth* I.i.96; *2H6* II.iii.59–98; *Mac* II.iii.24–28), and a healthful generator of blood and bodily heat (*MAAN* I.i.240–44; *A&C* I.ii.25; *Temp* IV.i.171). It was also a source of national pride:

> IAGO   I learned it in England, where indeed they are most potent in potting. Your Dane, your German, and your swag-bellied Hollander—Drink, ho!—are nothing to your English.

CASSIO   Is your Englishman so exquisite in his drinking?

IAGO   Why, he drinks you with facility, your Dane dead drunk; he sweats not to overthrow your Almain; he gives your Hollander a vomit ere the next pottle can be filled. (*Oth* II.iii.76–85)

Whatever else could be said about Englishmen, they congratulated themselves on their ability to hold their liquor. One can almost hear the groundlings at the Globe laughing, nudging each other knowingly, and roaring approval at this characterization of their capacity.

Ale and Beer

Both ale and beer began with barley, which was turned into malt, according to William Harrison, in *The Description of England*, by the following procedure: the grains were steeped for three days, drained, and left on a floor in a round heap for at least twenty-one days, or until the grains began to sprout small roots. It was imperative that they be turned and the heap thinned four or five times a day, and that they not sprout leaves. The grains were then put into a kiln and dried over a slow fire, "For the more it be dried . . . , the sweeter and better the malt is and the longer it will continue." If even a small amount of moisture was left in the grain, it would be devoured from the middle by weevils known as maltworms, leaving only an empty husk. Properly dried barley should be golden yellow "and will write like a piece of chalk after you have bitten a kernel in sunder in the midst." The malt was best if made over a straw fire; a wood fire was believed to make for a worse hangover.

Making ale (*2GV* III.i.298, 300; *1H4* I.iii.231; *2H4* II.iv.132; *MND* II.i.50; *H5* III.ii.13, IV.vii.37, 44; *WT* IV.iii.8) from the malt was a relatively simple procedure. First, the malt was ground in a quern (*MND* II.i.36), or hand-mill, a time-consuming job performed by the housewife and her maids. Alternatively, the malt could be sent to the miller, but some preferred to save the miller's toll and grind it themselves. Water was heated and poured over the malt in huge batches; Harrison's wife added 80 gallons (303 l) of water to 8 bushels (.29 m³) of malt. The malt was allowed to steep for a few hours, and then the resulting brew was drained off, mixed with a little yeast, and allowed to age for about five days. The physician Andrew Boorde's *Dyetary of Helth* declared that good ale "must be fresshe and cleare, it muste not be ropy nor smoky, nor it must have no weft nor tayle."

Ale was often made at home, despite the hard work involved in brewing; indeed, many alehouses were the enterprises of housewives who brewed especially good ale or were in especially dire straits. Unlicensed alehouses were legion, but the authorities made an effort to locate and license the principal establishments, sending "ale-conners," or ale inspectors, to the various houses to verify quality and quantity. Pewter containers bearing the inspector's or borough's seal were known as "sealed quarts" (*TS* Ind.ii.88), and were thought of more highly than ale that arrived in an unlabeled vessel.

Ale was considered a laudable and healthful drink by many, including Boorde, who disdained water but had no objection to "good Ale." In times of plague, the bitter herb rue was added to the ale, in the belief that it would ward off disease. Ale was also the central feature of village celebrations, whose names paired the word "ale" with the name of the party benefited by the ale's sale: church ale, bride ale, christening ale (*H8* V.iv.8–10), and so on. In the case of the bride ale, which raised funds for the establishment of a newlyweds' household, the bride often brewed the ale herself. While plenty of people objected to public drunkenness, few were bold enough to challenge the esteem in which ale was held. Foreigners, too, approved of the brew; the Flemish cartographer Abraham Ortelius wrote in his *Theatrum Orbis Terrarum* that the English "drinke . . . of malt, is indeed very good, holesome and pleasant; much sought after in the Low countries, and therefore conveied thither in great abundance." The chief problem with ale was that it kept badly and spoiled within several days of its brewing.

This deficiency was addressed by the advent of beer (*2H6* II.iii.64; *Ham* V.i.204, 210–12), which added hops to the standard ingredients of malt, yeast (*Ham* V.vii.194), and water. Hops lent the brew a bitter taste and acted as a preservative. At first, there was resistance to the new drink, and beer brewers (*2H4* III.ii.268–69; *Lear* III.ii.83) were barred from the Brewers' Company. Boorde joined the general outcry, declaring beer unhealthy for those with colic or "the stone," and claiming—no surprise to modern victims of "beer belly"—that it fattened. Eventually, however, it met with general favor, probably because women no longer had to go to the trouble of brewing every few days. Queen Elizabeth, who certainly never had to handle an 80-gallon cauldron herself, nevertheless concurred with popular opinion and called beer "an excellent wash." Most people drank their beer within a month, though the nobility, who could afford the storage space, kept theirs for up to two years.

William Harrison's wife made beer by adding 2 pounds (.75 kg) of hops to a second 80 gallons of water and letting it rest over the used malt for 1½ hours in the winter or 2 hours in the summer. After draining, boiling, and re-steeping this wort, she boiled a third 80 gallons of water and poured it over the twice-used malt, adding another 1½ pounds (.56 kg) of hops and a little orris, powdered bayberry, and wheat flour. This third brew, because it had a weaker flavor, was called "small beer" (*2H6* IV.ii.69; *2H4* II.ii.5–6, 9–11; *Oth* II.i.158); if the hops were omitted, it made "small ale" (*TS* Ind.ii.1, 23, 75). Brewing, like cheese-making or butter-churning, involved a certain element of chance, and the housewife's hopes that it would yield "barm" (*MND* II.i.38) or froth were not always realized. The odds of success could be increased by using good ingredients. Harrison stated that the best water was the "fattest" or most mineralized, and averred that the quality of the hops, more than any other factor, determined the beer's shelf life. Some people bypassed the entire question of preservation by drinking the unfermented liquid, or "wort" (*LLL* V.ii.234).

Beer was the daily drink of courtiers and commoners alike, though it was a socially inferior drink to wine (*H5* III.v.18–22); it was meted out to inmates at St. Thomas's Hospital in London and to Elizabeth I's maids of honor, in quantities that would give pause to a strong man today. For those who had to buy their ale and beer, it went for 1d per quart (.95 l) and only ½d per quart for small ale or beer, according to a 1603 statute that regulated the price. Small wonder, then, that moralists objected to the level of drunkenness in everyday life. Drunkards were fined and set in the stocks, to no avail; Harrison called the habitually drunk maltbugs and said that they drank themselves into a stupor. He listed various slang names for strong ale and beer: "huffcap, the mad-dog, father-whoreson, angels'-food, dragons'-milk, go-by-the-wall, stride-wide, and lift-leg, etc."

Wine

Wine (*1H6* II.iii.79; *2H6* II.iii.98; *R3* I.iv.164, 165, V.iii.63, 72, 133; *MAAN* III.v.53; *H5* II.ii.41–42; *JC* IV.iii.155; *Oth* II.iii.279–81, 307–8; *A&C* I.ii.14–15; *Cor* IV.v.1; *Mac* II.iii.95–96; *AYLI* III.ii.201–3), like ale, was generally acknowledged to be good for the health. Andrew Boorde listed several varieties as aphrodisiacs and recommended washing the penis in white wine as a cure for sexually transmitted diseases. Clary, a wine infused with the herb of the same name, was felt to be good for the stomach and mental disorders. The botanist John Gerard listed a whole catalog of reasons to imbibe in his *Herball*:

> Wine doth refresh the inward and naturall heate, comforteth the stomacke, causeth it to have an appetite to meat, moveth concoction, and conveyeth the nourishment through all parts of the body, increaseth strength, inlargeth the body, maketh flegme thin, bringeth forth urine, cholericke and watery humours, procureth sweating, ingendreth pure bloud, maketh the body well coloured, and turneth an ill colour into a better.

All of this was true, he said, provided wine was consumed in moderation, rather than to excess. Boorde agreed in the main with Gerard, with a slightly more personal tone; he would drink, he maintained,

> good Gascon wyne, but I wyl not drynke stronge wynes, as Malmesey, Romney, Romaniske wyne, wyne Qoorse, wyne Greke, and Secke; but other whyle, a draught or two of Muscadell or Basterde, Osey, Caprycke, Aligant,

Tyre, Raspyte [raspis, or raspberry wine], I wyll not refuse; but white wyne of Angeou, or wyne of Orleance, or Renyshe wyne, white or read, is good for al men.

White wine, he claimed, nourished, engendered heat (an important consideration in an age that thought of the body as a furnace—see *Tim* IV.iii.430–31), combated heaviness, and cleansed wounds.

Boorde listed many of the wines imported into England in the sixteenth century. Writers had different means of classifying wines, but they tended to divide them according to their place of origin, their contents, or their alcoholic strength, with some overlap between the categories. Boorde considered Gascon, French, Rhenish (*MV* I.ii.84–85, III.i.39–40; *Ham* V.i.179), and claret (*2H6* II.iii.71) wines "meane" or less alcoholic wines and noted that they paired well with food. Strong or "hot" wines, he considered ill-suited for meals but acceptable afterward, especially for old men, who were considered naturally cold and in need of the warmth provided by these wines. In this category he places malmsey (a sweet wine that had a long shelf life—see *LLL* V.ii.234; *R3* I.iv.158, 273; *2H4* II.i.38), course, greke (*T&C* V.i.1), romanysk, rumney (a sweet Spanish wine), sack, alicant (a Spanish mulberry wine), bastard (a sweet Spanish wine—see *1H4* II.iv.74–75; *2H4* II.i.48; *MM* III.ii.3–4), tyre (another sweet wine), osay (also sweet), Muscadell (a sweet, richly flavored wine—*TS* III.ii.171), caprycke (still another sweet wine), tynt, and roberdany. William Harrison estimated that the English consumed 20,000 to 30,000 tuns of imported wine yearly, and he divided his list of wines into fifty-six weak and thirty strong varieties.

Various other sources tell us that canary (*2H4* II.iv.25–28; *TN* I.iii.78; *MWW* III.ii.82) was a sweet white wine imported from the Canary Islands, and "cute" was a boiled, and thus thickened, but little-fermented, wine. Piment was wine mixed with honey and spices. Charneco (*2H6* II.iii.63) was probably a kind of port. Hippocras was a spiced cordial, and wormwood wine, as its name implies, was distilled from wormwood and resembled absinthe, which is made from the same principal ingredient. (Given the potential toxicity of wormwood, it seems odd that in his *Whole Art and Trade of Husbandry*, Conrad Heresbach recommended this beverage, like barley water, for laborers.) A recipe for hippocras, undated in the source, calls for 5 ounces of aqua vitae, 2 ounces of pepper, 2 ounces of ginger, 2 ounces of cloves, 2 ounces of "grains of paradise," 5 grains of ambergris, and 2 grains of musk, to be steeped for 24 hours; three to four drops of the mixture should be added to 1 pound of sugar and 1 quart of red wine or cider. The same source indicates that hippocras was often served hot and was a favorite beverage at weddings and during the winter. Bordeaux (*2H4* II.iv.63–66) was a fine wine, contrasted with the peasant's "sour milk" and extolled as a worthy beverage for the fashionable throat in Thomas Heywood's 1633 play *The Wise Woman of Hogsdon*.

Of all the wines, sack (*1H4* II.ii.44–46, II.iv.116–17, 460, 542–43, V.iii.54–57 s.d.; *2H6* II.iii.60; *TS* Ind.ii.2, 6; *2H4* II.iv, IV.iii.88–125; *H5* II.iii.27; *Temp* III.ii.12–13, 29) deserves special mention and exposition because of its importance to any play in which Falstaff is a character. Sack was a general term for white wine or, more specifically, Spanish white wine, and still more specifically, "sherris sack," the white wine of Jerez, Spain. The name probably came from the French phrase *vin sec* (dry wine). It was probably not naturally sweet, since Falstaff sweetens it by adding sugar (*1H4* I.ii.114). Over time, "sack" came to mean the wine that is today called sherry. It could be drunk plain, sweetened, topped with a floating crouton (*MWW* III.v.3–4), heated ("burnt"—see *TN* II.iii.189; *MWW* II.i.203–4), or heated and mixed with egg (*MWW* III.v.28–32). Though it seems odd to modern tastes to float things in wine, the practice was quite common in the Renaissance, with "sops" of bread or cake being soaked and eaten (*TS* III.ii.169–75). A less esteemed addition to wine was lime, which was used to make bad wine seem clearer (*1H4* II.iv.125; *MWW* I.iii.10).

Wine, for those who could afford it, played a prominent role in revelry. A good example is the post-wedding banquet of *The Taming of the Shrew*, in which healths are drunk back and forth (III.ii.169, 185, 195). A great deal of alcohol might be consumed at wedding feasts, such as the 1,000 gallons (3,785 l) purchased for the wedding of Lord Burghley's daughter in 1582. Healths (*TN* I.iii.37; *R&J* I.iv.85; *H8* I.iv.38–40), which were toasts to the welfare of a particular person, were one way of adding ceremony to the practice of drinking. These courtesies might be phrased as "I drink your health, sir," "Good cheer!" or "I pledge you, madam." Another was to sing a drinking song (*Oth* II.iii.69–73) or to cry "Hem!" a rough equivalent of "Bottoms up" (*2H4* III.ii.222, II.iv.30; *MAAN* V.i.16). Many people drank their wine in taverns, but some could afford to keep a wine cellar (*Tim* II.ii.166–68) full of casks, or "pipe[s]" (*MWW* III.ii.83), and kegs, or "anker[s]" (*MWW* I.iii.50).

Aqua Vitae

Strong liquor was not usually drunk in England at this time. Not until the eighteenth century would gin and rum be widely, even epidemically, consumed. The one exception was aqua vitae (*MWW* II.ii.298), Latin for "water of life." This was brandy, and it was typically a woman's drink, preferred by the nurse in *Romeo and Juliet* (III.ii.88, IV.v.16) and by a hypothetical midwife in *Twelfth Night* (II.v.191–92). The mention of a midwife is not coincidental, for one of the most common occasions for female drinking was in the room where a woman was in labor or had just delivered a child. The midwife, the laboring woman's "gossips" (close friends), and occasionally the new mother refreshed themselves with aqua vitae in the long hours during and after the delivery.

Brandy had various medicinal uses. John Gerard recommended it to the impotent or the old; the latter were thought to be cold by nature and in need of the warming of this "hot infusion" (*WT* IV.v.792). Hot, in this case, did not necessarily mean warm to the touch. Instead, it signified that aqua vitae was both strong and likely to imbue the body with internal warmth. However, brandy could be, and often was, served literally hot. Unlike ordinary wine, it could be set alight, and a favorite drinking game was floating a burning raisin, called a "flapdragon" (*WT* III.iii.96; *LLL* V.i.43; *2H4* II.iv.251), in brandy and swallowing it.

Metheglin and Mead

Both metheglin (*LLL* V.ii.234; *MWW* V.v.161) and mead were made with honey and water, and both were popular in Wales and certain English counties. Boorde stated that mead was made with fermented honey and water only, while metheglin was augmented with herbs. Others claimed that mead, too, could be spiced, and in some cases it was hard to tell the difference between the two concoctions. William Harrison seemed to think the two beverages were identical. He scorned "a kind of swish-swash" made in some places of honeycomb, water, and spices, which he said "differeth so much from the true metheglin as chalk from cheese." One recipe for "the true metheglin" called for 9 gallons (34 l) of boiling water, 28 pounds (10.44 kg) of honey, the peels of three lemons, 2 tablespoons of yeast, and small amounts of ginger, mace, cloves, and rosemary, the whole mixture to be fermented for six months and then bottled.

Cider and Perry

Cider, made of fermented apples, and perry, made of fermented pears, were popular in certain regions of the country, particularly in Kent, Sussex, and the western counties. Both drinks, along with beer and aqua vitae, were commonly consumed by women. William Lawson, in the 1648 edition of his *New Orchard and Garden*, explains how to make cider. One should remove the stems, upper ends, and galls of the apples, then stamp and strain them and allow the juice to sit for 24 hours. Then

> in you hang a poakefull of Cloves, Mace, Nutmegs, Cinnamon, Ginger, and pils [peels] of Lemmons in the midst of the vessell, it will make it as wholesome and pleasant as wine.

Perry, he wrote, was made in the same manner. Both were good cures for the ague.

Possets and Caudles

Possets (*Mac* II.ii.6; *MWW* I.iv.8, V.v.172) and caudles (*Tim* IV.iii.227; *2H6* IV.vii.91) were mixtures of alcoholic beverages with other substances. They were considered suitable for invalids, babies, new mothers, people about to retire for the night, and anyone else who needed soothing nourishment. The posset was a mixture of warm wine or ale and milk; Boorde considered the "posset ale," a blend of hot milk and cold ale, augmented with herbs, a good cure for fever or an overheated liver. A recipe from Shakespeare's era for a "Sack Posset" called for cream, sugar, mace, nutmeg, sack, and ale, the total volume of the sack and ale to be equal to the volume of the cream. The whole mixture was to be set in a hot pewter dish, covered with a basin, and placed by the fire to stay hot for 2 to 3 hours. *See also* Food.

Ducat

One of the most respected and widespread currencies of the late Middle Ages and the Renaissance, the ducat originated in twelfth-century Sicily, in the duchy (in Latin, *ducatus*, hence the name) of Apulia. It was originally a silver coin invented to fill a need, in a newly prosperous society, for larger denominations than the old denier (which corresponded to the English penny). However, in 1284, the city of Venice decided to mint a *ducato d'oro*, a gold ducat, and this was the form that became famous throughout Europe.

Venetian ducat. Actual size is 20 mm in diameter. © 2002 The American Numismatic Society. All rights reserved.

The ducat's quality was so exceptional that it became, in some regions, nearly synonymous with "gold coin." It also inspired imitations in Rome,

Hungary, Serbia, Padua, Greece, Rhodes, and elsewhere, causing anxiety in Venice over its own coin's reputation. Who knew how pure those non-Venetian copies might be? The worst fears were never realized, however, and the ducat remained, with the florin, Europe's dominant currency until the end of the fifteenth century. In some areas even the florin, which, as its name suggests, originated in Florence, became generally known as a ducat.

The design of the ducat was copied to a greater or lesser extent by the foreign coiners, but in its Venetian incarnation its obverse showed the doge (Duke of Venice) kneeling before a haloed Saint Mark. The reverse showed Christ surrounded by a mandorla (almond-shaped arrangement) of stars and the legend SIT TXPE DAT QTV REGIS ISTE DVCAT (abbreviated Latin for "May this duchy which you rule be given to you, O Christ").

Venice was still using the ducat in the sixteenth century, and its Italian origin made it a natural currency choice for Shakespeare when he was setting a play in Italy. It thus appears in *Much Ado About Nothing*'s Messina (II.ii.49–50), *Romeo and Juliet*'s Mantua (V.i.59), and, unsurprisingly, in the *Merchant of Venice* (I.iii.1–10, II.iii.4, II.vi.50, II.viii.15–24, III.i.86, III.ii.306–7, IV.i.84), in which the debt to Shylock is 3,000 ducats and in which Shylock divides his grief between the disappearance of his daughter and the loss of his ducats. However, the popularity of the ducat in northern Europe, central Europe, and the Mediterranean as far away as the Levant makes it quite plausible that the coin should also crop up in Ephesus (*CE* IV.i.30; IV.iii.82; IV.iv.13, 86; V.i.232, 390), Illyria (*TN* I.iii.21), Denmark (*Ham* III.iv.25, IV.iv.20), and Vienna (*MM* III.ii.127). A group of German visitors to England in 1592 mentioned nothing about Venetian ducats, but they noted that the Hungarian ducat was worth 6s. 8d. *See also* Money.

Duel

The elements of the duel (*TN* III.iv) were a casual acceptance of violence in everyday life, the inclusion of deadly weapons as male costume accessories, and a fanatical obsession with personal reputation. The result was a climate in which disagreements were, at least in the upper classes, settled by brawling—at times highly formalized brawling, at other times nothing more than impromptu street fighting. Duels were fought for many reasons, avoided for nearly as many, and attended by various consequences for the participants.

A duel was usually precipitated by an insult to the family, masculinity, integrity, or political allegiance of a gentleman or nobleman. Rank and gender were critical to the duel, for women and commoners were considered to have no personal honor to defend. A woman's honor was the property of her husband or father, and a remark reflecting negatively on her chastity was supposed to be resented and physically refuted by the man who was legally responsible for her (*MAAN* V.i.54–192). A servant was associated with the family for whom he worked, and mistreatment of him was similarly expected to be avenged by the master of the household. Furthermore, the combatants had to be of equal rank (*2H6* IV.x.43–55). An earl could not challenge or be challenged by a knight or an untitled gentleman, and the same was true of soldiers of differing ranks, for example, a captain and a sergeant. To challenge a man of higher rank was ambitious, even insolent; to accept such a challenge was inappropriate, for it implied an equality between the two men that contradicted the entire social order. Just such a case arose in 1577, when Sir Philip Sidney was forbidden to challenge the Earl of Oxford. A man of higher rank had no need to defend his insult with his life; he could merely refuse to fight on the grounds of rank, adding a second offense to the first in perfect safety and with public approval. That Cloten bothers to fight an inferior is one instance among many in which his ill-breeding is apparent (*Cym* II.i.15–16).

However, theory and practice were not always identical. Just because commoners were assumed to have no honor did not mean that they did not quarrel, or that when they quarreled, they did not copy the formalities of the duel. However, these scenes are usually played for laughs, and one suspects that gentlemen looked with condescending amusement upon the "duels" of their social inferiors. Francis Bacon attempted to use the descent of dueling through the social ranks as a deterrent, offering the hope "that men of birth and quality will leave the practice, when it begins to bee

A duel with rapiers from the *Roxburghe Ballads.* Reprint from *Shakespeare's England.*

vilified and come so lowe as to Barbers-surgeons and Butchers, and such base mechanicall persons."

Duels could be fought over the sexual deportment of women, or for their love (*TA* II.i.25 s.d.–100; *MND* III.ii; *H5* II.i.56–60, 99–102 s.d.). Yet in real life, as in Shakespeare's works, an insult against a man himself was more likely to lead to a quarrel than an insult against his country or dependents. The insult, or cause (*LLL* I.ii.173–74; *R&J* II.iv.26), could take a number of forms, as Touchstone indicates:

> O sir, we quarrel in print, by the book, as you have books for good manners. I will name you the degrees. The first, the Retort Courteous; the second, the Quip Modest; the third, the Reply Churlish; the fourth, the Reproof Valiant; the fifth, the Countercheck Quarrelsome; the sixth, the Lie with Circumstance; the seventh, the Lie Direct. All these you may avoid but the Lie Direct. (*AYLI* V.iv.90–97)

Shakespeare lists seven degrees of "the lie" (in Italian, *mentita*), though other contemporaries listed as many as thirty-two, each of which called for a response ranging from the retort courteous, acknowledging an honest difference of opinion, to a formal challenge. Furthermore, an insult was not always an imputation of dishonesty. Accusations of bastardy, treason, blasphemy, heresy, and cowardice were just as serious (although, in some circumstances, such a remark might not be an avengeable insult; a recognized royal bastard, for example, could take no offense at having his status known by others, and a former but forgiven traitor could tolerate a remark about his past crime, but not an imputation of continuing disloyalty). An insult could be any conscious, intentional, competent gesture of contempt, spite, or insolence, meaning that honest mistakes and the acts of women, children, drunkards, animals, and men under physical duress did not count as insults.

An insult could be as simple as a fierce glance or rude gesture, or as grievous as a slap to the face or an actual wound. Several of the more serious causes of duels are listed in *Hamlet*:

> Am I a coward?
> Who calls me villain? Breaks my pate across?
> Plucks off my beard and blows it in my face?
> Tweaks me by the nose? Gives me the lie i' th' throat
> As deep as to the lungs? (II.ii.577–81)

Removing another's mask, barring someone's entry into a public place, or forcing one's way into another's house constituted an insult. Words were usually held to be somewhere in the middle of the continuum, though some considered them more serious than blows, since they wounded the soul rather than the body. The insult (*ingiuria* in Italian) was magnified if offered by one who had an advantage, such as being attended by more followers or being armed while his victim was weaponless. For example, Tybalt considers himself injured (*R&J* III.i.67) by Romeo because Romeo has invaded his house in disguise, and because Tybalt was not able to resent the insult at the time because of his duties as a host and because of his uncle's direct command. His honor therefore demands that he resent the intrusion at the first possible opportunity, and he raises the stakes by offering Romeo two insults: that he is his "man" or inferior and servant (possibly unintentional) and that he is a villain (decidedly intentional). Romeo's unwillingness to respond, especially considering the presence of his friends Benvolio and Mercutio, appears dishonorable in the extreme (*R&J* III.i.57–75).

Today, we would consider spreading rumors more dangerous than a face-to-face taunt, for rumors are harder to refute, but the reverse was true in Shakespeare's time. Secret slander was less serious than an open affront, for the former could be judiciously ignored while the latter required a response or the further imputation of cowardice (*MAAN* V.ii.57–59). Ironically, an insult could be, and was expected to be, followed by a challenge, even if both parties knew the accusation to be true. A particularly sad example, which may have been of this nature, was the duel between two esquires in 1384, in which one accused the other of raping his wife. They fought, and the husband was killed.

Preparations and Procedures for the Duel

If possible, an insult was to be resented immediately. In Touchstone's case, the first step, if possible, was to turn the insult aside or offer the speaker a chance to retract his words gracefully:

> I did dislike the cut of a certain courtier's beard. He sent me word, if I said his beard was not cut well, he was in the mind it was: this is called the Retort Courteous. If I sent him word again it was not well cut, he would send me word he cut it to please himself: this is called the Quip Modest. If again, it was not well cut, he disabled my judgment: this is called the Reply Churlish. If again, it was not well cut, he would answer I spake not true: this is called the Reproof Valiant. If again, it was not well cut, he would say I lie: this is called the Countercheck Quarrelsome: and so to the Lie Circumstantial and the Lie Direct. (*AYLI* V.iv.71–80)

If the speaker (A) did not retract, the insulted party (B) said, "You lie, sir," or something very like it; otherwise he was assumed to have conceded the truth of A's statement. Simply giving the lie in return, the *ritorcimento*, was not considered an adequate response. Neither was applying the same terms of opprobrium to the speaker (the *ingiuria volta*) or returning it and adding another (*ingiuria rivoltata*). This was "giving the lie," and A was now honor-bound to issue a challenge (*H5* IV.i.200–21, IV.vii.118–77, IV.viii.6–71) or to produce proof of his original assertion.

The challenge was, if properly handled, written out (*MWW* I.iv.103–4) and delivered by A's second, a friend or acquaintance who served as a helper, a message bearer, a mediator (*H5* II.i.99–102 s.d.), and, sometimes, a co-combatant. B had the choice of weapons, and one of the jobs of the second was to relay this choice to A and to help the two men agree upon a consistent length for their weapons (*Ham* V.ii.266–67; *MWW* II.i.197–98), using a stick for comparison. Seconds were supposed to take every opportunity to patch up the quarrel before it came to bloodshed, using the numerous methods of settling a duel beforehand (*2H6* II.i.178–79). Among these were litigation, arbitration by judges or clerics, the speaker's belated acceptance of the injured party's denial, the injured party's acceptance of an apology (often accompanied by some form of self-humiliation) from the speaker, and possibly an embrace or handshake as a symbol of renewed amity. An offender of lower rank could back out of the duel by putting himself into the victim's power in some way; the offended party could then give him a token slap or a light blow with a rod, though he was not supposed to cause serious injury. Sometimes the quarrel could be averted by a rephrasing of the insult or lie as a conditional statement—"*If* you were to say X, then you would be lying." This course is Touchstone's ace in the hole. He knows that one may avoid even the Lie Direct

> with an If. I knew when seven justices could not take up a quarrel, but when the parties were met themselves, one of them thought but of an If: as, "If you said so, then I said so"; and they shook hands and swore brothers. Your If is the only peacemaker. Much virtue in If. (*AYLI* V.iv.98–103)

If mediation failed, they met at a prearranged location, usually a street, square, or field, and fought until one died or yielded. To prove that neither had cheated by wearing a mail shirt beneath his doublet, both men usually stripped to their shirts (*LLL* V.ii.691–708).

Sometimes the encounter had royal sanction and served in place of a trial. At various times, women, clergymen, the blind, citizens of London, and men sixty years old or older were protected from having to participate and could choose a substitute to champion their cause, but able-bodied men in the prime of life were expected to fight for themselves. Trial by combat (*R2* I.i.69–83, I.iii, IV.i.19–106; *Lear* V.iii.110–55; *2H4* IV.i.115–37; *2H6* I.iii.210–22, II.iii.47–106) was supervised by a constable, marshals, and the monarch, and followed a strict procedure. The appellant (or his substitute) arrived at the field of battle, fully armed, and named himself and his purpose; then the defendant, who had been given the choice of arms, did likewise. Both swore that their cause was true, that their weapons were equal, and that they would use no magic to prevail but would do all else in their power to win. The onset was sounded by a trumpet and a call in French, and the combatants fought until one was killed or forced to yield. If one yielded, or if the monarch cried out for the combat to cease, the opponents were separated, and the constable or marshal noted their position in case the fighting should be resumed. If the defendant had not yielded or been slain by the end of the day, he was found not guilty. These rules were much the same from the late Middle Ages all the way through the Tudor period, though trial by combat was seldom used during Elizabeth I's reign.

Consequences of Dueling

Trial by combat was an accepted and perfectly legal form of the duel, in which formality was carried to an extreme. The more duels departed from the rituals of accusation, verbal challenge, refusal to recant, written challenge, mediation, and encounter before witnesses, the more they resembled murder or revenge. The duel that took place spontaneously at the moment of insult (*R&J* I.i.4), or by ambush, or with general brawling by seconds and spectators, or with departures from the verbal formalities, was much more likely to be prosecuted as murder, assault, or breach of the peace. The penalties could range from a substantial fine to banishment (*2GV* IV.i.23–29, 51–52) to execution. Lucentio, for example, claims to have killed a man in a duel and to have fled justice afterward (*TS* I.i.230–31), and, in the real world, Bacon prosecuted a pair of duelists and secured fines of £500 and 500 marks from them. If charges were filed, the seconds were subject to the same penalties as the quarreling pair, giving seconds good cause to think carefully before accepting their role and to devote themselves wholeheartedly to the task of mediation. The best course was to arrange things so that the other party struck the first blow, giving oneself grounds to claim self-defense (*TN* III.iv.157–70; *R&J* I.i.40–41), or to leave the country entirely so as to evade English law, though Bacon was all for prosecuting Englishmen who fought duels in any nation. It was also important to resent an insult to the corrrect degree, so as not to exceed proper recompense and appear too vengeful. *See also* Fencing.

Dwarf

The dwarf (*1H6* II.iii.23; *MND* III.ii.328; *MWW* III.ii.6) was a celebrated rarity in Europe, and people of small stature were commonly employed by the nobility and royalty. The powerful "collected" dwarfs; Charles IX of France was given three as a gift in 1572, and his mother Catherine de' Medici had five. A 1566 banquet at Cardinal Vitelli's, in Italy, featured thirty-four little people as waiters. English monarchs did not escape the mania for dwarfs. Mary I had a 3'8" page, John Jarvis; Edward VI is said to have had a royal dwarf named Xit; and Elizabeth I made a gift of gilt plate on New Year's, 1584–85 to "Mrs. Tomysen, the dwarf." Dwarfs, like giants, often made a living by exhibiting themselves at inns and taverns.

John Stow saw a show of this kind in 1581 that featured a direct comparison between two Dutchmen of 7'7" and 3' tall. John Ducker, a little person 2'6" tall, was making money by exhibiting himself in 1610. A common profession for people of short stature was that of jester or fool, a trade that evolved out of exhibitions and turned the ridicule directed at dwarfs into an asset.

Earthquake

Earthquakes would seem an unlikely subject for Shakespearean discourse, and indeed he mentions them infrequently (*Temp* II.i.319; *V&A* 648). However, he had good reason to introduce the topic now and then, for a notable earthquake had startled London on April 6, 1580, and had been the subject of four ballads, one of which began "Quake, quake, 'tis tyme to quake, / When towers and townes and all doo shake." Another began, "Come from the playe, come from the playe, / The house will fall, so people say." Some have used the Nurse's reference to an earthquake eleven years before (*R&J* I.iii.23) as a way of dating *Romeo and Juliet* to 1591, though the 1580 earthquake was not the only one of that decade, merely the worst, and most experts presume the play to have been written in 1594 or 1595.

Education

To speak of an educational "system" in Shakespeare's day is to imply that there was a national plan for the education of the general populace, which was not the case. There was a national plan for the education of some and a consensus that laborers and the most menial servants needed little or no education. Therefore, while many people could read, fewer could write, and fewer still could understand the Latin that was emphasized in grammar schools and universities. Much teaching was still done at home by parents, servants, or private tutors, and many people who entered a grammar school never reached a university. Those who matriculated at a university often never took a degree. Schooling was therefore far from universal, far from consistent, and often far from complete.

Learning began at home. The rich, especially peers, hired private tutors for their sons and daughters (*TS* I.i.91–99, 186–93, II.i.108–10; *LLL* IV.ii.74–77), while others taught their children themselves. Another course was to send the children, at about age five, to "petty schools" where the rudiments of reading, writing, and arithmetic were taught. Girls were permitted to attend these schools (*MM* I.iv.47–48; *MND* III.ii.324) with their brothers, and some did, but fewer girls than boys were literate, implying that they attended school less often and for fewer years. Reading was the skill most stressed; arithmetic was seldom considered an important subject in any school during the Renaissance, being a merchant's skill best learned on the job (*LLL* I.ii.40–41; *Cor* III.i.244; *2H6* IV.ii.86–92), and writing was more difficult than reading. Furthermore, the ability to read was often the only entrance requirement for a grammar school, and religious orthodoxy—one of the main goals of Protestant education in England—required the ability to read Scripture but not to write.

Reading was taught first with a hornbook (*LLL* V.i.46; *TNK* II.ii.40), a framed paddle covered by a thin sheet of transparent horn. An example from Charles I's reign shows the lowercase alphabet with a cross before the *a*. This symbol was apparently such a common feature of horn books that the first row was called the cross row (*R3* I.i.55). After the lowercase alphabet, the uppercase letters appear, followed by syllables such as "ab eb ib ob ub" and "ca ce ci co cu," followed by the Lord's Prayer and the phrase "In the name of the Father, & of the Son, & of the Holy Ghost, Amen." The child would say each letter, syllable, or word either in chorus with others or individually as the teacher pointed to him with a small stick called a fescue (*TNK* II.ii.33–35). Once the child had mastered the alphabet, he moved on to the "Absey-book" (*John* I.i.195–200, *2GV* II.i.23), a pamphlet with the A B C, a catechism, some moral epigrams, and few short prayers such as the grace before and after meals. If this was mastered he moved on to the *Primer and Catechism*, which contained prayers, psalms, a calendar, an almanac for calculating the dates of Easter and the other movable feasts, and other religious material.

Grammar Schools

Once they could read and perhaps write a little, boys (*MAAN* II.i.214–16; *JC* V.i.61, V.v.26–28; *Cor* III.ii.116; *TNK* Ep.2–3) moved on to grammar school (*2H6* IV.vii.33–35, 72–77), where they were at first known as "petties" and perhaps subjected to some remedial classes until their writing skills were acceptable. The grammar schools were free, but students were expected to provide their own pens, paper, candles, and in some schools, special fees or perquisites due to the master and his usher. The teachers—mostly priests (*3H6* I.iii.ch.) and unbeneficed scholars called clerks (*Per* V.Cho.5, *H8* II.ii.92)—needed all the fees they could get, for though their housing was often provided by the school, their pay was not high. Masters (*A&C* III.xi.71, III.xii.ch.; *TS* IV.ii.55–56; *Lear* II.iv.301; *TNK* II.40, III.v.ch.; *2H6* IV.ii.88) received about £20 per year and ushers £10 at the end of the sixteenth century, a salary that had approximately doubled since 1500, while the cost of living had gone up by a factor of six. There was little that they could do to improve their situation, however, for while the universities were turning out ever-increasing numbers of scholars, the number of schools in which to teach was growing at only a moderate pace. There were only a few hundred grammar schools in England around the turn of the sixteenth century, scattered about so that there was one in almost every town and about one every twelve miles. This distance excluded many, for twelve miles was too far to walk each way, and not all families could afford to pay extra to board their sons with the schoolmaster.

Though the grammar schools had been founded to teach poor boys free of charge, they were being invaded in greater and greater numbers by the sons of the gentry and the richer mercantile classes. Thus, the typical student population might contain a very few truly poor boys, but was more likely to be composed of the sons of yeomen, tradesmen, esquires, and knights. Unlike the petty schools, which were usually held in the church (*TN* III.ii.73–74) or in a private home, grammar schools usually had their own buildings. Furthermore, they had to have a license from the diocese, and the master had to take an oath of religious conformity. He was supposed to be a man of good character, a regular churchgoer, and a decent scholar, free from the vices of lying, stealing, or swearing, and unlikely to "infect" the minds of his students with unsound doctrine.

The grammar school taught mostly Latin grammar (*TS* III.i.28–44; *TA* IV.ii.22–23). English was used but not extensively studied, for the study of the English language was just beginning to develop. The boys spoke in Latin, especially when studying that language, read Latin, and composed and translated sentences. There was some work that did not center on Latin—mainly religion, logic (*TS* I.i.34; *R&J* III.v.150), rhetoric (*AYLI* V.i.44; *LLL* IV.iii.236, and the "rope-tricks" of *TS* I.i.35), letter-writing, and probably a modern foreign language such as French (*2GV* IV.i.33–34; *TS* II.i.81)—but Latin was the chief subject of study. Greek was considered a laudable language to study, as was Hebrew, both because they could shed light on early Christian and Jewish texts, but they were only rarely undertaken at the grammar-school level. Most boys encountered them only in the form of the Greek alphabet, which was printed at the beginning of the Latin Accidence and Latin Syntax. Their appearance there was designed to familiarize the boys with the alphabet so that later they could make use of it in their university studies; how well the plan succeeded may be judged from the fact that whenever Shakespeare mentions Greek, it is as a synonym for something unintelligible (*JC* I.ii.277–82; *AYLI* II.iv.55).

The 100 to 150 boys sat on benches, or "forms," their position in the one-room school being determined by their abilities (hence the "Degrees [ranks] in schools" of *T&C* I.iii.104). For the first few years, they sat in the back of the room and were taught by the usher, the master's assistant. Here they learned grammar, translated, composed "Latins" (sentences in Latin) and "vulgars" (sentences in English), and acquired a wide vocabulary. After they had learned all that the usher had to teach them, pupils moved to the front to study with the master, where they read Latin authors such as Cicero, Cato, and Terence, and began composing Latin orations and essays of their own.

One of the leading texts for this study was William Lily's *Shorte Introduction of Grammar* (1549), popularly known as Lily's Latin Grammar. Shakespeare's familiarity with it is evident from certain passages in the plays (*MWW* IV.i), and he even repeats a mistake of Lily's (*TS* I.i.162). Though it was far from being the only text used in the grammar schools, the popularity of Lily's work is reflected in the £100 per year fee paid by a publisher to sublet the monopoly on its printing, and in the printing of up to 10,000 copies a year of the book when 1,250 was a standard edition size.

At no time was the school day easy. Aside from the sheer volume of work, the student-to-teacher ratio was high, the teaching methods were the deadening ones of drill and repetition, the teachers were in many cases either pedantic or bitter, and discipline was by the rod (*R2* V.i.31–32). The day was also a long one. Students arrived at about six or seven in the morning, worked until eleven with one fifteen-minute break midway through the morning, ate dinner, returned at one in the afternoon and worked until five or six, with a second fifteen-minute recess at about three. The day was slightly shorter in the winter, but it was still arduous, and boys looked forward eagerly to the occasional Thursday "remedy," or half-day holiday. Shakespeare's schoolboys were no doubt typical in their heavyhearted trudging toward school and their cheerful flight from it (*R&J* II.ii.157–58; *2H4* IV.ii.104–5; *AYLI* II.vii.144–46). Small wonder, too, that Iago, planning to deprive Othello of his greatest comforts, threatens that "His bed shall seem a school, his board a shrift" (*Oth* III.iii.24). Nonetheless, some students enjoyed the learning, even if they did not always appreciate the rigor. Some applied themselves with great dedication (*AYLI* I.i.5–6), and some even came to love their studies (*MWW* III.i.36–37); Prospero loses his dukedom because he neglects government in favor of academia (*Temp* I.ii.89–90). And while pedants (*TS* IV.ii.ch, iv.ch.; *TN* III.ii.73) of the Holofernes stamp must have been all too common, there were instances of teachers who made learning pleasant and who earned the love and admiration of their pupils.

Universities

England was generally acknowledged to have three universities (*TS* I.i.1–24, 28–40; *Ham* III.ii.99; *2GV* I.iii.10)—Oxford (*2H4* III.ii.9–12), Cambridge, and the Inns of Court. (The Inns of Court are discussed elsewhere in this volume, in the Law entry.) Oxford and Cambridge differed in some respects, but resembled each other enough that they can be described together. Both were evolving from a medieval style of instruction, in which undergraduates heard lectures in one of several halls, to a more college-centered approach, in which undergraduates lived in the colleges and dined with the masters and graduate students. In the new type of instruction, students attended university lectures given four days a week by university professors, were tutored by fellows of the college, and engaged in "exercises" on Monday, Wednesday, and Friday afternoon, in which they wrote and delivered speeches and defended their points through disputation. The required course of study for a bachelor's degree at either university was the same for doctors, lawyers, clergy, and dilettantes. At Cambridge, according to the statutes of 1570, this meant a year of rhetoric, two years of logic, and a year of philosophy (*TS* I.i.28, III.i; *R&J* III.iii.55–58), much of the reading material consisting of the Bible, theological works, and the works of Greek and Roman classical authors. Master's candidates continued for three more years, studying logic, Greek, natural philosophy, metaphysics (*TS* I.i.37), history, geometry, astronomy, and Hebrew. At Oxford the courses of study were similar, and Arabic was offered as well. Any additional subjects, like anatomy, were optional and cost extra money. Those who had completed advanced degrees were authorized to teach their subjects or to proceed to further professional training and were addressed, like physicians, as "Doctor" (*MAAN* V.i.201). Degrees were awarded in July in a solemn ceremony called an Act at Oxford and a Commencement at Cambridge. Friends and family swarmed to the respective towns in such numbers that it was extremely difficult to find room in the local inns.

Each university was divided into several colleges, each of which housed faculty, scholars pursuing advanced degrees, and, increasingly, undergraduates. In the 1580s, William Harrison's *The Description of England* listed the Cambridge colleges as Trinity, King's, St. John's, Christ's, Queen's, Jesus, Benet, Peter, Gonville and Caius, Magdalene, and Emmanuel. He also listed four remaining halls, vestiges of the medieval teaching and housing systems. At Oxford he named Christ Church (founded by Cardinal Wolsey—see *H8* IV.ii.58–59), Magdalen, New, Merton, All Souls, Corpus Christi, Lincoln, Oriel, Queen's, Balliol, St. John's, Trinity, Exeter, Brasnose, University, Gloucester, and Jesus, the last still being planned and built in Harrison's time. Wadham was added in 1610, after Harrison's list was compiled, and that notable Oxford landmark, the Bodleian Library, opened its east wing in 1603. Both universities had large libraries by contemporary standards. Cambridge University Library had about 950 volumes in 1600; the Bodleian, about 2,500 in 1602. Each of the universities had its own character; Oxford, for example, was fonder of old-fashioned May Day and Christmas revels. Each college also had its own character, a tendency reinforced by the colleges' habit, often specified by the founding articles, of recruiting heavily from particular regions of the country or from selected grammar schools.

During the period in question, three trends were evident in both university populations. The first was a general increase in size. In the 1560s, about 300 students matriculated each year at Oxford. By the second decade of the seventeenth century, the number was more like 400. Each had about 3,000 students in all by the late sixteenth century. The second trend was an increase in the age at matriculation. Entering scholars, or "sophisters," had usually been about fourteen to sixteen years old in the early sixteenth century but were now typically sixteen to eighteen. The third trend was a gradual gentrification of the student body. In the early sixteenth century, it had been customary for peers' sons, and to a lesser extent those of the gentry, to be educated at home and perhaps sent directly to the Inns of Court to study law. Increasingly, a few years at a university, if not an actual degree, became desirable, often more for the social connections and the experience than for the academic benefits. Accordingly, more gentlemen paid for their sons to go to the universities or bribed schoolmasters to recommend their sons for scholarships normally reserved for the poor, and the percentage of genteel and noble scholars increased to the detriment of yeomen's and tradesmen's sons. A reflection of this development, albeit not in a university context, can be seen in Shakespeare's boast that the virtuous schoolteacher Marina instructs a better class of student: "pupils lacks she none of noble race" (*Per* V.Cho.9).

Distinctions were inevitably made between the students of noble and the students of lesser birth. Gentlemen and peers, for example, were not required to wear the same "sober robes" (*TS* I.ii.131) as the other undergraduates, and unlike the poor scholars, they did not have to wait at table in the dining hall to earn their keep. Chief among the complaints about them was that they thought they could get away with any behavior, no matter how outrageous or disruptive. Harrison, typical of the critics, snorts that, "for excuse, when they are charged with breach of all good order, [they] think it sufficient to say that they are gentlemen, which grieveth many not a little." *See also* Books; Law; Literacy; Music; Travel; Writing.

Entertainment

The absence of mass media did not prevent Shakespeare's contemporaries from enjoying themselves. To some extent, their pastimes revolved around work and the cycle of seasons, but they also played games, invented stories, danced, played music, watched and listened to professional performers, went to plays (*JC* I.ii.203–4), celebrated rites of passage, and observed blood sports. Some forms of entertainment were sporadic, while others were enjoyed at regular intervals. Some took place in the home, others at a special location. Some had a paying audience; most were free of charge.

The professional entertainers included jugglers (*CE* I.ii.98; *2H4* II.iv.132–33; *MND* III.ii.282; *T&C* V.ii.24), masquers, actors, fortunetellers (*CE* V.i.239–40), and jesters, or fools (*CE* V.i.175; *MAAN* II.i.132–33; *AYLI* ch.; *TN* ch.; *Lear* I.iii.1–2; *Ham* V.i.179), but not all of these performed in a theater. There were very few permanent venues for paid entertainment. The masquers, the hired musicians or minstrels (*MAAN* V.i.129–30), the acrobats (*LLL* III.i.187), and the fools did their work in the homes of their wealthy patrons. The fools, in particular, were personal servants, paid and housed by a single employer; they entertained by poking fun at those present, by dressing in ridiculous outfits of motley (*MND* IV.i.210; *AYLI* II.vii.13, 42–43, V.iv.41; *TN* I.v.57; *Lear*

I.iv.148), or many-colored patches, and by engaging in tumbling or other physical antics. Their place of business was thus wherever the employer happened to be.

Others, such as itinerant animal trainers and exhibitors, did much of their business at fairs and in taverns and inns. These showmen displayed giants, dwarfs, rare animals, the preserved bodies of people from faraway places (*Mac* V.viii.25–27; *Temp* II.ii.33; *H8* V.iv.32–34), and monkeys, dogs, and horses that could perform a series of tricks (*TNK* V.ii.44–66; *LLL* I.ii.53; *WT* IV.iii.96). Puppeteers (*2GV* II.i.97; *MND* III.ii.288–91; *A&C* V.ii.208), displaying a primitive "motion" (*WT* IV.iii.97–98) or show of a well-known story, might work in the same sorts of places. Prince Lewis of Württemberg, visiting England in 1610, saw at least two exhibitions that might have traveled: one of monkeys that rode on horses, and another of "virginals which played of themselves."

A jester, from *Panoplia*, illustrated by Jost Amman. Reproduced from the Collections of the Library of Congress.

Some forms of entertainment were staged in streets or other public places as part of the pageantry of unique occasions, such as military victories or visits from foreign dignitaries (*LLL* IV.iii.369–77). Processions, fireworks (*LLL* V.i.109), jousts, or even mock sea battles were incorporated into such events. Other revels came around once a year, such as the Christmas festivities presided over by a facetious "Lord of Misrule," the traditional Shrove Tuesday football games, the Midsummer Day's morris dances and bonfires, and the church ales and wakes. The ales were held once a year to benefit the parish church. Locally brewed ale was sold, and the proceeds were used to repair church buildings and to buy books, cups, surplices, and other equipment. Similar parties, at which guests purchased ale, were held to benefit new brides or families in financial trouble, but these were not regularly recurring events. Church wakes (*WT* IV.iii.102) were festivals held once a year, usually on the local saint's day, with feasting, dancing, sports, and a good deal of informal courtship and flirtation.

Like juggling and puppet shows, contests involving animals could be traveling exhibitions that moved from town to town and from fair to fair;

unlike the former, however, they also had permanent arenas. Cockfighting (*A&C* II.iii.35–36; *Cym* II.i.22–25) was the pitting of roosters against each other in a ring, with the owners and spectators gambling on the outcome and shouting encouragement until one of the roosters was dead. The birds were trained by sparring with their spurs padded, and were fed white bread and other treats. Before a match, they were sweated by being covered in hay or straw and sometimes placed near a fire. The sport was a favorite pastime of schoolboys, who were given money to buy cocks; the schoolmasters kept the losing birds as a perquisite. In London, cockfighting was terrifically popular, and cockpits (*H5* I.Cho.11) were built in several places, including the future site of the Drury Lane Theater. Phillip Stubbes spoke in *The Anatomie of Abuses* of specially erected cockpits with "flags & ensignes hanged out" to advertise the fights.

Bearbaiting and bullbaiting pitted dogs against large, fierce animals. Bearbaiting (*MWW* I.i.274–86; *WT* IV.iii.103; *3H6* II.i.15–17), which Stubbes called "a filthie, stinking and lothsome game," began with the bearward (*2H6* V.i.149, 210; *TS* Ind.ii.20; *MAAN* II.i.37–38), or bear-keeper, fixing the bear by a chain to a stake in the ground (*Mac* V.vii.1–2; *TNK* III.i.68–69; *2H6* V.i.144–153, 208–10; *TN* III.i.120–22). A bear attached to a stake in this way was said to be "lugged" (*Lear* IV.ii.43; *1H4* I.ii.74). A number of dogs, usually four to six mastiffs, were let loose against the bear, and substitutes were released as necessary to replace any dogs grievously wounded by their prey. When the bear was subdued by the dogs or pronounced undefeatable, the match ended, and a new bear was produced. The old bear was led out of the ring to be nursed back to health, if possible, by the bearward. Particularly fierce bears and valiant dogs were much admired by the public, and the bears George Stone, Harry Hunks, Tom of Lincoln, Sackerson (*MWW* I.i.282), and Blind Robin, among others, became minor celebrities. Bulls could be just as deadly to their attackers as bears, for they often caught the dogs on their horns and flung them high into the air. In 1592, the Duke of Württemberg's secretary noted the persistence of the dogs, who would latch on so tightly "that one is obliged to pull them back by the tails, and force open their jaws." The cries of the spectators at such an event are captured by Shakespeare in *Troilus and Cressida*:

Now, bull! Now, dog! 'Loo, Paris, 'loo! Now, my double-horned Spartan! 'Loo, Paris, 'loo! The bull has the game; 'ware horns, ho! (V.vii.10–12)

The use of the word "Paris" is connected to the Southwark bearbaiting and bullbaiting arenas, collectively known as Paris Garden. The first ring, located near the eventual site of the Globe, was built in the reign of Henry VIII, and when a newer ring was added in 1570, the new arena was devoted to bullbaiting while the older one remained in use for bears.

However, not all forms of recreation required paid admission. Most people amused themselves at home with whatever materials were available. They sang songs while working, played games and sports, told stories by the fire on long winter nights (*R2* V.i.40–42; *WT* II.i.25–26; *Mac* III.iv.63–66), and asked each other riddles (*Lear* V.i.37; *Per* I.i.65–72; *AW* I.iii.218; *Ham* V.i.41–59; *LLL* IV.ii.35–41). The queen's ladies in *Richard II* offer a fairly standard catalog of such activities when they suggest bowls, dancing, storytelling, and singing as possible diversions for their mistress (III.iv.10–19). *See also* Dance; Games; Holidays; Jousting; Masque; Music; Theater.

Etiquette

In a society of strict class distinctions, small and sometimes inescapable social groups, and a growing tendency for offended gentlemen to settle their quarrels by dueling, etiquette was necessary to reinforce status, prevent misunderstandings, and soothe wounded feelings. Conduct books (*AYLI* V.iv.90–91) offered advice about the proper behavior in different settings, from making salutations and farewells in a suitably respectful way to conversing on appropriate subjects. Table manners, principles of basic hygiene, and even the correct way to walk or sit were discussed. The result of this instruction, according to a Dutch cousin of the Flemish cartographer Abraham Ortelius, was that the English were "full of courtly and affected manners and words, which they take for gentility, civility, and wisdom." Shakespeare might have agreed, at least in part, for he creates many opportunities to criticize.

Greetings took place either between equals or between an inferior and a superior. Two friends meeting on the street might embrace or, more commonly, remove and replace their hats at the same time. The timing was crucial, as we shall soon see. If one were being welcomed into the other's home, the guest would be expected to kiss the hostess and her daughters (*TS* IV.i.141; *T&C* IV.v.19–52) and to take their arms, perhaps to walk them in to dinner. Samuel Kiechel of Ulm, visiting England in 1585, said that this kissing was "the custome of the country, and if any one does not do so, it is regarded and imputed as ignorance and ill-breeding on his part." Shaking hands, which in later centuries would become the dominant mode of greeting between men, was in this period restricted chiefly to a ritual performed after the making of an agreement.

Greetings between people of different social rank varied according to the degree of difference, but in all cases it was the inferior's responsibility to make a salute first. The simplest gesture was to doff the cap or hat (*H5* IV.v.15; *Cor* III.ii.10–11; *Oth* I.i.9; *R2* I.iv.31, V.ii.19–20), ideally by holding the brim or band in the fingers of the right hand and sweeping it downward against the thigh so that the inside did not show. Contempt or disrespect could be shown by abbreviating the gesture (*Tim* II.ii.219).

Some sort of verbal greeting was also made, with the inferior using the superior's proper title, and the superior perhaps addressing the inferior as "sirrah" or "fellow." A polite greeting would be "God-den" or "Good den" (contractions of "God give you a good evening"—see *MAAN* V.i.46; *R&J* III.i.39), "Good day," "God ye good morrow" (*R&J* II.iv.114), or "God-amercy" ("God have mercy on you"—see *John* I.i.185).

Additional respect could be shown by adding a bow, varying from a simple inclination of the head (*Tim* II.ii.219) to a low *congé* (*H8* IV.ii.82 s.d.) or "courtesy" (*2H4* II.i.124; *R&J* I.iv.72; *MND* V.i.21; *TN* II.v.59; *AW* V.iii.323). The deeper forms of the bow were made by moving the left leg (since the right was generally steadier—see *TS* IV.i.83–84, *AW* II.ii.10); the leg moved backward in the late sixteenth century, forward by late in the seventeenth. In either case, the knee was then bent (*3H6* III.ii.57) and the head lowered (*MV* I.iii.120–21; *JC* III.i.43). The person bowing had to be mindful of the distance between himself and his acquaintance, for if they were too close, he might strike the other person in the chin when lifting his head. The salute ended when the bow was complete and the social superior bade the inferior to "be covered" (*AYLI* V.i.17–18), that is, to put his hat on again. However, in many cases of extreme difference in rank, the cap was to be removed again by way of humble acknowledgment if the superior complimented or paid special attention to the inferior, and the inferior was to take every opportunity to repeat his interlocutor's title, such as "your honor" or "your worship." He should speak when spoken to and never interrupt or ask pointed questions. If he had to ask questions, he was to do so in a hypothetical way and to apologize for his presumption. The degree of fawning that could be observed in some exchanges is evident in Shallow's shameless toadying (*2H4* III.ii). Courtiers tended to add the additional ceremony of kissing their hands (*2H6* IV.i.53; *TS* IV.i.85; *MAAN* IV.i.331; *TN* III.iv.33–34; *AW* II.ii.10; *AYLI* III.ii.44–49, *Oth* II.i.169–75) as they made their bows, although this custom was much ridiculed by ordinary Englishmen.

Women also made a dipping motion of the body in greeting, though they did not take a step in their courtesy, or curtsy (*LLL* V.ii.222; *MAAN* II.i.51, 53; *TNK* V.i.173 s.d.). Instead, they kept their legs together and bent both knees, the degree of the bend being again dependent on the difference in station between greeter and greeted. In cases of extreme difference, the inferior might make a token movement as if to kiss the other's knee, and in any case she would wait, bent-kneed and eyes downcast, until her superior indicated that she should rise. If the difference was not too great between them, the lady greeted would return the courtesy, either by inclining her head or by making a curtsy in response.

Farewells were made in much the same way as greetings. When groups of ladies paid visits to another, for example, to a new bride, a departing guest would curtsy to the assemblage upon leaving. If she were of high rank, she would receive a curtsy in response from all present, and the hostess would walk her to the door. If she were of equal or lesser rank, she would receive a curtsy only from the hostess, who would kiss her own hand, briefly touch the guest's, and take her seat again. A polite departure also usually included some verbal component, such as "Fare ye well" (*H5* V.i.80) or "God buy you" ("God be with you," the origin of the phrase "good-bye"—see *TN* IV.ii.102).

Walking or seating arrangements also reflected rank (*Mac* III.iv.1). In general, superiors or guests were placed to the right, inferiors or hosts to the left. The "top" of the dinner table, taken by the master of the house or a very exalted guest, was flanked on right and left by the most distinguished people present, though the seat to the host's right was more prestigious than that to the left. The middle of the table was occupied by a saltcellar, and it was a sign of one's high rank to be seated above the salt (*Tim* III.vi.66–70). Being seated below the salt was less honorable, though it was always better than being seated below the main table with servants and other inferiors. When walking, the person of highest rank occupied the right hand, the middle if more than two were present, and the place closest to the wall if the party was in the street. In bedchambers, the bed, or the point farthest from the door, was the "top" of the room, and people positioned themselves accordingly, right or left, top or bottom, making exceptions in the cases of comfortable chairs or positions convenient to the fire.

At the table, it was important to behave in a way that did not offend the other diners. One should not gape, pick the teeth with nails or knife, slouch, put one's elbows on the table, or shift the buttocks as if passing gas. The knife should be used whenever appropriate and, in upper-class homes, the newfangled forks, should be used if available. If one were eating with the hands, as was often the case, only the first two fingers and thumb of the left hand should be employed, and the fingers should be wiped on a napkin rather than cleaned on the clothing or licked. The mouth should be wiped before taking a drink, especially at meals or celebrations where participants shared a communal cup. Eating should be done quietly, with no gnawing of bones or licking of dishes. Carving of meat was done sometimes by servants, sometimes as a graceful compliment paid by the host to his guests; offering to carve for someone else was a gesture fraught with peril, for it might be taken as an admission of one's own servile inferiority or as a usurpation of the host's prerogative. The host's other privileges included being offered water at the table to wash his hands before and after the meal, opening his napkin before the other diners, and being presented with food before anyone else.

It was important for the host and hostess (*Mac* III.iv.4–7) to be assiduous in seeing to their guests' comfort. Perdita is chided by her adoptive father for being too reserved in executing her duties as hostess and compared gently but unfavorably to his late wife, who knew how to run a festival:

> This day, she was both pantler, butler, cook;
> Both dame and servant; welcomed all, served all;
> Would sing her song, and dance her turn; now here
> At upper end o' th' table, now i' th' middle;
> On his shoulder, and his; her face o' fire
> With labor and the thing she took to quench it,
> She would to each one sip. You are retired,
> As if you were a feasted one, and not
> The hostess of the meeting. (*WT* IV.iv.56–64)

Most important, then as now, was to make each guest feel especially welcome. Shakespeare writes disparagingly of the "fashionable host" who neglects one guest while favoring another. This bad example "slightly shakes his parting guest by the hand, / And with his arms outstretched, as he would fly, / Grasps in the comer" (*T&C* III.iii.166–68). A good host, in contrast, would speak directly to each guest in turn, perhaps adding the formula "Proface," which meant, "May it do you good," and was often spoken before the beginning of a meal (*2H4* V.iii.28).

In general, it was advised to be discreet about bodily functions, though the prohibitions offered by conduct book writers—such as not licking the dishes—tell us a great deal about the kinds of behavior widespread enough to generate disapproving commentary. Therefore, when the authors advise against blowing the nose loudly, or in the sleeve rather than a handkerchief, we may be reasonably sure that many people committed precisely these errors. We may apply the same standard to the rules against blushing, puffing out the cheeks, laughing too much, scratching the head and body in public, strutting, shuffling, urinating or passing gas in public, spitting ostentatiously, burping, yawning in the presence of superiors (*Cor* III.ii.11), exposing the upper thighs when seated, coughing in other people's faces, and eating with dirty hands. Children, who were virtually everyone's inferiors, were specifically admonished to be meek, silent, and obsequious. They were not to grimace, laugh, stick out their tongues, frown, or speak without being bidden. If possible, they were to doff their caps and give way to adults, even complete strangers, on the streets, advice that must have kept any child who observed it in a constant state of doffing, ducking, and dodging.

Other rules of good behavior concerned everything from proper posture when walking or sitting to the composition of letters. A lady or gentleman should sit with feet together on the ground; a lady was to make sure that her dress hem touched the floor, and a gentleman was to make sure that his legs were neither crossed nor spread wide. In an armchair, the left arm was draped along one chair arm, with the right elbow propped on the other and the right hand preferably holding some little accessory or bauble. If the chair had no arms, then ladies were to keep their hands folded in their laps. There was a general prejudice against the adoption of foreign modes of walking, talking, and bowing, and a specific embrace of such habits among courtiers (*LLL* I.ii.61–63; *MV* I.ii.66–74; *R&J* II.iv.29–36; *TNK* I.ii.55–58; *1H4* I.iii.35–63; *MWW* III.iii.69–71). Over time, many of these habits were absorbed into general practice, just as the southern English dialect and accent gradually became acknowledged as the proper way to speak, even by people in other parts of the country.

In such a context, when inferiors signed their letters "your very humble and obliged [or obedient] servant," and even superiors might end with "your humble and affectionate servant," deliberate rudeness was risky and even shocking. Among gentlemen, particularly if coupled with a blow or an accusation of lying, it could be cause for a duel. Among the humbler sort of people, who were presumed to have no honor to maintain, outright rudeness was safer, and therefore probably much more common. Putting the thumb between the index and middle finger was a contemptuous and obscene gesture, much as raising the middle finger is today. A similar gesture was "biting" the thumb, or bringing the thumbnail between the teeth and popping it out again against the upper teeth so that it made a clicking sound. Either gesture could be called the "fico" or "fig" (*2H4* V.iii.122; *H5* III.vi.57, 59, IV.i.60). *See also* Dance; Duel.

Eunuch

Eunuchs (*TA* II.iii.128; *TN* I.ii.56) were castrated boys or men, found in Shakespeare's day mostly in various parts of Asia and associated with exotic foreign barbarity. Though there were eunuchs at mosques to tend to visiting women and in the Sistine Chapel choir, they were associated in the popular imagination mainly with the Ottoman (Turkish) sultan and his harem.

Islam, ironically, forbade castration, so the palace eunuchs began as foreign slaves—white boys from Circassia, Georgia, or Armenia, and black ones from Egypt, Abyssinia, or Sudan. The African eunuchs were more common. Purchased from slave traders, they were castrated in Egypt by non-Muslims according to one of three methods: cutting off the penis and leaving the testicles intact, cutting off both the penis and testicles and cauterizing the wound, or crushing or severing the testicles only. They were then buried up to their necks in sand, in the belief that this would facilitate healing. Mortality was high, increasing with the eunuch's age.

The by-products of castration were relative hairlessness, a high voice, flabbiness, obesity, and urinary dysfunction. Those who had had their penises removed usually required a tube to be inserted into the urethra in order to urinate; some carried quills for the purpose tucked into their turbans. The castration inhibited sex and made the eunuchs' bodies more feminine. It did not, however, necessarily remove the capacity for, desire for, or enjoyment of sex. Eunuchs still could (and did) perform oral sex; those with intact penises, even without testicles, were capable of erections, and some had affairs with the harem women or even left the harem and took wives.

Boys who entered the sultan's service became apprentices and were disciplined by being bound and having their feet beaten with rods. They were paid well and given silk robes and various sorts of presents, according to a witness in 1608. They slept in dormitories and at the end of their apprenticeship were assigned to the care of a particular harem woman or royal child (*LLL* III.i.198). They were increasingly powerful from the second half of the sixteenth century until well into the eighteenth, though Shakespeare uses them as a metaphor for weak government (*2H6* IV.ii.165). Frequently ambitious and corrupt, they aspired to be *kizlar agasi*, "master of the girls," chief of the harem eunuchs (who were all African; white eunuchs served in the men's quarters). The *kizlar agasi* had free access to the sultan and the *valide sultana* (the sultan's mother), and he frequently carried messages between them and between the sultan and the grand vizier. His power approached that of the vizier, and he frequently took bribes.

Shakespeare recognizes the eunuch as a Turkish entity (*AW* II.iii.88–89), but his most famous eunuch does not serve the sultan at all. This is Mardian, Cleopatra's eunuch, who appears throughout *Antony and Cleopatra* as a character.

Execution

There were numerous capital crimes in Shakespeare's England and four principal methods of execution (*CE* V.i., 120–21, 127; *2H6* III.i.58–59; *R2* III.i.28–35; *JC* IV.iii.170–72). The most commonly used, by far, was hanging, for this was the manner of executing almost all commoners who were found guilty of capital felonies such as theft (*1H4* I.ii.61, 65–67, II.i.64–70, II.iv.328; *AYLI* III.ii.327–29) and murder (*LLL* V.ii.679–80; *2H4* V.iv.1–2). Its dominance can be judged by the fact that though Shakespeare's characters are disproportionately noble, the executions in which method is mentioned are disproportionately hangings (*2H6* I.iii.199, 220, II.iii.5–8; *TS* I.ii.196; *TA* IV.iii.81–83, IV.iv.45, 47–48, V.i.47–53, 145–51; *2GV* II.v.3–4; *R&J* III.i.58; *John* IV.ii.147–57; *WT* IV.iv.459–61). Samuel Kiechel of Ulm described the procedure in 1585:

> For hanging, the English have no regular executioner; they take for this business a butcher, and whoever is called upon is obliged to perform it. The

criminal, seated in the cart, has one end of a rope tied round his neck, and the other is fastened to the gallows; the cart then moves on, and the condemned wretch is left hanging; friends and acquaintances pull at his legs, in order that he may be strangled the sooner.

Kiechel might also have added that after the cart (*1H4* II.iv.501) and rope had done their work, the hangman was paid and entitled to the dead man's clothes (*1H4* I.ii.72–73; *Cor* I.v.6–7) as a perquisite.

The gallows (*2H6* IV.ii.122; *LLL* IV.iii.51, V.ii.12; *1H4* I.ii.39, 58) was later usually triangular in form, though in Shakespeare's day it appears to have been composed of two upright beams topped by a third; hence its nickname "the two-legged mare." On this mare (*2H4* II.i.77) the unfortunate criminals rode, never to dismount alive. The gibbet (*MWW* II.ii.16; *Cym* V.iv.168–69) was a slightly different contraption, having only one upright and a projecting arm, and looking more like the rough figure drawn for the game of Hangman than the traditional gallows. Bodies of executed felons were sometimes left on the gibbet as a warning to passersby (*1H4* IV.ii.36–38); the

A man riding the "two-legged mare," in a detail from a *Roxburghe Ballads* woodcut. Reproduced from *Shakespeare's England*.

diplay of bodies or body parts was, as we shall see, a popular form of deterrent. Gallows and gibbet were so much in use that references to hemp, the substance of which rope was made, were widely understood to be allusions to hanging (*2H6* IV.vii.91; *TS* V.i.45). The hangman's rope was also sometimes called the cord (*1H4* I.iii.164; *H5* III.vi.40–48; *Cym* V.iv.136–37) or the halter (*MV* II.ii.105, IV.i.378).

One of the privileges of nobility was the exemption from the indecency of hanging, with its slow suffocation and its evacuation of the bowels before a mob. Aristocrats merited the quicker death afforded by beheading (*1H6* I.iii.87–88; *2H6* II.iv.49, IV.vii.91–92, 110–113; *3H6* II.i.197, IV.v.26; *R3* III.i.193, III.ii.43, 90, III.iii.38, 75–77)—the fate to which Elizabeth I's mother and one of her stepmothers had gone, and the fate to which Elizabeth herself had sentenced Mary Queen of Scots. A noble condemned to be beheaded, usually for the crime of treason or perceived treason (*2H4* IV.ii.122–23; *R2* III.iii.13–14), made confession (*MM*

II.i.33–36) and was led to a platform called a scaffold (*R3* IV.iv.240). There he or she was allowed to make a brief statement. It was usually an assertion of innocence or admission of guilt, followed by a prayer or statement of faith and perhaps an avowal of loyalty to the king or queen. It was also customary for the executioner to beg pardon for taking a life, and for the prisoner to grant forgiveness in advance (*AYLI* III.v.3–6). Then the condemned laid his or her head on a large block (*MM* II.iv.179–80, IV.iii.37; *TNK* V.iv.38 s.d.; *R3* V.i.28) of wood, moving or removing any clothing or hair that might interfere with the headsman's work (*MM* IV.ii.179–81). An ax (*R&J* III.iii.22–23; *Ham* IV.v.217) was the usual implement, although some executioners used swords. While a good executioner could sever the head in one blow, some took two strokes or even several to complete the task. Afterward, the head was displayed to the assembled witnesses (*R3* III.v.21 s.d.), and, in most cases, the body was buried. The heads of traitors, however, were usually retained and hung on spikes above the Southwark entrance to London Bridge, where they served as a grim monument to royal power. Shakespeare, following this tradition, often uses the display of a severed head as a dramatic device (*2H6* IV.vii.96–97, 113, 131–38, IV.x.84–85, V.i.135; *3H6* I.i.17 s.d., I.iv.179–80, II.vi.51–54, 84–85).

The other two methods of execution were burning at the stake (*1H6* V.iii.44, V.iv; *2H6* II.iii.5–8; *MAAN* I.i.226–29), reserved for witches, heretics, and wives who poisoned their husbands; and drawing and quartering (*1H6* IV.ii.11; *MAAN* III.ii.20–26; *John* II.i.504–9), used for commoners found guilty of treason. Prisoners who were drawn and quartered were first hanged until nearly dead, then cut down and attached by each leg and arm to a different horse, each of which pulled in a different direction, pulling the body into four "quarters." Christopher Norton and his uncle were executed in this manner in 1570. The uncle went first, and then Norton,

> being hanged a little while, and then cut down, the butcher opened him, and as he took out his bowels, he cried, and said, "Oh Lord, Lord, have mercy upon me" and so yielded up the ghost. Then being likewise quartered, as the other was, and their bowels burned, . . . their quarters were put into a basket, . . . and so carried to Newgate. (from a Contempoary Account)

The quarters, "parboiled" for the purpose of preservation, were then mounted on stakes at London Bridge.

All the methods of execution sound horrific, and indeed they were, but the horrors were an accustomed sight. Hangings were attended by large crowds whose mood incorporated equal parts of holiday cheer and morbid curiosity. Hanging was so ubiquitous in Renaissance life that a traditional punishment for wolves and dogs who attacked people was trial and hanging (*2GV* IV.iv.15, 21–22). England had no wolves, but the trial, sentencing, and execution of dogs still happened from time to time. Executions of humans were unusual enough for a special mythology to arise from them, yet common enough to sustain the mythology, in which things associated with the hanging of a murderer were held to have magical properties (*Mac* IV.i.65–66).

Samuel Kiechel's observations aside, England's executioners (*2H6* III.ii.217; *3H6* V.v.67, V.vi.30, 33; *R3* I.ii.119, 185, I.iii.338; *AW* IV.iii.313; *MM* IV.iii.26; *TNK* V.iv. ch.; *John* IV.i.ch.) appear to have been professionals, though they were probably not employed full-time in this trade and may, in many cases, have been butchers the rest of the time. Those who performed beheadings were supposed to be experts, and an especially gifted practitioner might be granted to the condemned as a final gesture of mercy. Hangmen, to judge from Shakespeare's works, were also trained in their work. To "Serve by indenture to the common hangman" (*Per* IV.vi.180) is adjudged superior to pimping, which implies that hangmen took apprentices, and indeed, we see a facetious version of just such an apprenticeship in *Measure for Measure* (IV.ii). In this scene, the "mystery," or compilation of trade secrets, of hanging is likened to that of pandering, and Pompey is admitted into the trade, which in this case appears to encompass both hanging and beheading skills. Elsewhere, the executioner is described as one "Whose heart th' accustomed sight of death makes hard" (*AYLI* III.v.4), implying that he had had quite a bit of practical experience.

Shakespeare appears to have been uncertain of the methods of execution used in other times and places. He seldom specifies a method of execution, for example, in the Greek or Roman plays. (An exception is the execution by half-burial in the earth and starvation in *TA* V.iii.179–83). On the subject of contemporary execution, however, he offers plenty of details, from the issuing of the warrant (*MM* IV.ii.155) and the building of the gibbet (*TA* IV.iii.81–83; *Ham* V.i.43) to the confession of the prisoner and the pardon and payment of the hangman.

He even includes the two methods by which a condemned prisoner could escape execution—at least temporarily. One of these was "benefit of clergy," a privilege descended from the historical separation of church and common law. In the Middle Ages, priests, monks, friars, and so forth could be tried and sentenced only by the church, and they could evade execution by secular justice simply by proving their membership in the clergy. At the time, when few other than the clergy were trained to read, they could do so by proving their literacy. By Shakespeare's time, literacy itself, rather than clerical status, was sufficient as an exemption from certain types of death sentences. Often, the benefit applied only to a first offense, and the prisoner would be branded as a sign that he had used up his one reprieve, so that if he committed the same crime in a different jurisdiction, the justices there would have license to execute him. Another type of reprieve applied only to women. If a woman could prove that she was pregnant, she received a stay of execution until after the baby was born. Sometimes a pardon also followed (*Temp* I.ii.267–70), but sometimes it did not, and the new mother was hauled to the scaffold as soon as she had recovered from the delivery.

Almost all of Shakespeare's references to execution refers to methods still in use in his day. There is, however, a notable exception. In *Coriolanus* he mentions "the steep Tarpeian death" (III.iii.88), a specific type of execution used in ancient Rome. It was the hurling of convicted traitors and murderers, when they did not merit the gentler punishment of exile, from a nearby cliff called the Tarpeian Rock. *See also* Law; Prison.

Fabric

If England was known for any one commodity throughout Europe, that commodity was fabric. In the 1580s, William Harrison bragged in his *Description of England*, of its exports of broadcloth, kersey, cotton, frieze, wool, baize, and mockado. Some of these types of cloth sound familiar today, but others sound strange, even fictional. It would be a brave person indeed who ventured into a fabric store today asking for "mockado" or "kersey."

Yet all these fabrics, and many others, were produced from just five raw materials: wool, cotton, hemp, silk, and flax (which yielded linen). Hemp was reserved for the roughest, cheapest, coarsest material, like sackcloth (*Per* IV.iv.29) and the homespun garments of peasants (*MND* III.i.76). Silk (*MND* V.i.340; *Lear* III.iv.94, 102–3; *Cym* III.iii.24; *WT* IV.iv.322; *Cor* I.ix.45) was, with one exception, the most expensive material, especially when made into velvet (*1H4* II.ii.2, III.i.254; *AW* IV.v.94–97; *MM* I.ii.30–35; *WT* IV.iii.13–14; *LC* 94) for use in clothing, cushions, book covers, bed hangings, and other items. Still more expensive was cloth of gold, which was woven of a silk weft and a gold warp (*A&C* II.ii.201; *MWW* II.ii.65); sometimes the term was used to refer to cloth woven entirely of gold threads, with the silk-and-gold combination called tinsel instead. Less costly varieties of silk included sarcenet, which was thin, soft, and somewhat shiny (*1H4* III.i.249; *T&C* V.i.31–36); damask; satin, which was used for bed hangings, counterpanes, cushions, cloaks, and the baggy hose called slops (*2H4* I.ii.29–30; *MM* IV.iii.10–11); and taffeta (*AW* II.ii.23, IV.v.2; *1H4* I.ii.10; *TN* II.iv.74–75), a showy fabric that Shakespeare represents in the cited examples as "flame-colored," "snipped" (slashed), and "changeable" (varying in color with the angle of the light). Taffeta could be one color, changeable, or striped; sometimes it was tufted. Cypress (*WT* IV.iv.220; *TN* III.i.123) was a thin, gauzelike silk that, when dyed black, was associated with mourning clothes both for its color and for its name; the cypress tree was often planted in graveyards. As with many of the fabrics that follow, silk had a composite form, "satin of bridges [Bruges]," which was less expensive than regular satin because it was made of a silk warp and a cheaper linen weft (or "woof"—see *T&C* V.ii.150). It apparently would not do for the exterior of fine clothes or furnishings but was adequate for linings.

Cotton fabrics were somewhat unusual, for most ordinary clothing, and even some very fine clothing, was made of linen or wool. Wool took the forms of felt (*Lear* IV.vi.185), frieze (*TNK* III.v.8; *Oth* II.i.123–25), stuff (worsted, made of combed, long-staple wool), woolens (made of carded, short-staple wool), and kersey (*MM* I.ii.34; *LLL* V.ii.414), which were coarse fabrics. Wool, especially as frieze and the flannel-like kersey, was associated with the russet-colored clothes of farmers (*Cor* III.ii.9). Serge (*2H6* V.vii.26) was not cheap but was often worn by working people because it was so durable; a fabric called say was similar and might be a blend of wool and silk. The coarse linsey-woolsey was, as its name suggests, compounded of linen and wool (*AW* IV.i.12). Penistone was a coarse wool fabric from Yorkshire that was occasionally napped and felted; mockado was a cheaper woolen with a short pile. Various rough, sometimes shaggy fabrics called ruggs, blankets, and fledges were used in large pieces as bed blankets, and the ruggs and fledges were occasionally used on the floor as well.

Some wool was put to loftier uses. It could be employed, for example, in the making of carpets, tapestries, and velvet; Angora wool, in combination with other materials, was used to make the expensive ribbed fabric called camlet (*H8* V.iv.88). But wool velvet never fetched as high a price as silk velvet, and silk tapestries likewise were more expensive than the wool variety, which were all too susceptible to moths. Nevertheless, Bess of Hardwick, who was a countess and loved fine furnishings, had bed hangings of "bay" (baize, a napped fabric woven of worsted and woolen, the best of which was made in Colchester) and "scarlet," the one wool fabric that was typically more expensive than silk velvet. Scarlet was usually, but not always, dyed the color that gave it its name.

Wool was England's most prized commodity, but it was unsuitable for certain kinds of clothing and furnishings, notably undergarments and table coverings. For items such as shirts, smocks, napkins, tablecloths, pillowcases, and sheets, therefore, people used linen, and the word "linen" eventually became a synonym for such goods (*2H4* II.iv.125, V.i.35–36; *MND* IV.ii.38). It came in several grades of quality. On the rougher, cheaper end were buckram (*1H4* I.ii.177; *2H6* IV.vii.26), lockram (*Cor* II.i.211–12), and dowlas. Holland (*1H4* III.iii.76) and

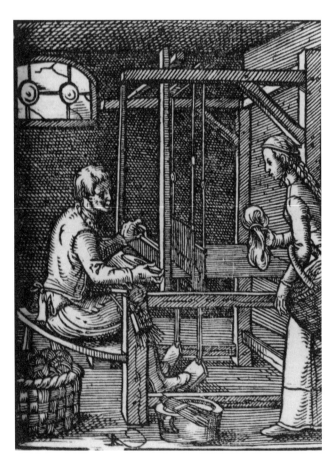

A weaver, from *Panoplia* illustrated by Jost Amman. Reproduced from the Collections of the Library of Congress.

cambric (*WT* IV.iv.207; *Cor* I.iii.85) were better, and lawn (*WT* IV.iv.207; 219; *Oth* IV.iii.77) was the finest of all, so soft and white that it was often almost transparent. Fustian, which had a linen warp and a cotton weft, was made in England but could also be imported; it took its name from Fustat, Egypt, which was its original port of shipment. It was a versatile fabric, used for clothing, quilt linings, and blankets which were called, unimaginatively, "fustians."

Fabrics were often made at home by the women of the family, but there were many professional manufacturers of cloth as well. The carders (*H8* I.ii.33) or combers aligned the wool to prepare it for spinning, using toothed tools made by a cardmaker (*TS* Ind.ii.19). Then spinsters (*H8* I.ii.33; *TN* II.iv.43) spun it into thread or yarn, weavers (*2H6* IV.ii.ch.; *1H4* II.iv.133–35; *TN* II.iii.59; *MWW* V.i.22–23) wove it or knitters (*TN* II.iv.43) knitted it into fabric, fullers (*H8* I.ii.33) beat the fabric to clean it, and dyers gave it color. Nick Bottom, who is given the head of an ass in *A Midsummer Night's Dream*, is a weaver by trade, and his name comes from the tool used to wind the yarn. *See also* Clothing.

Fairs

See Market and Fairs.

Fairy

Belief in sprites (*CE* II.ii.191–93), elves (*R3* I.iii.227; *Mac* IV.i.42), and fairies (*CE* IV.ii.35) was widespread, so much so that a Fulham couple, John and Alice West, ran a temporarily successful con game in the early seventeenth century based on their claim that they knew the king and queen of the fairies. Charms and spells were devised to enlist the aid of the fairies in locating lost items or buried treasure, and many a housewife set out a bowl of curds as payment to Robin Goodfellow, or Puck, for his nighttime help with the housework. Reginald Scot, in his *Discoverie of Witchcraft*, wrote of the common belief in such creatures, perpetuated by nursemaids, who told their charges tales of

> bull-beggars, spirits, witches, urchens, elves, hags, fairies, satyrs, pans, sylens, Kit with the cansticke, tritons, centaurs, dwarfes, giants, imps, calcars, conjurors, nymphs, changling, *Incubus*, ROBIN GOOD-FELLOW, the spoorne, the mare, the man in the oke, the hell wain, the fier drake, the puckle, Tom Thombe, Hob gobblin, Tom Tumbler, boneless, and such other bugs, that we are afraid of our owne shadowes.

He noted the payment to Robin Goodfellow of milk or white bread, in exchange for which he was supposed to sweep the floors or grind mustard-seed or malt. The Puck (or "puckle") was, however, deeply offended by gifts of clothes, which he took as a slight on his nakedness, and if such an insult was offered, or his gifts of food were suspended, he would take out his anger by bringing the household bad luck, burned food, and failures in the making of cheese, butter, and ale. The helpfulness and the capricious cruelty of Puck are both described by Shakespeare in *A Midsummer Night's Dream* (II.i.32–57, III.ii.6–34, 120–21, V.i.386–89). His role as "Kit with the can[dle]sticke," better known as Will-o-the-wisp, ignis fatuus (fool's fire—see *1H4* III.iii.41–42), or Jack-a-lantern, is to lead travelers astray with false lights (*MND* III.i.105–10).

Folk beliefs about fairies varied from place to place, but some aspects of the myth were reasonably constant. Fairies were believed, first and foremost, to have magical powers (*A&C* IV.viii.12). Oberon's love potion and its antidote are consistent with this belief, as is Puck's ability to give Bottom the head of an ass. Accordingly, they could offer incredible gifts to the mortals they favored (*Lear* IV.vi.29–30) and could punish transgressors with equal fervor. They held revels, usually at night (*Cym* II.ii.9–10), and usually on hilltops, leaving rings of mushrooms or bare earth in the grass as evidence of their dances (*Temp* V.i.37–40; *MWW* IV.iv.49–51). They were ruled by a king, a queen (*R&J* I.iv.53–95), or both, who, like other fairies, might take a mortal lover, often to the lover's detriment (*MND* II.i.68–80). They could be, like Puck, helpful or, like Hobgoblin (another of Puck's incarnations—see *MWW* V.v.43; *MND* II.i.40), mischievous. Their powers, for good or evil, were thought to be especially strong on Fridays, Lady Day (the Annunciation), Lammas (August 1), Christmas, Midsummer Night, and any night between midnight and one o'clock (*MWW* IV.iv.58, V.v.76).

Usually perceived as small, sometimes as human-sized, fairies had a world of their own, sometimes identified with the land of the dead, and it was dangerous to partake of anything from this world, especially food. The link between the fairy world and death was reinforced by legends in which time passed differently in the real world and the fairy realm, with the result that those emerging from a single night's revel found the real world advanced by hundreds of years, or returned to the real world only to crumble into dust or bones. Perhaps it is this association with death that prompts the question to a character in *Pericles*, "Have you a working pulse, and are no fairy?" (V.i.158); then again, perhaps the question comes from a popular belief that fairies had no souls.

Fairies sometimes grew fond of mortal children, and exchanged them for fairy children, or changelings (*WT* III.iii.115, IV.iv.691; *1H4* V.i.76; *Ham* V.ii.53; *MND* II.i.22–27, 120–37; *TNK* IV.ii.44), in the cradle. Unbaptized children were thought to be especially vulnerable, as were unchurched women, who were sometimes stolen, it was thought, to serve as wet nurses to fairy infants. Numerous charms were devised by villagers to ward off fairy kidnappings, though these charms were clearly thought to be fallible, for human children with birth defects or behavioral oddities that became apparent after the first few days might be suspected of being changelings. In the popular imagination, the fairy world was at once alluring and dangerous, just as it is in the works of Shakespeare. *See also* Magic.

Falconry and Fowling

Falconry (*WT* IV.iv.14–16; *TNK* II.iv.11–12; *TS* Ind.ii.43–44), unlike deer hunting, was a sport that could be pursued by almost anyone, and its terminology was as familiar to Shakespeare's audiences as the language of football, baseball, or basketball is to Americans today. Phrases like "stoop," "pitch," "bate," and "tercel gentle" would have been as recognizable then as "touchdown," "stolen base," and "slam dunk" are now. Today, the language of falconry, except to the few remaining enthusiasts of the sport, seems complex and mysterious. There are so many kinds of hawks and so many pieces of equipment, and the very idea of capturing a wild creature, taming it, and shaping it to our own purposes is an alien concept for most.

Falconry

The Types of Hawks

An often-published list gives the types of birds of prey appropriate to every social rank, but, as John Cummins has pointed out in *The Hound and the Hawk*, the list is more of a literary device than a practical tool. Many of the birds named, such as eagles and vultures, would make poor captive hunters. The most commonly used birds could be divided into two groups: hawks of the tower, or long-winged hawks (Falconidae), and hawks of the fist, or short-winged hawks (Accipitridae). Most popular of the hawks of the tower was the falcon gentle, the female peregrine falcon; females were larger and supposedly braver than males, and were thus generally preferred. George Turberville, in *The Booke of Falconrie or Hawking* (1575), calls them "more ventrous, hardy, and watchfull." The male peregrine, also a much-used bird, was called the tercel gentle; when Juliet calls Romeo a "tassel gentle" (*R&J* II.ii.159–60), it is this bird she has in mind. Other hawks of the tower included the lanner, which was not as pretty as the peregrine but sturdier and willing to fly at a wider variety of prey, and its male, the lanneret; the saker, an eastern European and Middle Eastern bird sometimes imported into western Europe; and the hobby, a poor man's or child's hawk, not very useful except against very small birds such as larks.

Hawks of the fist included the gyrfalcon, which was less pretty than the peregrine but sturdier and willing to attack a wider variety of prey. Its male was called a jerkin. The merlin, whose male Turberville calls a "Jacke," looked like a small peregrine and was easily tamed. The goshawk, whose male was a tercel (*T&C* III.ii.50), was difficult to tame but extremely effective once trained. The sparrowhawk could be a useful bird and was favored by aristocratic ladies, but it could seem healthy one day and be dead the next; its male, the musket (*MWW* III.iii.21), was temperamental and even more delicate than the female. Both birds were somewhat unreliable and were used most when other hawks were in molt and could not fly. The trainer of almost all hawks was called a falconer, though a goshawk trainer was called an austringer and a sparrowhawk trainer an austringer or sparviter.

In addition to being divided by wingspan, species, and sex, hawks were also distinguished by their age. Age was not much of a concern once a bird was thoroughly trained, but it mattered a great deal when choosing a hawk in the first place. The older the bird, the better it would have learned to hunt in the wild; the younger the bird, the easier it would be to "man," or accustom to the presence of humans. Turberville called the hawk an eyas (*MWW* III.iii.21) when it was still in the nest, a "ramage Falcon" from May to August, a "sore" or soar hawk from August to November, a "Marzaroly" from November to May, and a hawk "of the first coate" or an "Entermewer" from mid-May to December. Entermewers had begun but not completed their first molt; when that molt was finished, they were "haggards" (*MAAN* III.i.35–36; *TS* IV.i.182, IV.ii.39; *Oth* III.iii.259), which because of their age could be difficult to train and often simply untamable. An unmannable bird was called a "buzzard" (*TS* II.i.206–8). Nonetheless, because of their advanced hunting skills, Turberville valued them highly and placed them second in his esteem to the soar hawk, which he thought best balanced tamability and skill.

Training and Equipment

A newly captured falcon had to learn three main skills: to tolerate humans calmly, to fly at and kill its prey, and to return to its owner with the bird it had killed. A falcon that was at ease in the presence of people was said to be "manned," hence Juliet's play on words when she calls herself "unmanned"—shy and skittish as a wild falcon, and also a virgin about to lose her virginity (*R&J* III.ii.14–16). An unmanned or nervous bird would "bate" (*H5* III.vii.115), or flap its wings, while held on the fist, and would thus be likely to tire or injure itself, so manning was an essential first step. There were several ways to go about this, and generally a combination of the methods was employed. One method was to accustom the hawk to a leather hood (*H5* III.vii.114; *R&J* III.ii.14) that covered its eyes, calming it. Falconers were advised to accustom the bird to having the hood put on and taken off by performing this action several times a day, rewarding the bird with food each time until it no longer bated when the hood was removed.

Another method was seeling (*A&C* III.xiii.112; *Oth* III.iii.210), which involved putting a stitch through the insensitive lower eyelid on one side, bringing the thread over the head, and stitching through the other lower eyelid. The thread could be tightened or loosened as necessary to close the bird's eyes to a greater or lesser degree, and this had much the same calming effect as the hood. The thread was gradually loosened as the bird became tamer, until finally it was removed altogether. The hood, on the other hand, continued to be used long after the training of the hawk was complete.

Still another method of manning a hawk was to keep it awake for several nights after its capture, which apparently exhausted it and broke its tendency to aggression (*TS* IV.i.179–85; *T&C* III.ii.41–42). (This approach exhausted the falconers, too; lords were advised to make special provision for the falconers' comfort during this time.) The hawk was also brought repeatedly into the presence of humans to accustom it to their noises and movements.

Falconer with falcon on the fist, from the 1611 edition of George Turberville's *Booke of Falconrie or Hawking.* Reproduced from the Collections of the Library of Congress.

The essential equipment for this training period, and for the years of hunting that followed, were a perch, a mews (falcon houses, with compartments one to two feet square for the falcons to roost in), a leather glove to protect the falconer's fist from the bird's talons, a lure of leather covered in feathers, a hood, and a retrieval system. This last consisted of jesses (*Oth* III.iii.260), leather strips about 6 to 10 inches (15 to 25 cm) long, knotted around the legs and ending in varvels or tyrits, silver rings sometimes inscribed with the name of the hawk's owner. Bells (*TNK* III.v.71–72), often paired so that they had the same weight but different and harmonious notes, were also attached to the legs with leather straps called bewits. Finally, a leash, or *creance*, was attached to the varvels and could be used to link the bird to its perch or to the falconer's fist, though when a falconer wanted to keep a bird close, he simply held the jesses.

Birds were trained with food rewards for flying to the perch, to the falconer's fist, or to the lure. Sometimes the lure was baited with meat and the hawk exercised by chasing the lure as the falconer spun it and pulled it away at the last moment. This training process took about a month, and at its end the hawk was supposed to be able to fly at and seize the lure even in noisy, distracting environments. When the hawk would reliably fly at a lure (*V&A* 1027) and return, it was ready to be flown at live prey.

Methods of Hunting

There were two styles of hawking, and different birds were adapted to each of the styles. Some birds specialized in the pursuit of herons, which they were trained to hunt by being released in the last phase of another hawk's kill and being given a piece of the heron as a reward. The peregrine and the gyrfalcon were especially adept at this mode of hunting, and the lanner could be used for it as well. They would chase the soaring heron higher and higher, spiraling upward almost out of sight, until they reached a "pitch" (*R&J* I.iv.21; *TN* I.i.12; *TA* II.i.14; *1H6* II.iv.11; *2H6* II.i.5–12) or height above the heron's. It then swooped down on the heron, falling on it even as it dived to escape, catching it and plunging downward.

The other type of falconry was called hawking "at the brook" (*2H6* II.i.1). In this sport, the hawk, usually a lanner, merlin, goshawk, sparrowhawk, or peregrine, would rise and hover above the hunting party, proving its worth by height, steadiness, and patience (*RL* 506–8). Men or dogs "put up the fowl" (*2H6* II.i.45), flushing them into the air, and the hawk would stoop upon them and bring them back to the falconer. This method could be used on a variety of birds, including partridges, pheasants, and bustards.

Smaller falcons, probably including the "fine hawk for the bush" of *The Merry Wives of Windsor* (III.iii.224), could be

"To flye at the Hearon according to Martine," an illustration of a falcon flying at the heron, from the 1611 edition of Turberville's *Booke of Falconrie*. Reproduced from the Collections of the Library of Congress.

set to catch little birds like larks, thrushes, and blackbirds. Several birds a day could be taken by a single hawk, for these flights were usually too short to tire the hawk very much. An exception was the merlin's flight against the lark, which resembled the peregrine's pursuit of the heron in miniature. In some cases, the prey was simply too big for the hawk, as when a goshawk tried to take a rabbit. Then it was imperative to have a dog, for the falcon could often hold the prey down, at least, until the dog could run up and kill it.

Fowling

Not all bird hunting was accomplished with falcons. Birds could be hunted with guns (*1H4* IV.ii.20; *MND* III.ii.20–24), though firearms were seldom very accurate at this period, or with blunt arrows called bird-bolts (discussed in Bow entry). They could be stalked and netted (*MAAN* II.iii.94; *Mac* IV.ii.34) or lured to twigs smeared with the sticky substance called birdlime. To entice the birds to approach, fowlers (*MND* III.ii.20) imitated bird calls, used decoys called stales (*TS* III.i.89; *Temp* IV.i.187), or set up a fake owl that would be mobbed by a flock of birds. Another technique was "batfowling" (*Temp* II.i.189), hunting the birds by night with a lantern and bell. The birds became so confused by the unaccustomed light and noise that they were temporarily stunned and could be netted or struck on the head with a bat.

Some birds could be caught in traps. The springe (*Ham* V.ii.308) or gin (*Mac* IV.ii.35) caught the bird with a noose attached to a flexible stick, while the pitfall (*Mac* IV.ii.35) caught the bird in an enclosure, slamming a door shut behind it. Notoriously susceptible to all these snares was the woodcock, which could also be caught in a "cock-shut" (*R3* V.iii.70), a net spread high across the wooded alleys through which the bird was wont to fly at twilight. This was such a common method of catching woodcock that the name of the trap, as in the example cited above, became synonymous with the time of day at which it was used. *See also* Birds; Bow; Hunting.

Farming

Running a farm in Shakespeare's time was extremely hard work. Selective breeding of livestock to maximize wool or meat production was a brand-new idea, hardly universally implemented, and all farm tasks were done by human or animal power. Fertilization was primitive and inadequate, leading to low crop yields that could not sustain a farmer's entire stock over the winter. Thus there was a wholesale slaughter of livestock in the late fall, leaving only a few animals with which to begin again in the spring. Crop rotation was practiced, but the innovations that would really help to improve the soil lay in the future, and fields usually had to lie fallow for a year or two to regain their nutrients. Most farmers had to do the work themselves, with the help of their children and perhaps a couple of hired hands, and they were always subject to the evils that have befallen farmers everywhere in every historical period. Pests, drought, unexpected cold, and even too much rain could spoil everything (*MND* II.i.93–97). It was a hard life, and a huge number of people lived it. There were craftsmen and actors and noblemen in Shakespeare's world, but servants and farmers were the norm. And farmers, because they provided the seasonal cycle of food that people ate every day, controlled to some extent the pattern of everyone's daily life.

Crops

All farmland was divided into arable land or pasture. Pasture (*H5* II.Cho.5, III.i.27) was devoted to grasses that fed the livestock in summer and, as mown and dried hay (*WT* IV.iii.12), through the winter as well. Animals could be kept alive—barely—on straw (*2H4* V.v.83), the bottom stalks of grain, but they needed hay to thrive and produce the manure that made a good grain harvest possible. Grasses and other pasture crops, including sainfoin, rye, cat's tail or timothy, clover, and vetch (*Temp* IV.i.61), were typically grown in natural wet lowlands near streams and rivers, and in man-made extensions of those areas created by ditches and dams. Pasture land was pretty and often sweet-smelling, but was full of ravenous pests like leather jackets and wireworms, the larval forms of crane flies and click beetles.

The arable land, about one-fourth of England's total farm acreage, was devoted to a variety of crops for both human and animal consumption. Wheat (*Lear* III.iv.116; *TNK* I.i.1 s.d., 64–65), also called corn (*AYLI* V.iii.17–18; *Temp* II.i.158; *TNK* II.ii.79–80; *Mac* IV.i.55) and not to be confused with New World corn or maize, was strictly for humans. It was too expensive to feed to animals, and too expensive even for many farm families to use in their bread. It came in several varieties: white, red, main (mixed), Turkey (or Purkey), gray, flaxen, pollard, English, and peak. Different types grew best in different soils. Barley (*Temp* IV.i.61) came in sprot, longear, and bear (big, bigg, or beer) varieties. Oats were "naked" (which did not need milling), black, red, white, and so on. Farmers might also plant rye (*AYLI* V.iii.21); horse, field, or tick beans; or white, green, grey, hotspur, or runcival peas. Sometimes mixed grains were sown together. Miscelin or maslin, a mixture of wheat and rye, and was often used to make cheaper bread. Thomas Tusser, an expert on husbandry, disapproved of sowing the two grains together and recommended that they be mixed when milled instead. Bullimong was a blend of oats, peas, and vetches (*Temp* IV.i.61—"fetches, oats, and peas") grown as cattle feed.

Less common crops were grown for specialized purposes. Wetland was especially well suited to rape seed or coleseed. Buckwheat was grown by

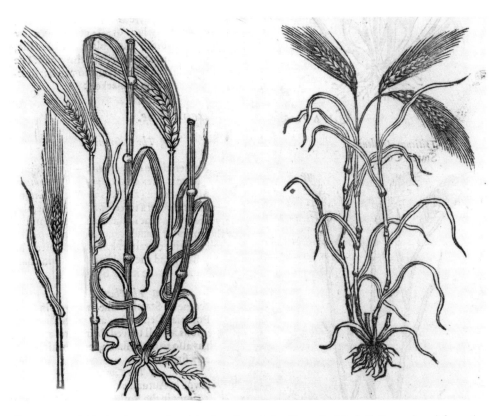

Common and big (or beer, or bear) barley, from John Gerard's *Herball*. Reproduced from the Collections of the Library of Congress.

some as a feed grain for chickens and sheep. Mustard choked out weeds and provided seed for making the prepared mustard that always accompanied roast beef. Some plants were grown for use as dyes, though these were unpopular crops. Madder, which yielded a red dye, and woad, which yielded a blue, were of this kind. Saffron, made of the stamens of flowers, could be used as a yellow dye or as a seasoning. Because only three small stamens per blossom were used, saffron had incredibly small yields; a satisfactory yield for an acre was twenty pounds of saffron per year. Nevertheless, it was much valued as a food ingredient, and many farmers continued to produce the little kiln-dried cakes. Hops were a relatively new crop grown for use in beer, which kept better than hopless ale. Hemp was grown for its fibers, which were used in sackcloth, rope, musket match, shoestrings, halters, canvas, coarse garments, and bowstrings; the stalks could be used as kindling. Flax fibers (*MWW* V.v.154; *Lear* III.vii.108–9; *TNK* V.iii.97–100) were turned into linen, musket match, and bowstrings. Those with more than sixty acres were required by law to grow flax, but many ignored the order. There were some vineyards in England (*H5*

V.ii.41–42, 53; *Temp* IV.i.68, 112), but the wine they produced was of poor quality, and imported wine was actually cheaper.

Livestock

The livestock were the heart of a farm, accorded much more daily attention than the crops. Most important were the sheep for wool, milk, and meat, then the cattle for beef, leather, and milk, then horses or oxen for hauling and plowing. There might also be brownish-gray asses to carry loads, though these were uncommon (*CE* III.i.14–18; *LLL* III.i.52, 54; *TS* II.i.199, III.ii.231; *R2* V.v.93; *MND* III.i., IV.i.78; *JC* IV.i.21, 25–27; *MM* III.i.26; *Cor* II.i.90–92). They were fed, according to Shakespeare, on "good dry oats," hay, or "a handful or two of dried peas" (*MND* IV.i.29–39). Mules (*AW* IV.i.43; *Cor* II.i.250; *T&C* V.i.61) were more common, since they could be used for either plowing or hauling. Stronger than horses, they could carry five to six hundred pounds at a rate of thirty miles a day, but they were not as good as oxen at plowing.

Goats (*1H4* III.i.38–39, IV.i.105; *AYLI* III.iii.1–2; *Oth* III.iii.400–401; *Cor* III.i.176) had the advantage of giving more milk than sheep (*TA* IV.ii.179), for which reason they were rather common in the West. "Goats" is used as a contemptuous term in *Henry V* (V.i.28) for Welshmen, whose nation abutted England's western edge. However, they were also more destructive. They would crop not just grass but anything they could find, including the kitchen garden. Goat herds rarely numbered more than a hundred and were kept far from the house if possible.

Most farms had a sow (*2H4* I.ii.11–12; *H5* III.vii.65; *Mac* IV.i.64–65), which might bear three to eight piglets at a time, and at least a couple of young pigs. These swine (*TS* Ind.i.34; *MWW* IV.ii.102; *John* V.ii.142) were fed a miscellaneous diet than included grain, brewing waste, acorns, and kitchen scraps. Rings in their noses kept them from grubbing in the garden or fields, but they were sometimes collected by a local swineherd (*1H4* IV.ii.35–36; *WT* IV.iv.327) and led out to forage in the woods for mast (fallen nuts—*Tim* IV.iii.420). Beginning at Michaelmas, hogs (*R3* I.iii.227; *AYLI* I.i.37–38; *Lear* III.iv.92–93) were housed in hard-floored pens and fed barley, malt, oats, peas, water tinged with ale, and whey. This regimen hardened the fat, which became a dish called brawn after the hogs were slaughtered. Pig-killing time began November 1 and continued through the fall and winter as necessary. Children inflated the bladders and filled them with dried peas to make rattles.

Each farm also had a dog—usually only one—for herding and guard duties and a cat to hunt mice (*2GV* II.iii.7–8; *MND* II.ii.30; *H5* I.ii.172). Cats not fortunate enough to have a farm to call home were often mistreated. Some people disliked their clinging ways (*MND* III.ii.260) and drowned them or shot at them (*Oth* I.iii.330–31; *MAAN* I.i.250–52).

Even Conrad Heresbach, an expert on husbandry, disliked having them around the farm. He cursed them, for

> besides the sluttishness and loathsomenesse of the Catte (you know what she layes in the Malt heape) she is most dangerous and pernitious among children.

Rabbits were sometimes kept in warrens for their fur and for food. Bees were kept for their honey and wax; their hives were carefully tended and placed in warm, sheltered locations. Every few years the bees were driven out into a new hive and the old one burned for the wax inside.

Poultry consisted of some chickens (*2H6* III.i.24, 251) and perhaps a few geese (*2GV* IV.iv.32; *LLL* III.i.90, 96, 98, 100–103, 121; *MWW* III.iv.40–41). A "green goose" (*LLL* I.i.97, IV.iii.72) was one about half a year old and ready to breed. A "barnacle" was a specific type of arctic goose (*Temp* IV.i.248–49), wild rather than domestic, which was thought to be hatched either from trees or from the barnacles on the submerged parts of ships or rocks. Geese were kept for their meat, their eggs, their wing feathers (which made quill pens), their smaller feathers and down (which stuffed mattresses), and their territoriality, which made them good "watchdogs." They were either fed at home or tended by a village gooseherd, who collected them from individual farms, using a paper rattle to attract their attention.

Chickens, at least the ones that were kept for their eggs rather than eaten while young and tender, were often given names like "Lady Margery" or "Dame Partlet" (*WT* II.iii.75, 159); the typical name for a rooster or cock (*2GV* II.i.27–28; *Temp* II.i.32–33; *TS* II.i.223–25)

The barnacle goose, from Konrad Gesner's *Icones Avium Omnium*. Reproduced from the Collections of the Library of Congress.

was "Chanticleer" (*Temp* I.ii.388–89; *AYLI* II.vii.30). Capons, the less fortunate male chickens, were castrated, either by cutting or burning out the testes, and fattened for eating (*Ham* III.ii.93–94; *Cym* II.i.22–25). Heresbach explained how to tell if the operation had been a success: "if they be right Capons, their Combs becommeth pale, neither crowing, not treading any more." Chickens were yellow, black, gray, or white. They were fed barley, vetches, peas, millet, and kitchen scraps. Other, less common, poultry included ducks, swans, turkeys (*TN* II.v.28–30; *TNK* II.ii.29–30), guinea fowl, peacocks, and pigeons. Turkeys had been introduced to England in the 1530s, and some experts on husbandry, including Leonard Mascall, found them too troublesome, greedy, and hard to keep healthy.

Animals required a great deal of daily attention, and even the best care, feeding, and housing could not always keep them healthy. Disease was always a concern. Chicks got "the pip," pigs contracted measles, and various diseases of livestock were classed under the heading of "murrain" (*Cor* I.v.3; *Temp* III.ii.83). When pestilence struck, it was important that the village act quickly to quarantine or destroy infected beasts, bury them deeply, and, if possible, stick one of their heads on a pole near the road to warn passing drovers not to tarry.

Farm Tasks

The typical farmer rose at dawn, said his prayers, and began his round of daily tasks, possibly carrying with him a little notebook in which to write down things he saw that needed his attention. If he was illiterate, he might instead carry a stick and make notches on it as reminders. If he was lucky, he might have a couple of hired out-dwelling servants to help him with his chores; if he was luckier, they might actually know what they were doing. There was a labor shortage in Shakespeare's day, and "mean servants" could do only a few farm chores—and those not particularly well. Farmers who could afford them treasured "chief servants in husbandry," who could plow, mow, sow, thresh, make a hay rick, thatch a roof, hedge, and butcher animals expertly. Unlucky farmers, like James Bankes of Winstanley, found themselves with hands who didn't care how well their work was done, so long as "they have meat, drink, and wages. Small fear of God is in servants."

Sometimes, a farmer's day might include special tasks, like hunting for ducks, fishing for eels, or gelding (castrating) cattle or horses (*MV* V.i.144; *2H6* IV.ii.164). Shallow's man presents him with various bits of farm business, including sowing, a blacksmith's bill for horseshoes and plow irons, the mending of a bucket (yoke), and the docking of another servant's pay for lost goods (*2H4* V.i.19–20). Some chores were done every day, like feeding the animals. Usually, however, the tasks were determined by the season.

Plowing and Planting

At certain times of year, there was plowing to be done (*LLL* V.ii.881–82; *A&C* II.ii.230; *Per* IV.vi.149–50; *TNK* II.ii.28). Fallow (unused) fields were plowed three times: in April, in May or June, and again in July or August (*H5* V.ii.43–46). Wheat and rye were planted in the fall. Barley, peas, beans, vetches, and oats were sowed in the spring.

The plowing itself was done by a wooden plow reinforced by iron fittings. It had three basic parts for cutting and turning furrows in the soil. The coulter (*H5* V.ii.45), usually of steel, made a vertical cut in the soil. It was followed by a plowshare, also of steel, that made a horizontal slice along a plane some inches down from the top of the soil, and a moldboard that flipped this twice-cut slice of earth over so that it fell onto the previous furrow and lay at an angle. A competent plowman (*MND* V.i.372; *LLL* V.ii.901; *T&C* I.i.61) could turn over one continuous strip of earth, foot by foot twisting up and over on its side, the entire length of a field—a "furrow long," the origin of the measurement "furlong," though at this time a furrow long could be any length at all.

There were different sorts of plows for different needs: rocky soil, wet soil, dry, chalky soil, and so on. Light soil might not be turned at all, simply agitated with a straight plow that had no moldboard. Some plows had wheels; others did not. A few, especially in Kent, were "turnwrest" plows, with a movable moldboard that allowed the plowman to switch turning directions at the end of each furrow. Most plows did not have this feature, which meant that if the plowman wanted all his furrows to lie the same way, he would have to plow one furrow (flipping the earth, say, to the right), reach the end of his row, then walk back across the field to plow the next row. Clearly, this was a waste of labor, so most fields were plowed "crown-and furrow," with the plowman walking in a spiraling oval, lifting the plowshare out of the ground at the turns, so that two furrows pointed toward each other in the middle of the field and two rows pointed away from each other at each side.

This system had the added advantage of creating "water furrows" at the edges of the field for drainage, an especially important consideration in wet soil, which had to be stacked in taller furrows to allow the soil to dry out a bit. Wet soil might also require drains and gutters to carry water

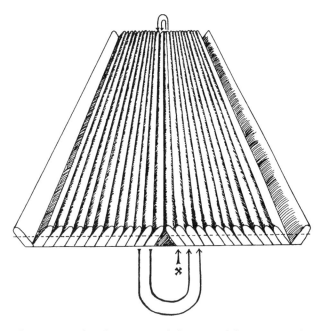

A compressed and exaggerated diagram of the crown-and-furrow plowing system. The plowman begins at the X and plows one furrow, then turns and plows the other way, creating a "crown" in the middle. He turns again at the end of each row, working out from the center in an outward-spiraling oval, until he reaches the edge of the field, where the furrow slices leaning in the opposite direction create a "water furrow" for drainage. The dotted line represents the original level of the ground before plowing.

away; these gutters could be dug by hand with a trenching spade or by animal power with a huge trench-plow that required up to twenty horses or oxen to pull. It cut a furrow 12 inches (30.5 cm) deep by 12 inches wide at the bottom and 18 inches (45.7 cm) wide at the top. Drains made of bushes, stones, or wooden pipes might also be installed if necessary. Dry soil, on the other hand, could be plowed with fewer water furrows, combining two fields in a single plowing pattern called "two-in-and-two-out." In steep areas, it was necessary to follow the contours of the land or even to terrace with greensward "linchets" between the level strips.

Often, plowing was followed by other ways of preparing the soil. Clods of earth were broken up by hand. Stones were removed and set aside to build field walls or farm structures. The soil might be fertilized with animal manure set aside from the winter stable or deposited by the sheep in their fold, compost from the kitchen compost heap, marl (a crumbly substance composed mostly of calcium carbonate—in other words, a soft limestone), burnt lime, coal ashes, soot, waste from pickling and tanning, sawdust, and bits of horn or leather (*2H4* IV.iii.119–21; *R2* IV.i.137; *Tim* IV.iii.441–43; *Ham* III.iv.152–53). Conrad Heresbach, in *The Whole Art and Trade of Husbandry*, advised having two dung heaps, "one of them newly thrown out of the stables, an other old, and serving for the field: for new doung is nothing so good as the old, for manuring of the ground." He further added that the dung heaps should be covered with straw or twigs, and soaked with the laundry water, to keep them moist. The soil was smoothed by a harrow, a wooden frame with vertical and horizontal strips studded on one side with ash or metal teeth; ash was considered better for very stony soil. This toothed side was laid on the ground and dragged behind a team of horses or oxen; in some cases a heavier harrow was used first, followed by a finer one. A roller, usually just a heavy log or a stone cylinder, was sometimes pulled across the field to flatten it.

Plowing took two men, one to hold and direct the plow and another to lead the horses or the yoked oxen (*MV* III.iv.13; *3H6* IV.vi.49; *MAAN* I.i.196; *R3* V.ii.2; *TA* I.i.30). The one holding the plow had three ways of controlling the depth of the furrow. He could use a plow with wheels, allowing the height of the wheels to determine furrow depth. Wheels were not always practical in wet clay soils, however, for in this case the wheels tended to become caked with dirt. Plowmen working this kind of soil used a plow with a foot. The hardest type of plow to control was a "swing plow," in which the depth was controlled not by the equipment but by the strength and skill of the operator. The efficacy of the plowman could be tested, wrote Heresbach, by putting a stick into the earth of the new furrows in various places to see if it sank to an even depth.

Sometimes the lead plowman carried a mattock to uproot bushes, weeds, and tree roots. If sowing (*MM* IV.i.76; *Cor* III.i.71; *2H4* V.i.15–17) was to be done at the same time, children were often enlisted to do it, scattering the seed by hand. Sowing was timed according to the weather and the crop, of course, but also according to the phases of the moon and the positions of the planets. Almanacs gave advice as to the best time to sow for maximum growth, usually when the moon was waxing—for the moon was supposed to control plant growth as well as tides—and placed in a favorable sign of the zodiac. Conventional wisdom also dictated which crops to sow in which fields; the preferred rotation was barley in the first year, peas in the second, and wheat in the third, with the field lying fallow for the fourth.

Amount of Seed Sowed per Acre, in Bushels

Barley	4–5
Beans	4
Oats	3
Peas	2
Rye	2
Wheat	2

In some areas, a special section of land was sown with peas for the poor. Once the crops were planted, the chief task of the farmers—particularly the children—was to keep the crops safe from birds and weeds. Though there were inanimate scarecrows (*1H4* IV.ii.38; *MM* II.i.1–4; *1H6* I.iv.43), a boy or girl as "crowkeeper" (*R&J* I.iv.6) was always helpful. Once the crops were well sprouted, weeding (*LLL* I.i.96; *Lear* IV.iv.3–6) took place by means of a weeding hook with an inch-wide blade or a pair of wooden tongs.

Harvesting

The harvest (*Temp* IV.i.114–15; *MAAN* I.iii.24; *R3* I.iv.245, II.ii.115–16; *Mac* I.iv.33) of both winter- and spring-sowed crops took place in summer. Reapers with scythes mowed the mead grass, pitchforked it into large carts called farm wains, hauled it home, and stacked it as hay for winter fodder (*H5* V.ii.49; *T&C* V.v.24–25; *A&C* III.vii.35; *Cor* I.iii.35–37). They cut the "plough-torn leas" (*Tim* IV.iii.194) as well, stacking grain in upright sheaves that dotted the landscape until they were picked up by an ox-drawn wain or cart and carried back to the barn. Each acre yielded about one to three dozen bushels of grain (depending on the type of grain and the success of the crop) or a little less than a ton of hay. Peas, beans, and vetches were also stacked, but were covered with wood or straw and kept on raised platforms called "hovels" to protect them from animals.

Suddenly the land looked utterly different; where tall stretches of grass or wheat or barley had shivered in the wind, there was now only stubble (*Cor* II.i.260–61). The last cartload was brought home with cheers, pulled by animals often decked with flowers, and everyone celebrated "harvest home" (*1H4* I.iii.33–34; *MWW* II.ii.269) with dance, song, and feasting (*Temp* IV.i.134–38). Sometimes the farmer chose this time to give presents to all his laborers.

The work, however, was far from done. First, the land had to be gleaned—searched for any fallen grains or "broken ears" that might have been left behind during the reaping (*H5* I.ii.151; *AYLI* III.v.101–3)— usually with a rake. This was a privilege sometimes given to the poor. At about this time, if the parish was one where peas had been sown for the poor, a bell was rung, and anyone with a license from the parish was allowed to go into the field to pick peas. Back at the barn, the work of threshing began (*TA* II.iii.123; *3H6* II.i.131). With wooden flails, the hands lashed the cut grain to separate the kernels of wheat from the stalks. Then the grain was winnowed, with the lighter chaff (*TNK* Pro.19; *2H4* IV.i.192–94; *MV* I.i.115–16; *MV* II.ix.47; *T&C* I.iii.27–28; *H8* V.i.111– 12; *Ham* V.vii.195; *Cor* V.i.26) being blown away with a fan and the heavier grain saved. The straw stalks were kept, to be used for fodder, bedding, stuffing, and fuel.

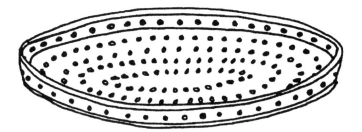

Sieve for winnowing corn, mid-sixteenth century.

The grain was then sorted. Sometimes a casting shovel was used to toss the grains; the heaviest would go farthest, and these were set aside for use as seed in the next growing season. Sometimes children were simply set to pick through the grains and choose the best and biggest ones. Some of the grain, particularly the wheat, was sold, and whatever the family wanted to keep for its own personal consumption was taken to the mill to be ground. The miller was usually paid in kind, with a set percentage of the flour.

Women's Work

Most of the tasks above were done by men, but the wife and her maid-servants were often called upon to help during the busiest parts of plowing and harvesting. In the meantime, they had plenty of other chores to do. Women—the wife or her dairymaid (*2GV* III.i.268), if she had one—was responsible for milking the cows and sheep (*WT* IV.iv.453), making the cheese, tending the poultry, and cleaning out the sty in which fattening hogs were kept. They spun flax and hemp, tended the garden that supplied much of the family's food, distilled syrup for cakes, and concocted medicines. They brewed, cooked, cleaned, made soap, made and mended clothes, did the laundry, watched the children, kept the hearth lit, and swept out the ashes.

The Rural Calendar

January	Wild doves fed and not killed; dovehouse (humorously referred to as an almshouse or a den of thieves, because of the tendency of birds to steal grain) cleaned. Hopyard weeded and manured with pigeon guano. Oats sowed. Hedges tended.
February	Wild doves fed. Grey or runcival peas sown.
March	Hops planted as seedlings in hopyard. Sometimes done as early as February. Housewife and her maids pay special attention to the garden. Barley sowing begins. More peas sowed. Garden vegetables planted.
April	First plowing of fallow fields. Housewife and her maids pay special attention to the garden. Timber collected. Making of butter and cheese begins. Late April, cattle permitted to graze in fields; this is sometimes postponed until early May.
May	May 1: lambs weaned; ewes milked from now until August. Sheep folded—put out to pasture inside an enclosure called a fold, which is moved from place to place to spread their manure around the fields. Second plowing of fallow fields, called "twy-fallow." Sometimes postponed until June. End of barley-sowing season. Winter wheat weeded. Buckwheat sowed. Calves set to graze. Stones picked from fields.
June	Sheep folded and shorn, except for yearling lambs. A feast follows the conclusion of the shearing. Spring-sowed crops weeded. Hay harvest begins.

July	Sheep folded. Yearling lambs shorn.
	Third plowing of fallow fields, called "thry-fallow." Sometimes done in August.
	Saffron plants uprooted, cleaned, separated, and replanted, every few years, between July 22 and August 15.
	Buckwheat reaped or plowed back into the ground as fertilizer.
	Hay harvest ends. Grain harvest begins.
	Ditches cleared.
August	Sheep folded.
	Hops harvested, dried in a kiln, and stored in canvas or hogsheads.
	Grain harvest ends.
September	Saffron blossoms picked.
	September 29: Michaelmas. Hogs are stied for the formation of brawn.
	Apple harvest begins.
October	Plow barley fields.
	Sort wheat seeds and sow wheat.
	End of October: all wheat now planted.
November	November 1: Hallowtide. Pigs slaughtered between now and Shrovetide as needed. At about this time, statute fairs are held at which servants can be hired for the coming year.
	Green peas sowed.
	November 11: Martinmas. Annual slaughter of cattle before winter.
	November 20: St. Edmund's Day.
	Garlic and beans sowed.
December	Wild doves fed.
	Firewood split.
	Tools mended and sharpened.
	December 25: Christmas.
	Plant new fruit trees.

Farm Equipment

The well-equipped farm had a house for the family and perhaps a separate building, set at right angles or across a courtyard from the main house, for the servants. A barn (*Temp* IV.i.111; *TA* V.i.133; *TS* III.ii.230; *1H4* II.iii.5; *MAAN* III.iv.45–47) held produce and perhaps the horses or oxen used to pull plows and carts. Fences of wood or stone might encircle fields and yards; usually these had gates to let animals through and stiles, sets of steps on either side, to let people climb over (*MAAN* V.ii.4–7; *MWW* III.i.32; *Lear* IV.i.56; *WT* IV.iii.127). Alternatively, the farmer might divide his property with hedges of whitethorn, crab, holly, hazel, oak, ash, or elm, but not blackthorn, which damaged the fleece of sheep. The plants were allowed to grow for about ten years, and then the branches were "plashed" or "pleached" (*H5* V.ii.42)—cut partly through, bent down, and twined with their neighbors to fill any gaps in the hedge.

The farm might also have a sheepcote (*AYLI* IV.iii.76), comprising a pen and a shed for lambing time, hung with sweet herbs, bedded with fern or straw, and hung with two-foot-high fodder racks. One or more sties (*Ham* III.iv.95) for pigs, a poultry house with roosts for the chickens above and the geese and ducks below, a stable, a dunghill (*2H6* IV.x.83; *H5* IV.iii.99; *AYLI* I.i.14; *LLL* V.i.75–76; *Lear* III.vii.99; *MWW* I.iii.62), and a supply of water from well, pond, or river completed the picture.

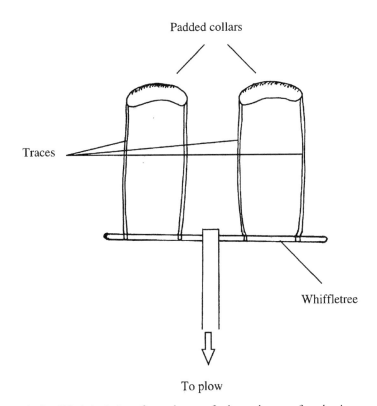

A simplified depiction, from above, of a horse harness for plowing. Padded horse collars have rope or leather traces, running along the horses' sides and joining a bar called a whipple tree, whiffletree, swingletree, swing bar, or splinter bar. This bar in turn connects to a beam that leads to the plow.

Numerous tools were needed to do the work of the farm. At least one plow was needed, plus the harness to attach it to the animals that pulled it. For oxen, yokes were necessary; for horses, a combination of poles, rope or leather traces, and padded collars. Wains were needed to haul dung,

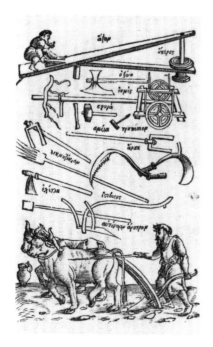

Farm tools and plowing from Konrad Gesner's *Icones Animalium Quadrupedam*. Though this illustration was supposed to represent ancient agricultural equipment, the essential tools for farming had not changed all that much. Texts on husbandry from the sixteenth century mention the same assemblage of scythes, plows, yokes, and so forth. Reproduced from the Collections of the Library of Congress.

hay, and grain; these were equipped with wooden wheels for places with soft earth, and with iron-bound wheels for places with harder ground. There were harrows, a trench plow or trenching spade, pitchforks, rakes, flails, ladders, troughs, and perhaps a roller. *See also* Animals; Bees; Cattle; Dog; Food; Holidays; Horse; Land; Occupations; Tools.

Farthing

The farthing was an extremely small coin, worth only one-quarter of a penny, that was introduced during the 1279–80 recoinage of Edward I. At that time, the silver coin had a facing portrait bust of the king on the obverse, with the legend EDWARDVS REX, and on the reverse a "long cross" (a cross that continued beyond the central portion of the coin and into the margin), three round pellets in each quadrant formed by the cross, and the legend LONDONIENSIS, which indicated that the coin had been struck in London.

Farthings continued to be minted until the reign of Edward VI, Elizabeth I's half brother, but they became too expensive to make and were too small to handle easily, so Elizabeth considered issuing the farthing, along with the penny and halfpenny, in a cheaper (and therefore larger) copper version. However, she scrapped this idea, and it was not until well into the reign of James I, after Shakespeare had retired, that the government issued copper farthings and half-farthings. The minting was done through a contractor, Lord Harington, who was given a monopoly on production, rather than through the royal mint.

However, despite the fact that farthings were absent from England's coinage during Shakespeare's entire career, the word "farthing" does crop up occasionally. This is because in 1561 Elizabeth did order the minting of a three-farthing piece, in other words, one worth ¾ of a penny or "halfpenny farthing" (*LLL* III.i.147). To distinguish this and other new additions to the coinage from previous small coins, the new coins (6d, 3d, ½d, and ¾d) added a small rose behind the queen's head on the obverse (*John* I.i.143). It is this odd little coin that is given as a tip ("remuneration") to Costard by Armado:

Remuneration? O that's the Latin word for three farthings. Three farthings—remuneration. "What's the price of this inkle?" "One penny." "No,

Three-farthing coin, 1561. Actual size is 13 mm in diameter. © 2002 The American Numismatic Society. All rights reserved.

I'll give you a remuneration." . . . Why, it is a fairer name than French crown. I will never buy and sell out of this word. (*LLL* III.i.135–41)

That Costard is a native of Navarre and Armado a Spaniard makes it odd that they exchange an English coin, except for the fact that it is such a piddling little coin that it makes Armado's parsimony all the plainer. *See also* Money.

Fealty

As it evolved during the Middle Ages, feudalism was a hierarchical system of landownership, military recruitment, and personal loyalty. In theory, all land, even that of powerful nobles, was granted by the king (the liege lord) in exchange for an oath of loyalty (fealty) (*2H6* V.i.50; *R2* V.ii.39, 45; *TA* I.i.257). Along with his oath, the noble (the vassal) gave a promise to defend the king in wartime by fighting and supplying a specified number of troops. The noble, in turn, granted portions of land (fiefs) to knights, who swore the same oath of fealty, defense, and recruitment, and the knights then distributed their own land to tenants who swore fealty and service. Tenants did not always offer military service alone, but often a combination of tithe goods, farm service, and soldiering. The essence of the system was the personal bond between liege lord (*2H6* III.ii.134) and sworn vassal (*2H6* IV.i.111; *2H4* IV.v.175; *R3* II.i.123; *R2* III.iii.88). Legally, the bond had to be renewed in every generation; when a father died, his land technically reverted to the liege lord, and the dead man's son or other heir had to swear fealty on bended knee (*2H6* I.i.10, III.i.11–12, 16) in order to be granted the fief anew.

It was this direct bond that made the system so dangerous to the monarchy, and even to basic civil order. On the one hand, order was preserved within a lord's domains because of his absolute power; on the other, the ability of individual lords to muster their own private armies at will led to conflicts between lords and to the ability of a cadre of lords to threaten, usurp, or control the monarchy itself. The men fought for their lord, and their oath was to him. If the lord chose to oppose the king, it was no fault of theirs. His disloyalty could not excuse their own. The king, therefore, with no substantial standing army of his own, had to rely on a combination of rewards, punishments, charisma, traditional authority, church sanction, and the unwillingness of the majority of his nobles to break their vows to him. It is against this backdrop that the breaking of oaths by vassals in Shakespeare's history plays must be viewed.

The feudal system had regional variations and changed over time. It was tempting to break one's word when the betrayal was especially advantageous, and it took only occasional ruptures to weaken a hierarchy based in large part on personal honor. Moreover, even well-intentioned vassals could have a legitimate conflict of interest, for they often held parcels of land from two different lords. To eliminate this problem, the concept of "liege homage" was introduced. The vassal paid ordinary homage (*1H6* IV.ii.7; *TS* Ind.i.135), perhaps, to many lords, but only one was his liege lord, to whom he owed paramount obedience in case of war between his different masters. This adaptation achieved a temporary clarification of loyalties, but ties were gradually clouded again as liege lords gave permission to their liege men to offer liege homage to other lords as well.

The rise of the professional army in the Renaissance, combined with the decreasing importance of knights in warfare, further undermined the feudal system. In England, which had avoided the worst complications of liege homage by making the king everyone's liege lord, the system survived mainly in the manorial courts, certain aspects of land tenancy, a general deference to social superiors, and the literature and mythology of heraldry and knighthood. The last of these survivals, combined with a widespread reverence for religion almost unimaginable today, would have made the self-serving breaking of oaths by Shakespeare's lords thoroughly reprehensible to his audiences. *See also* Government; Jousting; Knight.

Fencing

Almost all English fencing fell into one of two styles. The more old-fashioned of the two was the sword-and-buckler technique (*1H4* II.iv.178–79; *2H4* III.ii.23), in which the combatants slashed with the cutting edges of a long sword—the "swashing blow" (*R&J* I.i.65)—and only occasionally thrust with the point. For defense they used a small shield called a buckler, held in the off hand or strapped to the forearm. By the late sixteenth century, because of the ineffectiveness of both the buckler and the slashing style, this English school of "fence" (*MWW* II.iii.14; *2H6* II.i.52, II.iii.80; *TN* I.iii.89–92, III.iv.289; *Per* IV.vi.60) was being rapidly displaced by the Italian school, in which a light sword called a rapier was used for attack and a matching dagger for both parrying and short-distance stabbing. By the time the First Folio was published, however, the dagger also was being replaced, this time by a mail gauntlet. A third school, promoted by a Spanish master named Carranza, was preoccupied with intricate, geometrically determined postures designed as complements (*R&J* II.iv.21) to an enemy's anticipated attack. It was impractical for actual fighting, and though many in England had heard of it and knew some of its techniques, never became popular outside of Spain. A possible reference to its elaborate poses occurs in *Antony and Cleopatra*, in a description of Octavian's uselessness in battle:

> Yes, my lord, yes. He at Philippi kept
> His sword e'en like a dancer, while I struck
> The lean and wrinkled Cassius. (III.xi.35–37)

The speaker, Antony, must have been using either the sword-and-buckler method, which Shakespeare often uses nostalgically, or the rapier-and-dagger style. The swashbuckling English style, despite a spirited defense by its proponents (*MWW* II.i.212–17), lapsed into use by boasting, shield-banging street performers and then into complete obscurity. It appears in

Fencing with long swords, from the title page of Joseph Swetnam's *Schoole of the Noble and Worthy Science of Defence*, 1617.

Guarding with the short sword and dagger against an attack by rapier and dagger, from Swetnam's *Schoole of the Noble and Worthy Science of Defence.*

Shakespeare in the armament of Sampson and Gregory in *Romeo and Juliet* I.i, in the customary award of one's buckler to a victorious rival (*MAAN* V.ii.16–22), and in the "dry-beat[ing]" of a sparring partner with nonlethal blows with the flat of the long sword (*R&J* III.i.80).

In order to learn the new style of fencing, gentlemen read texts by master swordsmen and took lessons, often taught by Italian expatriates, at fencing schools. Practice bouts, or "veneys" (from the French *venues*—see *MWW* I.i.270–73), used weapons blunted either by sticking golf-ball-sized foil buttons on the tips or by bending the tips back and hammering them somewhat flat. As Horace Craig points out, the final duel in *Hamlet* (IV.vii.134–39, V.ii), in which Laertes surreptitiously substitutes a sharp weapon for a practice foil, must have employed the second method of blunting, for Hamlet could hardly have failed to notice the absence of a sizable button on his opponent's sword.

To the modern reader, Shakespeare's fencing scenes seem littered with unintelligible terms, but he actually used only a small percentage of the available buzzwords. He passes over, for example, *botta lunga, caricado, imbrocatta, incartata, mandritto,* and the like. However, those he includes indicate the rising popularity of the Italian style. The *passado,* which makes its appearance in *Romeo and Juliet* (II.iv.27, III.i.86) and *Love's Labor's Lost* (I.ii.174), was a means of lessening the distance between oneself and one's opponent. The distance (*MWW* II.i.213, II.iii.24–25; *R&J* II.iv.22) between the combatants was all-important, since it determined which weapon (rapier or dagger) would be favored, whether the sword thrust would have sufficient force, and whether a tall man or a man with a longer weapon would have an advantage of reach. The goal was to stay just out of reach of the opponent's sword while being able to close and thrust at will with a single step. To close the gap for an attack, a man might take one or more steps toward his opponent, thus passing one foot in front of the other (hence *passado*), usually thrusting or lunging at the same time (*MWW* II.i.213). There were other types of footwork as well, such as the slip, in which one foot moved to the side and behind the other, turning the body to avoid a blow; and the traverse (*MWW* II.iii.23), in which a sidestep took the fighter to the left, to the right, and sometimes forward or backward at the same time.

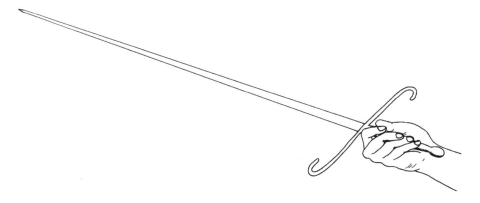

The position of the hand for the stoccata. The simple quillons are based on a contemporary woodcut, but rapiers often had far more complex quillons with ring guards above the quillons through which the index finger could be safely looped.

Shakespeare mentions several types of thrusts. One of these is the "foin" (*MWW* II.iii.22; *MAAN* V.i.84), which was simply a generic term for a thrust of any kind. A more specific type was the "punto reverso" (*R&J* II.iv.27), or *punta riversa*, which took the "point" in its name from the thrust with the sword point and the "reverse" portion from the fact that it was struck from the left side, usually though not necessarily with the left hand. The attacker thrust with the dagger, with the rapier in the left hand, or with the rapier in the right but pointed toward his left. If successful, it ran under or over the enemy's sword, achieving the basic goal of sword fighting in earnest—to kill or incapacitate the rival as swiftly as possible. Shakespeare does not speak of the *imbrocatta*, a thrust from above the opponent's sword, but he does use the *stoccata* (*MWW* II.i.214), which struck from below with the hand supinated (palm and fingernails pointed up, as opposed to pronated, in which they were pointed to the left or down). Stoccata rarely appears in its Italian form in the plays, though the "alla stoccata" of *Romeo and Juliet* (III.i.75) simply means "at the stoccata," and uses the original term. More commonly, it is anglicized as "stock" or "stuck" (*MWW* II.iii.24; *TN* III.iv.280; *Ham* IV.vii.162). The "montant" (*MWW* II.iii.25), made into the faux-Italian "Mountanto" (*MAAN* I.i.29) by Shakespeare, was a thrust of some kind, though sources differ as to its exact nature. The "reverse" spoken of by the Host in *The Merry Wives of Windsor* appears in a series of fencing terms, along with foin, traverse, punto, stock, montant, and distance (II.iii.21–25), and since both punto and reverse are used as separate terms, the Host must be using "punto" to mean either a thrust with the point (in which case it would be redundant with foin) or the *punta riversa*, and "reverse" to mean either the *punta riversa* (in which case it might be redundant with "punto") or the *rinverso*, a left-to-right, palm-down, horizontal slash that ideally caught the opponent's left side. Perhaps Shakespeare meant for the list of terms to be internally consistent, perhaps not. Certainly Falstaff's fictitious account of his fight with highwaymen (*1H4* II.iv) is meant to be humorously contradictory and confused. Falstaff freely mingles terms of sword-and-buckler fighting with those of rapier fencing, clearly demonstrating to the contemporary audience that his only knowledge of his sword is how to buckle it on.

The goal of any fight was to win, and to win by any means. There were no rules in a real fight except those determined by pragmatism. For example, few cuts or thrusts were made to the legs, since even a blow that went entirely through the thigh would neither seriusly cripple the opponent nor prevent him from making a counterattack to a much more vulnerable area, such as the abdomen, armpit, or face. Feet, because they were so important to balance and movement, could pose a serious problem if hit, though most fencers did not expend much effort in aiming for them. The face was a favorite target less because it was a lethal area than because scalp wounds bled so profusely, discouraging the enemy and perhaps partially blinding him. Permanent blinding was also possible. English boys usually agreed when practicing not to strike at each other's faces, leaving them with psychological barriers to the proper defense of the face, and many an English fencing master had only one eye as a result of facing opponents without such scruples.

As the combatants circled each other, searching for a line of attack, they adopted wards (*1H4* II.iv.196; *WT* I.ii.33; *Temp* I.ii.474), or postures, that offered defense while simultaneously positioning the arms in readiness to strike a blow. Most attacks consisted of a forceful thrust or cut. The goal of the opponent was then to divert the blow with the buckler or gauntlet or to parry it with the dagger or rapier. When parrying, it was best to use the portion of the blade near the hilt, since this was sturdier than the tip of the blade. Some methods of parrying allowed the defender to capture the tip of the attacker's sword between the dagger and rapier or between the dagger blade and its quillons. Some daggers were made with triple blades or curved quillons for the express purpose of pinning a sword blade between two of these prongs and, with a twist of the hand, snapping off the point. Some defenses were purely psychological, such as the yelling of some loud word or noise (for example, the "hay" of *R&J* II.iv.27, from the Italian for "Thou hast [it]") or the taunting of an enemy to enrage him and cause him to make a mistake. However, the emphasis was always on attack, with the chief method of defense being the maintenance of a proper distance from the enemy. *See also* Duel; Sword.

Fire

For people living in a cold climate before the advent of electricity, lighting a fire was as natural and common, though not nearly so simple, as opening the refrigerator or turning on the blender is for us. It was an everyday task, not an occasional chore designed to introduce an atmosphere of romance or rusticity. It was also an indispensable part of the manufacturing trades and a constant source of danger.

For most people, fire meant the house fire, and in most houses there was only one chimney and one hearth. Some houses might have two hearths—one on the ground floor and one directly above it on the next floor. Only large houses had more. The house fire was kindled in the morning by the maidservant if there was one—perhaps from the embers of the previous night's fire if any remained, blowing on the coals to see if they would glow (*John* IV.i.105–11; *H8* II.iv.76–77). More commonly the fire had to be lit anew; Shakespeare speaks of "wasted brands" glowing in their last heat at midnight (*MND* V.i.374), and these would surely not last until morning. In this case, the maid would rake the ashes to save any bits of fuel that could be used again and sweep out the hearth (*MWW* V.v.45–48), saving the ashes, if she worked on a farm, to be used as compost or as a component of homemade soap. Next she built a pile of logs from a stack made by one of the men of the house (*LLL* V.ii.910; *R&J* IV.iv.17), augmented it with smaller sticks called faggots (*1H6* V.iv.56; *TA* III.i.69) and twigs or straw for kindling, and started the flame by striking a piece of hard stone called flint against metal to generate sparks (*LLL* IV.ii.89; *RL* 176–79). The sparks were meant to land in some light, flammable substance called tinder (*Oth* I.i.137; *Cor* II.i.51); flax (*2H6* V.ii.54–55; *TNK* V.iii.97–98) or straw (*JC* I.iii.107–8) was a common choice.

It was not easy work. Hauling wood and ashes was dirty and tedious. Nurturing the spark from the flint was tricky; Shakespeare speaks of a character

> That carries anger as the flint bears fire,
> Who, much enforcèd, shows a hasty spark,
> And straight is cold again. (*JC* IV.iii.110–12)

The spark, so hard to make, must light the tinder. Then one had to blow on it just right to encourage the flame to creep higher. There must be enough wood, but not so much that the flame was smothered, or the entire process must begin again. And it must all be done with stiff, cold hands before the rest of the family awoke, chilled and ready to begin their day. Then the fire must be maintained with fresh wood all day, monitored for just the right amount of heat during cooking, and made all over again the next day. Some householders could afford to pay a woodmonger (*H5* V.i.67) to fetch firewood, but others had to find, cut, and carry it themselves.

There were other disadvantages to the household fire. In many cases, the ventilation was not quite right, particularly in the cheapest hovels, where there might not be a chimney at all but only a hole in the roof. In these cases, the house was smoky, dirty, and smelly as a result (*1H4* III.i.155–57). Sometimes the fire was too hot; in one case in Shakespeare, a lady's page stands between her and the fire at dinner to keep her back from becoming too warm (*LLL* V.ii.477), and one feels enormous sympathy for the slowly roasting page. Stray sparks, especially in houses without chimneys or with thatch roofs, could easily result in house fires that swept from one timber-framed building to another. It was this danger that led many to build or rebuild brick chimneys in the Tudor era.

Nonetheless, the fire was a great comfort, especially in winter, when its warmth forced the family to gather around the hearth (*MWW* V.v.241; *Cor* I.i.193–94; *AW* IV.v.47–49). Here, stories were told, political issues were discussed, and mending was done. The family's food was cooked there. In a bedroom, it was a cozy sight, and in houses of the rich, sweet-scented wood might be burned there to serve as a Renaissance air freshener (*TS* Ind.i.49). Fires were also built outdoors. For heating and cooking, they were necessary in army camps (*H5* IV.Cho.8–9; *Cym* IV.iv.18). For their joyous, convivial properties, they were an essential part of celebrations (*2H6* V.i.3; *WT* V.ii.24; *Oth* II.ii.3–5; *Cym* III.i.32).

Fires were also required for certain agricultural and industrial processes. Brewers, including the multitude of home brewers, needed slow, low heat to dry their sprouted malt. Dyers used fire, as did glassmakers, saltmakers, smelters, blacksmiths, and armorers. The fire for these purposes was sometimes fueled with wood, but more often with charcoal or coal. Coal was sometimes called "sea coal" (*2H4* II.i.87; *MAAN* III.iii.13–14; *MWW* I.iv.8–9) to distinguish it from charcoal, but often it is hard, in Shakespearean references, to sort out charcoal from sea coal or from the wood coals to be found in the last stages of a wood fire (*V&A* 337–38), since all three can be called "coals" (*H5* III.ii.46–47; *R&J* I.i.1–2; *T&C* II.iii.196; *WT* V.i.68; *2H6* V.ii.36; *MV* III.v.23–26; *Cor* V.i.17). In glassmaking, sea coal was the preferred fuel, but it had to be kept covered in the furnace (*Cym* I.vi.66; *AYLI* II.vii.146–47; *H8* I.i.140), for otherwise the sulfur in the coal combined with the lead in the glass and turned it black. Though the smoke of a coal fire could be unpleasant, a shortage of wood spread the use of coal into homes as well as shops by the end of the sixteenth century.

Sea coal was mined in many places in England, including the west Midlands, Somerset, Nottinghamshire, Yorkshire, Northumberland, Durham, and Leicestershire. It was shipped by boat—hence the name "sea coal"—to London, usually from Newcastle, hence the proverbial redundancy of sending coals to Newcastle. Then it was hauled and sold by colliers (*TN* III.iv.121; *R&J* I.i.3; *LLL* IV.iii.264), who were often likened to devils because the coal dust made them appear black. In some cases it was dug near the surface or in shallow tunnels into hillsides. The more adventurous and ambitious dug a deep pit, then hollowed outward all around the bottom of the pit without shoring up the roof, going as far as they could until the roof collapsed. By the mid-sixteenth century, deeper, timber-lined shafts were being dug, seven to ten feet square and up to a hundred feet deep, with side tunnels also lined with timber. Men ascended and descended either by a ladder or by a rope and windlass cranked by men or a horse. Falls, ventilation, water seepage, and methane gas were recurring problems. *See also* Alchemy; Architecture; Lighting.

Firearms

Pistols and rifles were increasingly common in the Renaissance, both for warfare and for hunting. Nevertheless, they were still cumbersome and inaccurate. Muskets (*AW* III.ii.105–11), which had a long barrel and fired a one-to-two-pound ball, were often so heavy that they had to be rested on a forked stand to be fired. However, there were lighter varieties such as the harquebus (or hackbut, which used a walnut-sized one-ounce iron or lead ball) and the caliver (*1H4* IV.ii.19; *2H4* III.ii.275, 277). The musket was over five feet long, with a barrel of just over four feet; the caliver was just under five feet, with a barrel of about three and a half feet, and, unlike the musket and harquebus, did not need to be rested on a stand to be fired accurately.

These guns were almost universally muzzle-loaders, which is to say that they were loaded down the front of the gun, one shot at a time. The butt of the gun, which existed to counteract recoil, was balanced on the ground, and powder was poured into the barrel from a waterproof flask (*R&J* III.iii.132; *LLL* V.ii.614) worn on the belt. Musketeers often wore bandoliers of small powder bottles, each containing a measured quantity of gunpowder. Next a wad and an iron or lead ball were pushed in with a long bar called a ramrod, another wad was pushed in to hold the ball in place, and the ramrod was stored in a tube running parallel to the barrel of the gun. It was a complicated process. Breech-loading rifles, loaded in the part of the barrel near the trigger, were faster, but they were also rare and costly. Because the powder was loose in the barrel, and because of the wadding tamped in after it, it was too messy and difficult to unload a gun, so hunters coming home with loaded guns simply fired them up the chimney to empty them.

There were two principal mechanisms for igniting the powder to make the gun fire. Most common was the matchlock, which employed a slow-burning hemp or flax fuse called a match, held by the clamp called a cock (*H5* II.i.54). Pressing the trigger brought the glowing match into contact with a small amount of priming powder that in turn lit the charge behind the bullet. An improved form of the matchlock, the snap-matchlock, used a spring to snap the cock into place and allowed the musketeer to devote more time and attention to aiming the gun. Another way of lighting the priming powder was with a wheel-lock trigger, introduced in the early sixteenth century. This system used a toothed wheel that rotated against a cock holding a piece of iron pyrite, producing sparks that lit the priming powder.

A wheel-lock hunting pistol, south Germany, 1578. Steel with a stock of walnut and engraved stag horn. Note the round pommel or ball butt, which served to counterbalance the weapon and to provide a handle when unholstering it. Pistols were introduced in the 1530s and acquired their name in the 1540s. *Wheel-Lock Hunting Pistol.* South Germany, 1578. Steel, walnut stock with engraved stag horn; ball butt, length 54.6 cm. © The Cleveland Museum of Art, 2001, Gift of Mr. and Mrs. John L. Severance, 1916.672.

Both types of gun were slow and unreliable by modern standards. In 1600, the very best musketeers could still only fire two rounds every three minutes, whereas archers could fire eighteen yard-long arrows in the same amount of time. Muskets were heavy; they tired the men. They misfired when powder or dirt clogged their mechanisms and barrels. They required gunpowder that was highly susceptible to damp. They were expensive. Why, then, did the musket, in one form or another, become the dominant infantry weapon in Europe? The answer was range. A crossbow's maximum range was about 130 feet, compared with the musket's 250. The advantage of distance from the enemy more than made up for the slow rate of fire, the weight of the weapon, and the care of powder.

Firearms were also used for hunting, and for this purpose it made little difference how long it took to reload. Aristocrats ordered guns with elaborate inlays, engravings, and gilding, and decorated powder horns and flasks made of metal, ivory, hardened leather (*cuir bouilli*), horn, and wood. Most gun barrels were cast in clay molds, the powder chamber reamed out, and the touchhole drilled by hand. From the 1540s, there was a tendency to bore the barrel hole rather than cast it, because this produced a more accurate gun. The "birding pieces" of *The Merry Wives of Windsor* (IV.ii.53) are no doubt lesser examples of the gunsmith's art. The pistol (*1H4* II.iv.348–49; *2H4* II.iv.112–19; *MWW* IV.ii.47; *Per* I.i.167–68), with its ornate barrel and heavy, round pommel, became as much a symbol of wealth and rank as an elegant rapier. *See also* Army; Artillery; Weapons.

Fishing

Fishing (*A&C* I.iv.4–5, II.v.10–17), or angling (*TNK* IV.i.32–34), was in most respects similar to fishing today. The equipment was more primitive in form and materials, but the basic elements were the same: a line that could be let out (*WT* I.ii.180–81) or taken up as the occasion required; tied to the water end was either a bent or covered hook (*A&C* II.v.12; *R&J* II.Pro.8; *MAAN* II.iii.110–11) with bait (*TA* IV.iv.91; *R&J* II.Pro.8; *MAAN* III.i.26–28) or a handmade artificial fly meant to look like an insect. Shakespeare does not mention fly fishing, though he does talk once of "tickling," or groping for fish by hand (*TN* II.v.19–20). For the most part, he sticks to metaphorical uses of the line, bait, and hook (or "angle"—see *WT* IV.ii.47; *Ham* V.ii.66; "angle" could also mean the line), using them, alone or in various combinations, to stand for stratagems and deception. In his more specific moments, he mentions dace (*2H4* III.ii.335), flesh (*MV* III.i.51), and worms (*Ham* IV.iii.27–29) as types of bait; calls the quick-biting gudgeon a foolish fish (*MV* I.i.102); and contrasts the tiny minnow, hardly worth the catching, with the large and nourishing salmon (*TNK* II.i.4–5).

Professional fishermen (*Lear* IV.vi.17; *Per* II.i.chs.; *R&J* I.ii.40–41; *TA* IV.iii.7) often fished in the ocean, though Shakespeare appears to have known little of their craft other

Fisherman's net, mid-sixteenth century.

than that they employed nets (*Per* I.i.41, II.i.14, 121–23) and wore oiled boots (*MWW* IV.v.94–96). An engraving by Jost Amman for *Panoplia*—admittedly a Continental rather than an English work—shows a fisherman standing in a small boat, using two different kinds of nets. One is square and dangles horizontally from ropes attached to its corners and to a pole. The other resembles a vase, narrow at one end, widening as it approached the entrance, abruptly narrower again, and then wider at the mouth.

Shakespeare appears to have been more familiar with freshwater fishing. When he mentions a venue for the activity, it is almost always in a lake (*TNK* IV.i.33) or a fishpond (*WT* I.ii.195). In *The Description of England*, William Harrison wrote that even the humblest homes were likely to have such a pond, stocked with "tench, carp, bream, roach, dace, eels, or suchlike as will live and breed together." He also noted that fishing was limited by the government, partly to ensure that adequate populations of fish survived to breed, and partly to keep laborers from sitting idly on the banks of rivers and lakes.

Five Wits

As there were five senses, so, according to Renaissance thinkers, were there five wits (*MAAN* I.i.63). These were wit (or common sense), imagination, fantasy, estimation, and memory.

Flags

The flags, or colors (*3H6* I.i.91, 251–52; *H5* III.vi.87 s.d.; *2H4* V.v.90; *R2* IV.i.99–100), of opposing armies had several purposes. Their chief purpose was to announce the position of each lord and his troops, so that tactics could be planned and soldiers protected from accidental assault by their allies. More specifically, flags identified individual knights when their faces had been obscured by their closed helmets. For the victors, captured enemy flags served as concrete proof of their opponents' defeat and helped, along with the bodies left on the field, to calculate the extent of the damage. One's own flags could be hung on the walls of a captured town to emphasize that possession had changed. Flags could also be used to request a truce (*1H6* III.i.139), though a parley or conference was signaled with a horn.

The largest of the usual flags was the standard (*1H6* II.i.23; *LLL* IV.iii.364; *R3* V.iii.22, 265, 349). It was triangular, with a slit in the narrower end and rounded tips on the two points created by the slit. Standards were enormous. The king's, in battle, could be eleven yards long; his peacetime standard was eight to nine yards. Other standards varied by rank.

Funeral certificate of Sir John Spencer (d. Jan. 9, 1599/1600), showing a standard, guidon, helm with crest and mantling, shield, and tabard. Reproduced by permission of the College of Arms.

Rank of Standard-bearer	Length of Standard in Yards
Duke	7½
Marquess	6½
Earl	6
Viscount	5½
Baron	5
Knight banneret	4½
Knight bachelor	4

No one below the rank of knight bachelor; or ordinary knight, was entitled to a standard. The standard showed the cross of St. George and the bearer's motto and badges.

The guidon was two-thirds as large as the standard and was also triangular but without the split end. Any armiger might carry one, placing his arms at the wide end and a plain or patterned field in the tapering area. The pennon (*H5* III.v.49) was half as big as a guidon and followed the same shape and design. It was carried furled around the lance and flown, unfurled, as the lance was held erect before a charge. It might also be hung on tents during encampments or displayed on the field during jousting tournaments.

Horsemen who distinguished themselves in battle could receive a field promotion to knight banneret. If this happened, the pennon would be torn vertically, leaving only a roughly square portion with the knight's arms. The lucky warrior would later replace this impromptu flag with a genuine banner (*Oth* III.iii.350; *John* II.i.308; *H5* IV.viii.81), a square flag with colored fringe that might be carried only by knights banneret and above. *See also* Army; Heraldry.

Flowers

Sometimes, in Shakespeare, a flower is just a flower, an indication that the action is taking place outdoors or in a particular season. Therefore, there are nosegays (*TNK* IV.iii.25; *WT* IV.iii.42–43) that have no particular symbolic significance, flowers tossed at weddings or woven into garlands that may or may not mean anything, flowers placed on graves (*R&J* V.iii.9, 12; *Per* IV.i.15–17) or in caps (*Mac* IV.iii.172) simply because they are pretty, and even a character named after a flower (Peaseblossom, in *Midsummer Night's Dream*) whose name is simply chosen, as almost any flower could have been, to indicate that he is small. Yet such is not always the case. Flowers, to Shakespeare's audiences, were often imbued with special meanings that might come from their nicknames, their scents, their colors, their blooming seasons, or their uses in "kitchen physic." Most people were familiar with the more common wildflowers, and most housewives

Harebells, from John Gerard's *Herball*. Reproduced from the Collections
of the Library of Congress.

kept a garden filled with flowers to use in recipes, cosmetics, medicines,
and the mixtures of fresh sweet herbs strewn on floors.

Some flowers were notable for their colors or shapes. Lark's heels (*TNK*
I.i.12), or larkspurs, are thrown at the interrupted wedding of Theseus and
Hippolyta. These were a deep blue, with buds made of five petals and a
long slender "tail" facing away from the rest of the petals. When the petals
opened, they curled gently backward, with the tail remaining, and both
bud and blossom could be seen to resemble the shape of a bird's foot,
hence the flower's name. Other blue flowers included the harebell (*TNK*
I.i.9; *Cym* IV.ii.220–25), or English hyacinth, which had slender, bell-
shaped flowers; and violets (*MM* II.ii.166; *V&A* 125; *LLL* V.ii.892),
which were as notable for their sweet fragrance (*H5* IV.i.102; *WT*
IV.iv.120–22) as for their appearance. Like many flowers, violets were associated with springtime. *Orchis mascula*, like the violet, had a purplish
blossom, but the flower in this case was elongated. Ophelia mentions that
the blooms were known as "dead men's fingers" or "long purples" or by
another name, unspecified, that from context is clearly phallic (*Ham*
IV.vii.169–71).

Yellow flowers included "cuckoo-buds," also known as crowfoot or
crowflower (*Ham* IV.vii.169), a small, buttercup-like flower. John Gerard's *Herball* (such an influential text in its time that, to this day, inclusion
of a substance in its pages is acceptable to the FDA as proof of historical
safety) also lists "cuckoo-floures" in addition to crowfoot, but Shakespeare

Cowslips and oxlips, from Gerard's *Herball*. Reproduced from the Collections of the Library of Congress.

specifies that the flower he means is "of yellow hue" (*LLL* V.ii.894), and Gerard's cuckoo flowers are white. Cowslips (*MND* V.i.331; *Temp* V.i.89), too, were yellow, with tiny reddish spots on the petals (*Cym* II.ii.38–39), a combination of colors that brought to Shakespeare's mind the uniforms of Queen Elizabeth's bodyguard, the Gentlemen Pensioners (*MND* II.i.10–13). Cowslips were small and grew in bunches at the tops of tall stalks. Incidentally, they should be thought of not as "cow slips" but as "cows' lips" a division made clear by Gerard's pairing of them with a similar flower of similar name, the oxlip. Oxlips (*WT* IV.iv.125; *TNK* I.i.10; *MND* II.i.250) were paler than cowslips and less fragrant, with each stalk bearing fewer blooms scattered more widely apart.

White or whitish flowers were often associated with maidenly purity. The primrose, with its whitish yellow color, is often referred to by Shakespeare as "pale" or "faint" (*MND* I.i.215; *WT* IV.iv.122–24; *2H6* III.ii.63), its hue, in one case, explicitly likened to a young woman's fashionable pallor (*Cym* IV.ii.221). The primrose, another spring-blooming flower (*TNK* I.i.7–8), was common in both wild and cultivated varieties. Like the primrose, the even whiter lily was associated with virginity and with compliments about fair skin (*2GV* II.iii.20; *LLL* V.ii.353; *Cym* IV.ii.201; *H8* V.v.61). The lily is a type of iris, and the Madonna lily specifically is a pure white flower. Shakespeare mentions lilies (with the connotations of whiteness and innocence), the "flag" (another term for iris—see *A&C* I.iv.45), and the "flower-de-luce" or fleur-de-lis, a type of iris—or, as Gerard would have it, a name for several types of iris—that was a national symbol of France (*1H6* I.i.80, I.ii.99; *2H6* V.i.11; *H5* V.ii.212; *WT* IV.iv.126–27). The iris and the flower-de-luce were not necessarily white. However, lady-smocks, another name for Gerard's cuckoo-flowers, are identified as being "silver-white" (*LLL* V.ii.893).

Roses, too, were often used as examples of a particular color. Roses came in red and white, and a pale red or pink rose was known as a damask rose (*WT* IV.iv.221; *LLL* V.ii.294–98). The colors of roses were especially important politically, for the white version had long been a badge of the house of York (*2H6* I.i.252; *3H6* I.ii.33) and the red rose similarly indicated the house of Lancaster (*1H6* II.iv.27–76, 104–11, 121–31; *3H6* V.i.81 s.d.); the battles between the two houses for control of the English throne were called the Wars of the Roses because of these badges. When Henry VII, Elizabeth I's Lancastrian grandfather, married a daughter of the house of York, he expressed the marriage symbolically by adopting a double rose, red and white, as the badge of the Tudor dynasty. The Tudor rose remained a prominent emblem to the end of Elizabeth's reign and was supplanted in James I's by the Scottish thistle.

Roses were considered the world's finest flower and were prized for their scent, which could be distilled into waters and oils for use in cooking, medicines, and perfumes. Varieties included not only the damask rose but also the musk rose, noted, as its name implies, for its heady aroma (*MND* II.i.252, II.ii.3, V.i.3) and the canker rose, considered an inferior variety because its scent was not as sweet and could not be usefully distilled (S 54; *1H4* I.iii.174; *MAAN* I.iii.25). It did not help that its name was also associated with disease and with a kind of garden pest, the canker worm, that destroyed flowers. Shakespeare typically uses it as a symbol of something inferior or flawed. Roses also brought to mind, then as now,

thoughts of love and of beautiful young women (*TNK* I.i.1–3, II.i.192–200, V.i.162 s.d.; *R3* IV.iii.12). Roses were not the only flowers that came in a variety of colors. Carnations, called "gillyvors" by Shakespeare (*WT* IV.iv.79–83) and gillofloures by Gerard, also bloomed in a multiplicity of shades. Gerard gives several related varieties, which he names carnations, clove gillofloures, sops in wine, pinks, Sweet John, and Sweet William.

Some flowers, like the rose and the violet, were remarkable for their scent or lack thereof. Into the former category falls woodbine (*MAAN* III.i.30; *MND* II.i.251), also known as honeysuckle (*2H4* II.i.49; *MAAN* III.i.7–9). "Woodbinde" could also mean ivy or another climbing plant, however, which is why it seems to refer to a plant other than honeysuckle in *A Midsummer Night's Dream* (V.i.43–44). Eglantine, a five-petaled flower associated in Catholic times with the Virgin Mary and in Elizabethan times with the queen, was also a sweet-smelling flower (*Cym* IV.ii.223–24; *MND* II.i.252). The daisy (*Ham* IV.vii.169; *Cym* IV.ii.398; *TNK* I.i.5), which Gerard gives the alternate name of

Field primrose, from Gerard's *Herball*. Reproduced from the Collections of the Library of Congress.

"maudlin-wort," and the pink (*TNK* I.i.4; *R&J* II.iv.60–61), on the other hand, were pretty but had no strong fragrance.

Other flowers, particularly those of herbs, had medicinal uses. Among these were "Hot lavender, mints, savory, marjoram" (*WT* IV.iv.104), and thyme (*MND* II.i.249; *TNK* I.i.6). Gerard, who usually identifies flowers and plants according to the four alchemical characteristics of moist, dry, cold, and hot, says that lavender is a hot and dry plant, and can be used to heal ailments associated with cold and moisture. Savory, he says, sould be eaten with foods that cause gas in order to minimize flatulence. He confirms Perdita's (*WT* ch.) claim that these are summer bloomers; marjoram, for example, he says should be sown in May and will, in August, "bring forth their scaly or chaffie husks or ears." The physician Andrew Boorde wrote in his *Dyetary of Helth* that thyme was good for breaking up kidney stones, reducing flatulence, and increasing the output of urine. Boorde also noted that rosemary was good for palsy, falling sickness, coughs, and colds.

Rosemary was one of many flowers with symbolic significance as well as therapeutic uses. Because it was an evergreen whose plucked leaves retained their scent for an impressively long time, it was an emblem of memory and was sometimes given as a

Pinks, from Gerard's *Herball*. Reproduced from the Collections of the Library of Congress.

silent way of saying, "Remember me" (*WT* IV.iv.73–76; *Ham* IV.v.175; *R&J* IV.v.79–80). A bud symbolized promise of youth; rue, repentance or grace (*WT* IV.iv.73–76; *Ham* IV.v.181–82); anemones, the mythical Greek youth Adonis (*V&A* 1168); daffodils, springtime or the Greek youth from whom they took their alternate name, narcissus (*WT* IV.iii.1, IV.iv.118–20; *TNK* II.i.176). The pansy, because of the similarity of its name to the French word *pensées*, or "thoughts," symbolized sadness, love, pensiveness, and tender feelings (*MND* II.i.166–72). It was, for this reason, a common ingredient in love charms. Perhaps when Ophelia says that "there is pansies, that's / for thoughts" (*Ham* IV.v.76–77), she has a specific kind of thought in mind. The pansy's nicknames, heart's-ease and love-in-idleness, reflected its connotations of romantic love. Like the pansy of today, the Renaissance flower could have purple, yellow, and white or blue all in the same bloom, but in shape and size it resembled a violet more than a modern pansy. The marigold (*Per* IV.i.15) was symbolic either of the sun or of those who followed a great leader or cause, because, according to the compiler of emblems Claude Paradin, "it openeth and shutteth itself at the rising and falling of the sunne." Shakespeare repeatedly links the flower to sunlight (*WT* IV.iv.105–6; *RL* 397; S 25). The connection between sun and marigold was so well known that Gerard calls the sunflower, recently discovered in the New World, "the Floure of the Sun, or the Marigold of Peru," because of reports that its heavy blossom turned from east to west to follow the sun's path each day. *See also* Garden; Plants; Trees.

Food

The Renaissance diet was, in many ways, surprisingly varied. Obviously, there were far fewer prepared and packaged foods, fewer foreign dishes, and few or none of the New World foods that eventually became common in Europe, such as maize and the Virginia potato. The latter of these was discovered in 1538 but not brought to Europe until 1588, and in Shakespeare's day it was still a rarity. On the other hand, people ate far more types of game and a far greater number of identifiable pieces of the larger animals. Fruits, vegetables, dairy, meat, and desserts were all consumed, though the types of food eaten by an individual were largely dependent on social and economic class.

Meals

There was some dispute about how many meals a day were best for the health and morals of the English. The more restrained preferred two—dinner (lunch) and supper. Both William Harrison and Andrew Boorde fell into this camp. In *The Description of England* Harrison disapproved of "breakfasts in the forenoon, beverages or nuncheons after dinner, and thereto reresuppers generally when it was time to go to rest." Breakfast meant then what it does now; a nuncheon was an afternoon snack akin to the modern English tea; a reresupper was a small meal served late at night. Boorde, in his *Dyetary of Helth*, made an exception for those whose work demanded extra caloric intake, but he agreed in the main with Harrison:

"Two meales a daye is suffycyent for a rest[ing] man; and a labourer maye eate thre tymes a day; & he that doth eate ofter, lyveth a beestly lyfe."

Shakespeare appears to have had no moral or medical opposition to breakfast, for it is a meal he mentions often (*2GV* II.iv.141, III.i.321, V.ii.34; *H5* II.i.11, III.vii.148; *1H4* II.iv.105; *R3* IV.iv.177; *Per* IV.vi.127–28; *Tim* I.ii.76). To judge from his works, it might be eaten at home, in a tavern (*1H4* III.iii.178), or in house of a friend (*MWW* III.iii.222–23); hunters often ate a picnic breakfast in the woods while planning the day's strategy. Apprentices were apparently given a breakfast of some kind, though it might be often interrupted by their duties; one of the apprentices in Thomas Heywood's play *The Four Prentices of London*, probably written in the 1590s but not published until 1615, complains of how

> I cannot goe to breake-fast in a morning
> With my kinde mates and fellow-Prentises,
> But he cries *Eustace*, one bid *Eustace* come.

That he expects to eat "breake-fast" may reflect the actual feeding of apprentices or the fact that his family has fallen in the world and once ate this meal. One suspects it is the former, for many people, like Boorde, associated the extra meal with those who had to labor for a living. The typical farmer's breakfast was pottage—a stew of meat broth, vegetables, oatmeal, and salt; Boorde claimed in his *Brevyary of Health* that the dish had a tendency to make the eater gassy. He listed other kinds of pottage as well, including frumenty, a dish made with wheat and milk, sometimes with a piece of meat stewed in it, that he declared hard to digest but nourishing; pease pottage and bean pottage, both of which also produced gas; and rice pottage with almond milk, which "doth restore and doth comforte nature."

Dinner (*1H6* II.iv.133; *3H6* II.ii.122–23; *2GV* I.ii.67, 131, II.i.169–70; *LLL* IV.ii.155; *MAAN* II.iii.207; *R&J* I.i.176; *JC* I.ii.288–89; *TS* IV.iii.187) took place around 11 A.M. or noon (*R&J* II.iv.146–47, II.v.78; *AYLI* IV.i.178–79), though Harrison noted that university scholars ate at 10 A.M. "out of the term," and was the largest meal of the day. Heywood's play *The English Traveller* (1633) lists a bill of fare for a gentleman's son in which many items are selected for their delicacy and high cost: duck, capon, turkey, green plover, snipe, partridge, lark, cock, pheasant, widgeon,

> Caviar,
> Sturgeon, anchovies, pickle-oysters. Yes,
> And a potato pie. Besides all these
> What thou think'st rare and costly.

The sheer variety was in itself an extravagance, for the typical gentleman had one to three dishes at his table when dining alone, and four to six when he was joined by guests. A dinner of the more ordinary kind might begin with a salad in summer, continue with meats, bread, and broth, and end with fruit and fortified wines. In *The Merry Wives of Windsor*, dinner ends with "pippins and seese" (apples and cheese—I.ii.12). In *The Whole Art and Trade of Husbandry*, Conrad Heresbach advised farmers to eat a moderate dinner of "an egge, a chicke, a peece of kid, or a peece of veale, fish, butter, and such like," and to sit at the table no more than an hour.

Supper (*TS* IV.i.41, 128, 131 s.d., IV.iii.189, IV.iv.86; *2GV* II.i.45; *1H4* I.ii.130–31; *MAAN* I.i.269; *R&J* II.iv.134; *JC* I.ii.286, II.ii.238; *R3* III.ii.120; *Oth* I.i.96; *A&C* IV.ii.44) began at five (*MV* II.ii.113–14) or six (*LLL* I.i.234–36) in town and on great estates, but not until seven or eight on smaller farms, where the housewife had many tasks to occupy her before she could turn her attention to cooking. It was supposed to be a lighter meal (*2H6* II.ii.2), and Boorde warned against eating rich food at this time, but on the farm the plowmen, who had worked hard all day, expected roast meat now and then. Workers went to bed promptly, but the aristocracy might stay up late, burning expensive candles, socializing, and eating a reresupper or "aftersupper" (*MND* V.i.32–34). The best descriptions of suppers can be found in *The Taming of the Shrew* (IV.iii.15–46), where Kate desires to be fed, and *1 Henry IV* (II.iv.540–44), where Falstaff reviews his tavern bill.

The most complex term was "banquet" (*AYLI* II.v.58; *TA* V.ii.76, 193, 202, V.ii.114–15, 128, 192; *A&C* I.ii.13–14, II.vii.1 s.d.; *Tim* III.vi.47 s.d.; *TNK* III.i.109, V.iv.22; *R&J* I.v.124; *Temp* III.iii.17 s.d.), which usually meant what we would now think of as a dessert course (*R2* I.iii.67–68). It included fresh fruit, dried fruit, and various dishes made with sugar *1H6* III.iii.18; *2H6* III.ii.45; *1H4* II.iv.4–5; *WT* IV.iii.38–39; *R2* II.iii.6; *R3* I.iii.241), often served with sweetened or spiced wine. The meal was eaten buffet-style from a table full of footed dishes piled high with sweets—jellies, custards (*AW* II.v.37), candied (*Ham* III.ii.60; *1H4* III.iii.168–69) citrus peel, preserved fruits (*TS* Ind.ii.3, 7) either sweetened and dried ("sucket" or "sucket candy") or still swimming in honey (*LLL* V.ii.232; *H5* I.i.50, II.iii.1; *R&J* II.vi.11–12; *1H4* III.ii.71; *R3* IV.i.79) or sugar syrup ("wet sucket"), sugared aniseed or caraway seed (*2H4* V.iii.3) "comfits" to sweeten the breath, sweetened biscuits, shortbread, "jumballs" or knots (pretzel-like, interlaced cookies), gingerbread (*LLL* V.i.69; *1H4* III.i.253), white gingerbread (made with almond paste and sometimes gilded), stiff and sliceable marmalades of quince or orange, small cakes (*CE* III.i.71; *TS* I.i.108; *2H4* II.iv.149; *TN* II.iii.117; *T&C* I.i.14–26), and leaches (jellies made with milk or cream and flavored with spices or rosewater). The centerpiece was often a "marchpane" (*R&J* I.v.9), or marzipan, shaped into a large, thin disk, iced, and decorated with complex designs, such as the figures and names of the zodiac constellations. Sometimes the ingredients were suspected aphrodisiacs; "kissing comfits," for example, were made from "eringoes" (*MWW* V.v.20), the roots of sea holly, which the botanist John Gerard described in *The Herball* as "the bignesse of a man's finger, and very long." The eringo root, which was candied with a distilled water of roses or orangeblossoms, or sometimes with cinnamon and musk, was widely thought to enhance sexual arousal. All of these sweetmeats (*R&J* I.iv.76) were collectively known as "banquetting stuffe," "junkets" (TS III.ii.247) or junkeries, or "cates" (*CE* III.i.28; *1H6* II.iii.79; *TS* II.i.189), the last of these terms being applicable to any kind of fine and costly food, sweet or otherwise.

The liberal use of sugar and "warm" spices such as nutmeg and cinnamon was thought to aid digestion after the main meal; it was also the reason that such banquets or *voidées* were the province of the rich (*TS* Ind.i.39). Because England had no colonial source of sugar until after 1616, all sugar had to be imported from places such as North Africa and Madeira and was therefore quite costly. Loaves of it were given as lavish gifts or used as bribes, and the sugar and spices were kept locked up (*R&J* IV.iv.1) and given to the cook only as he needed them. The sweets for banquets were either made by the lady of the house and her daughters and maids from ingredients purchased from grocers, or bought ready-made from comfit-makers (confectioners—see *Tim* IV.iii.261; *1H4* III.i.246).

However, a banquet, in addition to being this light and expensive final

A middle-class dinner, from the *Roxburghe Ballads*. Reproduced from the Collections of the Library of Congress.

course, could also be a banquet in the modern sense: a large feast (*LLL* II.i.40; *R&J* I.ii.20, 84, 100, I.v.76; *TS* III.ii.184–247, V.i.139, V.ii.8– 10; *TNK* I.i.219; *AYLI* II.vii.114) of the kind served after a wedding, at a church-ale, or at a trade guild's annual meeting. It could also mean a light snack between meals, perhaps simply of preserved and fresh fruits. If this was the bill of fare, it was called a running banquet, and if only fresh fruit was served, a fruit banquet. Because fruit in season was much cheaper than the sugar and spices necessary to produce candies, the fruit banquet had extended to the middle class by the time of Shakespeare's career.

Middle-class people also enjoyed pies (*H8* I.i.52) and tarts (*TS* IV.iii.90), which could be made with fruit and perhaps a little sweetening. The crust of the pie, because it had a bottom and lid that enclosed the filling, was called a coffin (*TA* V.ii.188; *TS* IV.iii.83; and indirectly, in *R2* III.ii.154). There were meat pies as well, and Shakespeare is not always perfectly clear about whether he means sweet or savory pies, but in at least one instance his intention is plain, for he explicitly mentions a pie of war-den pears in a crust colored with saffron (*WT* IV.iii.46–50). Another dessert available to the middle class was white-pot, a white cream custard flavored with spices and apples; for a long time, dishes made with cream or milk were considered peasant food. These dishes, however, were rarely called desserts. The term "dessert" was still unusual in 1600 and would not be in common usage until the second half of the seventeenth century.

Fish and Flesh

Of all the foods eaten in Shakespeare's lifetime, bread was perhaps the most ubiquitous and essential, but meat was the one most widely desired. There was nothing like a good roast, slowly spit-turned over the kitchen fire, from a freshly butchered animal, particularly since fresh meat was a seasonal treat, not always affordable by the poor, and in any case restricted by the numerous fish, or fast, days in the Elizabethan calendar. There were 153 fish days each year after 1563, including the entire period of Lent and every Wednesday, Friday, and Saturday (*LLL* I.ii.126; *MM* III.ii.180–81). Almost all meats were divided into the categories of fish or flesh (*Per* II.i.85–86), with poultry falling on the side of flesh and a few foods, such as oysters (*TS* IV.ii.102; *Lear* I.v.25), edible on either type of day.

The fish that were eaten included cod (*Oth* II.i.153), sole, herring (*2H6* IV.ii.36–37; *MWW* II.iii.11; *Lear* III.vi.31; *TN* I.v.120–21; *R&J* II.iv.38), pilchard (a fish like a herring but smaller and rounder—see *TN* III.i.34–36), conger eel (*1H4* II.iv.246; *2H4* II.iv.250); plaice, flounder, sprat (*AW* III.vi.107), turbot, haddock, trout (*MM* I.ii.92), smelt, mack-erel (*1H4* II.iv.363), dory, carp, pike, perch, gurnet (*1H4* IV.ii.12), the dried hake called "Poor John" (*Temp* II.ii.27), bream, barbel, chub, loach, and what William Harrison called "lumps, an ugly fish to sight and yet very delicate in eating if it be kindly dressed." Shellfish, such as crayfish, lobsters, oysters, prawns (which Shakespeare serves with vinegar—see *2H4* II.i.92–97), shrimp (*1H6* II.iii.23), crabs, whelks, mussels (*MWW* IV.v.26), and cockles (*TNK* III.iv.14, IV.i.130), were also consumed; Duke Frederick of Württemberg's secretary noted the presence, in 1592, of oyster sellers crying their wares in the streets and of markets where fresh and salt fish were sold.

Fish was prepared in several ways; it could be salted (*MWW* I.i.21), smoked, or fried fresh in butter (*AW* V.ii.7–8), and the physician Andrew Boorde declared in the *Dyetary of Helth* that it could safely be "sod, rostyd, bruyled, & baken." Sometimes thin pieces of desiccated cod, called "stock-fish" (*1H4* II.iv.247; *Temp* III.ii.74; *2H4* III.ii.33; *MM* III.ii.110), were stewed in water to make a fish broth; this may be what he meant by "sod," or boiled. Boorde was of the opinion that saltwater fish were more healthful than freshwater fish, and that river fish (*Cym* IV.ii.35–36) were better than those from ponds or other standing water. Porpoise, which some ate, he thought an improper food, and he also warned against eating the skin, heads, or fat of the fish, and against eating fish and flesh at the same meal. He does not render an opinion on fish pies, but they were certainly made, for Shakespeare mentions eels in "paste," or pastry (*Lear* II.iii.119–22). Harrison noted that river fish were sold by the inch, measured from eye or gill to the "crotch" of the tail.

Fish was, in the language of the time, a "cold" food, which meant not that it was served cold but that it had a natural essence of coldness and could thus counteract "hot" influences on the body, such as anger, fever, and alcohol (*2H4* IV.iii.92). Meat, on the other hand, was naturally "hot," even if served cold (*Cym* III.vi.38), and was good for most people, because heat was believed to aid digestion. The poor were seldom able to benefit from the heating qualities of meat, but almost everyone else ate it a few times a week, and the rich ate it in great variety: mutton (*TS* IV.i.149–64; *2H4* II.iv. 354; *2GV* I.i.97–101, often served with capers as in *TN* I.iii.116–17), lamb, veal (*LLL* V.ii.248), brawn, souse, bacon (*1H4* II.i.25, II.ii.85–86; *MWW* IV.i.47; *TNK* IV.iii.37), hare (*R&J* II.iv.137–45), rabbit (*LLL* III.i.18–19; *TS* IV.iv.99–101—like the hare, thought of as poultry rather than red meat), venison from their private deer parks (*AYLI* II.i.21; *Cym* IV.iv.37; *TNK* III.iii.27; *MWW* I.i.75, 77), beef (*1H6* I.i.9; *TS* Ind.ii.7, *H5* III.vii.152; *TN* I.iii.83), kid, and pork (*MV* III.v.23–26). Most of these meats are self-explanatory, but brawn and souse are a bit obscure. Souse consisted of preserved pig parts, such as ears and feet. Brawn (*1H4* II.iv.111) was a delicacy produced by fattening a boar in a hard-floored pen, boiling the flesh from its front legs, and preserving the cooked, softened meat as a kind of pickled paste. This unappetizing description belies its extraordinary popularity, especially in the countryside, where it was a standard winter dish.

Most meat (*CE* II.ii.54–62; *2H6* IV.x.39–42; *R2* II.i.76; *Cym* V.iv.123;

TNK IV.iii.86) eaten during the winter was preserved in some way, because most livestock simply could not survive on the limited dried fodder stored during the summer and fall. Accordingly, there was a butchering season in the late autumn, near Martinmas, and most farms killed off a large percentage of their animals at this time. The beef produced at this time, called Martylmas beef (*2H4* II.ii.100), was hung on hooks in the smokehouse or chimney and preserved; other meats were salted and smoked as well, and the family had to get by on this fare until well into the spring and summer, when veal, lamb, and "grass beef" fattened on pasture were available. Those who were able, supplemented their home-grown meats with wild game and meats purchased from butchers (*2H6* III.ii.189, 195, IV.ii.ch., IV.iii.ch., IV.vii.ch.; *2H4* II.i.92–95; *H5* V.ii.142–44; *JC* II.i.166, 175–76; *MWW* III.v.4–6; *Cym* III.iv.96–97; *Cor* IV.vi.96); town dwellers, of course, got all their meats from a butcher. There might be many such tradesmen in a single town; Manchester, for example, had fifty butchers' stalls in 1599. Throughout the year, meat consumption was higher in England than almost anywhere else in Europe, and "meat" was in fact synonymous with "food" in many contexts (*TS* IV.iii.9; *2GV* I.ii.68, II.i.173; *MM* I.ii.14–16). This is its meaning in the phrase "spoon-meat" (*CE* IV.iii.59), which simply meant any soft food—whether it contained flesh or not—that could be eaten with a spoon.

Meat was prepared simply. Usually it was roasted on spits (*Cym* V.iv.122; *Per* IV.ii.132–33; *A&C* II.ii.181), though it might also be baked into savory pies (*TA* V.iii.60; *TS* IV.iii.83; *T&C* I.i.263–64; *AW* I.i.161) called pasties (*MWW* I.i.186; *TA* V.ii.189; *AW* IV.iii.125), boiled, or stewed, and accompanied by mustard (*TS* IV.iii.23, 25–30; *2H4* II.iv.246; *MND* III.i.192–92; *AYLI* I.ii.61–65) or, in a new innovation imported from the Continent, by sauces (*TN* III.iv.148–49; *H5* V.i.34; *JC* I.ii.298–300; *TNK* III.iii.25–26). Harrison said that meat could be baked in suet or roasted and basted either with butter or with its own juices. The muscles of the cow were eaten as today, but the chine (*backbone*—see *2H6* IV.x.58; *H8* V.iv.25), feet (*TS* IV.iii.17), tongue, head (*MAAN* V.i.155), organ meats, and tripe (stomach lining—*TS* IV.iii.20) were also widely consumed. Sometimes the animal was roasted whole; pigs were sometimes cooked in this way with fruit in the mouth (*MV* IV.i.47), and a whole roast boar was the special delicacy of the annual Bartholomew Fair (*2H4* II.iv.234–35). Sometimes meat was cut into small slices called collops (*WT* I.ii.137), and sometimes it was simply slashed, or "carbonadoed" (*1H4* V.iii.60; *AW* IV.v.101; *Lear* II.ii.39; *WT* IV.iv.265; *Cor* IV.v.195–96), and broiled. It might also be made into sausages, which were called "puddings" (*2GV* IV.iv.30; *MWW* V.v.154; *MM* IV.iii.15; *Per* II.i.86; *Oth* II.i.252; *AW* II.ii.27), by being chopped, seasoned, stuffed into washed intestines, tied at intervals, and boiled. Because of the use of intestines as sausage casings, the intestines of a living creature, particularly if it had recently fed, were sometimes referred to as puddings (*1H4* II.iv.458; *H5* II.i.88–89; *MWW* II.i.30–31).

Boorde found boiled meat easier to digest than that which was "rosted," and he forbade that which was baked or fried. Young beef was a healthful food, he determined, but old beef engendered melancholy. He acknowledged that veal was the favorite meat of many people (though he preferred kid), warned that lamb was bad for old men, and was generally suspicious of mutton because sheep were susceptible to so many diseases. Bacon was "good for carters and plowmen," but bad for the urinary tract; hare engendered melancholy, but rabbit was fine; tongues (*1H4* II.iv.247; *MV* I.i.112; *MAAN* II.i.264–65) were not nutritive, but the testicles of gelded animals were. As for the omnipresent brawn, he found it "harde of dygestyon," and judged that it couldn't hurt anyone who didn't eat it. Occasionally, as in the case of brawn, his judgments are often funny or disarmingly personal. Of pork, he says simply, "I dyd never love it." Of venison, he says that it is healthful but that "great men do not set so moch by the meate, as they do by the pastyme of kyllyng of it." And of the notorious "Martylmas beef, whiche is called 'hanged beef' in the rofe of the smoky howse," he has nothing good to say. It is "not laudable" and will serve a man better as an umbrella than as food:

> If a man have a peace hangynge by his syde, and another in his bely, that the whiche doth hange by the syde shall do hym more good, yf a showre of rayne do chaunse, than that the which is in his bely.

Nevertheless, he admits that many people enjoy smoked beef and seems resigned to the fact that they will go on eating it despite his advice.

Poultry, like meat, was usually boiled or roasted on spits. The variety eaten may be astonishing to twenty-first-century readers accustomed to seeing only chicken, turkey, and a few other less common fowls at the supermarket. Chickens were common enough and were divided into several groups, including pullets (young females), hens (adult females), and capons (gelded males—see *AYLI* II.vii.153; *1H4* II.iv.461–62; *MAAN* V.i.155; *2GV* IV.iv.9; *LLL* IV.i.57–58). The capon was the most commonly eaten, since hens could lay eggs and thus justify their continued existence. Turkeys (*1H4* II.i.228) were less common, having been introduced to Europe only in the 1530s; the agricultural expert Leonard Mascall did not like to raise them, for he found them greedy eaters and intolerant of cold and wet. Then there were duck, pheasant, swan, peacock, goose (*R&J* II.iv.81–85), pigeon (often served in pies—see *2H4* V.i.18–19, 27), partridge (*MAAN* II.i.144), quail, snipe, woodcock, turtledoves (*MV* II.ii.133), cranes, bitterns, plover, gulls (captured and fed beef for a while before butchering, to cleanse them of their fishy flavor), curlews, herons, blackbirds, thrushes, and larks. Boorde thought pheasant the best game bird, partridge the most digestible, capon the best and most digestible domestic fowl, and roosters suitable only for broth or "gely." Ducks were bad, young geese acceptable, young turtledoves good for the blood, and pigeons "good for coloryke & melancoly men." The birds were killed and brought to the kitchen (*MM* II.ii.85–86), where the cook or an assistant plucked them clean (sometimes scalding them in boiling water first to loosen the feathers—see *Tim* II.ii.75–76), chopped off their feet and heads, spitted them several at a time from throat to backside, and basted them over the fire with a ladle.

Dairy Products

The poor had no hired cooks, no large herds of livestock. They were lucky to have a cow, a pig, and a few chickens. Their protein therefore came mostly from fish, poached rabbits, trapped or arrow-shot birds, and "white meat"—eggs, milk, and milk products. The eggs (*R&J* III.i.23–25; *T&C* I.ii.137; *AW* IV.iii.254; *Lear* I.iv.157–61), gathered fresh and either eaten right away or stored for a while in salt or bran, were typically roasted (*TNK* II.ii.75; *AYLI* III.ii.36–37) or poached and sprinkled with salt and, if it could be had, a little sugar as well. Boorde recommended against fried eggs, probably the same "eggs and butter" found in *1 Henry IV* (I.ii.20–21, II.i.61–62).

The milk (*LLL* V.ii.911; *1H4* II.iii.32) of cows, ewes, and goats (*TA* IV.ii.178–79) was drunk fresh or as "whig," a term for sour milk, buttermilk, or whey (*Mac* V.iii.17). A particularly rich milk, and therefore much prized, was "beest" (*TNK* III.v.130), the milk produced soon after calving. Boorde thought that clotted and raw cream eaten together were tasty but not nourishing—a kind of Renaissance junk food—and that raw cream over strawberries, a common rural dish, was bad for the liver. Perhaps his disapproval came from the general perception that because dairy products were a staple of the poor, they were therefore inferior. Not until the seventeenth century was cream redeemed in the fashionable mind and absorbed into such delicacies as "syllabubs," confections made of sugar, wine, cream, and spices. Even then, there remained a declassé connotation to dairy foods; the affected foreign household servant Reignald, in Thomas Heywood's 1633 play *The English Traveller*, calls the common English servant Robin "cheese and onions" and orders him to

> Stuff thy guts
> With speck [bacon fat] and barley-pudding . . . ,
> Drink whig and sour milk, whilst I rinse my throat
> With Bordeaux and canary.

Reignald is hardly a sympathetic character, so Heywood seems to want his audience to approve of Robin's homely English fare, but its homeliness is nevertheless plain. A more positive, but still pastoral, view appeared in a 1619 poem by Michael Drayton. Here the "country cates" include "New whig," stream water, fresh fruit, cheese, "curds and clowted cream," syl-labubs, and cider.

Dairy products were made, according to Conrad Heresbach, by allowing the collected milk to sit in a bowl or pan. On the second or third day, the cream (*MV* I.i.89; *1H4* IV.ii.58–59; *WT* IV.v.161) was skimmed and churned into butter (*1H4* II.iv.121–24, 516, IV.ii.61; *MWW* II.ii.272, 295, V.v.143–45), "and eyther eaten fresh, or barrelled with Salt." The leftover buttermilk was either drunk or given as a treat to calves and dogs. Cheese (*T&C* V.iv.10–11) was made by pouring milk into a large vessel with a walnut-sized chunk of rennet (the lining membrane from an ani-mal's stomach used to curdle milk, often stored in birch juice to prevent infestations of mites—see *AW* I.i.144–46). When curds formed, they were pressed into molds with the hand or a weight, the goal being to remove the liquid, or whey, as quickly as possible. The pressed curds (*3H6* II.v.47; *WT* IV.v.161) were then placed in a cool, dark place, sprinkled with salt to draw out moisture, left for a while, and then pressed again. They were salted and pressed a third time, then allowed to sit in storage, packed in heaps of pulse or wheat, until they were needed in the kitchen. When it was time to serve the cheese, typically at the end of a meal to aid digestion (*T&C* II.iii.41; *MWW* I.ii.11–12), the hard rind was cut off and the inside eaten. The rind afforded some entertainment for those who were not too particular about their table manners; Shakespeare mentions the practice of carving it into little figures, perhaps for the amusement of children (*2H4* III.ii.313–14). Cheese could be eaten plain or laid atop bread and toasted (*H5* II.i.9; *MWW* V.v.142; *Lear* IV.vi.89; *2H6* IV.vii.12–13); it was as-sociated with Welshmen, who were supposedly particularly avid cheese eat-ers (*MWW* II.ii.296, V.v.83–84).

Cheeses were named according to their age, texture, or place of origin. Green cheese was not green in color, but was the youngest cheese, with some whey still present. There were soft and hard cheeses and "spermyse," which was made of curds and "the juice of herbs" mixed together. Heresbach considered that "In England the best Cheese is the Cheshire, and the Shropshire, then the Banbury Cheese, next the Suffolke, and the Essex Cheese, and the very worst is the Kentish Cheese." Of all these cheeses, Shakespeare mentions only the Banbury variety, noted for its thin-ness (*MWW* I.i.122–23).

Grains

Both rich and poor relied on grains for part of their diet, though among the poor they made up a greater percentage of the total. There were also differences in the types of grain eaten; the rich tended to consume the more expensive wheat (*T&C* I.i.14; *A&C* II.vi.37), while the poor relied more on the cheaper oats, barley, and rye. Regional specialization, too, influenced diet, for oats and barley tended to be the dominant grains in the northwest, while the northeast ate more rye; the south, wheat; and East Anglia and the west, barley. Peas and beans were grown, too, but these were mostly used as animal feed and the occasional poor man's pottage.

Several grades of bread were made by home and professional bakers (*1H4* III.iii.72–75). The finest was manchet, a soft white (*TNK* III.v.81) wheat bread that weighed 8 ounces (226.8 g) going into the oven and 6 ounces (170.1 g) coming out. Andrew Boorde admitted that wheat breads fattened the eater but confessed, "I do love manchet breade." Cheat was a lesser grade of wheat bread, made with slightly yellower flour that had had the coarsest bran (*MM* IV.iii.155) removed. The size of the loaf, 18 ounces (510.3 g) going into the oven, 16 ounces (453.6 g) after baking, was governed by statute. William Harrison mentions the assize of bread, the regular inspections of loaves performed at markets, but he also notes that the regulations were seldom enforced except against out-of-town bakers with a superior-tasting product. The bread called raveled cheat was rougher still, and "brown bread"

A miller, from *Panoplia*, illustrated by Jost Amman. Reproduced from the Collections of the Library of Congress.

(*MM* III.ii.183) might not be made of wheat at all. It was made sometimes with whole wheat, sometimes with the mixture of wheat and rye called maslin, mesclin, or, in Boorde's spelling, "mestlyng." This mixture, like the even less appealing flour made of rye and barley, produced a bread that only the laboring classes would eat. The truly poor made their bread of whatever they could get, even if that was the sort of food normally fed to animals—beans, peas, oats (*Lear* V.iii.39), and ground acorns. Boorde's *Brevyary of Health* recommends removing the upper crust of bread before eating it, consuming it when it was no less than 24 hours and no more than 5 days old, and salting it moderately. One should not eat stale bread, he warned, for stale bread dried up natural moisture, and people in the

Renaissance were terrified of anything that interfered with the balance of their bodily fluids. The poor, of course, ate crusts and stale bread if that was what they had, since they had not the leisure to accept Boorde's medical advice.

Shakespeare tends to mention bread without much elaboration, either as a specific food, without further details, or, like "meat," as a synonym for all food (*MAAN* III.v.38; *H5* IV.i.270; *R2* III.i.21, III.ii.175; *Tim* I.ii.46; *TNK* I.i.158). He does, however, write occasionally of the process of baking and eating it. This process began with corn (*1H6* III.ii.15; *2H6* I.ii.1; *LLL* IV.iii.380; *3H6* V.vii.3; *TA* V.iii.71; *Cor* III.i.114; *Per* I.iv.94)—not Indian corn, or maize, but a synonym for grain of any kind—that was harvested, threshed to remove the grains from the stalks, winnowed to remove the chaff, and hauled in sacks (*LLL* IV.iii.78) to the local mill (*WT* IV.iv.306; *Cor* I.x.31) to be ground. The miller (*TNK* V.ii.66), whose huge horizontal millstones (*T&C* I.ii.149) were usually turned by a waterwheel or windmill, and occasionally by horses, poured the grain so that it gradually worked its way between the stones and was crushed and driven out. As his pay, the miller kept a percentage of the flour, a system that, while helping cash-poor customers, occasioned much disagreement. Millers were continually accused of taking too much flour or of taking the finest-ground while sending the customer home with "chaff and bran, chaff / and bran" (*T&C* I.ii.247–48; see also *Cor* I.i.147–48).

A baker, from *Panoplia*, illustrated by Jost Amman. In the background, a baker kneads dough in a trough; in the foreground another, stripped to the waist because of the heat of the ovens, inserts bread into the oven using a wooden peel. Reproduced from the Collections of the Library of Congress.

Not all the grains of flour were of the same fineness, so they were "bolted"—sifted—and the finer flour, which Shakespeare calls "meal" (*Cor* III.i.321), was separated from the coarser. This step might also be performed at home or, in some households, omitted entirely. Some flour went to bakers, who apparently did their own sifting (*H5* II.ii.137; *Cor* III.i.320–22) with bolters, or sieves, made of coarse linen (*1H4* III.iii.72–75). They baked loaves and sold them for as little as a halfpenny (*2H6* IV.ii.67). Their results were probably more consistent than those of home bakers, who occasionally turned out a doughy mess or a "Cobloaf" (a loaf that was mostly burnt crust—see *T&C* II.i.37). Loaves of bread were sliced (*TA* II.i.87) at home, and people tended to prefer the "crum" (the soft part inside—see *Lear* I.iv.198) to the crust. Nevertheless, they would take a whole slice and eat it with cheese (*MWW* II.i.132), or perhaps toasted with butter (*1H4* IV.ii.21). Dry toast was broken into bits and soaked in wine; these "sops" could also be made of small bits of cake (*R3* I.iv.160; *TS* III.ii.172; *T&C* I.iii.45, 113; *Lear* II.ii.33).

Flour could also be made into the flat and extremely hard ship's biscuits (*T&C* II.i.38–39), fritters (*MWW* V.v.146), pancakes (*AYLI* I.ii.61–65; *AW* II.ii.23–24) or flapjacks (*Per* II.i.87), pie crusts, and small sweet cakes. The process of making a cake is described in *Troilus and Cressida*, from "the grinding" of the flour to "the / bolting," "the leavening," "the kneading, the making of the / cake, the heating of the oven, and the baking" (I.i.14–26). Porridge (*MWW* III.i.60; *T&C* I.ii.48; *Lear* III.iv.54), made of stewed whole grain, peas, or beans, was a common dish at rural breakfasts. Shakespeare implies that it was sometimes sweetened with dates (*AW* I.i.161–62).

Vegetables

Almost every housewife, in the country or the towns, kept a small garden in which she grew herbs and vegetables. Many (though not all) of these were meant to be eaten. Thomas Tusser suggested an array of vegetables that a woman ought to grow and categorized them by use. Among those for salads and sauces, he listed "alexanders" (horse parsley, the stalks of which were eaten like celery), artichokes, carduus benedictus (holy thistle), cucumbers, cresses, endive, mustard, mint, purslane, radish, rocket (a strong-tasting salad green), sage, sorrel, spinach, skirrets (water parsnips, which had edible roots), succory, tarragon, and violets. Salads (or "sallets"—see *2H6* IV.x.8–16; *AW* IV.v.13–19; *Lear* III.iv.130) were eaten with a very basic vinaigrette; they were also, because they required fresh and preferably tender leaves and stems, eaten primarily in the spring and early summer, hence Cleopatra's reference to her youth as her "salad days" (*A&C* I.v.73).

Vegetables to be boiled or buttered included beans, cabbage, carrots (*MWW* IV.i.52), citrons, gourds, navews (cole, a cabbagelike plant), pompions (pumpkins—see *MWW* III.iii.39), parsnips, runcival peas, rape (a turniplike plant), and turnips. Other sources added leeks (*MND* V.i.334), lettuce (*Oth* I.iii.315), onions (*A&C* IV.ii.35–36; *TS* Ind.i.124–28; *MND* IV.ii.40–42; *AW* V.iii.320), mures (sweet cicely, whose roots were used in salads), and sweet potatoes (*T&C* V.ii.55; *MWW* V.v.18–19) to these lists. Some fashionable people grew and ate mushrooms, cauliflower, and eggplants, vegetables that were out of the mainstream of English cooking. Some vegetables had additional significance. The leek, for example, was a symbol of Wales (*H5* IV.i.54, IV.vii.97–104, V.i.1–2, 8–12, 22–59), and sweet potatoes, which were not grown in England but imported from Spain, Portugal, and the Indies, were thought to have aphrodisiac qualities. The pea was such a commonly grown vegetable that there were names for each of its different phases of growth: peaseblossom for the flower, squash for the unripe pod, and peascod for the ripe pod (*MND* III.i.186–87; *2H4* II.iv.390; *TN* I.v.156–57; *Lear* I.iv.200; *WT* I.ii.160).

Andrew Boorde had a medical opinion of most vegetables. Turnips, for example, augmented the appetite when eaten raw and increased fertility when boiled with meat. He may not have been entirely mistaken about the latter, for anyone who could afford meat had a better chance of eating a balanced diet, which in itself would have aided conception. Several vegetables, according to Boorde, increased the production of semen, urine, or both; these included parsnips, radishes (which had the unfortunate side effects of worsening gas and gout), carrots, and rocket. Rape was nutritive but caused gas and stomach discomfort, while sorrel was good for the stomach and gourds, despite their popularity, were simply evil. Leeks increased urine output and could "open the breste" (clear the lungs), but they also increased "evyll blode." Naturally cool foods included lettuce and cucumbers; both could decrease the sex drive, and lettuce was good for inducing sleep, blood production, and lactation. Aphrodisiacs included artichokes boiled in beef broth (*Cym* IV.ii.50) and onions, which had the dual effect of inciting both sleep and "veneryous actes."

In *The Herball*, the botanist John Gerard had different advice, mingling the medical uses of plants with instructions for their cultivation and descriptions of their appearance. In most cases, the vegetables he describes resemble their descendants today, though radishes, according to his account, were not the red-skinned, rounded, walnut-sized roots we would recognize, but long tubers (*1H4* II.iv.187; *2H4* III.ii.314–16). Gerard mentions tomatoes but dismisses the "Apples of Love" as a source of food: "In Spaine and those hot Regions they use to eate the Apples prepared and boiled with pepper, salt, and oyle: but they yeeld very little nourishment to the body, and the same naught and corrupt."

Fruit

Fruit was fairly widely available, whether it was gathered wild, bought from a fruiterer (*2H4* III.ii.33), grown in gardens and orchards, or stolen from a neighbor's orchard. The most common varieties were apples, pears, and plums (*John* II.i.162; *V&A* 527–28), followed by peaches, melons, cherries (*MND* III.ii.140, 209–11; *John* II.i.162; *R3* I.i.94; *V&A* 1103), gooseberries (*2H4* I.ii.175), mulberries (*Cor* III.ii.79–80; *TNK* IV.i.68; *V&A* 1103), barberries, quinces (*R&J* IV.iv.2), raspberries, whortleberries (tiny dark-blue berries also called bilberries—see *MWW* V.v.47), strawberries (*R3* III.iii.32, 47; *H5* I.i.60–62), blackberries (*1H4* II.iv.240–41, 413–14; *T&C* V.iv.12), apricots (*MND* III.i.166), nectarines, currants (*WT* IV.iii.39), and figs (*A&C* V.ii.235; *Oth* I.iii.314; *2H6* II.iii.67; *John* II.i.162). Shakespeare also mentions "dewberries" (*MND* III.i.166), which may have been blackberries or gooseberries.

Some of the fruits mentioned in treatises for gardeners, or in Shakespeare's works, were varieties of more familiar fruits. Damsons (*2H6* II.i.97, 101, 102) and bullaces, for example, were types of plums; wardens (*WT* IV.iii.46) were a kind of pear; and pippins (*MWW* I.ii.12; *2H4* V.iii.2), costards (a large variety whose name was also a synonym for "head"—see *LLL* III.i.70, *MWW* III.i.14), and crabs (*LLL* IV.ii.6, V.ii.920; *MND* II.i.48; *Lear* I.v.15–16; *Temp* II.ii.169; *TS* II.i.226–28) were apples. Shakespeare's "pomewater" (*LLL* IV.ii.4) and "bitter sweeting" (*R&J* II.v.82) are sweet and tart apples, respectively, and his "leather-/ coats" are apples with reddish-brown skins (*2H4* V.iii.42–43). Lemons (*LLL* V.ii.645), yellowish Seville oranges (*MAAN* II.i.283–84), dates (*WT* IV.iii.47; *R&J* IV.iv.2; *AW* I.i.161), pomegranates (*AW* II.iii.262), grapes (*AW* II.iii.100; *Cor* V.iv.17; *TNK* IV.ii.95–96, *RL* 215), and raisins (*WT* IV.iii.50) were all imported, for they would not grow satisfactorily in the English climate.

Many fruits were eaten raw. Some were eaten preserved with sugar, dried, or as flavorings in cooked dishes. Plums, for example, were eaten fresh, dried as prunes (*MWW* I.i.273; *WT* IV.iii.50), and cooked into a dish called plum broth or plum porridge, which was made of stewed plums and barley (*TNK* II.ii.74, II.v.5). As prunes (*1H4* III.iii.119; *2H4* II.iv.149; *MM* II.i.87–92, 104), plums had a symbolic meaning, for a dish of stewed prunes was often put in the window of a brothel as a shop sign.

Boorde approved of figs, especially when served with blanched almonds; roasted or stewed, he thought them an aphrodisiac. Raisins, like capers, olives, oranges, and damsons, made a good appetizer. Currants were good for the back and for urine production, but bad for the spleen; strawberries qualified the natural heat of the liver and increased the production of good blood; wardens, when roasted, soothed the stomach. The medlar (*Tim* IV.iii.304; *R&J* II.i.34–38; *MM* IV.iii.174–75), a brown apple-like fruit eaten when overripe and pulpy, and the service, a small, round or pear-shaped fruit that was similarly eaten when nearly rotten, were said by Boorde to increase melancholy; perhaps this was because their decayed state reminded the eater of his own inevitable death. Medlars, like prunes, had sexual connotations, and Shakespeare uses them as symbols of the sexual organs or of prostitution.

The most common fruit was certainly the apple (*TS* IV.ii.101; *H5*

III.vii.147), which Boorde recommended eating with comfits, sugar, fennel, or anise to reduce its tendency to cause flatulence. Apples might be eaten raw, converted into cider, roasted (*LLL* V.ii.920; *MND* II.i.47–50), or picked late in the growing season and stored all winter in an apple loft above the kitchen or pantry. William Lawson, in *A New Orchard and Garden*, gave instructions for storage:

> For keeping, lay them in a dry Loft, the longest keeping. Apples first and farthest on dry straw, on heapes ten or fourteen daies, thicke, that they may sweat. Then dry them with a soft and cleane cloth, and lay them thin abroad. Long keeping fruit would be turned once in a moneth softly: but not in nor immediately after frost.

Pears could be preserved in the same way (*MWW* IV.v.97; *AW* I.i.163–64). The fruit should also be covered, Lawson advised, with straw, chaff, or bran. A 1613 song by Thomas Campion, "Jacke and Jone," lists the storage of apples as one of the quaint pleasures of rural life. Our married hero and heroine disport themselves at fairs, drink ale, tell stories in wintertime, and "Climbe up to the Apple loft, / And turne the Crabs till they be soft." These soft, shrunken apples from the loft are referred to by Shakespeare as "apple-johns" (*1H4* III.iii.4; *2H4* II.iv.2–3). Shakespeare does not usually mention the unripe phases of fruit growth, as he does with peas, but he makes an exception in the case of the apple "codling" (*TN* I.v.157), the term for the fruit before it is mature. (An illustration of fruit can be seen in Children entry, along with a plate of candied citrus-peel comfits.)

Nuts

Nut trees as well as fruit trees were cultivated in orchards. Some nuts (*MND* V.i.29–39; *AYLI* III.iv.24; *T&C* II.i.102; *AW* II.v.43), like filberts (*Temp* II.ii.173), were eaten plain and raw. Others, like chestnuts (*TS* I.ii.208; *Mac* I.iii.4–6), were roasted. Walnuts (*TS* IV.iii.66; *MWW* IV.ii.158) and almonds (*T&C* V.ii.192) were probably the most popular varieties, though Shakespeare also mentions hazelnuts a few times (*R&J* I.iv.67, III.i.20–22; *TS* II.i.249). Almonds in particular were favored for use in confections. Boorde was fond of almond butter flavored with sugar and violets, and almonds were the basis of much "banquetting stuffe," most notably marzipan. At least one nut mentioned by Shakespeare, the pig-nut (*Temp* II.ii.170), is not actually a nut at all. It is instead the rounded root of an umbelliferous plant, *Bunium flexuosum*.

Spices and Seasonings

Just because the food of the Renaissance was prepared relatively simply (with the notable exception of banquet dishes) did not necessarily mean that it was bland. Those who could afford to do so added a number of spices to their food, many of which were grown in the ubiquitous kitchen garden. Garlic (*MND* IV.ii.41; *MM* III.ii.183; *1H4* III.i.158), saffron (*CE* IV.iv.60; *AW* IV.v.2), rosemary (*R&J* II.iv.210–16; *Per* IV.vi.156), mint (*LLL* V.ii.653), hyssop, mustard, sage, savory, basil, marjoram (*AW* IV.v.16; *Lear* IV.vi.93), thyme, and fennel (*R&J* I.ii.29) were all home-grown, and were widely available, though saffron was a notoriously expensive spice and colorant, since it was made of only the dried stamens of the saffron flower and thus had extremely small yields. The spices that were not grown in the garden were purchased from a grocer, who either acquired them domestically or imported them from around the known world. William Harrison gave prices of some of these commodities in the late sixteenth century:

Sugar	5d per pound
Currants	6 to 10d per pound
Nutmeg	2½d per ounce
Ginger	1d per ounce
Raisins	3 pounds for 1d
Cinnamon	4d per ounce
Cloves	2d per ounce
Pepper	12 to 16d per pound

Currants he called "raisins," and grape raisins, "great raisins." Other flavorings commonly available included licorice, capers, parsley (*TS* IV.iv.99–101), caraway seeds, ginger (*1H4* II.i.26; *H5* III.vii.20; *TN* II.iii.118–19), nutmeg (*LLL* V.ii.644; *H5* III.vii.19), and mace (*WT* IV.iii.47), which was ground from the nutmeg hull. Ginger was sold by the "race" or "raze," which meant "root" (*WT* IV.iii.49).

The most commonly used seasoning was salt (*2GV* III.i.355–56; *MAAN* IV.i.141–42; *R&J* II.iii.71–72), which was made at various places around England. Harrison described the salt works at Wich and Nantwich, where salters drew water out of a well and boiled it in caldrons over a coal fire. The water might be boiled until nothing was left but salt, or it might be boiled until very thick, then the salt strained out of it with wicker baskets and left to dry. Salt was used in pickling brines, in the drying and smoking of meats, in the preparation of cheese and butter, and in the "powdering" or liberal seasoning of food (*1H4* V.iv.110). *See also* Architecture; Dishes; Garden; Housework.

Fortune

Like jewelry with skulls, which were supposed to remind Renaissance people of the uncertainty of life and the need to consider the hereafter, Fortune (*R&J* III.v.61–64; *2H6* I.ii.67; *3H6* IV.iii.46–47) was a powerful symbol of the relative helplessness of humankind. Portrayed as a goddess with covered eyes, she spun a wheel (*A&C* IV.xv.43–45) on which any one person's status was a fixed point. As the wheel went around, those with poor luck became fortunate and rose high, while those who seemed invincible were brought low. Particularly for those in high places, she was a constant reminder that chance, or the whim of the monarch, or a bit too much ambition, could result in disaster. Shakespeare's characters, whether suffering hard luck or afraid of it, fear the fickleness of Fortune, call her "turning and inconstant" and an "arrant whore" (*H5* III.vi.27–37; *Lear* II.iii.51), and beg her for her favor (*AYLI* I.ii.30–31; *Lear* II.ii.175–76).

France

England had a complicated relationship with the Continent in general and with France in particular. On the one hand, England was an insular, xenophobic nation, suspicious of things that came from abroad, fiercely protective of its economic interests, and justifiably concerned about foreign Catholic intrusion into its religious affairs. France was Catholic and had long been a military rival of England, for the most part because of a difference between English and French law regarding the inheritance of the throne. France, following Salic law, would not let the throne pass through the female line, whereas in England a woman could transmit this inheritance or even hold the throne herself, as demonstrated by Mary I and Elizabeth I. The result of this disagreement was that the English kings, who could claim descent from French royalty through the female line, claimed the French throne. The French refused to hand over their kingdom, and so began the Hundred Years' War, which forms the backdrop to the *Henry* plays. As if this were not enough, Henry VIII had fought against France within living memory, and resentment against Mary, Queen of Scots, a Catholic who had once been married to a French king and who had aspired to the English throne, was a freshly remembered source of annoyance.

Anti-French sentiment is easily found in Shakespeare's plays, particularly those in which war with France is part of the subject matter. Jack Cade's ignorant followers, who can be taken to embody the worst excesses of mass opinion, go so far as to consider speaking French a sign of treason (*2H6* IV.ii.165–72).

On the other hand, as much as the English derided anything that came from across the Channel, they often copied French manners and fashions. Furthermore, the whole basis of the Hundred Years' War was that France was really just a part of English territory, and though the last French city in English hands—Calais—fell to the French under Mary I, both Elizabeth I and James I continued to quarter the arms of France on their shields as if they were that country's crowned sovereigns. Even the mottoes on their coins proclaimed them the rightful rulers of it. For 500 years, England had also been ruled by the descendants of a Norman lord, and royal marriages with the French had maintained a connection intermittently ever since. French of a sort was still the language of the law, and everyone with a pretense to education could speak the language at least a little (*MV* I.ii.66–74).

This is not to say that people in general were fluent in French. Pistol, for example, cannot follow a conversation and requires an interpreter (*H5* IV.iv.2–67). However, it would appear from the dialogue assigned by Shakespeare that even very humble people spoke a few words of French; *adieu* was widely used and understood (*2GV* III.i.50; *R2* I.iii.305; *MND* V.i.346), in the same way that people today who are not fluent in Spanish or Italian might say *adios* or *ciao* as a farewell. Of course, it makes perfect sense that *adieu* should appear in plays actually set in French-speaking countries, such as *Love's Labor's Lost*, but it is scattered with nearly equal frequency throughout plays set in England, Italy, Austria, and even ancient Greece and Egypt, and it is spoken by characters of every social class (*MAAN* III.i.109; *H5* II.iii.60, 62; *R&J* V.iii.143; *MV* II.iii.10, 13, 14; *AYLI* IV.i.196, 198; *MM* I.iv.90; *A&C* I.iii.77).

Sans (without) and *monsieur* (mister) are also frequently used (*CE* IV.iv.72; *LLL* V.i.83; *John* V.vi.16; *MAAN* II.iii.34; *MND* V.i.10–25). Other words and phrases occur less often. Some are not so much French as "Franglais," anglicized French. Into this category fall such expressions as "Couple a gorge!," from *couper la gorge*, "cut the throat" (*H5* II.i.73); "foutra," from *foutre*, "fuck" (*2H4* V.iii.101); "gramercy," an elision of the words for "great thanks" (*TS* I.i.41, 163; *R3* III.ii.105; *TA* I.i.496; *Tim* II.ii.73); "kickshawses," trifles, a corruption of *quelque chose* (*TN* I.iii.111); "Pardonne moy" for *pardonez moi*, "excuse me" (*R2* V.iii.118); "bawcock" from *beau coq*, "pretty chicken" (*TN* III.iv.116); and "parley," a genuine English word descended from the French *parlez*, "to talk" (*TA* V.i.161; *2GV* I.ii.5).

Shakespeare undoubtedly expected at least some of his audience to be fluent in French, for he wrote some scenes that are almost entirely in that language, and he was too good a dramatist to leave most of his audience floundering and bored. It is perhaps possible to dismiss the French in *Henry V* III.iv. as irrelevant, since the humor comes from Katherine's attempts to learn English, and it would not have required a full knowledge of French to guffaw at her pointing to parts of her body while badly mispronouncing the English words for them. It would also have satisfied the patriotism of the audience to see her learning English in preparation for the inevitable French defeat. Even so, the scene is greatly enhanced if one does know French, and there is at least one pun that requires a knowledge of French obscenity to be fully appreciated. *Henry V* IV.v falls into the same category; there is French here, but it is not absolutely essential to an understanding of the scene. However, V.ii of the same play has dozens of lines in French, only occasionally translated by Alice, and Shakespeare must have expected at least the genteel portion of his audience to comprehend these lines.

𝔉urniture

"Furniture," to Shakespeare and his contemporaries, was a broader term than it is today. The word meant equipment or furnishings of any kind. In *The Description of England*, William Harrison included within its scope not only beds and tables but dishes and tapestries; Shakespeare uses it in one case to mean supplies for war (*2H6* I.ii.171). Here, it will be used in the narrower modern sense of substantial, movable household items exclusive of dishes, utensils, textiles, and art objects.

Whatever the people of Shakespeare's time called it, there was more furniture, and that of better quality, than at any time in living memory and probably than at any time in English history. Harrison spoke of how the old men of his day had slept in their youth on straw pallets with coarse coverlets and perhaps a log for a pillow, little dreaming that their grandsons would enjoy mattresses, flock beds stuffed with cotton or wool, and pillows filled with down. Even a person of ordinary means could expect, at the turn of the seventeenth century, to own a chest, a few chairs, beds, tables, stools, and perhaps a cupboard or "joynt presse," a cabinet made not by a mere carpenter but by a joiner.

Materials and designs changed gradually through the reigns of Elizabeth I and James I. For most of Elizabeth's reign, oak was the preferred wood, with apple, pear, holly, bog oak, and ebony (*LLL* IV.iii.244–46; *TN* IV.ii.39) used at times for inlay. Beech was often used for painted or upholstered furniture and for a specific type of chair called a coffer-maker's chair. Some items were made of chestnut, deal, elm, or imported Virginia cedar. During the Elizabethan age, however, walnut, usually in the form of uncarved veneer, became fashionable among the wealthy, and this popularity increased during the Jacobean period. Wicker was used for certain chair seats and for cradles, and leather, sometimes gilded, might be employed for covering chests. Upholstery was still uncommon; people were accustomed to hard, flat seats or chests covered with separate cushions. However, some pieces, particularly in the homes of the rich, had stuffed fabric seats or backs.

Gothic-style furniture survived into the mid-sixteenth century, but already a distinct Renaissance style was evolving as a competitor. It featured carving rather than painting and a variety of decorative multiple-wood techniques. These were lumped, at the time, under the general heading of marquetry (or "marke-tree," as one household inventory spelled it), though there were actually three distinct methods of manufacture. Inlay involved gouging a pattern out of the foundation wood and filling the spaces with precisely cut strips of different-colored woods. True marquetry employed the techniques of inlay to make an overall design, which was then cut into thin slices of veneer and glued to another piece of wood. Parquetry was made by attaching blocks of different-colored woods in geometric patterns, slicing the blocks into sections, and applying the design a section at a time rather than all at once. Popular design elements included strapwork (patterns of interwoven lines), arabesques (curves and flourishes), and caryatids. A common element of more elaborate tables was a huge, melonlike ball turned or carved into each leg.

Furniture Makers

Furniture was made by several different types of craftsmen who were frequently at odds with each other over which techniques were the exclusive "mysteries" of which trade. Generally speaking, carpenters (*1H6* V.iii.90; *MAAN* I.i.181; *JC* I.i.7; *MND* ch.; *Ham* V.i.42), wearing leather aprons, armed with their saws, hammers, and measuring tools, were the crudest craftsmen. Their trade was principally the framing of houses, not the precise cutting and finishing of fine furniture. They were prohibited from using glue, so their work was limited to items that could be manufactured from planks and nails or iron straps—chiefly chests, the cruder sorts of stools, and the kinds of basic tables found in taverns, alehouses, and countinghouses.

Turners were more specialized. They made "thrown" furniture by turning pieces of wood on a lathe and cutting away parts of it in a pattern. Their work was in demand for chair, stool, and table legs, chairs made almost exclusively of turned spindles, and

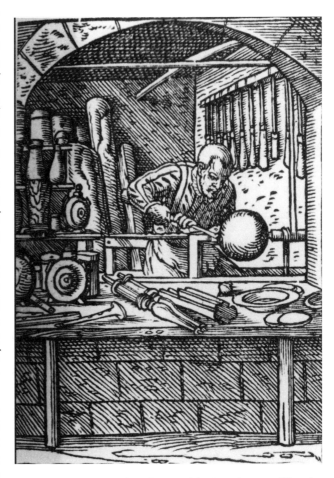

A turner, from *Panoplia*, illustrated by Jost Amman. The object on the lathe is most likely a table leg with the melon-shaped protuberance typical of this period. Reproduced from the Collections of the Library of Congress.

some cupboards that had spindles partially concealing their shelves. In addition, they made wooden shovels and scoops, bowls, measures, and parts of bushels and trugs (wooden trays for milk or other commodities).

The most highly regarded of the furniture makers was the joiner (*R&J* I.iv.68; *MND* ch.), who was permitted to use glue. His defining technique was the mortise-and-tenon joint, which gave its name not only to the craft but also to any piece of furniture made with such joints, which were dubbed with the adjectives "joint," "joined," or "jointed." The "joynt presse" mentioned above is an example of this type.

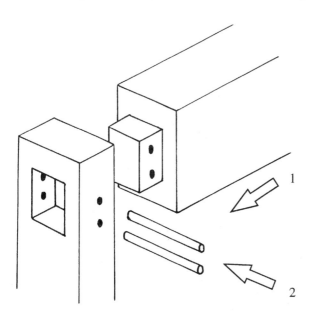

A mortise-and-tenon joint. (1) The tenon is slid into the mortise. (2) Dowels are inserted through holes drilled in both boards.

The mortise-and-tenon joint is made by cutting a slot (the mortise—see *Oth* II.i.6–9) near the end of one board and a correspondingly sized peg (the tenon) at the end of another. Aligned holes are drilled through the side of the mortised board and through the tenon itself. The pieces are then fitted together and secured with dowels or with dowels and glue. The mortise-and-tenon joint allowed joiners to make panel frames as well. They took a square or rectangular panel of wood and built a loosely fitted frame around it, composing various kinds of furniture, including chests and chairs, out of these panels. Panels made furniture lighter, reduced the need for huge individual pieces of wood, and helped to keep the wood from splitting or warping.

The carvers were a subset of the joiners. They were highly skilled craftsmen who seldom did any general joinery. An ordinary joiner could do a little carving, such as chip carving, in which the design was chipped out of the surrounding wood; sunk carving, in which the background was chipped away; or scratch carving, in which the design was merely scratched into the surface with a sharp tool. More complicated work, however, like reliefs or sculpture, required a specialist.

Softer materials were the purview of the basketmaker, who wove wicker seats and cradles, and the "upholder" or upholsterer. The upholsterer was a hybrid of the wood and textile craftsmen, for he made stuffed furniture as well as bedding and decorative hangings. In the Jacobean era, he was increasingly called upon to coordinate the hangings, bedclothes, and chairs of upper-class bedrooms.

Chairs, Stools, and Benches

The stool (*Cor* I.iii.1 s.d.; *2H6* II.i.140, 142, 148; *T&C* II.i.42) was the most common form of seat from the Middle Ages to the time of James I. Its dominance was so complete that when armless chairs first appeared, they were called "back-stools," for the word "stool" was practically synonymous with any one-person seat. In the early sixteenth century, the typical example was a trestle stool, composed of four interlocking planks, two vertical, two horizontal, on which a fifth plank rested and served as a seat.

Trestle stool in the Gothic style from the time of Henry VIII.

This was replaced during the century by the joint-stool (*R&J* I.v.7; *1H4* II.iv.383; *2H4* II.iv.253; *Lear* III.vi.51; *TS* II.i.197–98), assembled with mortise-and-tenon joints and having three legs and a round seat. It was typically 1'9" (53 cm) tall and was sometimes, in richer households, carved and upholstered in Turkey work. Late in the Tudor period there were also stools with turned legs and triangular seats, though these were never as popular as the round-topped variety. Some examples resembled backless, armless chairs, with four legs and upholstered seats.

Like the stool, the bench (*2H4* V.ii.86; *JC* III.ii.258–59) or form (*LLL* I.i.206; *R&J* II.iv.35–36) was a common type of seating in the Middle Ages, when it was placed against a wall or along one of the long tables in the great

Velvet-upholstered oak stool from late in the reign of Elizabeth I.

Armchair with carved back panel, c. 1600.

hall. A variant, the settle, had sides and a back like a church pew, and usually a storage area concealed beneath the seat. In Elizabeth's time, the bench remained ubiquitous, even in great homes; the settle had evolved into a padded two- or three-person seat called a couch. One version of the couch (*2H4* III.i.16), which had an inclined arm to serve as a pillow for napping, was called a daybed (*TN* II.v.46).

Chairs—seats with backs and arms—were less common than stools and benches. In ordinary homes, there was only one chair for the master; in somewhat fancier establishments, there might be one for the mistress as well. In Shakespeare's works, chairs often surface either as seating for invalids (*1H6* III.ii.51, IV.v.5; *Lear* IV.vii.20 s.d.) or as places of honor for important people (*1H4* II.iv.381; *JC* I.iii.143). The difference between the master's chair in a prosperous yeoman's household and the throne of a king was a matter of the rank of the occupant and the workmanship of the chair, but the chair itself was in both cases a symbol of the preeminence of the occupant in his or her particular social setting.

Early in the sixteenth century, chairs had been essentially boxes with sides that rose to become the arms and a straight back that rose to support the occupant's back without much comfort. This evolved, by the century's end, into a joined chair with turned front legs that rose above the level of the seat to support the armrests, square back legs, stretchers between the legs, a slightly reclined back, and a back panel decorated with inlay or carving. There were exceptions to this pattern, including child-sized chairs, spindle chairs without solid backs, chairs upholstered in velvet or Turkey work, and the cheap wicker chairs favored by old women. A couple of notable innovations were the upholsterer's or imbrauderer's chair, a wide, upholstered armchair dubbed a "farthingale chair" by the Victorians because of their assumption that its larger seat was designed to accommodate the hoop-skirted dresses of Elizabeth's time, and the coffermaker's chair, a leather-covered, X-framed wooden chair that was sometimes designed to be foldable. However, the turned-leg, solid-backed chair remained the most common type.

Beds

The bed (*TS* Ind.i.33, 72, Ind.ii.37–39, IV.i.189; *MND* II.ii.39, 42; *3H6* II.v.53) was the largest and often the most expensive piece of furniture in the house, as well as one of the hardest to live without. At their humblest, beds were the "uneasy pallets" (*2H4* III.i.10) of straw (*MM* IV.iii.35–36; *Lear* IV.vii.40) on which servants and the very poor slept, with a sheet to cover them and, if they were lucky, one below to keep the straw ends from sticking them too much. Some might be lucky

Armchair, c. 1600.

enough to have a wood frame, made like a shallow, open box, in which to lay a mattress (*A&C* II.vi.70) of straw, wool, cotton, or feathers. Middle-class farmers or tradesmen might have a simple bed with a head-board and a platform of boards or cords to support the mattress, and the more money one acquired, the more ornate this simple bed became, sprouting carved posts, a tester from which to hang valances and curtains, a decorated headboard, paint, varnish, and even gilding. Such, no doubt, are the beds belonging to Shakespeare's noble-born characters—in his imagination, at least, if not on the stage (*Cor* I.iii.5, II.ii.1 s.d.; *R3* I.i.142; *2H6* III.ii.11, 29; *RL* 301). The most famous of these bedsteads, in an age of massive and elaborate beds, was the Great Bed of Ware, built in the last quarter of the century and measuring almost eleven feet on each side (*TN* III.ii.46–47). These were all "standing" beds, so called because they were too huge to move. People with multiple houses might also have a "field" bed that, unlike the standing bed, could be taken apart and reassembled.

The bedchamber was not a private place. Indeed, in small homes, it might double as the main room. Even in mansions, it was a place in which guests were received and business was conducted; private acts such as dressing, eliminating waste, and writing letters took place in smaller side rooms called closets or cabinets. A wealthy woman might well have a bed-chamber or a suite of rooms to herself, but this did not necessarily endow her with privacy. If she was married, her husband might come and go as

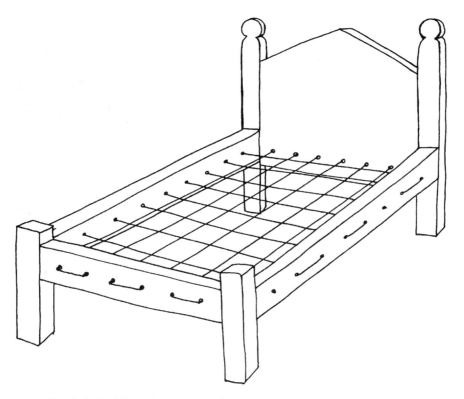

Simple bed with cords to support the mattress, early seventeenth century.

he liked (*JC* II.i.237–38). If she was single, a relative or servant would share her bed or room to ensure her chastity (*MAAN* IV.i.146–48). Servants were accommodated on straw pallets or "truckle" or "trundle" beds that could be rolled under the standing bed in the daytime (*MWW* IV.v.6).

Children might share a bed with a sibling or parent, as do the princes in the Tower in *Richard III* (IV.iii.14), but as babies they often had cradles for sleeping and for daytime rocking (*2H6* III.ii.392, IV.ix.3; *R2* I.iii.132; *MV* III.ii.69; *AYLI* I.i.106). Cradles might be made of wicker or wood. They either dangled between two posts or sat on curved rockers.

Tables

The dining table (*T&C* I.i.31, *Temp* III.iii.52 s.d.), when the sixteenth century began, was typically a trestle table, located in the great hall of large houses and the kitchen or combination kitchen and hall of smaller ones. In finer homes, the hall would have several such tables, with one raised on a dais and placed perpendicular to the others. The master and his family and guests sat at this raised table, on one side only, so that they could face the rest of the hall, where servants, guests' servants, and other lesser mortals took their fare. The table top rested on trestles and stretchers, sometimes with no means of attachment, sometimes atop dowels or tongues that matched holes in the bottom of the tabletop. The idea was that, after dinner, the tables could be taken apart to free the floor of the hall for dancing. In practice, many of these trestle tables, which could be more than 20 feet (6 m) long and 6 inches (15 cm) thick, were probably moved or disassembled only when necessary.

Trestle table, early seventeenth century.

In the second half of the sixteenth century, there was a transition to a different kind of table, a framed table with four to eight legs and stretchers. These tables, often with turned and carved legs and inlaid or carved friezes, were for use in the dining parlor, a smaller, more casual room that was replacing the great hall as the favorite place for the family to eat. The shift toward the dining parlor caused a trend toward smaller tables whose length could be increased by the addition of hinged or drawn leaves. Variations on the framed table were children's tables, "little" tables that were at normal height but had much smaller tops, card tables, and a few extremely expensive tables made of inlaid marble.

These tables were all for use in the homes of the prosperous. Tenant farmers and lesser artisans were still making do with the old trestle tables. Trestle tables were easier to move so that the limited space in a cottage could be utilized for cooking or chores, and they were cheaper because they could be made by a simple carpenter. The trestle table was also the well-known "board" of alehouse, inn, tavern, and shop; the phrase "room and board," still in use today, refers to this obsolete term for table.

Chests and Cupboards

The chest (*TS* II.i.344; *John* V.ii.141; *MV* I.ii.29–30) was the standard storage unit in the Middle Ages. A rectangular box with a flat lid, it did double duty as a seat when topped with a cushion and was thus rarely decorated on the lid, though the front and sides might be inlaid or carved. It was a common feature of the bedroom, hall, and kitchen, and was used to store linens, clothing, and even dishes. Difficulties arose, however, anytime someone wanted something from the bottom of the chest, and this inconvenience, especially when dealing with heavy or breakable items, drove chests out of fashionable bedchambers by 1600. An innovation that turned out to be a transition in disguise, the addition of drawers at the bottom of the chest behind a pair of lockable doors, led to the development of a host of closed storage units—presses, aumbries, armoires, and eventually—later than the period that concerns us here—the modern chest of drawers. These new pieces of furniture were eagerly adopted by the rich, while ordinary people usually made do in the second half of the sixteenth century with chests for linens and clothes and open cupboards for dishes.

The cupboard (*Cor* I.i.101) was a doorless unit, often with stepped shelves, that could hold almost anything but usually contained dishes and cups—hence its name. England's rising middle class, happy to display the tangible proof of its good fortune, set up its plate, glass, and brass for all to see. To exaggerate the splendor of these exhibitions, shelves were laid with Turkish or Turkish-style carpets, which were still much more common on tables and shelves than on floors. Even humble homes could

Court cupboard, third quarter of the sixteenth century.

sometimes afford a small wall cupboard with sides made of spindles or pierced panels for its glassware.

This was the basic cupboard, but it was only one representative of its family. "Sideboard" was a term applied to a unit used for table service. Beer or wine might be kept there, for example, and brought by a servant whenever a diner beckoned. The "court cupboard" (*R&J* I.v.8) had three shelves and might be used in the hall, dining parlor, or bedchamber. The top shelf was usually covered by a green cloth or Turkish-style carpet, while the middle and bottom shelves held a variety of items. While the court cupboard had no doors, it did sometimes possess knobless, handleless drawers located just below the top shelf. One of the most versatile storage pieces of its time, it often came apart so that it could be easily transported to another room.

Oak press, early seventeenth century. The two top drawers are false fronts, and the entire top lifts to reveal a shallow storage area.

Historians have inferred that the commonly mentioned "livery cupboard" and the commonly surviving court cupboard with an enclosed upper section are probably one and the same. In any case, there was a tendency, as time went on, to add doors and drawers to the standard open cupboard. The number of individual compartments varied, but such pieces of furniture were usually known by one of two names. "Aumbry" or "ambry" was a common term for a closed cupboard, particularly when it was used to store food. Another designation, "press" (*MWW* III.iii.204,

IV.ii.57), referred to two types of cupboards with multiple sections. One type had doors enclosing its bottom two-thirds, topped by a row of recessed panels with doors and a frieze jutting out over the recessed area, its front half supported and joined to the lower enclosure by spindles. The other type, found in as many rooms as one's income allowed, had a flush front, paneling, and one or two doors. It came in various heights; but the taller version, which usually held clothes, eventually evolved into the wardrobe. *See also* Architecture; Dishes; Household Objects.

Games

Considering the absence of electronic media, the paucity of ephemeral print media such as magazines and newspapers, the low population density outside London, and all the other impediments to entertainment that existed, Renaissance England had a culture rich in diversions. It has been said that all a child really needs is a ball, a box, and a stick; and with only a slightly larger and slightly more complex set of equipment, the people of Shakespeare's England created or perpetuated a host of games. Under this heading of "games," it should be noted, are activities that relied for their entertainment value solely on the participants' actions.

Dice and Cards

Some of the most portable games were those played with dice and cards. Dice had been around for centuries, starting with the knuckle-bones thrown for sport or divination by our ancient ancestors. Shakespeare's characters are fond of dice (*H5* IV.Cho.19, IV.v.10; *LLL* V.ii.234; *MWW* III.i.36–37; *A&C* II.iii.32). Some of the references are to particular throws, such as "treys" (threes—*LLL* V.ii.233), "ace" (one—*MND* V.i.305–6), "deuce-ace" (a one on one die and a two on the other—*LLL* I.ii.45–48), or "ames ace" (two ones—*AW* II.iii.79–80). The men of Shakespeare's time were perfectly willing to gamble on anything, from an archery contest (*2H4* III.ii.46–47) to a fight (*TS* V.ii.35) to a fencing match (*Ham* IV.vii.134, V.ii.149–54, 166–69), but dice were especially associated with betting. "Gaming," dice, and the attendant swearing upon losing were listed in various combinations as common sins (*Ham* III.iii.91, III.iv.46; *1H4* III.iii.15–19; *WT* IV.iii.26). No doubt some of the oaths were caused by false dice (*MAAN* II.i.270), for example the flat, the farger, the langret, and the "gourd and fullam" (*MWW* I.iii.84), being employed against inexperienced players. The fullam, or fulham, was weighted with lead in one corner and came in two kinds, one designed to produce high rolls and the other designed to produce low ones; of most other "cheting" dice we have no descriptions.

The mere existence of such unfair equipment, and its effect on the fortunes of unsuspecting players, was enough to turn some men against dice entirely. Roger Ascham, Elizabeth I's childhood tutor and the author of a classic archery text, despised such pastimes as dicing, bowling, "and hauntinge of tavernes." He blamed "werisome idlenesse" for the popularity of dice and cards and deplored the gamesters who, if a rube actually managed to get ahead, switched the rube's true dice for false ones, then pretended to discover the cheats, and used the confusion of the accusation to steal his winnings.

Specific games and rules are seldom referred to in the plays. There is one reference to novum, a game in which nine and five were important throws (*LLL* V.ii.540), and one to "tray-trip" (*TN* II.v.186), in which the winning roll was probably a three, but Shakespeare offers us no scene of dicing to rival in color and detail his descriptions of bearbaiting or theatrical performances. He does, however, employ terms associated with the game of hazard, which dated from at least the fourteenth century and was destined to be the ruin of many a young gentleman in the seventeenth and eighteenth centuries. The word "hazard" is usually used ambiguously, meaning possibly the game and possibly a risk of any sort, yet it often appears in a gambling, and specifically a dicing, context (*H5* III.vii.87–88; *R3* V.iv.9–10; *Tim* V.iv.34–35). Hazard, as it eventually evolved, used two dice that were thrown to set a "main" point of 5, 6, 7, 8, or 9, and a "chance" point of 4, 5, 6, 7, 8, 9, or 10. A set of rules governed the winning or loss of the stake on specific rolls while trying to set the chance point; a 2 or a 3, for example, always lost the stake, while a chance identical to the main won it, and an 11 or a 12 either won or lost it, depending on the number rolled for the main. If the stake was not won or lost during this procedure, the dicer continued to roll until he rolled the main again and lost, or the chance again and won. The terms "main" and "hazard" are used together in Shakespeare's works in a dicing context, though not unambiguously:

> To set the exact wealth of all our states
> All at one cast? To set so rich a main
> On the nice hazard of one doubtful hour? (*1H4* IV.i.46–48)

"Main," in this example, is used in the sense of the stake itself, not necessarily the first point set in the game of hazard, but the fact that a roll of the dice is meant is clear enough.

The deck of cards was not nearly as ancient as the cup of dice, being a relatively recent evolution from the medieval fortune-telling tarot deck. They were usually blank, not patterned, on the back, with suit spots and face-card pictures but no numerals. Cards (*A&C* IV.xiv.18–19; *TA* V.i.100; *John* V.ii.105–6; *TNK* V.ii.107) were used for several popular games, including cent or sant, the ancestor of piquet. Gleek was a three-player game in which certain cards had different names, such as "Tib" for the ace and "Tiddy" for the four; the deck had forty-four cards, which gave each player a hand of twelve with eight left over. Thirty-one, with its "tricks eleven and twenty long" (*TS* IV.ii.57), was also known as one-and-thirty or bone-ace; in this game, the ace of diamonds was the highest card, and the third card was dealt face-up. Primero (*MWW* IV.v.97–98; *H8* V.i.7) was popular in two forms, one played with face cards, the other with no cards higher than the seven. The cards had different values from their face values; each player's four-card hand was revealed, with hands being ranked according to score and suit. Post and pair was a game with three cards dealt to each player and multiple rounds of betting. In post and pair, the jack or knave was called a "pur" (*AW* V.ii.19), a term also sometimes applied to a boy or a male sheep.

Board and Table Games

Some games required more equipment than a pack of cards or a pair of dice. "Troll-my-dames" (*WT* IV.iii.88), also known as Trou Madame, Troule in Madame, trunks, or small trunks, was played on a board with numbered holes or arches in one end. Players tried to roll balls, made variously of lead, copper, tin, or wood, into specific holes. Another game that called for balls and a table was billiards (*A&C* II.v.3), which at this time used a curved, yard-long cue with a flattened, spoonlike tip. A seventeenth-century version had two obstructions on the table: an arch called a port and a pin called a king. The player needed to pass his own ball through the port, then force his opponent's ball to strike the king.

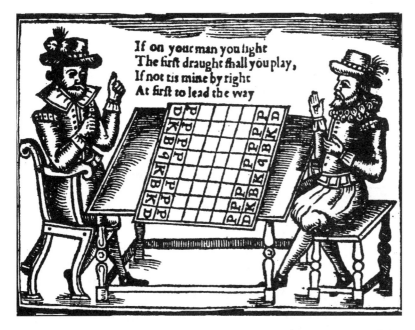

Chess players determine which of them will move first in an illustration from the title page of *The Famous Game of Chesse-Play*, 1614. The two pawns missing from the board are concealed in the hands of the player on the left.

A checkered board was used for chess (*Temp* V.i.171 s.d.) and draughts. Chess was fundamentally the same game as today, but draughts (checkers) was still evolving. Until about 1535, there was no rule that forced a player to take an opponent's "dame" or playing piece. When the rule was introduced, first in France and then eslewhere, draughts split into two separate games—*le jeu plaisant de dames*, without forced capture, and *jeu forcé*, in which the new rule applied.

A different but similarly sized board was used for backgammon, which was quite an old game. Originally called tables (*LLL* V.ii.327), it had been overtaken in popularity by other board games, which were also grouped under the name tables. Early in the seventeenth century, however, it enjoyed a new popularity throughout Europe due to rule changes, its new vogue reflected in the manufacture of fine sets with beautiful boards, dice cups, and pieces. A version with pegs and holes at the side for scoring was called tick-tack (*MM* I.ii.193–94).

A widespread board game, which was played in pubs for centuries, was shove-groat. The object of the game, as in modern shuffleboard, was to push one's piece, in this case a coin, between lines perpendicular to the piece's line of travel. The secondary object was to knock the opponent's piece away from the scoring area. In Shakespeare's time, shillings rather than groats appear to have been the preferred playing pieces, judging from his reference to the game as "shove-groat shilling" (*2H4* II.iv.195–96) and from Slender's complaint that his "two Edward shovel-boards" (*MWW* I.i.148–50) have been stolen, The "Edwards" were shillings of Edward VI's reign, and their suitability for the game can be seen in Slender's claim, unchallenged, that he paid more than twice face value for them. We are left to wonder what made these particular coins so desirable for the game. Coins' design and metal content (and thus weight) changed from reign to reign. Perhaps the Edward VI coins slid especially well.

Other games of Shakespeare's day included "span-counter" (*2H6* IV.ii.156), a game in which counters were tossed as close to the opponent's as possible, and nine men's morris (*MND* II.i.98), which was like a more complex form of tic-tac-toe played on a board of three nested squares linked by lines. The game's name came from the fact that each player had nine counters or "men." A "point" was a corner of any of the squares, or the intersection of a square and a line. The two players took turns placing their men on the open points and then, once all the men were placed, moving one counter one point at a time. Whenever

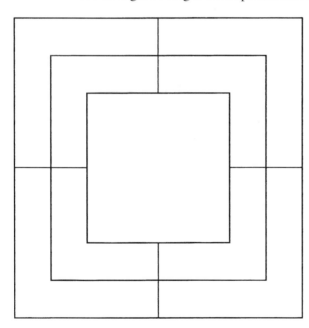

The board for nine men's morris.

placing or movement resulted in a "mill" of three of the player's men in a row, he could remove one of his opponent's men. The game ended when one player was unable to move or had only two pieces left. Nine men's morris could be played on a beautifully inlaid or gilded board or in a simple square cut into the turf or drawn in the soil.

Outdoor Games

More athletic sports were usually played outdoors. Robert Burton's *Anatomy of Melancholy* (1621) lists nineteen such activities available to ordinary people, including quoits (*2H4* II.iv.195, 250), "pitching of bars," hurling, wrestling (*TNK* II.ii.69; *T&C* IV.v.193; *AYLI* I.i.118–56, I.ii.97–215), jumping, running races (*TNK* II.ii.69), fencing, swimming, and fighting with wooden swords called wasters or singlesticks. Dun in the mire (*R&J* I.iv.39–41) was a game whose premise was that a cart horse, "Dun," represented by a log, was stuck in the mud. It seems to have been partly a tug-of-war and partly an excuse to drop a heavy log on a friend's toes. Fights for fun, such as wrestling and fencing matches, often had an umpire called a stickler (*T&C* V.viii.18) to separate the combatants if things got too rough. Contemporaries considered it axiomatic that if things got really violent, the stickler was likely to be the first injured.

Bowling games (*WT* IV.iv.332; *LLL* IV.i.140, V.ii.578–79) of one kind or another were popular with people of all classes. Some of these had a field with pins that the bowler attempted to knock down, but "bowls," on the other hand, had no pins but a smaller target ball called variously a jack (*Cym* II.i.1–2), master, or mistress (*T&C* III.ii.47). The winner was the player whose ball, evading obstacles or "rubs" (*LLL* IV.i.139–41; *H5* II.ii.187–88; *Ham* III.i.65), came closest to the jack. The best throw of all was one in which the player's ball "kissed" or lightly touched the target ball. Shakespeare often refers to "bias" in connection with bowls (*TS* IV.v.24–25; *R2* III.iv.3–5; *Cor* V.ii.20–21), but authorities differ as to whether this bias lay in a deliberate asymmetry of the ball, an accidental irregularity in the ball, or the design of the field itself. Another throwing game, loggets, was played with pieces of wood that were thrown at wooden pins; boys sometimes substituted bones for the wooden targets and tossing piece (*Ham* V.i.92).

Other sports included archery and similar target sports, sometimes with animals as targets. Cats were hung in baskets for this purpose (*MAAN* I.i.250–52). A similar game, but without arrows, was shying at cocks. In this sport, whose supporters included Henry VIII and James I, a rooster was tied to a stake by one leg, and sticks were thrown at it. The object was to knock the bird down and then run forward and seize it before it had a chance to stand up. One of the most popular games, especially at Shrovetide and in December (when it was thought to be good for the grass), was football (*CE* II.i.84; *Lear* I.iv.87). It had few rules, which was one of its chief attractions for rowdy young men. It was played by two teams whose size depended on the population and enthusiasm of the participating towns. The game consisted of running a ball to one of two goals, which might be the church, a particular tree, or two houses on opposite ends of a town or street. Kicking, biting, trampling, punching, and elbowing were common tactics. Sir Thomas Elyot, in 1531, called the game "nothing but beastely fury and extreme violence," and Phillip Stubbes, fifty-two years later (in *The Anatomie of Abuses*), thought that "it may rather be called a friendly kinde of fight, then a play or recreation. A bloody and murthering practice, then a felowly sporte or pastime." Injuries like broken bones, dislocations, and bloody noses were frequent.

Football was considered a lower-class sport. The rich had their own favorite pastimes: fishing, bird-snaring, falconry, archery, and bowls. Large houses might possess a shovel-board of up to thirty feet long for playing the full-size version of shove-groat. Horseback riding was a part of some kinds of hunting, and those who rode often raced for fun. Sometimes, they engaged in a type of follow-the-leader race called "the wild-goose chase" (*R&J* II.iv.74–75). Another sport that required a horse was jousting. Working-class people had their own form of jousting, running at the quintain. They used a stick for a lance and ran at the target or quintain, which sat at one end of a swinging arm. The object was to hit the target without being hit by a heavy weight or sack attached to the arm's other end.

One of the most fashionable sports for the gentry was tennis (*TNK* V.ii.55; *H8* I.iii.30; *Per* II.i.62–64), which could be played indoors or out. Henry VIII built four courts, two open and two covered, at Westminster. The rectangular court was surrounded by walls. The walls on the short sides and one long side had a second, shorter wall in front of them, covered by an inward-sloping roof. Points were scored by hitting a ball into various small holes in the inner walls or by forcing an opponent to let the ball bounce twice on his side of the net (called a "chase"), but the rules regarding the number of points scored were rather complicated. The net, more like a thick fringe than a modern tennis net, curved from about five heet high at the edges to about three feet high in the middle. The balls, usually stuffed with hair, often dog hair (*MAAN* III.ii.41–44), are sent as an ironic gift by the French dauphin to Henry V to symbolize the English king's former pursuit of frivolity. Henry's reply is full of terms used in the game, such as "set," "match," and "chases." Another tennis term was "bandying," which meant the rapid passage of the ball back and forth between the players (*LLL* V.ii.29; *R&J* II.v.12–15). Tennis was a young man's game, sometimes associated with other supposedly dissolute pursuits. A 1633 play by Thomas Heywood, *The Wise-Woman of Hogsdon*, includes a speech of resignation and disappointment by a father with a rogue of a son, who says, "Enquire about the taverns, ordinaries, / Bowl-alleys, tennis-courts, gaming-houses, / For there, I fear, he will be found."

Children's Games

Some games were chiefly, though not exclusively, played by children. These included leapfrog (*H5* V.ii.140); hide-and-seek (*LLL* IV.iii.75); prisoner's base (*2GV* I.ii.97; *Cym* V.iii.19–20), a form of tag with teams; and blindman's buff or hoodman blind (*AW* IV.iii.121; *Ham* III.iv.78), in which one player was hooded, then approached and hit by the others until he caught and correctly identified one of his assailants. Children also played "cherry-pit" (*TN* III.iv.120), a game that involved tossing cherry stones into a hole. The "wild mare" could mean a seesaw (*2H4* II.iv.252) or an identified rural and Christmas game called shooing or shoeing the wild mare. *See also* Entertainment; Theater.

Garden

The kitchen garden (*Oth* I.iii.315–19; *TNK* II.i.275), in city or country, on large estates and by small cottages, was an important source of food, medicines, cosmetics, and plants grown simply for their lovely scent or smell. Only wealthier families, however, could afford something beyond this kitchen garden. They planted orchards that yielded fruits and nuts, and devoted whole swathes of land purely to aesthetic pleasure. The area behind a substantial home might be divided into a series of squares or rectangles, arranged along a grand central avenue, each section having its own type of plants and its own decorative design. One or several of these areas might be planted with low-growing herbs and flowers in a

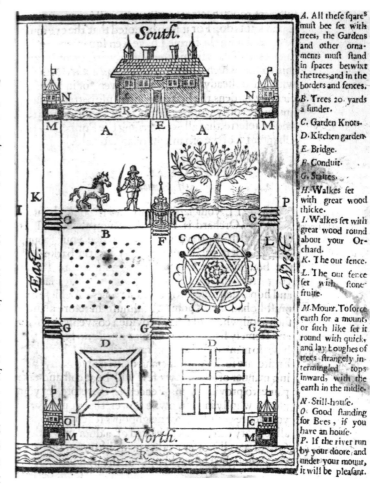

A. All thefe fqareS muſt bee ſet with trees, the Gardens and other ornaments muſt ſtand in ſpaces betwixt the trees, and in the borders and fences.

B. Trees 20. yards a ſunder.

C. Garden Knots.

D. Kitchen garden

E. Bridge.

F. Conduit.

G. Staires.

H. Walkes ſet with great wood thicke.

I. Walkes ſet with great wood round about your Orchard.

K. The out fence.

L. The out fence ſet with ſtonefruite.

M. Mount. To force earth for a mount, or ſuch like ſet it round with quick, and lay boughes of trees ſtrangely intermingled tops inward, with the earth in the midle.

N. Still-houſe.

O. Good ſtanding for Bees, if you have an houſe.

P. If the river run by your doore, and under your mount, it will be pleaſant.

William Lawson's plan of a garden. From *A New Orchard and Garden*. Reproduced from the Collections of the Library of Congress.

knotwork pattern (*LLL* I.i.244–45)—an intricately interwoven arrangement of shapes and paths. Another area might be devoted to a hedge maze; the maze at Hampton Court, one of Henry VIII's palaces, still stands, and paying visitors can attempt, with great frustration, to make their way from its entrance to its exit.

One of the most important considerations in planting a garden, large or small, was location. The authors of the time, including William Lawson, Conrad Heresbach, and Thomas Tusser, had a good deal to say on this subject. Tusser said the garden should face south or southwest. Lawson warned that the soil must be well-drained and never boggy. He advocated square plots, with tall plants along the walls and borders, short plants in the middle of each bed, and herbs of middle height in between. Heresbach pointed out the need for an enclosure of some kind to discourage thieves and vermin. This could be a wall of limestone, rubble, dead wood, or brick (*2H6* IV.x.7; *MM* IV.i.28–33). Some, he said, "making earth in mould doe counterfeit Brickwals." Another type of fence could be made of quick-set hedges, composed of closely planted shrubs of "beeries of sharp thornes, briers, holly, and wilde Eglantine," but hedges took longer to grow than other fences took to build.

The most common type of garden was that supervised by the housewife and her maids (*TS* IV.iv.99–101). Here they planted most, if not all, of the green stuff that the family (and in some cases, the livestock) would consume for the entire year: asparagus, lettuce, endive, colewort, spinach, beets, cresses, radishes, onions, garlic, strawberries, leeks, gourds, artichokes, cabbages, carrots, turnips, parsnips, and "pompions" (pumpkins). Notably absent from this list was the common potato, which was first imported by Sir Walter Raleigh in 1586 but had not, by the time of Shakespeare's career, achieved general popularity. They also sowed herbs and flowers: rue, roses, lavender, rosemary, hyssop, sage, thyme, fennel, elecampane, lilies, poppies, lovage, angelica, cowslips, daisies, peonies, pinks, parsley, sweet cicely, anise, coriander, carduus benedictus, savory, pennyroyal, dill, mint, basil, chervil, cumin, sorrel, mustard, and many, many more. Some of these yielded cooking spices, others were cut and strewn on the floor along with rushes, used for decoration, made into medicines, or distilled for cosmetics and food flavorings.

The bulk of the work in the garden took place in the spring and summer, though some tasks took place earlier in the year. Cabbages and parsnips, for example, were planted in February, as was garlic. Each "clove set in the latter end of *February*," wrote Lawson, "will increase to a great head before *September*." Lawson gave detailed instructions to his readers for the sowing, care, and harvesting of each type of plant. According to his *Country House-Wives Garden*, carrots and turnips should be planted in late April or May, pumpions in late March. Tusser noted that March and April were generally the busiest months.

The housewife spent her gardening hours weeding, picking, digging, planting, and looking for pests, in much the same way that gardeners do today, and with much the same tools. Some plants required extra care. Cabbages were especially suscepible to worms, strawberries to frost. In cold weather, strawberries were protected by a framework of arched sticks covered with straw.

Orchards

For apples, pears, plums, and the like, one needed an orchard (*TS* II.i.111; *John* V.vii.10; *MAAN* I.ii.8–9). As with the garden, the right sort of land in the right sort of place was critical. Lawson noted that the ground could be moister than that of the garden, but not too moist. If necessary, the paths that ran through the orchard could be raised a little to keep them dry, using a layer of earth, another of walnut-sized stones, and one of gravel on top. Trenches could be used to drain excess water from the soil. Low ground was preferred, both because it was more fertile and because it was better protected from the wind, which could damage trees and fruit. The plot should be sunny and, like the garden, it should be enclosed with a wall and entered through a gate (*2H4* I.i.4–6).

The trees should be planted far enough apart so that their branches would not rub together when they were mature. Lawson insists that pits for transplanted trees be fertilized with manure first (*H5* II.iv.39–40), that the transplanted trees be watered thoroughly to help the roots spread, and that trees never be moved except when absolutely necessary. He advises great care of the roots, disapproving of the practice of some gardeners of trimming away the main roots when replanting a tree. Every seven years, he advises, a new layer of manure, 6 inches (15.2 cm) thick, should be spread around each of the trees.

Because only more prosperous people could afford to plant an orchard, Lawson gives some instructions for the hiring of gardeners. The ideal gardener, he writes, should be religious, honest, and candid about his skills and deficiencies. He needs to be skilled at planting seeds, saplings, suckers (which spring from the roots of an existing tree), and the twig clippings called scions. He should be able to prune the tree so that it will grow most efficiently, with no boughs so low that they cannot get sun and bear fruit, no "fretters" (branches that rub together), and no dominant top bough. The gardener should also discourage the growth of suckers, which Lawson likens to drones, because they consume sap yet bear no fruit for many years. He should be alert for signs of disease or moss, weeds (*2H6* III.i.31–33), moles, deer, cattle, birds, and thieving neighbors. Finally, he should be able to harvest and to graft.

Grafting (*JC* II.i.184; *R3* III.vii.126; *2H4* V.iii.1–3; *2H6* III.ii.213–14; *Per* V.i.60), according to Lawson, was "The reforminge of the fruite of one tree with the fruit of another, by an artificial transplacing or trans-

The gardeners were kept busy in the orchard in nearly every season, grafting, planting, and harvesting. Note the orchard wall, an architectural feature most notably mentioned in the balcony scene of Romeo and Juliet. From William Lawson's *A New Orchard and Garden*, 1648. Reproduced from the Collections of the Library of Congress.

posing of a twigge, bud or leafe . . . taken from one tree . . . and placed or put to, or into another tree." The result was fruit with a new appearance or taste, or a single tree that bore different kinds of fruit. Lawson describes several methods of grafting. Incising involved the making of two cuts in the bark. A scion (*H5* III.v.5–9), also called a slip (*2H6* II.ii.59), was shoved into the gap and the gap was closed. "Packing on" was cutting the tree branch and the scion so that they matched like puzzle pieces, placing them together, and sealing the wound. Inoculating (*Ham* III.i.118) was "an eye or bud, taken bark and all from one tree, and placed in the room of another eye or bud of another, cut both of one compass, and there bound"; this method, he specified, was appropriate in the summer only. The most common method was to take a top twig and sever it below its highest knot, so that it was about 5 to 6 inches (13 to 15 cm) long, with three or four "eyes" ready to sprout.

> It is thus wrought; You must with a fine, thin, strong and sharpe saw, made and armed for that purpose, cut off a foot above the ground, or thereabouts, in a place without a knot, or as neare as you can without a knot . . . your stocke, set, or plant, being surely stayed with your foot and legge, . . . and then plaine his wound smoothly with a sharpe knife: that done, cleave him cleanly in the middle with a cleaver, and a knocke or mall [maul, a heavy wooden hammer], and with a wedge of wood, Iron or Bone, two hanfull long at least, put into the middle of that clift, with the same knocke, make the wound gape a straw bredth wide, into which you must put your Graffes.

The wedge was then carefully removed so as not to disturb the placement of the graft, and the cut in the bark was sealed with a poultice of chaff and horse dung. All this effort was more than repaid by the results, according to William Harrison. He was impressed by the accomplishments of gardeners who could make their trees yield better, sweeter, more varied, and even seedless fruit.

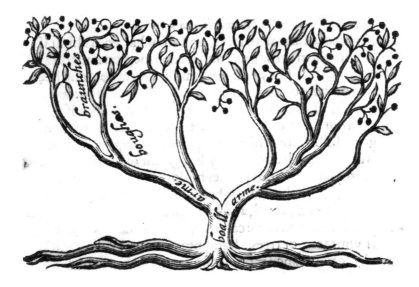

Lawson's diagram of the perfect shape of a fruit tree. From *A New Orchard and Garden*. He preferred short trunks or "boales," though he allowed for longer trunks near paths, where low-hanging branches might pose a hazard. Reproduced from the Collections of the Library of Congress.

The most common types of trees were apples, pears, cherries, plums, damsons (small, dark plums), bullaces (wild plums), walnuts, and filberts. Lawson insisted that in England, "we meddle not with Apricockes nor Peaches, nor scarcely with Quinces," but Harrison listed apricots and peaches, along with almonds, figs, and the even rarer capers, citrus, and olives, as novelties grown in noblemen's orchards from the mid-sixteenth century on.

There was much work to be done in the orchard; Shakespeare offers a detailed exchange between the Duke of York's gardeners on the nature of the required tasks. They are to "bind up young dangling apricocks" (*R2* III.iv.29), trim "the heads of too fast growing sprays" (32), weed, prune, hedge, restore order to the knotbeds, remove caterpillars, and tend to the grafting (40–47, 57–64). Guides to husbandry indicate that these, with a few additions, were the typical tasks required. Harvest took place in summer and fall, with the gardeners climbing platformed ladders to fill baskets or pouches with fruit. The easiest way to harvest the fruit was to train the trees to grow splayed flat along a wall, but Lawson disapproved of this method. It allowed the branches, he admitted, to be more exposed to "the Sun, which is commendable, for the having of fair, good, and soon ripe fruit. But let them know, it is more hurtful to the trees then the benefit they reap thereby, as not suff[er]ing a tree to live the tenth part of his age," because the proximity to a wall damaged both roots and bark. He recommended picking fruit for immediate use as it ripened, usually between midsummer and Lammas; fruit to be stored over the winter, however, should be harvested no earlier than Michaelmas. Damsons and bullaces should be picked at the first full moon after the first frost. It was of the utmost importance to preserve the stem and to handle the fruit gently, for "Every bruise is to fruit death."

Lawson was skilled at describing the pleasures and advantages of keeping an orchard. It was easier to maintain than a garden; could be enhanced with moats, fountains (*AYLI* IV.i.149–50), or fishponds; delighted the senses; and offered a place for recreation. Shakespeare's characters would seem to agree; they are often to be found walking, reading, or working in their gardens and orchards (*TN* III.i., III.iv., IV.iii.; *Cym* I.i.81; *JC* II.i., III.ii.247–51; *R&J* II.i, II.ii, II.v, III.v; *AYLI* I.i; *R3* III.iii.32; *R2* III.iv.1–3; *MAAN* II.iii.2–3, III.i.5–16). *See also* Farming; Flowers; Trees.

Ghosts

Belief in ghosts (*R3* I.ii.8, I.iv.37, III.i.144; *MM* V.i.437; *V&A* 933) was widespread. The ghost was the soul itself (*1H6* I.i.67; *2H6* III.ii.161, 231, 373–74; *Lear* V.iii.315), severed from the body and driven to walk on the earth for some reason. Part of the popularity of belief in ghosts was connected to the theology of the Catholic Church, which had been England's state religion in the time of Shakespeare's father and grandfather, and which was still present in parts of the country where recusants hid priests and said Mass in private. Catholicism, unlike the Church of England, held that some souls stayed in a place called purgatory, neither heaven nor hell, where they had to atone for their sins until they were cleansed and could proceed to heaven. They could be assisted in this by the prayers of those on earth, which was why many people left provisions in their wills for Masses to be said on their behalf.

The Anglican Church did away with purgatory, but not with the lingering belief that souls with unfinished business might lurk somewhere, waiting for some reason to move on. It was most common to think of ghosts as those who had died suddenly or violently, either without time to prepare themselves spiritually for death or in a manner—for example, murder or suicide—that cried out for justice against the hand that had done the deed. Suicides were, in fact, buried with a stake through the heart in the belief that this would keep the ghost from walking at night. Apparitions, such as that of Herne the Hunter in *The Merry Wives of Wind-*

sor (IV.iv.27–42), were said to show themselves most often at night (*2H6* I.iv.20; *H5* IV.Cho.28), and especially at midnight (*MND* V.i.378–81). They were sometimes said to groan or to speak (*TA* I.i.126; *JC* IV.iii.271 s.d.–83, V.v.17). Shakespeare's ghosts tend to haunt their killers (*R&J* IV.iii.55; *R3* V.iii.119–77) or to seek justice for their killers, as in *Hamlet*, but not all Renaissance ghosts were so logical. Ghosts were reported in mines, dressed as miners and mocking the living miners for no apparent reason, and there was a general belief in appearances by large, black, spectral dogs that bore no connection to a past murder or suicide.

Giants

Giants (*MM* II.ii.108–9, III.i.80; *MAAN* V.i.200; *John* I.i.225; *2H4* I.ii.1; *T&C* II.iii.137–38; *Mac* V.ii.21) fell into two categories: the mythological and the real. Fictional giants included the costumed performers at midsummer revels, ancient Greek Titans, and the legendary British giants Gog and Magog, or Gogmagog, supposedly defeated by Brutus. Real giants, including a 7'6" individual who worked for Elizabeth I, and a man of similar stature named Walter Parsons, who worked for James I, were often recruited as royal porters and guards. Other giants, like John Middleton of Hale, Lancashire, had to settle for an introduction to the king but no employment. There were a few extraordinarily tall women as well. "Long Meg" was a possibly fictional but much celebrated rogue of Henry VIII's time who was supposed to have kept a bawdy house in Southwark. Other than royal service, giants might find themselves in any occupation that required great strength, or they might travel the country exhibiting themselves. On July 17, 1581, John Stow saw a show in London based on the difference in height between a 7'7" giant and a 3' dwarf; he marveled at the fact that the dwarf, who wore a hat with a feather, could pass untouched between the giant's legs, or stand on a bench on which the giant sat and still be the shorter of the pair.

Glasses

See Spectacles.

Gloves

English gloves (*2GV* II.i.1–6; *R2* V.iii.17; *MV* IV.i.425; *R&J* II.ii.24–25; *Cym* I.iii.10–12; *T&C* V.ii.77) in Shakespeare's day were made from domestic deer, lamb, or sheepskin, or from imported kidskin (the "chev'ril" of *TN* III.i.12) produced and dressed in France. The French kidskins, due to their fine quality, could be dressed on the hair or "grain" side of the skin, resulting in a smooth, fashionable, and desirable glove. The English skins were rougher, with a less pleasing grain, so they were usually dressed on the flesh side of the skin, resulting in a suede finish. The skins were usually left a whitish color (*LLL* V.ii.412), though some were dyed, or dyed only on the cuff or "gauntlet" section. After a lengthy tanning process, the skins were delivered to the glover (*MWW* I.iv.19–20), who with skillful cutting could get one and a half pairs from a kidskin, one to two from a lambskin, and at least three from a sheepskin. Cutting the gloves required not only conservation of the leather but also placement of the pieces to maximize the fit and flexibility (*AW* V.iii.277–78) of the gloves.

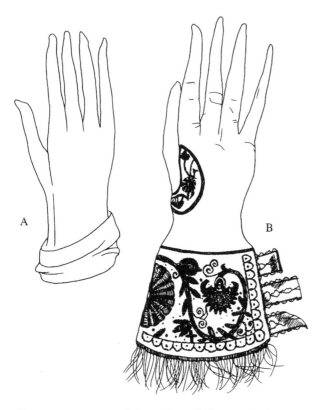

A

B

The finger and hand sections were often assembled separately from the wide gauntlet, the two parts being joined at the very end of the process. One of the principal differences between the gloves of the sixteenth century and those of today is that today, the glove fingers are designed to accommodate the differing lengths of the actual fingers on any given hand, whereas on sixteenth-century gloves, all the fingers tended to be the same length, thus artificially lengthening the shorter fingers. The cuff was the part most likely to be decorated in some way, either by dyeing or by embellishment such as beadwork or embroidery. When it was folded down toward the hand, as was increasingly the case from the 1590s, the gloves were said to be "gauntlet-style." Once the gloves were cut and sewn, they could be perfumed at extra cost (*MAAN* III.iv.60–61; *WT* IV.iv.221). In 1583, Phillip Stubbes disapproved of "sweet washed gloves imbrodered with gold, silver, and what not," but he was probably in the minority. Not all gloves were made of leather; some were made of linen, silk, or cotton, but these gloves were typically produced not by glovers but by dressmakers or milliners (*WT* IV.iv.192). In places without a local manufacturer, gloves might be sold by a peddler (*WT* IV.iv.602).

Two common sorts of gloves from Shakespeare's day. (A) The ordinary, natural-leather glove for everyday use, with a white or colored cuff. (B) A fancy presentation-style glove from the first decade of the seventeenth century with an embroidered gauntlet and silver gilt fringe.

Gloves were a common gift. They were a traditional favor for wedding guests or an intimate gift from one lover to another (*LLL* V.ii.47–49; *T&C* IV.iv.63; *Lear* III.iv.85; *Cor* II.i.266; *Tim* V.iv.49–50; *TNK* III.v.46). Monarchs, including Elizabeth I and James I, routinely received elaborately decorated pairs, including a pair given to James I in 1605 trimmed with pearls and worth £6. Other ceremonial gloves were embroidered or trimmed with velvet, ribbons, braid, or lace. Prices varied widely. Apprentices in James's time were theoretically limited to leather or woolen mittens that cost less than 1 shilling a pair. Prince Henry of Wales, on the other hand, owned thirty-one pairs in 1608, most of them worth 3 shillings a pair. In 1618, the custom of wearing gloves was so widespread, and the sumptuary laws so widely disregarded, that an Italian visitor claimed to see "very costly gloves" on everyone in London, "even the porters." *See also* Clothing.

Government

England was governed on a national level by the queen or king, her or his officials, the Privy Council, and the Parliament, and on a local level by parish and town or borough (*3H6* II.i.195) officials. The sovereign could issue all sorts of edicts, proclamations, and warrants, collect certain taxes, and order executions without anyone's consent, though unpopular decisions were liable to result in angry petitions from the people or even open rebellion (*H8* I.ii.30–36). Conversely, rulers perceived as good rulers were greeted in the streets with cheers, banners, and caps flung high (*R2* V.ii.1–36; *3H6* II.i.196).

In making decisions and executing commands, the monarch relied upon the advice the Privy Council (*H8* V.ii.16–18), which had fewer than twenty members under Elizabeth I. It dealt with matters of foreign policy, poor relief, supervision of justices of the peace, treason, and breaches of the peace, and was limited only by the queen's or king's will. The council contained several members of the royal household, including the Lord Chamberlain (*H8* I.iv.64 s.d.), the Lord Treasurer, and the Lord Chancellor. The last of these bore a large purse that held the Great Seal (*H8* I.i.114 s.d., III.ii.318–20), the sign of his office; it was not supposed to leave England, even if the Lord Chancellor traveled abroad. Other high officials included ambassadors (*H8* III.ii.318–20; *LLL* I.i.133–39, III.i.51–52), the Lord Privy Seal, the Lord Admiral, and the queen's (or king's) secretary.

If the king was a child, the most important member of the royal household was the protector (*1H6* I.i.36, 170–72; *2H6* I.ii.44, 56) or regent (*1H6* I.i.84; *2H6* III.i.290, 294, 305), appointed by the previous ruler to govern during the new king's minority. Protectors often struggled to keep their temporary authority; Richard III apparently murdered to do so. If

The purse that held the Great Seal, symbol of the office of Lord Chancellor.

more than one protector was appointed, to prevent the rise of a tyrant, then there might be deleterious squabbling among them.

When rulers needed more money than their traditional privileges allowed, or when they wanted to pass legislation that overrode all other authority, they needed to turn to Parliament (*2H6* III.i.set, IV.vii.15–16; *3H6* I.i.35, 39, II.i.118, 173; *2H4* IV.ii.18). This legislative body was composed of the House of Lords and the House of Commons. The Lords were composed of bishops, archbishops, and nobles, numbering about eighty or ninety, with the spiritual lords making up about a third of the total. The Commons were elected by boroughs and counties, which got one or two representatives each, and London, which got four, for a total of 439 in 1583 and 462 in 1603. Parliament was called by the monarch (*2H6* II.iv.70, V.iii.25; *2H4* V.v.105) forty days before the beginning of the session, and on the first day, she or he sat in the chair of state (*3H6* I.i.22–26, 51, 168) in the House of Lords, with the spiritual lords seated on her or his right and the temporal lords on the left. Nearby, judges, secretaries of state, and the Master of the Rolls sat on wool sacks to offer opinions if called upon. Next the ruler met with the Commons, where the Speaker gave a traditional address requesting the continuation of the house's "liberties and privileges," freedom of speech for the members in debate, the right to punish its own members for violations of decorum, access for the Speaker to the ruler, and forgiveness in advance for any offense the Speaker may give in the course of his duties.

During the session, bills were presented and voted upon three times; in the Lords, they were read by the clerk of the Parliament, and then the members might rise, one by one, to speak for or against the bills. After the debates were concluded, the proper form for voting was either "Content," or "Not content." Some lords voted by proxy.

In the Commons, the Speaker sat in an elevated chair, with a clerk to read the bills. Members gave notice that they wished to speak by standing up and removing their hats. Each member could speak only once per day on a particular bill (*H5* I.i.1, 7–19, 70–71), and if he wished to rebut an opponent's rejoinder, he had to wait until the following day. He had to watch his tongue, for abusive language was punished. In this house, voting was by a simple mass "yea" or "no," with no proxies allowed; if the voice vote was indecisive, yeas were asked to sit down, and the sitters and standers were counted individually. Bills from the Lords that were read in the Commons and passed all three times were signed, "Les commons ont assentus." The reverse form, for approving a measure that originated in the Commons and passed the Lords, was "Les seigneurs ont assentus."

At the end of the session, the monarch appeared again and was thanked by the Lord Chancellor and the Speaker. The Lord Chancellor then thanked both houses on behalf of the monarch, and all acts passed during the session were read, with the ruler assenting to ("Il nous plaist"—I like it) or rejecting ("Il ne plaist"—I don't like it) each one. The ones that had been authorized were published and distributed.

In addition to the king or queen and members of Parliament, the national government had a host of minor officials in its employ. These included tax collectors, torturers, executioners, spies, secretaries, porters, postboys, and purveyors. The accounting was done by auditors (*1H4* II.i.60), who took their name from the fact that in the past they had heard oral reports of the finances from those under them. Less educated but just as important in their way were the whifflers (*H5* V.Cho.12), who walked before processions to clear the path of pedestrians and coaches.

Local Government

The towns, counties, and parishes were governed by several bodies and individuals whose duties or territories often overlapped. There were road surveyors, who maintained the highways that ran through the parish; justices of the peace, who ran most of the courts; local lords, who held a great deal of traditional and economic authority; church officials; overseers of the poor; sheriffs (*2H6* II.iv.ch.), who collected taxes and supervised the courts through the undersheriff, and the execution of writs and warrants through bailiffs; and beadles, who rounded up and whipped vagrants. Towns generally had a mayor; Shakespeare includes the mayors of St. Albans (*2H6* II.i.ch) and York (*3H6* IV.vii.ch) as characters, though it was generally agreed that the Lord Mayor of London (*1H6* I.ii.ch., III.i.ch.; *2H6* IV.iii.13–14; *R3* III.i.ch., III.v.ch., III.vii.ch.; *H8* V.v.69) was the grandest specimen of his breed. Contemporaries thought that for sheer pomp and splendor on public occasions, he had not his equal throughout Europe. Second in state only to the mayor was the alderman (*3H6* IV.vii.ch.; *R3* III.vii.65), the leader of a guild or member of the town's ruling council.

Non-English Governments

Since many of Shakespeare's plays are set outside of England, it is not surprising that many of his government officials hold foreign offices. The term "senate" was applied to many of the governing bodies of nations and cities during his life, so it is appropriate that he applies it to the governments of Venice and Athens (*Oth* I.i.115, III.ii.2; *Tim* IV.i.5), but most of his references to a senate and senators are to the government of ancient Rome (*TA* III.i; *Cor* I.i.58, V.vi.82). During Rome's Republican period, the city and its territories were governed by the Senate and a handful of magistrates.

A political hopeful began with about ten years of military service, ending with a term as a military tribune or a tribune of the plebs. At this time, the citizenry of Rome was divided into an upper class (the patricians—see *Cor* I.i.16) and a lower (the plebeians). Membership in a particular tribe determined to which class a person belonged; it was the same as his father's (even if, according to a law passed in 445 B.C.E., his mother was a plebeian and his father a patrician). The tribune of the plebs (*Cor* I.i.217) was usually born a patrician, but once elected by the plebeian tribes (*Cor* III.iii.11), he served as their representative, arguing their concerns before the magistrates and protecting them, if possible, from abuses of authority. In return, the plebs protected him from arrest or illegal seizure by the patrician government. Becoming a tribune of the plebs (along with sponsoring a lot of expensive gladiatorial spectacles) was an essential step in securing popular support, and with popular support came power, as the success of Sicinius and Brutus in discrediting Coriolanus demonstrates. Flavius and Marullus, the tribunes in *Julius Caesar*, also appear to exert a great deal of authority.

Once he had successfully completed a tribuneship, the aspirant tried for a praetorship. Praetors acted as deputies to the consuls (*Cor* II.i.225–39), two of whom served as Rome's highest temporal authorities. The praetors oversaw the individuals who decided civil lawsuits, published rulings on areas of the law that were unclear, and nominated the praefecti who had jurisdiction over Italian cities. If he were lucky, a praetor would be elected consul for as many terms as he could manage. His duties, with his co-consul, would be to govern Rome and its territories, and to defend and extend those territories in the field of battle. The importance of the consulate was so great that Romans dated occurrences as happening either in "*n* years from the founding of the city" or "the consulship of *x* and *y*." The consuls' authority was symbolized by the lictors (*Cor* II.ii.36 s.d.; *A&C* V.ii.214) who accompanied them, carrying the fasces, a bundle of rods topped with an axe whose presence warned that the consul could chastise or execute, as he chose. In 180 B.C.E. a minimum age, probably forty-two, was set for the consulship.

Rome also had a censor (*Cor* II.iii.246), who ruled on the class membership of citizens based on both their wealth and their behavior, and who drew up the list of Senate members, excluding any he felt had proven unworthy to remain in office. Quaestors, who served as financial administrators to the consuls, were elected by the tribal assembly; from 421 B.C.E., when their number was raised from two to four, they could be either plebeians or patricians. Aediles (*Cor* III.i.172) controlled streets, markets, and public festivals.

The constant among these officials, who served short terms, was the Senate. The senators, unless they were removed by the censors, served for life, and though their decisions were purely advisory, their moral and traditional authority was such that few magistrates dared rebel against them. The Senate's period of greatest power came to an end with the rise of two triumvirates, or triple (rather than double) consulships—the first, of Julius Caesar, Pompey, and Crassus; the second, of Octavius Caesar, Antony, and Lepidus. Their rule and internal squabbles succeeded in crumbling the old consular traditions, and at the end of the fighting, Octavius Caesar, now Caesar Augustus, emerged as Rome's first emperor (*TA* I.i.205). *See also* Court; Law.

Griffin

The griffin was a legendary beast with the body of a lion and the wings and head of an eagle. Griffins were rumored to live in Scythia or India, building nests of gold in the mountains and guarding them with a fierceness that made griffins a popular emblem in heraldry. Female heraldic griffins had wings; males had no wings but a series of spikes along the back or sometimes a pair of long, straight horns on the head. Archeologists now think that belief in the griffin may have arisen from discoveries of the fossilized skeletons of beaked, four-legged, lion-sized dinosaurs (*MND* II.i.232; *1H4* III.i.148).

Groat

The groat (*AW* II.ii.21; *MWW* I.i.148), or fourpence, was already an ancient type of coin by Shakespeare's day. It was first introduced in the reign of Edward I and soon afterward withdrawn, then reissued nearly three-quarters of a century later by Edward III. The name was similar to those of large Continental coins, such as the Dutch groot (from the word for great or large) or the French gros tournois (literally, big thing from Tours, for this multiple-denier coin was minted at the abbey of St. Martin of Tours). The groat was minted for circulation for the last time in 1582, though the half-groat, now called a twopence, continued to be produced during the reign of James I. The groat remained a familiar small coin for some time, however, judging from the frequency with which it appears in Shakespeare's plays. Perhaps because it had been discontinued, and perhaps because of its long history, it had a whiff of the archaic, and as such it is often found in the history plays (*2H6* III.i.113; *H5* V.i.59–60; *R2* V.v.68; *John* I.i.94; *2H4* I.ii.237–40) and, anachronistically, in *Coriolanus* (III.ii.10).

Silver groat issued during the reign of Henry VI (1422–61). Actual size is 26 mm in diameter. © 2002 The American Numismatic Society. All rights reserved.

In its last incarnation, from 1561 to 1582, the groat bore a portrait of Queen Elizabeth on the obverse, framed by the legend ELIZABETH D G ANG FR ET HIB REGINA—Elizabeth, by the grace of God (D[ei] G[ratia]) Queen (REGINA) of England (ANG), France (FR), and Ireland (ET HIB). The reverse bore the royal arms quartered by a "long cross" that extended into the rim and the legend POSVI DEVM ADIVTOREM MEVM (Behold, I have made God mine helper). Legends on coins tended to be in Latin and to be much-abbreviated, particularly on the smaller coins.

The half-groat or twopence (*MWW* I.i.150; *TN* IV.i.32; *2H4* I.ii.238) looked like the groat until 1582 but was somewhat smaller. It also, co-incidentally, looked the same as the half crown of the time and was the

Half-groat, also known as twopence, 1604–5. Actual size is 17 mm in diameter. © 2002 The American Numismatic Society. All rights reserved.

same size as the half crown, the only difference between the two being that one was made of gold and the other of silver. It was a well-known stratagem to gild a twopence and pass it as a half crown (*2H4* IV.iii.51).

From 1583 to 1603, the twopence had a different style. It retained the bust of Elizabeth, but the legend was replaced with another common motto, E D G ROSA SINE SPINA (Elizabeth, by the grace of God, rose without a thorn), and the reverse legend read CIVITAS LONDON. James I altered the design still further. From 1603 to 1604 the coin bore his portrait with the legend I D G ROSA SINE SPINA (the same as Elizabeth's, but with an I for Iacobus, his Latin name, substituted for the E) on the obverse. The reverse bore a new coat of royal arms, containing the symbols of England, France, Scotland, and Ireland, and no legend at all. The twopence of James's second coinage (1604–18) bore a crowned thistle, a symbol of Scotland, on the obverse, with the legend TVEATVR VNITA DEVS (May God protect united things). The reverse had a crowned Tudor rose and the rose-without-thorn legend. *See also* Money.

Gypsy

The gypsies (*AYLI* V.iii.13–14; *TNK* IV.ii.44), a nomadic race that specialized in trading and fortune-telling, first appeared in England in the early sixteenth century. Their name came from the belief that, with their dark hair, comparatively dark skin, and strange language, they must originally have come from Egypt. Shakespeare accordingly identifies them with Egypt by calling Cleopatra a gypsy (*A&C* I.i.9–10, IV.xii.28–29; *R&J* II.iv.43) and uses them as a symbol for unattractiveness (*MND* V.i.10–11), since dark hair and skin were the direct opposite of the Renaissance ideal. The gypsies traveled throughout England from a home base in the Derbyshire Peak, attended by much suspicion of their supposedly habitual thievery and delight in the trinkets and the false knowledge of the future that they peddled.

Hair

Men's hairstyles, which had remained almost entirely unchanged for much of the sixteenth century, underwent only a few changes during Shakespeare's writing career. During the second quarter of the century, the longish hair of Henry VII's time had been replaced by a short cut, usually swept back from the face. In the 1580s, however, the short haircut developed curls on top, assisted by the curling irons (or tongs—*TN* I.iii.89–100; *Lear* III.iv.85; *Tim* IV.iii.161) of one's barber (*Lear* II.ii.34) or servants.

By the 1590s, fashionable men were wearing their hair longer, sometimes growing "lovelocks"—individual bunches of hair allowed to grow long and dangle near the ear, sometimes loose, sometimes gathered with a cord or ribbon. Shakespeare simply calls this fashion a "lock" (*MAAN* III.iii.168, V.i.307–8), not a lovelock; it is not frequently mentioned, though the vague references to Pericles' unshorn hair may apply to the hair all over his head, his beard, or a lovelock (*Per* III.iii.30, V.iii.74). The short styles of the past were no longer daring—witness Shakespeare's characterization of tradesmen as "smooth-pates" (*2H4* I.ii.38)—but short, nonetheless, was still how the vast majority of men wore their hair. Petruchio's servants do not curl or plait their hair for their master's return, but simply comb it (*TS* IV.i.81–82).

Women's hair was sometimes augmented by wigs or periwigs (*H5* III.vii.62–63; *CE* II.ii.75), made of horse-hair or hair purchased from the poor, but usually it was simply propped up on pads or frames, frizzed and curled to build it up still more, and decorated with jewels called bodkins that could be stuck into the mass or headbands, called biliments, studded with jewels. The rest of the hair was gathered at the back of the head and tied into a little bun. Phillip Stubbes, writing in *The Anatomie of Abuses* (1583), was appalled by the fashion:

> . . . their haire . . . whiche of force must be curled, frisled, crisped, laid out (a World to see) on wreathes & borders, from one eare to an other. And least it should fall down, it is under propped with forks, wyers, & I cannot tell what, rather like grime sterne monsters, than chaste Christian matrones. Then, on ye edges of their bolstred heir . . . there is layd great wreathes of gold and silver, curiouslie wrought, & cunninglie applied to the temples of their heades. And for feare of lacking any thing to set foorth their pride withal, at their heyre . . . are hanged, bugles (I dare not say bables), ouches, rings, gold, silver, glasses, & other such gewgawes and trinckets besides.

He also accused them of dyeing their hair.

Not all women wore their hair this way, however. In the first place, not every woman could afford all these "bugles" or the time it took to arrange them. The country lass in *A Lover's Complaint* wears a simpler hairstyle, consisting of loosely braided hair tied with a cloth headband and partially concealed by a straw hat, with a few loose strands danging here and there, not by design but simply because the braids had come partly undone (29–35). Brides had a completely different style, wearing their hair loose around their shoulders (*TNK* I.i.1 s.d.); this is also the way Anne Boleyn wore her hair at her coronation (*H8* IV.i.36 s.d.).

Blonde hair was generally prized, and red hair was considered a sign of a dishonest or unsavory temperament (*AYLI* III.iv.7; *CE* III.ii.48, 102). Eyebrows were plucked, and if this was skillfully done, it could make up even for the disadvantage of being a brunette (*WT* II.i.8–11). Hair could be symbolic. It was torn in grief and mourning (*John* III.iii.45–75), shaven off at the crown by the monks England had forsworn (*2H6* II.i.51). *See also* Clothing; Hat; Jewelry.

Halfpenny

Introduced in 1279–80 by Edward I after a long absence from English coinage, the halfpenny was always, in a time when coins were made of real silver, a very small coin. As such, it had little room for Latin mottoes or elaborate royal portraits. Elizabeth I's halfpenny of 1583–1603 had no words on it at all. The obverse had a picture of a portcullis; the reverse, a cross with three tiny pellets (round bumps) in each quadrant. James I's was the same until 1604, when its design was altered to a thistle on one side and a rose on the other, also with no words.

Halfpenny, 1609. Actual size is 10 mm in diameter. © 2002 The American Numismatic Society. All rights reserved.

Not surprisingly, when the halfpenny is mentioned in Shakespeare's works, it is in reference to very small things: "halfpenny loaves" (*2H6* IV.ii.67), a "halfpenny purse of wit" (*LLL* V.i.71), bits of a shredded letter (*MAAN* II.iii.142–43), and a ridiculously one-sided wager ("my hat to a halfpenny," *LLL* V.ii.556). One example, the selling of a stolen lute case for "three halfpence" (*H5* III.ii.42–44), might be a reference not to three halfpenny coins but to one three-halfpence, a coin produced between 1561 and 1582 and looking very much like a penny of the same era. Another possible reference is the "ob." on Falstaff's tavern bill in *1 Henry IV* (II.iv.544); this stands for "obolus," a term for any coin of small value, and might be a halfpenny. *See also* Money.

Ḥat

Men's headgear fell into three principal categories: coifs, caps, and hats. The coif was a tight-fitting skullcap that covered most of the head, including the ears, and was usually worn under some kind of cap or hat. The coif could be made of velvet or silk and was often black, though lawyers typically wore white.

Caps (*3H6* II.i.196; *R3* III.vii.35; *MAAN* I.i.193) were brimless, low, and often soft. They might be decorated with jewels, brooches (*LLL* V.ii.617), ribbons (*Ham* IV.vii.77), flowers (*Mac* IV.iii.170–72), or badges; Shakespeare indicates that gloves or daggers might be worn on them as well, as a sign of a quarrel (*H5* IV.i.56–57, 200–21). Other symbols, such as a Welsh leek (*H5* IV.vii.97–104) or a lover's token, might be worn there instead. Because the cap was highly visible, the symbolism of items worn there was emphasized. Taking off one's cap could carry meaning as well. The cap was doffed in the presence of a social superior (*1H4* IV.iii.68) and flung into the air as a sign of joy (*Ham* IV.v.108; *A&C* IV.xii.12).

Some caps were meant for special uses. Simple knit wool caps were supposed to be worn by nearly everyone seven or older on Sundays, according to a statute in effect from 1570 to 1597. Because their use was mandated by law, they were called "statute caps." Judges, scholars, and clergy sometimes wore a coif covered by a flat triangular kind of cap that Shakespeare calls a "corner-cap" (*LLL* IV.iii.50). Men of most classes also wore two kinds of nightcaps (*Oth* II.i.306)—one that was decorative and meant to be worn at home in the evenings, and one that was made of simpler fabric, usually of white

Low soft cap, c. 1585.

wool or linen. The simpler version, often provided with strings that tied under the chin, was called a biggin (*2H4* IV.v.26) and was meant to be worn while sleeping.

Hats (*2GV* II.iii.21; *LLL* I.i.302; *MAAN* III.ii.38–40) had brims and crowns of varying shapes and sizes. One type of hat was the copotain or capotain, a hat with a medium-sized brim and a tall, tapered, almost conical crown. Its resemblance to the most prominent feature of churches lent it the nickname "steeple hat." The moralist Phillip Stubbes loathed the capotain, which might stand 9 inches (23 cm) tall. He was not much more fond of the other hats men wore, because they were often made of costly materials such as silk, velvet, taffeta, sarcenet, wool, and beaver-fur felt, which he called "a certaine kind of fine haire, far fetched, and deare bought you maye bee sure." Part of what offended him was that hats, as fancy as one's purse allowed, were worn not only by gentlemen but also by servants and peasants.

Gardener's hat, 1577.

Stubbes probably exaggerated a good deal. The countryman in Robert Greene's *Quip for an Upstart Courtier* (1592) is shown not in a fancy hat, but in an unadorned, broad-brimmed hat clearly meant to keep the sun out of the eyes and off the head. His headgear is possibly made out of straw, as many country hats were (*Temp* IV.i.136; *LC* 8–9, 29–35). The courtier, on the other hand, wears a tall plumed hat of the kind described by Stubbes. He might equally have worn a narrow-brimmed, round-crowned felt bowler, whether colored, black, or gray and edged with colored trim. The courtier's hat might be made of any of the materials in Stubbes' list, or it might have been "thrummed," woven with a nap or pile, though thrummed hats were unfashionable by the time of Shakespeare's London career.

Hats, like caps, could be used to convey messages. They could be used for concealment, either respectful or furtive (*MM* II.ii.188–89; *JC* II.i.74–75). They could be used to emphasize a gesture (*Cor* II.iii.169) or be doffed to show respect for a superior (*Ham* V.ii.94–95). Like caps, they could be decorated with jeweled bands, brooches, or feathers (*AW* III.v.77, IV.v.104–6; *Tim* III.vi.113–14; *H8* I.iii.25). And they could, as in the case of cardinals, indicate occupation and rank (*1H6* I.iii.36).

Women's headdresses were similar to men's. They, too, wore caps (*TS* IV.iii.63–85, V.ii.123; *2H4* II.iv.281; *AW* I.i.157–60; *Oth* IV.iii.78) and coifs (*WT* IV.iv.225), though, unlike men, they sometimes wore cauls, or net coifs, that might be jeweled or expensively lined. The coif might be topped with a bongrace, a kind of flat hood meant to keep the sun off the face and often attached in the back to a veil (*TN* I.v.163–64; *T&C* III.ii.44–45; *Cor* II.i.218–21; *TNK* I.i.24 s.d.). Unlike men, they wore jeweled biliments and bodkins; like men, they wore caps and hats. One type of popular hat was small, with a short, pleated crown and a narrow brim. Called a "taffeta pipkin" and worn at an angle, it was especially fashionable from 1565 to 1595. The court bonnet, popular from 1575 to 1585, was similar but had no brim. Both of these styles were succeeded by the bowler, virtually identical to the man's bowler, and the topper, which had a tall crown like the copotain but grew wider rather than narrower toward the top. Shakespeare also mentions a "porringer," a scallop-edged cap shaped like a soup basin (*H8* V.iv.47). Emanuel van Meteren, a Dutch resident of England from 1558 to 1612, wrote that women went about without a hood or mantle to cover their heads and that "Married women only wear a hat both in the street and in the house; those unmarried go without a hat." *See also* Clothing; Hair.

Helmet

Shakespeare's helmets, like most items of armor mentioned in the plays, present problems. Helmets are mentioned most frequently in plays set in the Middle Ages, ancient Greece, or ancient Rome. However, Renaissance actors were costumed in contemporary, not historically accurate, clothing and armor. Nevertheless, it seems appropriate to describe both the thing itself—the Corinthian helmet, the barbute, and the bascinet—and the substitute that probably was seen onstage in Shakespeare's day.

The Greek examples are the earliest—the "helmet" (I.ii.210), "helm" (V.iv.4), and "plumes" (I.iii.385) of *Troilus and Cressida*, and the "casque" (III.vi.62) of *The Two Noble Kinsmen*. This is not necessarily inaccurate usage. Greek soldiers did wear helmets of hammered bronze, sometimes with hinged cheek flaps, and usually topped with a crest of metal or metal and horsehair. Achilles' "plumes," then, could be a crest of this type, although it seems more likely to be the identifying plumes of a Crusader's or jouster's helm. And Nestor's announcement that "I will hide my silver beard in a gold beaver" (*T&C* I.iii.296) is clearly anachronistic. Corinthian helmets covered the whole face, whereas the bevor (or beaver) was a separate piece that covered the throat and lower face. It might be a type of visor attached to a helmet or a tall, separate, gorget-like piece worn with a hatlike helmet, but in either case it was invented long after the days of the Trojan War.

There are passing references to helmets in *Coriolanus* (the "casque" of IV.vii.43, for example), but we meet with helmets again in earnest in the tragedies and histories set in the Middle Ages. At the time of the Norman Conquest, the standard knightly garb was a suit of chain mail topped by a pointed metal cap with a "nasal"—a long, thin piece of metal descending in front to protect the bridge of the nose. By the time of King John (*John* II.i.254), this basic metal helmet was evolving into different shapes, and throughout the thirteenth century it appears as conical, high and oval, or round and close-fitting, with or without the nasal. Another version looked more like a medium-brimmed hat, its resemblance to an overturned metal dish giving it the name "kettle helmet." The kettle's crown might be rounded, with crown and brim barely changing angle as they met, or it might have a flatter top, giving it the appearance of a truncated triangle or an early pith helmet. Both the rounded and kettle helmets perched on

Top row: thirteenth-century helmets. (A) Mail coif and kettle helmet. (B) Rounded helmet with nasal, worn over a mail coif. (C) Helm. Bottom row: fourteenth-century helmets. (D) Bascinet and aventail, the aventail hanging from staples underneath a plate running along the sides of the bascinet. (E) Peaked bascinet and pointed bevor.

the top of the head; the ears, throat, and sometimes the chin were still covered in chain mail. For increased protection, some thirteenth-century knights adopted a closed helm, shaped rather like an upside-down bucket, with long, narrow eye slits and small ventilation holes across the front. Worn over a padded lining, the helm could be decorated with identifying emblems—for example, plumes, metal wings, a crown, or a metal lion's or eagle's head affixed to its flat top.

The helm had certain advantages, notably its improved protection against blows to the side and back of the head. The relative safety it afforded to the eyes must also have been attractive. No knight was likely to forget the story of King Harold, slain by an arrow to the eye in 1066. However, the helm was hot, heavy, and hard to see out of. When not worn—for example, while on the march—it was hung from a chain over the knight's shoulder, an arrangement that could hardly have been comfortable. Most crucially, the flat top allowed a sword or mace to find purchase too easily, and the flat helm was therefore destined to be replaced by a superior device.

The fourteenth century saw the development of the bascinet, an improved version of the rounded helmet. Instead of perching atop the head, the bascinet enfolded it, extending below and around the ears. Worn with a dangling chain-mail aventail to protect the chin and throat, it offered a rounder surface that resisted the biting edge of an enemy sword. There were bascinets of varying shape, as armorers sought to find the form that offered the best protection. Some bascinets were nearly round on top. Others were tall and shaped like the pointier end of an egg. A favorite shape rose to a point near the back, sometimes with a central ridge for better sword deflection. A version of the bascinet, the barbute, remained popular in Italy until the end of the fifteenth century.

The chief weakness of the bascinet, however, was the same as that of the kettle helmet. It did little to protect the eyes and face. For this reason, it was worn exclusively under the helm as a second layer of defense. Toward the end of the fourteenth century, knights began to discard the great, unwieldy helm and to adapt the lighter bascinet for their primary use. Accordingly, they had their armorers add a visor or bevor to replace the aventail. The bevor might be a separate piece of armor, rising from the throat and jutting out around the chin and cheeks, or it might be a pivoting visor with eye slits and ventilation holes. It was often pointed and beaklike at first, but a rounder version soon developed. This bascinet with a rounded visor, the bicoquet, evolved gradually into the armet, a helmet with a round crown, a ridge running along the middle from front to back, and a two-piece visor that hinged on either side and overlapped in the middle.

There were several variations on the theme of a bascinet-like headpiece with a visor. One version, popular in the last third of the fifteenth century,

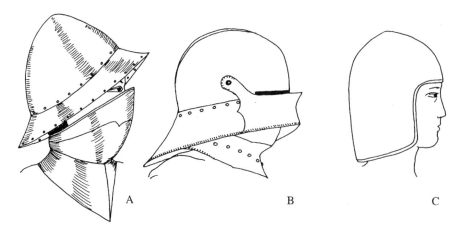

Fifteenth-century helmets. (A) Kettle helmet with separate bevor. (B) Sallet with bevor and visor, c. 1480. (C) Barbute, mid-fifteenth century.

was called the "frog head" helmet for its jutting throat piece. Helmets for the joust, which was an asymmetrical and anomalous form of combat, had no ventilation holes on the left-hand side, where the opponent's lance was most likely to strike. In the sixteenth century, the armet, with its overlapping visor, was gradually replaced by the burgonet (*2H6* V.i.200, 204; *A&C* I.v.24), which had a brim over the eyes and two hinged cheek flaps that tied under the chin. An adjustable face protector called a "buffe" could be attached as well. Employed by both cavalry and infantry, the burgonet remained in use into the seventeenth century.

The burgonet, then, was one type of helmet still in use in Shakespeare's day. Other common helmet types in the late sixteenth and early seventeenth centuries were the close helm, which had a one-piece visor, and the sallet, a round helmet wider at the brim, with the brim lower, wider, and pointed in back. It might be open-faced, visored, or fitted with eye slits in the front brim so that it could be tipped down to protect the face. The sallet, particularly the "sighted" or "French" version with eye slits, was popular in England and could be decorated with plumes, crests, or streamers. Another common sort of helmet was the morion, a rounded helmet with a brim that rose to a point in both front and back. It had a high front-to-back comb and is today associated chiefly with Spanish conquistadors, although it was worn in England, for example, by pikemen.

It is difficult to know which of these helmet types Shakespeare usually intended. With few exceptions, helmet references are general—"helm," "casque," "headpiece," or "helmet" (*R3* III.ii.11, III.iii.81, V.iii.352; *R2* IV.i.51; *H5* I.Pro.13–14, III.vii.140–42, IV.vi.6, V.Cho.18; *3H6* II.i.163; *Lear* III.ii.26). Occasionally, we know that the helmet is visored, either by context (for example, in the joust) or because the bevor is mentioned specifically (*3H6* I.i.12; *R3* V.iii.50; *1H4* IV.i.103–4). *See also* Armor.

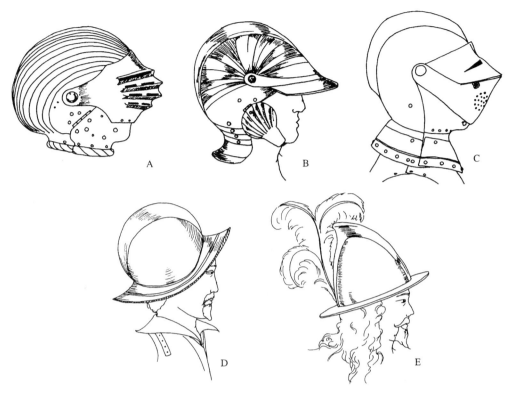

Sixteenth- and seventeenth-century helmets. (A) Armet in the Maximilian style, c. 1520. (B) Burgonet, c. 1510–40. (C) Close helm and gorget, c. 1590–1625. (D) Morion, c. 1575–1600. (E) Pikeman's helmet with plumes, c. 1608.

Heraldry

Originating as a means of identifying knights on the battlefield, heraldry took its name from the heralds whose job it was to research and authorize the use of specific symbols for families, towns, guilds, religious jurisdictions such as bishoprics, government departments, and other organizations. Heralds (*2H6* IV.ii.175; *H5* III.v.36, IV.viii.ch.; *LLL* III.i.69; *Lear* V.iii.108–22) also made proclamations, carried messages between rulers, and helped officiate at tournaments by announcing combatants and carrying challenges. For official duties they wore a ceremonial tunic called a tabard (*2H6* IV.x.71–72; *H5* III.vi.114; *1H4* IV.ii.42–45) covered with their master's emblems.

The College of Arms, led by the Garter King of Arms and composed of two provincial "kings," six heralds, and four junior heralds called pursuivants, recorded new designs and changes to old ones. The chief set of symbols was composed of several parts, which taken together were called armorial bearings or armorial ensigns, and the people authorized to use them were called armigers.

The right to use arms was one of the principal and most visible privileges of a gentleman, and it was greatly prized. Petruchio and Kate play on its importance:

PETRUCHIO   I swear I'll cuff you if you strike again.

KATE   So you may lose your arms:
If you strike me you are no gentleman,
And if no gentleman, why then no arms.

PETRUCHIO   A herald, Kate? O, put me in thy books. (*TS* II.i.219–22)

In the following two lines, they discuss what his "crest" will be, continuing their discussion from the right to display arms to the individual parts and symbols.

The Components of Armorial Bearings

The most important part of the armorial bearings was the shield at its center, called the coat of arms (*MWW* I.i.13–15). The top of the shield was the chief; the bottom, the base. The right side was called dexter; the left, sinister (the words for "right" and "left" in Latin), but the directions were given as if from behind the shield, so the dexter side is actually on the left as we look at it on the page. The "dexter chief" corner, then, is the top left corner as viewed from the front of the shield, and "sinister base" is the bottom right.

The shield bore designs in various colors (discussed below). Above the shield there was often a wreath (*Per* II.ii.29), represented as a six-bunched twist of cloth in alternating colors; a helmet with a crest (*MND* III.ii.212–14) such as feathers, a fan-shaped plate, a dragon's wing, or an animal head; and mantling that looked like leaves or slashed fabric in two colors, hanging down from the top of the helmet and often held in place by a cap, coronet, or wreath. Below the shield there was usually an undulating ribbon bearing a motto, most often written in French but occasionally in English or Latin. The Percy family motto, "Esperance," is mentioned in *1 Henry IV* (II.iii.73, V.ii.96), and a variety of mottoes are given in *Pericles* II.ii.

A few coats of arms had supporters—figures of people, animals, monsters, or birds—at each side of the shield, but this honor was usually reserved for royalty or for honored families or organizations. The official description of the bearings, complete with colors, mottoes, geometric divisions of the shield, and the position of symbols, was called the blazon (*TN* I.v.291), and it was legal property, much like a copyright or a patent.

Not all family symbols were part of a coat of arms. Some were "badges" (*1H6* IV.i.105, 177; *2H6* V.i.201–10), animals, objects, or designs that symbolized a family or a particular individual and were used in architecture, decorative objects, jewelry, and servants' livery. Some of the most promi-

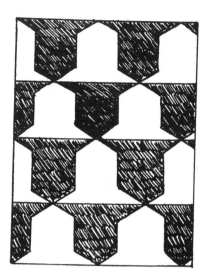

Two fur patterns: ermine on the left, vair on the right.

n Shakespeare's time, the colors were also associated with particular
es, an idea used explicitly in *The Rape of Lucrece*:

heraldry in Lucrece' face was seen,
d by Beauty's red and Virtue's white. (64–65)

re has a slightly different symbolism attached to many of these
example, associating red with beauty rather than with magna-
k he associates with night and evil (*LLL* IV.iii.251–52); yellow,
holy or jealousy (*TN* II.iv.113; *WT* II.iii.106); white, with
eraldry (*1H6* II.iv.); purple, with blood (*R&J* I.i.88; *John*
.i.158); "ruddy" or red, with blood also (*JC* II.i.289); and
h, growth, or immaturity (*LLL* I.ii.85; *R3* II.ii.127, 135;
ohn III.iii.145; *H5* V.ii.146; *A&C* I.v.74).

ble Ordinaries, and Ordinaries

of decorating a shield or escutcheon (*LLL* V.ii.560)
artitions. When describing the tinctures of a parti-
with whatever color included the dexter chief (top
o one section of the coat contained the majority
n that contained the majority of the chief was
inaries were designs that usually took up about
ften echoed the divisions in shape.
inaries had variations, each with its own name.
ar in multiples. When pales covered the entire
"paly"; a field covered in bars was "barry";

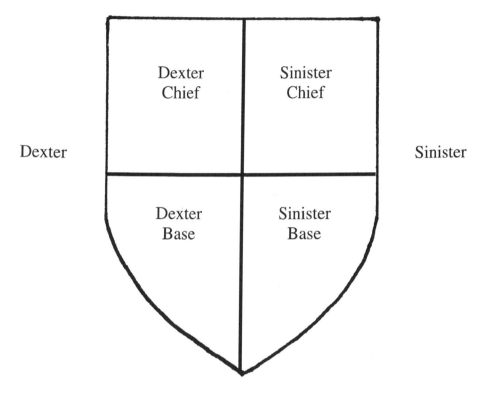

The sides and quarters of a shield.

nent symbols of famous people were actually their badges, not part of their
coats of arms. Prince Hal's ostrich plumes (*1H4* IV.i.97), Richard III's
boar (*R3* I.iii.227), the Yorkist white rose, the Lancastrian red rose, and
the Tudor red-and-white rose were all badges, not coat-of-arms elements.
The royal arms, for most of the period covered by the history plays, and
during much of Shakespeare's lifetime, were three lions on red, quartered
with fleurs-de-lis on blue (*1H6* I.i.81).

Nonetheless, the symbols were well known, as were the coats of arms
themselves, which were incorporated into signet rings, carpets, tapestries,
funerary monuments, stonework, and stained-glass windows (*R2* III.i.25–
27). Knights of the Garter had one more opportunity to display their arms,
on stalls in St. George's Chapel at Windsor Castle, where they hung a

The royal arms of James I, bordered by the motto and symbol of the Knights of the Garter. From the first English translation of Abraham Ortelius's atlas, *Theatrum Orbis Terrarum.* Reproduced from the Collections of the Library of Congress.

picture of their "coat, and several crest, / With loyal blazon" (*MWW* V.v.65–66). Thus Shakespeare could count on his audience's associating Edward IV with suns (*3H6* II.i.25–40; *R3* I.i.2), Henry IV with the mole, Percy with the lion, Glendower with the dragon (*1H4* III.i.145–49), and Warwick with the bear (*3H6* V.vii.10).

Tinctures

Arms were displayed in colors called tinctures, of which there were three types: metals, colors, and furs. For black-and-white sketches of arms, such as those made by the heralds when recording the designs, the colors a metals were indicated by abbreviations. A system of hatchings for us silver and glass was developed in the early seventeenth century. Th had their own unique patterns and needed no additional hatch ma

Tincture	Color	Hatching	Vir
Metals			
Or	Gold—drawn as yellow	Dots	
Argent	Silver—drawn as white	Unhatched	
Colors			
Gules	Red or orange-red	Vertical lines	
Azure	Blue	Horizontal lines	
Vert	Green	Diagonal \\\	
Purpure	Purple	Diagonal ///	
Sable	Black	Vertical a lines	
Proper	The natural color of an animal, plant, or person		
Furs			
Ermine	White spotted with black		
Ermines	Black spotted wi white		
Vair	Blue and white squirrel-skin p		
Vairy	A squirrel-s in any oth		

Some added te
the list of col
on black) to
ture was listed
a Dragon rampan.

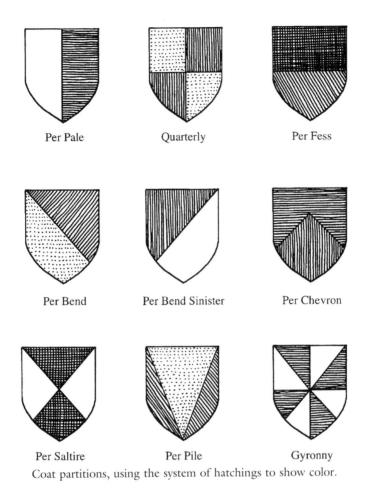

Per Pale   Quarterly   Per Fess

Per Bend   Per Bend Sinister   Per Chevron

Per Saltire   Per Pile   Gyronny

Coat partitions, using the system of hatchings to show color.

one covered in chevrons, "chevronny"—as long as there was an even number of pales, bars, or chevrons. Odd-numbered elements were described as if the tincture in the majority were the field and the tincture in the minority laid atop it. Another way that the honorable ordinaries (or partitions, for that matter) could be varied was by drawing them with wavy, embattled (crenellated), engrailed (concavely scalloped), indented (sawtoothed), or invected (convexly scalloped) lines. A third type of variation was in width. Some figures could be drawn half, a quarter, even an eighth as wide as their normal sizes. On the Continent this usually occasioned no change of name, but in England there were terms for each of these diminutives.

Honorable Ordinary	Half	Third	Quarter	Eighth
Pale	Pallet	—	Endorse[1]	—
Bend	Bendlet	Garter[2]	Cotise[1]	Riband

Honorable Ordinary	Half	Third	Quarter	Eighth
Bend Sinister	Skarpe[3]	—	Baton[4]	—
Bar	Barrulet	—	Cotise[1]	—
Chevron	Chevronel	—	Couple Close[1]	—

[1]Used only in pairs on either side of a full size honorable ordinary; [2]May bear only flowers or foils as charges; [3]Or skarfe; [4]Associated with illegitimacy and usually "couped," with the ends cut off before the edges of the shield; batons Or or Argent were associated with royal bastards.

A fourth type of change was made by "voiding" the center of a figure to turn it into an outline. There was also another set of shapes called ordinaries or subordinaries. They included triangles or squares placed in one corner of the shield, variations on the honorable ordinaries, and areas defined by curved lines.

Charges

Charges were pictures of animals, people, plants, or objects that could be placed on the field, an honorable ordinary, or an ordinary. The lion (*1H6* I.v.28) was the most popular animal, but other animals, such as leopards (*LLL* V.ii.544), stags, boars, horses, bears, dogs, wolves, camels, crabs, goats, and even fish were used. Mythical beasts, some of which appeared in legends and some of which were the creations of heralds, also appeared as charges, crests, and supporters. These included griffins male and female, dragons, wyverns (two-legged dragons), basilisks, phoenixes, unicorns, and the yale, which had cloven hooves, ears, curved horns, and a lion's tail. Animals could be shown in a variety of positions.

Combatant	two rampant animals facing one another
Couchant	lying flat with only the head raised (*AYLI* IV.iii.114); when a deer is shown in this position, it is said to be "lodged"
Couped	part of the animal, usually the head, shown cut off at the bottom with a straight line
Courant	running
Coward	with tail between legs
Demi	upper half of body only
Displayed	with outstretched wings
Dormant	sleeping
Erased	cut off, as in "couped," but with an irregular edge
Guardant	looking at the spectator (*1H6* IV.vii.9; *Cor* V.ii.62)

Chief

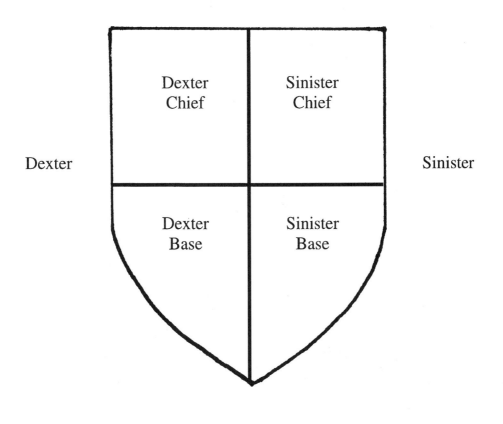

Dexter

Sinister

Base

The sides and quarters of a shield.

nent symbols of famous people were actually their badges, not part of their coats of arms. Prince Hal's ostrich plumes (*1H4* IV.i.97), Richard III's boar (*R3* I.iii.227), the Yorkist white rose, the Lancastrian red rose, and the Tudor red-and-white rose were all badges, not coat-of-arms elements. The royal arms, for most of the period covered by the history plays, and during much of Shakespeare's lifetime, were three lions on red, quartered with fleurs-de-lis on blue (*1H6* I.i.81).

Nonetheless, the symbols were well known, as were the coats of arms themselves, which were incorporated into signet rings, carpets, tapestries, funerary monuments, stonework, and stained-glass windows (*R2* III.i.25–27). Knights of the Garter had one more opportunity to display their arms, on stalls in St. George's Chapel at Windsor Castle, where they hung a

The royal arms of James I, bordered by the motto and symbol of the Knights of the Garter.
From the first English translation of Abraham Ortelius's atlas, *Theatrum Orbis Terrarum*.
Reproduced from the Collections of the Library of Congress.

picture of their "coat, and several crest, / With loyal blazon" (*MWW* V.v.65–66). Thus Shakespeare could count on his audience's associating Edward IV with suns (*3H6* II.i.25–40; *R3* I.i.2), Henry IV with the mole, Percy with the lion, Glendower with the dragon (*1H4* III.i.145–49), and Warwick with the bear (*3H6* V.vii.10).

Tinctures

Arms were displayed in colors called tinctures, of which there were three types: metals, colors, and furs. For black-and-white sketches of arms, such as those made by the heralds when recording the designs, the colors and metals were indicated by abbreviations. A system of hatchings for use on silver and glass was developed in the early seventeenth century. The furs had their own unique patterns and needed no additional hatch marks.

Tincture	Color	Hatching	Virtue
Metals			
Or	Gold—drawn as yellow	Dots	Faith
Argent	Silver—drawn as white	Unhatched	Innocence
Colors			
Gules	Red or orange-red	Vertical lines	Magnanimity
Azure	Blue	Horizontal lines	Loyalty
Vert	Green	Diagonal \\\	Love
Purpure	Purple	Diagonal ///	Temperance
Sable	Black	Vertical and horizontal lines	Prudence
Proper	The natural color of an animal, plant, or person		
Furs			
Ermine	White spotted with black		
Ermines	Black spotted with white		
Vair	Blue and white in a squirrel-skin pattern		
Vairy	A squirrel-skin pattern in any other colors		

Some added tenné (orange) and sanguine (murrey, mulberry-colored) to the list of colors and erminois (black spots on gold) and pean (gold spots on black) to the types of fur. In the blazon, the field or background tincture was listed first, then the tinctures of any design elements. Thus *Sable a Dragon rampant Or* meant a black shield with a gold rampant dragon.

Two fur patterns: ermine on the left, vair on the right.

In Shakespeare's time, the colors were also associated with particular virtues, an idea used explicitly in *The Rape of Lucrece*:

This heraldry in Lucrece' face was seen,
Argued by Beauty's red and Virtue's white. (64–65)

Shakespeare has a slightly different symbolism attached to many of these colors, for example, associating red with beauty rather than with magnanimity. Black he associates with night and evil (*LLL* IV.iii.251–52); yellow, with melancholy or jealousy (*TN* II.iv.113; *WT* II.iii.106); white, with purity, as in heraldry (*1H6* II.iv.); purple, with blood (*R&J* I.i.88; *John* II.i.322; *JC* III.i.158); "ruddy" or red, with blood also (*JC* II.i.289); and green, with youth, growth, or immaturity (*LLL* I.ii.85; *R3* II.ii.127, 135; *2H4* IV.v.203; *John* III.iii.145; *H5* V.ii.146; *A&C* I.v.74).

Partitions, Honorable Ordinaries, and Ordinaries

One of the ways of decorating a shield or escutcheon (*LLL* V.ii.560) was to divide it into partitions. When describing the tinctures of a partitioned coat, one began with whatever color included the dexter chief (top left as viewed). When no one section of the coat contained the majority of that corner, the section that contained the majority of the chief was listed first. Honorable ordinaries were designs that usually took up about one-third of the field and often echoed the divisions in shape.

Many of the honorable ordinaries had variations, each with its own name. They could, for example, appear in multiples. When pales covered the entire field, the design was said to be "paly"; a field covered in bars was "barry";

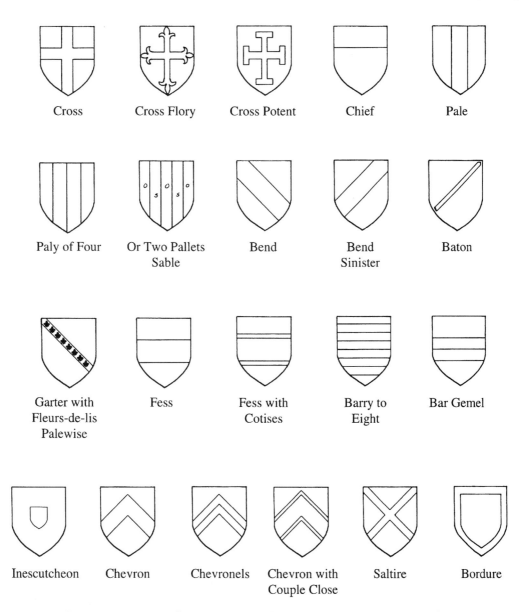

Cross

Cross Flory

Cross Potent

Chief

Pale

Paly of Four

Or Two Pallets
Sable

Bend

Bend
Sinister

Baton

Garter with
Fleurs-de-lis
Palewise

Fess

Fess with
Cotises

Barry to
Eight

Bar Gemel

Inescutcheon

Chevron

Chevronels

Chevron with
Couple Close

Saltire

Bordure

Honorable Ordinaries. Some of the variants have been shown, and the shield with five pales has been marked, with Or and Sable. The term "palewise" refers to the fact that the charges are aligned vertically, rather than parallel to the lines of the garter. "Bar gemel" refers to two barrulets placed side by side.

Haurient	vertically, of a fish
Issuant	rising, of nonwinged animals
Passant	walking with right foreleg raised (*MWW* I.i.18); a deer in this position is "trippant"

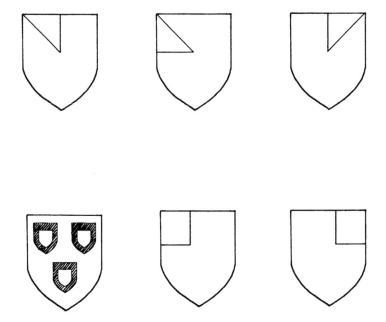

Ordinaries. Top row: three of the four possible versions of gyron.
Bottom row: three orles, canton, canton sinister. Other ordinaries
included the flaunch and flasque, vertical lines curving inward on
each side toward the center of the shield.

Rampant	standing on one hind leg with forelegs raised (*2H6* V.i.203; *3H6* V.ii.13; *1H4* III.i.149); a griffin in this position is "segreant"
Regardant	looking back over shoulder
Salient	jumping or rearing; a horse in this position is "forcene"
Sejant	seated on haunches with forepaws but not forelegs on ground

The eagle was the most popular bird on coats of arms, but the hawk,
owl, dove, rooster, heron, martlet, and others were used also. Flowers,
especially roses and fleurs-de-lis, were often employed, sometimes "semy"
(scattered across the field like a wallpaper pattern). Foils, which could represent leaves or flower petals, were identified by number; a trefoil had three
lobes; a quatrefoil, four; a cinquefoil, five. When a foil or flower had a
stem, it was said to be "slipped."

Inanimate objects used as charges included the escallop (a scallop shell,
a symbol of Christian pilgrimage), estoile (a wavy-rayed star), garb (wheat
sheaf), lozenge (diamond), mascle (voided or outlined lozenge), pheon
(arrowhead), annulet (ring), tressure (narrow orle around the edge of the
shield), and fret (mascle interwoven with a St. Andrew's cross). Roundels
(circles) had different names, depending on their color:

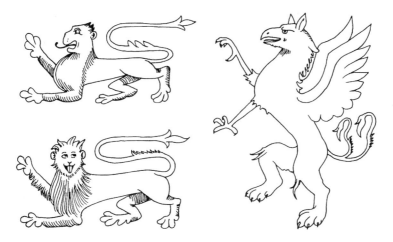

Animal postures. Clockwise from top left: lion passant, griffin segreant (the same position as rampant), lion passant guardant. The heraldic leopard was sometimes a spotted creature, and sometimes, particularly in the Middle Ages, merely a lion passant guardant.

Or	bezant
Argent	plate
Gules	torteau
Sable	pellet or ogress
Vert	pomme
Azure	hurt
Purpure	golp

Charges were chosen either for their symbolism or because their names sounded like something significant, for example, the family name or home.

Miscellaneous charges and cadency marks. Top row, left to right: crest wreath, estoile, clavichord, escallop, coronet, maunch (sleeve), cross moline. Middle row: label with three points, label with five points, crescent, mullet, martlet, annulet, fleur-de-lis, roundel, lozenge. Bottom row: garb, slipped trefoil, cinquefoil, rose, mascle, fret, pheon, quatrefoil.

A family with the syllable "burt" or "hart" in its name might, for example, incorporate a burt (turbot, a kind of fish) or hart (deer) in its coat of arms. Mottoes might contain similar puns, using a Latin word that resembled the family name in sound, spelling, or meaning. Towns and corporations tended to pick symbols of their industries; the arms of the Company of Miners Royal, drawn in 1568, showed a miner digging in a tunnel with a pick and hammer on the coat and had two human supporters, one holding a hammer and the other carrying a smelting fork. A variety of charges, including a hand, torch, sun, knight, and branch, are used by the knights at the tournament in *Pericles* (II.ii.20–43).

A small charge or cadency mark might be used in the chief of the shield to differentiate between the head of the family, his heir, and his younger sons. The father's coat of arms appeared without a cadency mark, and his sons each used a mark as shown below.

1st son	label with 3 points (horizontal bar with three short vertical bars descending)
2nd	crescent
3rd	mullet (five-pointed star)
4th	martlet
5th	annulet
6th	fleur-de-lis
7th	rose
8th	cross moline
9th	double quatrefoil

The first son's first son, during the lifetime of his grandfather, used a label with five points.

The Use and Combination of Arms

Numerous rules governed the design and use of arms. The chief design rule was that a color could not be placed on a color nor a metal on a metal. Equal divisions of a field, such as quartering, barry, per pale, and so on, did not count as placing anything on top of anything else, and so could be composed of colors and metals at will. But when placing a charge, an honorable ordinary, or an ordinary, it was necessary to follow the rule, and it was also followed when the field was made of an odd number of equivalent shapes. A field of Or, therefore, could not have an Argent ordinary laid upon it, but it could have an ordinary of blue, black, green, red, or purple, which could then bear a charge of Or or Argent but not another color. Furs were not concerned in this rule, nor were "proper" colors.

Women had limited rights to use arms. They could not, for example, use a coat of arms topped by a helmet, which was a sign of war. They could not pass on the use of a crest to their children, for the crest was part of the masculine helmet. Women used their fathers' cadency marks, with no distinction between their arms and their sisters'. And a woman's rights varied depending upon whether she was single, married to another armiger, married to someone without arms of his own, widowed, with a living father or brothers, or left as the sole surviving member of her birth family. In general, a woman bore her father's arms, often on a field that was not shield-shaped, until she married; then she used her husband's arms. If both the wife and husband had arms, they might represent their union by impaling their arms—that is, placing the husband's arms on the dexter side and the wife's arms on the sinister side of one shield, both sets of arms being compressed to fit into half the shield's width. Impaled arms could not be used by the husband in battle, however, if his wife had any surviving male relatives. The presumption was that they would send along their own representative to fight under the family ensigns.

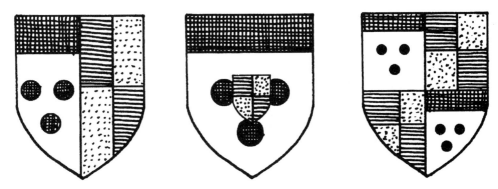

Combinations of arms. Left to right: impaling, escutcheon of pretense, quartering.

If the wife's father was dead and she had no living brothers, her husband might bear an "escutcheon of pretense," a small shield with his wife's arms, placed in the center of his own. He might bear these arms in battle, since his wife's family no longer had a man of its own to send to the wars. Widows bore their husband's arms, or the impaled arms of their husbands and fathers, on a lozenge rather than on a shield.

The children of two armigers might use quarterings, placing their father's arms in the dexter chief and sinister base, and their maternal grandfather's in the other two quadrants. While women could not bequeath crests to their children, they could pass on any quarterings that they had inherited from their own fathers. In this case, the father's arms came first, followed by the mother's arms and any quarterings she brought to the marriage, followed by, in order of ancestry, any other quarterings that had come through previous marriages in the direct male line. The result was that some coats of arms bore eight, twelve, even thirty quarters. A younger son might distinguish himself from the heir by developing his own coat of arms, "compounding" the elements of his mother's and father's arms in a new coat that resembled both in some way.

Holidays

January

One of the difficulties in describing the Elizabethan and Jacobean cycle of holidays is determining where to start, for beginning at the logical date, January 1, places us right in the middle of a festival season that began at Christmas and ended on January 6, Epiphany. Epiphany, marking the arrival of the three kings at Christ's cradle in Bethlehem, was the twelfth night of the festival, so it was called Twelfth Night and gave rise both to the Shakespeare play of that title and to today's carol "The Twelve Days of Christmas." January 1 was the Roman New Year, not the English, but though Rome had not ruled England for centuries, the importance of the date persisted, and gifts were exchanged in noble households on this date (*MWW* III.v.8–9), a custom that may have spread downward through the social classes during the sixteenth century. On January 6, the Christmas season closed with religious services and, in the royal household at least, a festive dinner.

With the morning came a return to work and preparations for the winter plowing. In Catholic England, this season had been formally ushered in by a blessing of plows on the first Sunday after Twelfth Night, and feasting and collections for the parish church on the following day, Plough Monday. The Reformation put an end to the supposedly superstitious blessing of plows, though the date remained associated with some church functions in some locations until the end of Shakespeare's life.

February

Another casualty of the Reformation was Candlemas, February 2. This feast commemorated the purification of the Virgin Mary and was thus associated with the devout Mariolatry of the Catholic Church. Historically, candles had been lit and blessed on this date, but this practice was discontinued under Protestant rulers. The date, however, was still common knowledge, and people probably still used it as a point of reference in the same way that they used Lammas and Michaelmas.

A different festival, St. Valentine's Day, remained a part of the post-Reformation calendar. Valentine's Day, falling then as now on February 14, was associated with the first courtship flights of birds—especially crows and similar species—and thus with the very first intimations of spring (*MND* IV.i.140–41). The holiday was chiefly observed among the nobility, who exchanged gifts among their circles of friends with partners drawn by lot, in a precursor of today's "Secret Santa" exchanges at Christmas. Though these exchanges were often platonic, the holiday was already associated with superstitions about love and courtship (*Ham* IV.v.48).

The chief preoccupation of February, however, was the rapid approach of Lent (*TN* I.v.9), the six-week period of restraint preceding Easter. Since Easter is a movable feast, the actual dates of Lent shift from year to year, but it usually begins somewhere between mid-February and early March. The period preceding Lent was called Shrovetide—for Shakespeare, "merry Shrovetide" (*2H4* V.iii.36), a period in which meat, revelry, and sexual antics could be enjoyed before the long, voluntary self-deprivation to come. The most important days of the festival were the Sunday before Lent and the three succeeding days: Collop Monday, Shrove Tuesday (*mardi gras* in French), and Ash Wednesday (*MV* II.v.26), which was the first day of Lent. As might be expected, Shrove Tuesday was often filled with last-minute sinning of one kind or another—overeating (especially of bacon, fowl, and pancakes—see *AW* II.ii.23–24), fighting, drinking, football (sometimes played by a team of bachelors against a team of husbands), and blood sports such as cockfighting and shying at cocks.

Ash Wednesday was the first Wednesday in Lent; the second began the first of four quarterly "embers" or fasts. Each began on a Wednesday, ceased on Thursday, and resumed on Friday and Saturday. Each of the four embers constituted a kind of mini-Lent, with the evening before (*Per* I.Cho.6) being filled, if possible, with merriment and good eating (though in the case of this first ember, meat could not be consumed).

Shakespeare also makes mention of a non-Christian holiday in February, recounting Caesar's refusal of a crown (*JC* I.i.68, III.ii.96) on the Lupercalia, February 15. This holiday, whose name literally means "wolf festival," had obscure origins but was at least in part associated with the adoption of the Roman founders Romulus and Remus by a she wolf. It was also, to some extent, a fertility festival. Plutarch describes the rites as a sacrifice of goats, followed by the touching of two noble youths' foreheads with bloody knives, "while others at once wipe it off with wool dipped in milk." The youths were supposed to laugh at this juncture, and the goats' skins were sliced into bloody strips, which were given to the Luperci, the priests of Faunus, who then ran dressed only in loincloths through the streets, lashing women who wished to conceive with the goatskin thongs.

March and April

Much of March was occupied by Lent, during which meat was forbidden (*2H4* II.iv. 354; *R&J* II.iv.137–42) except to the sick (*2H6* IV.iii.6–7) and sexual relations, even between husbands and wives, much discouraged. That the latter prohibition was widely but not universally observed can be seen by a corresponding drop in (but not absence of) births approximately nine months later. Shakespeare mentions Lent a few times, usually in the context of abstaining from meat or using the "Jack-a-Lent" (*MWW* III.iii.25, V.v.130), a puppet or effigy of a man that served as a target for rocks and other missiles.

March was an important month for other reasons as well. March 1 was "Saint Davy's day" (*H5* IV.i.55, IV.vii.97–104, V.i.1–2, 8–12, 22–59) and the anniversary of a Celtic victory over the invading Saxons in 540. It was significant to the Welsh, who wore leeks (a symbol of Wales) in their caps on that date. The connection to leeks is not precisely clear, but St. Dewi or David was the patron saint of Wales. March 25 was the legal beginning of the English year, and the Ides of March, March 15, was the date on which Julius Caesar was assassinated (*JC* I.ii.18). This was a Roman, not an English, holiday and coincided with the full moon.

Sometime in March or April, Easter arrived. As Lent neared its conclusion, a rising spiritual tension culminated in a series of days marking important moments in Christ's life and death. Many of the Lenten rituals were eliminated after the Reformation, but the sixth Sunday in Lent, Palm Sunday (in some regions known as Branch, Yew, Willow, or Sallow Sunday, depending on the type of foliage locally available), still marked Christ's entry into Jerusalem and officially began Holy Week. The following Thursday was Maundy Thursday, commemorating the Last Supper. On this day, Elizabeth I washed, dried, crossed, and kissed the feet of a selected group of paupers, afterward making them a present of money. Elizabeth typically gave each a white purse filled with a penny for each of her years and a red purse filled with twenty shillings. The next day, Good Friday (*John* I.i.233–35), commemorated Christ's crucifixion, and on this day the monarch blessed "cramp rings" as magical cures for epilepsy, apoplexy, and labor pains. Two days later, Easter Sunday celebrated Christ's resurrection and the return to a diet that included meat. The next day, oddly, was "Black Monday" (*MV* II.v.25), so called, perhaps, because of a general, superstitious fear of Mondays and because of a similarly superstitious conviction that great joy was sure to be followed by some equally great misfortune.

Black Monday and the Tuesday that succeeded it were known as Hocktide. A popular pre–Reformation custom gave one of these days to the men to capture and bind women that they found in the streets, who had to pay a fine to the parish coffers to be released. The other day, the women did the same to any men they captured. The day that the women were the captors typically resulted in much more enthusiastic fund-raising. The custom was abolished in many places after the Reformation, but it persisted in some locations, notably Oxford and the rural areas near London, into Shakespeare's lifetime.

The chief April holiday (except for Easter, when Easter fell in April) was St. George's Day, April 23. George was England's patron saint, and the occasion was part religious and part patriotic and secular. Traditional celebrations included parades and the display of an effigy or costume of a dragon. The date was also important to the Order of the Garter, England's highest order of knighthood, whose patron was St. George and whose emblem bore his image.

May

May 1 (*MND* IV.i.105; *TNK* II.ii.36–41, III.i.1 s.d., III.v.124) was celebrated with a conscious appreciation of the approach of summer. It was customary for young adults to go out the night beforehand to gather flowers and greenery (*TNK* II.iv.48–49) to decorate the streets and houses, a practice that Puritans claimed encouraged premarital sex and illegitimate births. In the morning (*TN* III.iv.146; *H8* V.iv.11–14), people danced around a maypole (*TNK* III.v.142–43; *MND* III.ii.296) topped by a garland of flowers (*A&C* IV.xv.64–65), sometimes painted, and, according to Phillip Stubbes in *The Anatomie of Abuses*, trailing "strings," or ribbons, down to the ground. Morris dancers cavorted with bells and handkerchiefs (*AW* II.ii.24). Plays, pageants, appearances by a couple dubbed Robin and Marian or the Lord and Lady of the May, and bonfires crowned the holiday in some areas. The role of summer lord was often attended with much pageantry, the lord being dressed in fine robes for the day, attended by a "court" of picked friends, crowned in a mock coronation, and entitled to issue orders and to preside over the festivities.

Not everyone approved of May games, and they were partially suppressed in some areas, usually against the will of the local populace. The maypole was derided by some as an idol, and all the May games were considered peasant pastimes for much of the late sixteenth century. It has been asserted that Shakespeare was one of those who considered the rites of May a peasant celebration, and it is true that he typically shows and discusses them with working-class participants only, but he also implies that many in the upper classes enjoyed observing the dances and listening to the music. This seems to have been the case, for the battle over suppression of May games was fought largely between members of the ruling classes, with the peasantry being fairly universally in support of the celebrations. By the first years of the seventeenth century, some people were writing in defense of the May games, refuting the charges of religious reformers that they were dangerous and impious.

May and June were the high season for church ales (*2GV* II.v.52), parishwide parties with food, ale, and music that served to raise funds for the local church. Like the May games, these festivals often drew criticism for the supposedly disorderly conduct of the participants. The condemned behavior ranged from drinking and dancing in moderation to antics so lewd that the critics would not commit them to paper for fear of shocking their readers. Gradually, for reasons that are still unclear, the church ales began to disappear, and their fund-raising duty was replaced by additional tithes and rates levied on the people of the parish. They did not vanish altogether, however; in the eighteenth century, critics were still leveling the same complaints of disorder against them and calling for their abolition. A scene that illustrates the sort of disorder that could arise in large crowds of festivalgoers appears in *Henry VIII* (V.iv.50–65).

Shakespeare makes frequent reference to the May 1 celebrations, and he includes one reference to "Philip and Jacob" (*MM* III.ii.202–3), apparently meaning the joint feast of the apostles Philip and James on May 3. Interestingly, the date is mentioned because an illegitimate child will be "a year and a quarter old, come / Philip and Jacob," meaning that the child in question would have been conceived out of wedlock on or about May 1 two years before. Perhaps there was something more than flower-picking going on in the woods, after all; at least there was a belief that something else was afoot.

June

Church ales continued into June. The sixth Thursday after Easter was Ascension Day (*John* IV.ii.152, V.i.22–29), preceded on the previous three days by the Rogation, or the "beating" of the parish "bounds." The beating of the bounds was a procession, led by the local priest (in secular dress after the Reformation) along the boundaries of the parish. The group stopped at each stone marker to read prayers. The ceremony itself had government sanction, but there was much controversy over the priest's costume and over anything that smacked of superstition or idolatry. The end of the following week (*2H4* II.i.87–88) was Whitsun or Pentecost (*R&J* I.v.38; *2GV* IV.iv.158–66; *CE* IV.i.1), commemorating the inspiration of the apostles by the Holy Ghost, and Whitsunday and Whit Monday were the most popular days for church ales. Revels similar to those of May Day were held at this time (*H5* II.iv.25; *WT* IV.iv.133–34), and indeed, since Whitsunday was also a movable feast, it might fall in May rather than in June. So might the second ember, or three-day fast, which took place on the Wednesday, Friday, and Saturday after Whitsunday. Another holiday with a variable date was Corpus Christi, the second Thursday after Whitsun. It had been an important day in the Catholic English calendar, marked by plays, pageants, and a grand procession with a canopied Host, but displays of this kind were suppressed under the Protestant monarchs.

Two feasts with fixed dates were those of St. John the Baptist (June 24, Midsummer) and St. Peter's Eve (June 28). They were celebrated almost identically, with bonfires, garlanding of houses with flowers and branches, pageants, and torchlight processions. It was customary to stay up late, even all night, for the revels, and this practice, along with the belief that the fairies were particularly powerful at midsummer, makes the timing of *A*

Midsummer Night's Dream so appropriate. Like the May games, the midsummer festivals were much loved by much or most of the general populace. A mayor with a Puritan streak might try to ban them, but his successor was just as likely to restore them by popular demand.

July and August

The end of summer was a busy and, in the popular mind, a dangerous time. Harvests came in, the hot weather of the dog days (*H8* V.iv.40–41) set in, and fairs were held. The dog days, so called because of the apparent near-conjunction of the sun and Sirius, the bright star found in the constellation Canis Major (Great Dog), ran from July 3 to August 15. Medicinal bleeding was forbidden during this period, as were most other kinds of medical treatment. Sex was discouraged, and great care was taken to avoid the increased risk of pestilence, poison, and death that came with this time of year.

A Midsummer Night's Dream is not the only play set in the summertime. *Much Ado About Nothing* begins on "the sixth of July" (I.i.275), and *Romeo and Juliet*, too, takes place in the dog days. We know this because the Nurse points out that Lammas—the "Loaf Mass," August 1, that marked the start of the season of harvests and fairs—is "a fortnight and odd days" away (I.iii.14, 17), placing the action in mid–July. One of the few non–Christian holidays mentioned by Shakespeare is also set in July. This is the Neptunalia (*Per* V.Cho.17), the feast of the Roman equivalent of Poseidon, which took place on the 23rd of Quintilis, the month later renamed July in honor of Julius Caesar.

August 5, during the reign of James I, was celebrated as his accession day; this patriotic holiday will be discussed in greater detail below. St. Bartholomew's Day (*H5* V.ii.310–12), after which the famous Bartholomew Fair was named, was on August 24. It should be noted that each town had its own patron saint and that the local church usually held a festival called a wake, similar in spirit to a church ale, on its local saint's day. Shakespeare speaks of local festivals collectively as "wakes . . . wassails . . . [and] fairs" (*LLL* V.ii.319); the first and last have been explained above, and the "wassail" was another fund-raising procession in which a bowl of liquor was carried from door to door and shared with residents in exchange for contributions.

September

September contained several holidays, but none of them were associated with widespread or noteworthy celebrations. Holy-Rood Day (*1H4* I.i.52), which honored the cross of the crucifixion, was September 14, and the third of four embers took place on the Wednesday, Friday, and Saturday that followed. St. Lambert's Day (*R2* I.i.199) was September 17, and Michaelmas (*MWW* I.i.195; *1H4* II.iv.55), a holiday that served more as a bureaucratic and agricultural milestone than as a religious holiday, occurred on September 29.

October and November

October had few holidays. St. Crispin's Day, October 25, was significant not so much because of Saint Crispin but because it was associated with the battle of Agincourt (*H5* IV.iii.40–67). However, the transition between October and November was of such importance that its rituals survived, in one form or another, beyond the Reformation and down to the present day. The actual holiday in question was All Hallows Day, or All Saints' Day (as "Hallowmass" in *MM* II.i.120–21; *2GV* II.i.27; as "Allhallowmass" in *MWW* I.i.194), November 1. On this date, in Catholicism, it was traditional to pray for souls in purgatory and to ring bells for the same reason. The feast of All Souls (*R3* V.i.10, 12, 18), similarly observed, followed on November 2.

In post-Reformation England, purgatory was no longer recognized by the state religion, and the ringing of bells was prohibited. The dead were either saved and in heaven, in which case prayers and bells were superfluous, or in hell, in which case prayers and bells were useless. The seriousness of the day persisted, however, as did the belief that the souls of the dead were particularly active on the night preceding All Hallows (*MM* II.i.123), or October 31—Halloween. The anxiety surrounding November 1 was almost impossible to root out, despite the best efforts of Protestant bishops, and the unauthorized ringing of bells and, where bells had been silenced, the private candlelight vigils in fields continued into James's reign.

With All Hallows Day, the last of the warm weather (*1H4* I.ii.157–58) passed, and winter began in earnest. Martinmas (*2H4* II.ii.100), like Michaelmas more of a record-keeping benchmark than a festival, came on November 11 and was the traditional date to slaughter most of the rest of one's flocks and salt down their meat for the winter. In early November, Elizabeth I, who usually spent the summer visiting noblemen, enjoying her country estates, and avoiding warm-weather outbreaks of the plague, returned to London to be surrounded by the largest possible crowds for her own Accession Day. This was not the anniversary of her coronation, which was not widely commemorated, but the day she had inherited the throne in 1558. From 1570, Accession Day was observed with bonfires, jousts, courtly salutes, and cannon fire. From 1588, St. Elizabeth's Day, November 19, was also observed in honor of the defeat of the Spanish Armada, and for the last several years of her reign, Elizabeth was lauded in mid-November with demonstrations of affection across the nation. The form of Accession Day celebrations varied by location but might include fireworks, bell-ringing, food, pageants, music, and processions. When Elizabeth I died, Accession Day changed to the date of her death and James's inheritance of the throne, but after 1605, November gained another patriotic holiday. This was November 5, the date of the failed Gunpowder Plot to blow up Parliament, which became known as Guy Fawkes' day.

December

Preparations for Christmas (*TS* Ind.ii.137; *LLL* I.i.105) began with the collection (or, in the towns, the purchase) of holly, ivy, and other greenery for decorating churches and homes. This practice diminished, but did not entirely disappear, after the Reformation. Throughout the season, there were plays (*LLL* V.ii.463), dances, music, and parties. As in the summer games, a Lord of Misrule was often named to preside over the festivities, and everyone, even the master of the house, had to obey him. Wassailing took place from door to door and within single households, with the huge bowl being passed around and transferred to the next drinker with a kiss. The Puritan Phillip Stubbes, who had an irritating disapproval for anything joyous, found the whole observance of Christmas badly done. There was nothing, he complained, "but cards, dice tables, masking, mumming, bowling & such like fooleries." Thomas Tusser, it appears from his *Five Hundred Points of Good Husbandry,* had more affection for the holiday, especially for the feasting:

> Good bread and good drinke, a good fire in the hall,
> > brawne, pudding & souse, & good mustard withall:
> Beefe, Mutton, and Porke, shread pies of the best,
> > pig, veale, goose, and capon, and turkey well drest,
> Cheese, apple, and nuts, jolly carrols to heare,
> > as then in the country is counted good cheere.

Some went wassailing in the orchards. Others sang "jolly carrols" that focused on the religious or the festive aspects of the holiday. Christmas continued into the beginning of January, bringing the cycle of the year back to Twelfth Night.

Horse

There were no doubt many breeds of horses in Shakespeare's time, but even writers about horses are frustratingly vague about how many and what they looked like. John Astley, the author of *The Art of Riding* (1584), was far more concerned with the abuses in horse training than in different breeds. Some German visitors in 1592 noted only that the English horses were small but swift and that those used for riding were mostly geldings. Shakespeare, following the trend, rarely gives an indication of breed. Richard III rides a "white Surrey" at Bosworth (*R3* V.iii.64), and these are references to "Galloway nags" and "jennets" (or "gennets"), both small types of horses, the former from Ireland and the latter from Spain (*2H4* II.iv.194; *Oth* I.i.110; *V&A* 259–64). In one case, an unnamed breed from northern England is mentioned (*H8* II.ii.1–4). The "Phrygian steed" of *Troilus and Cressida* (IV.v.185) calls to mind, deservedly or not, the horses with absurdly long, thin, graceful legs found on Greek vases. The "Barbary horse" (*Oth* I.i.108; *Ham* V.ii.150; *R2* V.v.78–94), whose name indicates an Arab or Moorish origin, was probably something like the slender, arch-necked Arabian horses of today, though how much like them it is difficult to say.

It is more common to see a mention of a horse's color—white (*TNK* III.iv.22; *TA* II.iii.76; *Tim* I.ii.186), roan (*1H4* II.iii.70, II.iv.108–9; *R2* V.v.78–92), black (*TNK* V.iv.47–81), or bay (*AW* II.iii.60; *Tim* I.ii.214). "Bay" meant reddish-brown, though it could range from a red-tinged golden brown all the way to a color resembling dried blood. "Roan" meant a mixed color, with hairs of gray or white, perhaps, evenly interspersed with hairs of black, reddish, brown, or some other color. Color, certainly, was what interested Thomas Blundeville, the author of *The Arte of Ryding and Breakinge Greate Horses* (1560), for to him it revealed the horse's temperament. Like most people of his time, Blundeville believed in four basic elements, earth, air, water, and fire, and that the preponderance of one element could have dramatic effects on everything from personality to health. For horses, this meant that

> if he hath more of the earth then of the rest, he is melancholy, heavy, and faint harted, and of Coulor a blacke, a Russet, a bright or darke donne. But if he hath more of the water, then is he flegmatique, slow, dull, and apt to lose fleashe, and of coulor moste commonlye milke white. If of the aire, then he is a sanguine and therefore pleasant, nymble, and of a temperate moving, and of coulor is most commonly a bay. And if of the fier, then he is cholorique and therfore light, whot, and fiery, a sterer, and seldom of any great strength, and is wont to be of Coulor a bright sorel.

In light of these considerations, Blundeville preferred horses that were "browne bay," dappled gray, black with silver hairs, "blacke lyke a moore," or "a fayre rone." Second best were similar colors, any color edged with black to counteract the "evill" predominant color, or sorrel, bay, or black with a little white "to mitigate his fearceness." Leonard Mascall, who wrote on a number of topics including husbandry, also favored bays, though he insisted that they have no more than one white foot. The Dauphin's horse in *Henry V* is "the color of the nutmeg" and is a superior horse because he is composed purely of the light elements of "air and fire; and the dull / elements of earth and water never appear in him, but / only in patient stillness while his rider mounts him" (III.vii.21–23). All riders could wish for such a horse.

Blundeville also had strong views on the subject of white feet and maintained that, of the eleven possible arrangements that included white socks or stockings, only four augured well for the horse's behavior. If we look at the horse from above, a **W** standing for a white foot and an **X** for a foot of any other color, the four acceptable combinations were those shown below.

Front	Front	Front	Front
X W	X X	X X	W W
X X	W W	W X	W W
Rear	**Rear**	**Rear**	**Rear**

All other combinations were evil, though either the good or the evil inherent in white feet could be intensified by the sprinkling of black spots. A white star or stripe on the nose was always a good sign.

Given all of the importance attached to the horse's color, it is almost surprising to find that Blundeville valued any other quality at all, but he did have other criteria, such as "Aptnes to learne," "Stout courage," and "Large continuaunce." As for the shape of the horse, it should have large, smooth, round, black hooves; small, heavy fetlocks (*3H6* II.iii.20–21); short pasterns to prevent foundering; broad, straight legs with large joints; "High thighes ful of sinewes" and with a good separation between them; a round rump; a short, level back; long sides and belly; large, fleshy shoulders; a large, round chest; sharp, straight withers (*Ham* III.ii.246–47; *1H4* II.i.7); a long neck that bent and tapered toward the head; small, sharp ears; large, black eyes; a lean jaw and large mouth; wide nostrils; a long mane (*R&J* I.iv.89) and tail; and a head that, overall, resembled that of a sheep. Adonis's horse comes close to the ideal:

> Round-hoofed, short-jointed, fetlocks shag and long,
> Broad breast, full eye, small head, and nostril wide,
> High crest, short ears, straight legs and passing strong,
> Thin mane, thick tail, broad buttock, tender hide. (*V&A* 295–98)

Blundeville spends little time discussing size, though he recommends that the larger varieties be used for war and the smaller ones for civilian riding.

Uses

The knight's "great horse" was certainly the most glamorous of all horses. These were the "foaming steeds" (*3H6* II.i.183), the "barbèd [armored] steeds" (*R3* I.i.10), the "neighing steeds" challenging one another across enemy lines before a battle (*TS* I.ii.203; *H5* IV.Cho.10–11), that made the knight's profession so picturesque and so ferocious. War horses were prized, armed, and highly trained (*JC* IV.i.28–33), for, if wounded or killed (*H5* IV.vii.77–80), they could immobilize their plate-mail-clad riders. One has only to look at the end of *Richard III* and Richard's famous, desperate cry for a horse, to understand the helplessness of a dismounted knight. The horse, like his rider, was armed in plate mail and decorated with heraldic insignia. In the horse's case, this took the form of a caparison (*R3* V.iii.178, 290; *V&A* 286; *Cor* I.ix.12), a velvet or brocade blanket embroidered with its rider's coat of arms or heraldic emblem. The civilian equivalent, purely for display rather than identification on the battlefield, was the "footcloth" (*R3* III.iv.83), a decorative trapping that hung all the way to the ground. Shakespeare does not use the term "great horse," but he does use the word "courser" (*3H6* V.vii.9; *Oth* I.i.109; *Per* II.i.164; *Tim* I.ii.214), and from context we can assume that this is the type of horse used in both war and the mounted joust.

For ordinary riding, there were lighter horses called palfreys (*2H6* IV.ii.70; *TA* V.ii.50), though in *Henry V* Shakespeare identifies the same horse as both a courser and a palfrey (III.vii.28, 45). Post horses were for fast riding by messengers, mail carriers, and others who valued speed (*R3* I.i.146; *2H4* IV.iii.35–36; *WT* III.i.21; *R2* I.i.56). The rest of England's horses were laborers, pulling or carrying on their backs as much weight as they could. They pulled plows, wagons, harrows, and rollers in teams (*2GV* III.i.266; *AW* II.i.32—in the second citation, a "forehorse" is the team's leader). They pulled carts, alone or together (*MV* II.ii.94–95; *Lear* V.iii.39); five or six horses could, as a team, pull up to 3,000 pounds. Pack horses (*R3* I.iii.121; *2H4* II.iv.166–69), rather than pulling, carried up to 400 pounds each on their backs. Brewers (*1H4* III.iii.9), millers (*TNK* V.ii.66), carters, merchants, miners, and bargemen all needed horses to pull, haul, or simply walk in a circle to move a gear that worked large equipment. Without horses, much of the basic work and travel of the preindustrial world became difficult or impossible.

Faults, Virtues, and Training

People complained or bragged about their horses in the Renaissance the way people complain or brag about their cars today. Sometimes the horse was a high-performance machine, capable of doing almost anything on command. Of these horses, it is said that "He will bear you / easily, and reins well" (*TN* III.iv.328–29) or "when I bestride him, I soar, I am a / hawk; he trots the air; the earth sings when he touches / it" (*H5* III.vii.15–17). Henry IV rides a good horse on his entrance into London; like the Dauphin's in *Henry V*, it is a "hot and fiery" horse, but can be calm even in a crowd if necessary (*R2* V.ii.7–10). We see signs of affection for good, hardworking horses in occasional mentions of their names—Cut, Dobbin, Barbary (*1H4* II.i.5–11; *MV* II.ii.94–95; *R2* V.v.78–92).

Unfortunately, just as there are few perfect cars today, there were few perfect horses then, and people were much more likely to complain than to brag. Horses had a limited range and could go only so long without tiring (*2H4* II.iv.166–69; *R2* II.i.299–300; *JC* IV.i.28–33). They bounced when traveling at anything but a walk, and they required constant effort from the rider, so that one arrived at a destination tired, sweaty, and covered with the dust or mud of the road. Horses' urine, feces, and sweat smelled (*Temp* IV.i.199), and they left their manure wherever they stood, in country fields or city streets. They stopped suddenly, threw their riders (*TS* IV.i.48–76), shook their heads, refused commands, and pulled on the reins. To John Astley, writing in *The Art of Riding*, a good horse should take pleasure in chomping at his bit, and any cessation of this activity was a bad sign (*H5* IV.ii.46–51). The bad horse, whether ill-behaved or just old and worn-out, was called a jade, and there are far more uses of this word in Shakespeare than there are loving references to good horses (*2H6* IV.i.3; *TS* I.ii.247, IV.i.1; *2GV* III.i.276; *MAAN* I.i.141; *R2* III.iii.178; *V&A* 391–92).

To minimize these faults, it was essential that a horse be trained well and corrected immediately (*AYLI* I.i.10–13; *H8* V.iii.21–24). This was especially important in the case of a war horse, which had to be able to charge fearlessly directly at an enemy, to turn quickly and precisely, and to stop instantly (*JC* IV.i.31–32). However, it was also important for riding horses to be well trained; Arcite dies because his is spooked by a spark from the iron horseshoes on the flinty pavement (*TNK* V.iv.47–81). Most writers on the subject advised kindness when training horses; Thomas Tusser said they should be admonished rather than beaten, and Astley vehemently condemned the use or overuse of spiked bits, musrolls, and spurs, which resulted in

> . . . horsses, that both without courage and comelines are ridden, with rawe noses, bloudie mouthes and sides, with their curbed places galled, turning their bodies one waie, & their heads another waie, which things are brought to passe by the violent and unskilfull use of the hand upon the chaine, *Cavezzan*, musroll, and such like, which were first devised to save their mouths; and not to marre their noses and muzzels.

A badly trained horse, Astley said, would soon grow immune to harsh treatment. He advised, instead, using gentler bits, teaching turns by making a clacking noise with the tongue, pulling in the bridle little by little rather than yanking on it to gain the correct neck position, and having only one rider on a given horse until it is fully trained. To teach the horse to back up, one should pull on the reins, apply pressure with the spurs, and tap him gently on the neck with a rod until he begins to back up. Then, as in all cases when the horse "hath done wel," one should "make much of him." One should use "gentle and curteous dealing." Thomas Blundeville agrees, specifying seven means of correction: voice, rod, legs, bridle, stirrups, spurs, and pacing in a ring. Like Astley, he says one should "cherishe" a horse when it does well, either by using a soothing voice or by scratching the horse's neck. Adonis tries both cherishing and admonishing, using "His flattering 'Holla' or his 'Stand, I say' " (*V&A* 284) with no success, since the animal he is trying to control is a stallion on the scent of a mare in heat.

When well trained, the horse should respond to a light touch, without coercion. It should be able, according to Astley, to pace (walk—*MAAN* III.iv.90), trot, gallop (*MAAN* III.iv.91), "carrier," stop (*MND* V.i.119–20), jump, hold its head properly, and stand still patiently. Astley's "carrier" is the same as Shakespeare's "passed the careers" (*MWW* I.i.170), a short gallop, as in a cavalry or jousting charge.

Tack

There was a great deal of equipment necessary to ride a horse. The most obvious and commonly mentioned items were the saddle, bridle, and spurs. The saddle (*2H4* II.i.26; *R2* V.ii.74; *Lear* I.iv.254; *V&A* 13–14; *TNK* II.iv.48) was something like a saddle today, made of wood covered in leather or another material, with a pommel rising in front. A saddle for warfare had other features, such as hooks or rings for hanging a sword or mace, armor plating, or a "hourd," a guardplate of leather or wood that protected the rider's knees, legs, and belly. A jousting saddle also had a high ridge in back to help keep its rider from being dismounted. The purpose of the saddle was to remove weight from the horse's vulnerable spine and rest it instead on the withers (shoulders) and hips; it was important to keep the saddle properly padded so that the skin over these bones did not become chafed and raw (*1H4* II.i.5–7). The saddle was held on with a belly strap called a girth (*TNK* V.iv.73; *TS* III.i.59) and often had a second strap called a crupper (*TS* III.i.60, IV.i.74) that passed under the horse's tail. Straps with stirrups hung down at either side (*2H6* IV.i.53; *TS* III.i.49).

The bridle (*H5* III.vii.52; *TS* IV.i.73; *V&A* 37) was only one part of

The perfect Stirrup.

The evil Stirrup.

A comparison of stirrup styles, from a treatise on horsemanship by Gervase Markham.

the harness that enabled the rider to control his horse. The bridle was slipped onto the horse's head with a bit (*MM* I.iii.20; *V&A* 269) of some sort that lodged behind the horse's back teeth; a cannon bit was smooth, a snaffle (*A&C* II.ii.63–64) usually smooth and jointed. Leather reins (*V&A* 31, 392; *R2* I.i.55) led back from the bridle to the rider's hands; Blundeville goes into great detail about exactly how the reins should be held.

Various kinds of straps were employed to control the horse's head and mouth to varying degrees. The head-stall (*TS* III.ii.56–59) was the bridle strap that went all the way around the horse's head. The curb (*TNK* V.iv.73; *AYLI* III.iii.78–79) was a piece that attached to the bit and passed under the lower jaw, and the musroll was a strap that passed around the upper jaw just above the nose. The martingale, one of the devices of which Astley approved for correcting faults, connected the bridle to the saddle to keep the horse from tossing his head. The cruelest device was undoubtedly the cavezzan, a strap across the nose that actually connected directly to the horse's nostrils.

Various devices were employed to make horses go faster, including whips (*AW* IV.iii.36), rods or switches (*John* I.i.140), and spurs (*R2* IV.i.72, V.ii.110–11; *MM* I.ii.163–65; *WT* I.ii.94–96; *LLL* II.i.118–20; *1H6* IV.iii.19). The prick spurs of the Middle Ages, with a single fixed point, had long ago been replaced by rowel spurs (*Cym* IV.iv.39–40; *TNK* V.iv.68–69), which had a rotating wheel studded by points, usually six points. The rowel was supposedly more humane because it did not dig as deeply into the horse's flesh. However, Shakespeare's descriptions of riders in haste do not make the rowel sound extraordinarily kind to horses. The spurs "make incision in their hides" (*H5* IV.ii.10), become "bloody" (*S* 50), and are driven so far into the skin as to be hidden (*JC* V.iii.15; *2H4* I.i.43–47). The kind of spurs one wore were an indication of status. Knights were permitted to wear gilded spurs; squires, silver; lesser horsemen, iron or brass. Copper (*MM* IV.iii.13) might be used as a cheaper substitute for gold.

Care and Feeding

Horses were fed grass (*2H6* IV.ii.70), oats (*TS* III.ii.203–5; *Lear* V.iii.39; *TNK* V.ii.64), hay (*TNK* V.ii.58), and sometimes peas and beans (*1H4* II.i.8–10; *MND* II.i.45). If they were too thin, they were fed wheat and barley moistened with ale or wine; fat horses got a combination of bran, honey, and warm water. Feeding and stabling were of special concern at inns, for the horses would have been traveling all day and need special attention, and there was a different ostler every time, who might be neglectful or scrupulous, honest or thieving (*2H4* V.i.63–64; *TNK* V.ii.58–59; *AW* IV.v.58–59). At home it was easier to make sure the horses got good food, a stall next to other horses they liked, a clean floor in the morning, a daily rubbing and combing, and fresh straw in the evening.

Shoeing was usually done by a blacksmith, though one of Portia's suitors brags that he can do it himself (*MV* I.ii.39–43). Gelding was often practiced to quiet the aggressive tendencies of stallions and make them suitable riding or plowing horses (*1H4* II.i.36–37; *MWW* II.ii.298–99). Conrad Heresbach recommended waiting until the animal was at least a year old; since the procedure was dangerous and might kill the horse, choosing the right time was critical. A gelding might be called a "cut" (*TNK* III.iv.22) for obvious reasons, although this term could also be applied, like the term "curtal," to a horse with a docked tail.

Horses were seemingly always getting sick (*Lear* III.vi.18–19; *TS* I.ii.80), sometimes with diseases like springhalt and spavin that affected the legs (*H8* I.iii.11–13). A catalog of their ailments can be found in *The Taming of the Shrew*, when Petruchio deliberately shows up at his wedding on the world's worst horse: it has a dislocated hip, glanders (an infection of mouth and nose), a swollen mouth, "fashions" (tumors), "windgalls" (leg swellings), spavin, "the yellows" (jaundice), "the fives" (swollen jaw glands), "the staggers" (a nervous disorder), "the bots" (worms), swayback, a dislocated shoulder or shoulders, and knock knees (*TS* III.ii.48–56). The only remedies or preventives were a "drench" or dose of medicine (*1H4* II.iv.108–9; *Cor* II.i.121) or, as with human patients, bleeding (*H5* II.iii.55–56). Thomas Tusser bled his horses every Christmas to ensure their continued good health.

The naturalist Edward Topsell provides a long list of equine ailments and cures in his *Historie of Foure-Footed Beastes*. He includes several types of fevers, mouth and throat ulcers, ague, pestilence, "the turnsick or staggers, the falling evill, the night mare, the Apoplexy, the palsie, and the convulsion or Cramp, the Catarre or Rheume, which in a Horsse is called the Glaunders," the "sleeping evill," watery or bloodshot eyes, the lampasse, and many others. The staggers, he says, causes dizziness, loss of appetite, dim sight, staggering, and apparent head pain, for a horse afflicted with the staggers will repeatedly bang its head against the stable wall. The night mare was a nighttime breathing disorder. "Palsie" resembled the staggers, with the horse walking crookedly, holding its neck oddly, and beating its head against the walls, but a palsied horse's appetite remained constant. The lampasse was a mouth disease in which a swollen, abscessed bit of flesh extended over the teeth and prevented eating; it was "cured" by cutting away the abscess "with a crooked hot iron made of purpose, which every Smith can do." *See also* Animals; Armor; Farming; Heraldry; Travel.

Household Objects

The average home, which had been quite bare and humble in the early sixteenth century, was by Shakespeare's day considerably more full of possessions. Some of these objects were designed for storage; some, for tending the fires in kitchens and bedchambers; some, for covering beds or tables; some, for cooking and other forms of housework; and still others, purely for decoration. Into the first category, we may put boxes (*Cym* III.iv.189), which were usually small enough to sit on some other piece of furniture rather than directly on the floor; jewel caskets (*Tim* I.ii.159; *John* V.i.40; *MV* I.ii.91, 103, II.vi.33); chests (*R2* I.i.180; *John* V.ii.141), which typically had flat lids, rested directly on the floor, and could double as seats; trunks (*TN* III.iv.373; *Cym* I.vi.196, II.ii.147); and coffers (*R2* I.iv.61; *Tim* I.ii.196; *H5* I.i.18; *JC* III.ii.90), which were boxes, often covered with leather or fabric and studded with brass nails, that held money or valuables and had domed lids. Some people also possessed writing caskets with little drawers to hold supplies or writing desks with angled tops.

Baskets carried a variety of objects. The "buck basket" (III.iii.2, III.v.86–90) of *The Merry Wives of Windsor* is designed to hold large quantities of soiled linen; its size may be judged by the fact that the fat Sir John Falstaff is able, with some discomfort, to fit inside it (III.iii.124–28). The basket is carried to a nearby meadow with the help of a "cowlstaff" (III.iii.143), a pole on which the basket could be suspened, with one man carrying the front and another the back end. Smaller baskets might be carried by servants (*MV* II.ii.30 s.d.) as they did the marketing or carried gifts or produce (*A&C* V.ii.338–39). Friar Lawrence uses an "osier cage" (*R&J* II.iii.7), or willow basket, to collect his medicinal herbs, and carriers and haulers often carried goods in baskets, such as the fellow on the London road with a load of live turkeys in a pannier (*1H4* II.i.228–29). Elsewhere, characters carry love tokens (*LC* 36–37, carried in a "maund," a wicker basket with handles) or flowers (*Per* IV.i.12 s.d.) in baskets.

Liquids were held in pails (*LLL* V.ii.911), buckets (which Shakespeare mentions in connection with wells—see *R2* IV.i.183–88; *John* V.ii.139), leather bottles, butts (*T&C* V.i.29), casks, tuns (large barrels), and vats. Shakespeare seldom offers specific details about containers for liquids, but he does mention that the bunghole of the standard beer barrel was stopped with a plug of loam (clay, sometimes mixed with other materials—see *Ham* V.i.204, 210–12).

Fire tools included andirons (*Cym* II.iv.88–91), shovels, pokers, and tongs. A broom or brush was optional, and for coal fires, which were in general use by 1600, a special grate was needed to lift the small chunks of coal off the floor of the fireplace. One of the great luxuries of the day, in houses without central heating, located in a cold nation, was the warming pan. This was a device that usually looked like two pie pans hinged together and fitted with a long handle. It could be filled with warm coals and inserted, closed, between the bedsheets. When the sleeper retired for the night, it was removed, leaving the bed warm and comfortable (*H5* II.i.85–86).

The comfort of beds was also enhanced by various sorts of linen and hangings (*2H4* II.i.145). The mattress was covered with sheets (*2H4* II.iv.228; *Lear* IV.vi.116; *Oth* IV.ii.104; *Cym* II.ii.16; *H5* II.iii.14), perhaps of coarse dowlas, perhaps of soft white Holland, and then with a wool blanket (*Lear* III.iv.64), fledge, rugg, white quilt (*1H4* IV.ii.49) from India, or coverlet (*RL* 394). Feather pillows (*2H6* III.ii.375; *2H4* IV.v.5, 30–33; *H5* IV.i.14; *R3* IV.iii.14; *Lear* III.iv.53–54; *RL* 387) covered with linen pillowcases lay at the head of the bed, against either the headboard or a decorative headcloth. In homes graced with a fine standing bed with four posts and a canopy called a tester, the top of the tester was hung with inner and outer valances and the posts draped with fabric. Curtains hung by rings on rods inside the valances and could be drawn around the bed for warmth and privacy.

Different types of bed hangings: (A) Valance, hanging from the tester; (B) Headcloth, hanging above the headboard; (C) Counterpoint or counterpane; (D) Curtains, hanging from rods inside the valances. The curtains are shown drawn back to the corners of the bed, but at night they would have been closed around the bed for privacy.

Linens for the table included napkins (*R&J* I.v.1 s.d.) and tablecloths. A servant waiting at table, or cleaning up afterward, might also carry a dishclout (*R&J* III.v.21; *LLL* V.ii.711), or dishrag, a limp and probably rather gray bit of linen or cotton.

Tools used in the performance of daily chores included the basin and ewer (*TS* Ind.i.55, Ind.ii.1 s.d.; *Tim* III.i.6–7), or pitcher, that were an essential part of the beginning of every meal. A servant offered the basin to the master of the house, allowed him to wash his hands, and offered him a towel (the "diaper" of *TS* Ind.i.57; this one probably had a "diaper," or overall pattern, woven in). Bakers needed a large flour-sifting bin called a bolting hutch (*1H4* II.iv.455) and an oven (*Per* III.Cho.7; *V&A* 331–32; *TA* II.iv.36–37) or kilnhole (*MWW* IV.ii.54), and cooks needed an assortment of pots, pans, ladles, cleavers, skewers, spits (*R&J* IV.iii.56–57, IV.iv.13 s.d., 15; *Lear* III.vi.15; *Per* IV.ii.132–33) hung on a rack that stretched from ceiling to mantel, and platters. A churn (*MND* II.i.37) was required for butter-making, a broom (*MND* V.i.388–89, the "besom" of *2H6* IV.vii.32) for sweeping, a pepperbox (*MWW* III.v.140–41) and salt-cellar for seasoning food, a spinning wheel (*A&C* IV.xv.43–45) for spinning wool or flax, a long-handled toasting fork for holding slices of bread over the fire (*John* IV.iii.99), and a quern (*MND* II.i.36), or hand mill, for grinding malt.

Decorative objects were chiefly textiles. The largest of these were wall hangings, and there were several types. The longest (*1H4* II.iv.505) was the arras, a floor-length tapestry that sometimes covered a door as well as a substantial part of the wall. When necessary, it could be drawn away from the door to allow passage. In Shakespeare's works, the arras often appears as a place of concealment (*MWW* III.iii.86–87; *TNK* IV.iii.52–53; *Ham* III.iii.27–28). Shorter tapestries (*2H4* II.i.140–42; *MAAN* III.iii.135–37) hung above the paneling that covered the lower part of the walls in fine homes; these tapestries were often made to fit a specific space, with devices or designs specific to the family that bought them, though Bess of Hardwick bought some secondhand and covered the previous owner's coat of arms with a patch. Silk tapestry, especially if made by Flemish weavers or adorned with details in silver and gold thread (*Cym* II.iv.68–72), was the most expensive. Wool was cheaper, and if even this was beyond one's means, there were painted cloths (*LLL* V.ii.572; *AYLI* III.ii.274–75; *T&C* V.x.45; *RL* 245). For these, the image was painted, often with an accompanying motto, on plain cloth, whereas in the tapestry the image was woven out of different-colored threads. In all these types of hangings, biblical and classical themes predominated, and a series of tapestries or cloths might illustrate a sequence of events from the life of a hero like Hercules, David, Susanna, Judith, or Odysseus. Late in the sixteenth century, it became fashionable to have custom-sized pictorial hangings of gilded leather, which served much the same function as tapestries.

Other textiles used in the home included curtains at the windows as well as on the four-poster beds (*MV* II.vii.78, II.ix.1, 83; *H8* V.ii.34). Those for the windows might be made of darnix or, in humbler homes, coarse wool; those for beds were made of such materials as mockado and tinsel.

Carpets, bought from carpetmongers (*MAAN* V.ii.32), were more commonly used on tables and cupboard shelves than on floors (*TS* IV.i.45). These were either "Turkey carpets," made in Turkey, or "Turkey-work," made elsewhere; Norwich, for example, had a thriving Turkey-work industry. The floors were covered not with carpet, but with braided mats of rushes or with hemp hall cloths about 4 to 6 yards (3.7 to 5.5 m) long.

One item that was both decorative and functional was the long cushion (*Cor* I.v.5–7; *MND* III.ii.203–5; *Lear* III.v.34), a rectangular pillow that was two to three times as wide as it was tall. It was frequently embroidered with hunting scenes, flowers, strapwork, or heraldic devices, and was used to top chests and wooden chairs to make them more comfortable to sit upon. Some, made by skilled amateurs or professional embroiderers, are examples of stunning artistry; others were less highly decorative and stuffed with humble materials such as hair. A few were covered with Chinese silk damask and not embroidered at all.

The ordinary home had a few mattresses stuffed with "flocks" (clumps of wool or cotton), enough linens to cover them (and not much surplus), perhaps a pair of candlesticks (*H5* IV.ii.46–47) or a chandelier of wood or iron that hung from the ceiling, and a tablecloth and napkins. A yeoman farmer, Thomas Gyll of Wardington, died in 1587 owning four candlesticks, eight brass pots and pans, two kettles, twenty-seven sheets, four tablecloths, three towels, and twelve napkins, as well as sundry dishes and other items.

Greater houses had many more items, including wicker or wainscot screens, carved or paneled chests, and chairs upholstered to match the velvet bed hangings in the principal chambers. Bess of Hardwick owned multiple tapestries, carpets, and a gilded bedstead with the family arms carved into the woodwork. Her bed hangings were made of such rich materials as velvet, cloth of silver, cloth of gold, damask, and fine cloth embroidered or trimmed with gold. One set that she owned in 1553 was made of black velvet "ymbos'd with clothe of golde and clothe of silv' " and embroidered with gold. A matching coverlet of black velvet and silver, and bed curtains of yellow and white damask, completed the set. In the same year Bess owned ten dozen napkins, twenty damask tablecloths, six dozen pillowcases, ten pairs of fine linen sheets, and fifty pairs of coarse linen sheets. Her collection of bed linens eventually included 250 coverlets, quilts, and counterpanes; 150 cushions; 40 Turkish carpets; and 70 carpets of cloth or Turkey-work. Fine embroidered linens were kept in chests with sachets of iridescent taffeta.

Housework

For the housewife and her maids, there was much to do every day. Almost every household had at least one servant, a "maid that milks / And does the meanest chores" (*A&C* IV.xv.77–78). This maid and her colleagues were responsible for a host of duties, beginning well before dawn and ending after sundown. They emptied chamber pots, built fires, hauled firewood and water, collected eggs from the henhouse, fed the pigs, weeded the garden, and milked the cows, goats, or sheep (*WT* IV.iv.244). They separated the milk they collected, if they didn't spill it on the way back to the kitchen (*AW* IV.iii.109–10), skimming off the cream and emptying it into large wooden churns.

The churn was shaped like a narrow barrel, tapered toward the top, with a lid that had a central hole. Through this hole ran a plunger that was pushed up and down until the cream solidified into butter and a little leftover liquid. The churning was exhausting and took seemingly forever, and sometimes the butter stubbornly refused to "come." When this happened, the hapless maid was likely to blame the failure on a witch or a fairy. In the former case, it was believed that the witch had somehow hidden herself in the churn; thrusting a hot poker into the churn, while saying a few words of banishment, was said to harm her enough to drive her from the cream.

Other kinds of food required substantial preparation as well. Cheese had to be made from curdled milk, drained, salted, and wrapped. Hams, bacon, beef, and herrings needed to be smoked in a smokehouse or, in smaller homes, in the chimney. Brewing ale and beer required a full day of work, boiling vats of water that held, in William Harrison's household, 80 gallons (303 l) each. The huge cauldrons were repeatedly filled—which required a lot of walking from a well, heavily laden—boiled over a hot fire, poured onto the malt and hops, drained off again, and stored in barrels. The malt itself, bushels of it for a single day's brewing, was slowly roasted and dried with great care, the fire of straw being fed through a "kiln-hole" (*WT* IV.iv.245), and might also have to be ground by hand.

Churning butter, from the *Roxburghe Ballads.* Reproduced from the Collections of the Library of Congress.

Serving a meal was a complex matter. The fire had to be built, tended, and kept at approximately the right degree of heat. Because the temperature was always somewhat inexact, foods were usually either boiled in pots that hung from hooks inside the fireplace or roasted on huge skewers called spits. Turning the spit (*MAAN* II.i.244–46) was the job of a kitchen maid, a boy, or a small dog inside a wheel (*CE* III.ii.147). A pan was usually placed below the meat to catch the drippings so that they could be used in the making of tallow candles. Meanwhile, the meat had to be basted and pots of stew keeled (skimmed—see *LLL* V.ii.915, 923). If the cook was especially adept, she might improve the presentation of the meal by cutting the harder root vegetables into attractive shapes (*Cym* IV.ii.49). Bread and pastries were baked in an oven that adjoined the fireplace. By the time the meal was ready, the kitchen was fiercely hot. Thomas Heywood describes it thus in *The English Traveller* (1633): "the meat stands hot upon the dresser, the kitchen's in a heat, and the cook hath so bestirred himself that he's in a sweat, the jack plays music, and the spits turn round to't." When it was time to eat, the "cover" (*2H4* II.iv.10), or tablecloth, was set out and topped with whatever the family possessed in the way of plate. Afterward, there were dishes and pots to wash; scouring pots was the most detested job in the kitchen and fell to the lowliest servant present.

The housewife and the maids also made the family's clothing, except in very wealthy households. This entailed carding or combing and spinning (*RL* Argument) wool, soaking and spinning flax (*TN* I.iii.98–100), dyeing, knitting stockings, weaving cloth (or buying it ready-made), and laboriously hand-sewing every seam, every buttonhole, every embroidered and ruffled cuff. In large establishments, the clothes came from a tailor, but servants and the woman of the house kept busy with fine needlework; there was always sewing of some kind to be done. When, in *Henry VIII*, Katherine of Aragon tells her visitors, "Your graces find me here part of a housewife" (III.i.24), it is probably some kind of sewing or spinning that occupies her.

Laundry, too, took great effort. First the soap must be made by hand from materials such as ashes and fat; it smelled terrible and took a long time to make. Then the water must be hauled and boiled, and the wet, heavy clothes stirred, wrung, and set out to dry. Even when laundry was done at the river's edge, the clothes must be carried back and forth. Great households had their own laundry houses, in which the heat and moisture could be somewhat confined, and middle-class housewives, like Mrs. Ford in *The Merry Wives of Windsor* (III.iii.124–28, 142–44), could send their soiled linen out to professional laundresses and whitsters (bleachers— *MWW* III.iii.11–13), but humbler folk had to do it all themselves, in the one large room their cottages afforded, or go dirty. Once the laundry was done, the linen was spread out to dry and whiten, not on clotheslines but on whatever bush or rock was convenient and relatively clean (*WT* IV.iii.5; *1H4* IV.ii.48).

All these tasks would seem to occupy the day fully, but there was much more to do. The house must be tidied and the floors swept, the maids reprimanded if they did wrong, the children dressed and taught their letters, the cat and dog fed and cared for. Birds had to be plucked by hand before they could be eaten, and the feathers saved for filling mattresses and pillows. The garden had to be sown, weeded, and guarded against pests, and the spices grown there had to be picked, dried, and ground. In busy farming times, the women were often enlisted to participate in the men's work, such as sowing grain, harvesting, threshing, and winnowing. If there were surpluses of the wife's butter, cheese, eggs, milk, and poultry, these must be hauled to market and sold, and typically it was the woman who performed this task. Finally, there were hosts of little seasonal jobs to do, such as decking the house with greenery at Christmas, distilling syrups and essences from the garden in summer, weaving rush mats, and turning stored apples in the winter. A song by Thomas Campion called "Jacke and Jone" (1613), celebrating the joys of rural life, describes the last of these tasks. The hero and heroine "Climbe up to the Apple loft, / And turn the Crabs till they be soft." Mistress and maid alike must have had no trouble falling asleep at night, for their days were filled with hard work. *See also* Dishes; Farming; Food; Needlework; Servants; Women.

Housing
See Architecture.

Humors
Renaissance medicine depended largely on the works of the second-century Greek physician Galen, who in turn based much of his theoretical doctrines on those of Hippocrates. It was Galen who developed and popularized the Hippocratic division of bodily fluids into four humors, and these categories remained dominant in medical thinking for nearly 1,500 years. The physician Andrew Boorde, for example, based his recommendations about sleep requirements on the sleeper's dominant humor.

Galen was fond of fours. He recognized four elements (earth, air, fire, and water) and four properties or qualities (hot, cold, wet, and dry). It makes sense, therefore, that his system should be based upon four humors—so much sense, in fact, that one of the humors, black bile, was invented to round out the group. Unlike the other three, blood, phlegm, and yellow bile, it does not exist in the human body. Later writers elaborated on Galen's ideas, and by the Renaissance there was an elaborate system in which elements, people, organs, herbs, and planets were categorized according to their essential qualities, and in which items with the same or opposite qualities were believed to strengthen or counteract each other.

Each of the humors was assigned two of the four qualities.

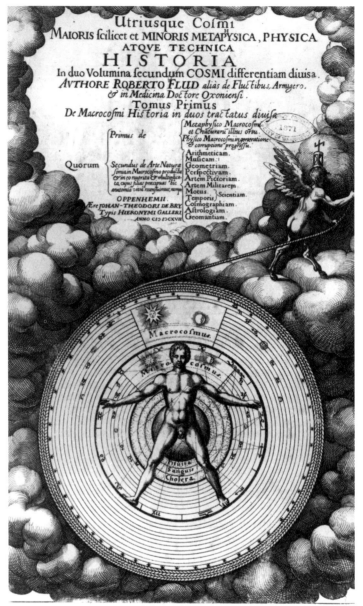

Title page of Robert Fludd's *Utriusque Cosmi Historia* (1624), showing the macrocosm—the solar system and universe—mirrored in the microcosm of the human body. The four humors are listed below the human figure's legs. "Melanche," otherwise known as black bile or melancholy, is the innermost humor, followed by "Pituita" (phlegm), "Sanguis" (blood), and "Cholera" (yellow bile). The diagram reveals the belief that people were affected not only by their bodily humors but also by the universe; the microcosm of the human body is influenced by the "planets"—the moon, Mercury, Venus, the sun, Mars, Jupiter, and Saturn—each of which is shown rotating in its sphere around the earth, represented by its astrological symbol just as the earth is represented by the humoral spheres. Around the planets swirl the stars, represented in the microcosm by the signs of the zodiac and in the macrocosm by six-pointed stars. Reproduced from the Library of Congress.

	Hot	Cold
Wet	Blood	Phlegm
Dry	Yellow Bile (Choler)	Black Bile

Each was presumed to have certain characteristics, to be attracted to certain organs, and to have certain effects on health and personality if it existed in the body in disproportionate amounts.

Phlegm was a clear, watery humor, so people with a preponderance of phlegm—caused, perhaps, by too little "heat" in their digestion—were dull and steady, like water. Phlegmatic, dull people made poor subjects for drama, and the only reference to a character as "phlegmatic" in Shakespeare is an ignorant malapropism for "choleric" (*MWW* I.iv.72), its direct opposite.

Choler was, for dramatic purposes, a much more interesting humor. It was another name for yellow bile, the hot, dry humor made by the liver and stored by the gallbladder. Its association with heat led to theories that it caused fever and was increased by too much heat in the digestive process. (Digestion was considered to be analogous to cooking, with the food being heated and purified by the body's natural warmth.) The choleric person was argumentative, angry, and impatient, traits seen in the use of "hot" as a synonym for angry and in such Shakespearean passages as "touched with choler, hot as gunpowder" (*H5* IV.vii.176). References to choleric temperaments are common (*2H6* I.ii.51; *2H4* II.iv.165; *CE* II.ii.61–62).

Blood was deemed the noblest humor, and medical theorists could find little to criticize in the ruddy-skinned, courageous, cheerful "sanguine" (*1H4* II.iv.244) temperament. The only potential negative consequence of being dominated by the blood was that too much blood was believed to cause serious health consequences, so sanguine people might need to have this plethora removed by bleeding (phlebotomy) more often than people of other temperaments.

The fourth (and fictitious) humor, black bile, was believed to reside primarily in the spleen. Associated with the planet Saturn, also a cold and dry entity, black bile supposedly produced people of dour and sullen temperament. This "melancholy" personality, sometimes called "allycholy" (*2GV* IV.ii.27) or "allicholy" (*MWW* I.iv.149), appears several times in Shakespeare's works, notably in *Love's Labor's Lost*:

> . . . besieged with sable-colored
> melancholy, I did commend the black-oppressing
> humor to the most wholesome physic of thy health-
> giving air. (I.i.230–33)

To judge from Shakespeare's works, however, black bile was not the only humor associated with the spleen. Splenetic characters are sometimes called choleric rather than melancholy (*JC* IV.iii.43–48), so it may be that some humoral terms were used rather loosely by laypeople, much as people today might say, "I have a temperature," rather than the strictly accurate "I have a fever." Ask someone today how a "Type A" person behaves, and often they will be able to list several characteristics of such a person. But ask the same respondent what it is, medically or psychologically, that makes a person Type A, and it is likely that they will have no idea.

Similarly, both Shakespeare and his audiences attributed people's behavior to their natural balance or imbalance of bodily fluids, without necessarily understanding every nuance that a medical practitioner would have known by heart. Their understanding of humors is therefore more general and metaphorical. Humor is frequently used to mean "mood" or "temperament" (*2H4* II.iii.30; *LLL* I.ii.59–60; *R&J* I.i.144), and there is a reference to "the four" types of "complexion" (*LLL* I.ii.78–83). Complexion meant personality, but it was also a reference to skin and features as well, since it was believed that humoral tendencies revealed themselves in personal appearance. For example, when Bardolph is bragging about his willingness to fight, he points to the "meteors" and "exhalations" in his face as proof of a choleric temperament. Prince Hal attributes the blotches to heavy drinking, instead, demonstrating that not everything could be laid at the doorstep of bodily chemistry (*1H4* II.iv.322–27). *See also* Bleeding; Disease and Injury; Medical Practitioners.

Hunting

Hunting in England was based on the French model. The two classic English texts on the subject, the medieval *Boke of St. Albans* and George Turberville's late-sixteenth-century *Noble Arte of Venerie or Hunting*, both drew on a French original. The names of calls on the hunting horn, the word "quarry," and even the cries of encouragement to the dogs, like *illo*—in Shakespeare, "alow" (*Lear* III.iv.75)—came from French words. There were some differences in practice between the two nations. It is said by some that the English, for example, made less use of tracking dogs called lymers to locate the hart, or male red deer (although when the Duke of Württemberg hunted near Windsor in 1592, his quarry, a fallow deer, was singled out with the use of a bloodhound, so the practice cannot have been entirely unknown). Nevertheless, the similarities were far more numerous than the differences, and the paucity of original English treatises on the subject makes it difficult to identify where most of the differences lay.

Title page of the 1611 edition of George Turberville's *Noble Art of Venerie or Hunting.* Reproduced from the Collections of the Library of Congress.

The **Par Force** *Hunting of Deer*

The deer (*2H6* V.ii.15; *AYLI* II.i.21–25, 31–40) was a gentleman's quarry, legally hunted only by those with sufficient lands and funds to build parks and fence them round with pales. This is not to say that deer hunting was entirely confined to the gentry and nobility, for landowners sometimes invited their guests, not always of noble birth, to hunt with them, and lower-born neighbors to the parks poached a deer from time to time (*TA* II.i.93–94). In *3 Henry VI*, it is a sign of the illegitimacy of Edward IV's rule that his own gamekeepers are defying the natural order and poaching the royal deer (III.i.1–8).

The venison that resulted from legitimate hunts served multiple purposes: it fed the master's family, was sent as a gift to friends and family, and served, through portions of the deer reserved as perquisites, as partial payment of the estate's huntsmen. William Harrison, in his *Description of England*, states that the park's keeper is entitled to the skin (*3H6* III.i.22), head, entrails, backbone, and shoulders, plus a present of a few shillings, though no doubt the standard recompense varied from place to place. It was clear to some, including the physician Andrew Boorde, that the meat, while probably quite valued by the huntsmen and their families, was of secondary importance to the lord. Boorde wrote that venison was a wholesome meat but that "great men do not set so moch by the meate, as they do by the pastyme of kyllyng of it."

There were three types of deer hunted in England (red, fallow, and roe), and two principal methods of hunting them (*par force* and "bow and stable"). Simply put, the differences between *par force* and bow and stable hunting lay in the number of animals hunted and the weapons used to kill them. The procedure that follows was identical for the hart (male red deer) and buck (male fallow deer), except that relays were less commonly used for fallow deer.

In *par force* hunting, the hunters had no weapons. A single animal—mature, male, fat and therefore presumably slow, with a good spread of antlers—was selected. In France, the quarry was chosen with the help of quiet trackers called lymers; in England, the huntsmen (*TA* IV.i.101) may have worked on their own or with bloodhounds. The huntsmen studied the tracks of the deer, which could say a great deal about its size; the "entries," or marks of its body's passage through grass and brush; the "port," or marks of the antlers' passage through the upper brush and branches, which indicated both the height of the deer and the width of the antlers; the "frayings," or scratch marks on trees apparent in the season when the velvet (*AYLI* II.i.50) was rubbed off the newly grown antlers; and the "fewmets," or droppings, which changed in shape depending on the season and were believed to reveal much about the animal's size, age, and even sex. This stage of the hunt was called the quest or harboring. Shakespeare turns the singling out of a quarry into a metaphor for the attack on Lavinia in *Titus Andronicus*, when Aaron instructs Tamora's sons to "Single you thither then this dainty doe, / And strike her home by force, if not by words" (II.i.117–18), "by force" being a translation of *par force* as well as a reference to rape.

Next, the huntsmen (*John* II.i.321; *TA* II.iii.278) rejoined the lord and his guests, who were waiting at rendezvous points with the other gamekeepers (*MWW* I.i.108) and the dogs. A strategy session, in which the hunters and huntsmen studied the possible quarries together, ensued. This stage, called the assembly or gathering, often involved a picnic breakfast and a good deal of socializing. Guesses were made as to which way the deer would run, and relays of four to six dogs, leashed in couples (*TS* Ind.i.18), were sent to points along the likely route, there to remain quietly hidden under the control of a huntsman until the deer ran by. It might seem strange to be able to predict the direction the deer would take, but the behavior of deer in certain circumstances was well documented, and in any case, deer parks were often designed to channel the animals' flight along a specific path.

Once everyone was in place, the deer was unharbored, or chased from its sleeping place (*T&C* II.iii.257–58). The challenge for the dogs, once the chase began, was to keep on the scent of the right deer. There were

The pursuit of the deer by dogs and a mounted hunter. Note the hunting horn, which would have facilitated communication between all the hunters and paid huntsmen. From Jost Amman's *Adeliche Weydwercke*. Reproduced from the Collections of the Library of Congress.

many such animals in a park, and a pursued deer would often dash past others of its kind. The huntsmen had to make sure that their dogs did not divert and follow a less noble beast. They also had to reprimand dogs that barked when not on the scent; such dogs were called babblers or brabblers (*T&C* V.i.93–95). Even worse were dogs who ran "counter" (*Ham* IV.v.110–11), or along the animal's trail but away from the quarry rather than toward it.

As he passed the deer's sleeping place, the huntsman felt it to see if it was still warm, indicating that the animal had left not long before; then he pounded on through the forest after his dogs, leaving marks for the other hunters to follow. Periodically, depending on circumstances, he withdrew his hunting horn from his baldric, or belt, and blew a signal. The hunters in the rear followed the sound of the horn and the baying hounds. As the deer passed relay points, the huntsmen waited for about half of the dogs to follow, then uncoupled (*MND* IV.i.108) their own hounds to join and lend new vigor to the chase, and blew a call called mote and recheat (*MAAN* I.i.234–36) on their horns to signal that they had released their dogs (*TN* I.i.16–24).

Other horn calls (*MND* IV.i.139; *TS* Ind.i.15 s.d.; *Lear* I.iv.7 s.d.; *TNK* III.i.95 s.d., 106 s.d.) might tell the hunters that the deer had gone into a stream, that a lost prey had been found and the chase begun again, that the hounds or hunters should assemble, or that the hounds were closing

Pursuing the deer through water. Deer could be hunted with bows or, as in this case, with a gun. From *Adeliche Weydwercke*. Reproduced from the Collections of the Library of Congress.

in on their prey. The call that everyone awaited was the mote and recheat blown simultaneously by all the hunters on site when the deer, exhausted (*V&A* 361–63), gave up running and turned, "embossed" (foaming at the mouth from exertion—see *AW* III.vi.101; *A&C* IV.xiii.3), to fight the dogs at bay (*JC* III.i.204; *TA* IV.ii.42; *R2* II.iii.127). Timing now became crucial. If the deer was too tired, it could not fight for long, which could pose a problem of etiquette if the lord had not yet caught up to the pack. A deer that had reserved some energy for the fight, however, might injure or kill a valuable dog, and to prevent this the huntsmen sometimes sneaked up behind it and cut its hamstrings, hastening death.

The death of the deer elicited another general blowing of horns, "The mort o' th' deer" (*WT* I.ii.118) and a baying of hounds. One version of this death call was a long note followed by six short ones; it was picked up by the other horns and then concluded with two long notes. Then came the unmaking, the butchering of the carcass (*Cym* III.vi.89). Using special knives, a tiny fork for the delicate bits, and a forked and pointed stick called a *fourchée* plunged into the ground, the deer was cut up by the highest-ranking hunter. In Turberville's 1575 book, Queen Elizabeth is shown as having the honor; in the 1611 edition, the illustration has been altered to make James I the royal butcher. The deer was placed belly-up in the dirt and flayed, with its skin, propped by sticks at the corners, making a basin to catch the blood. The hounds were given a taste of the kill and made to howl again, and then the carcass was cut into sections.

Some were reserved as the huntsmen's perquisites, while the best morsels, including the testicles, tongue, and large intestine, were pierced with a knife and stuck on one of the branches of the *fourchée* for the lord. The end of the hunt and the delicacy of the dowsets, or testicles, is described in *The Two Noble Kinsmen*:

> May the stag thou hun'st stand long,
> And thy dogs be swift and strong,
> May they kill him without lets,
> And the ladies eat his dowsets. (III.v.152–55)

Shakespeare gives another example of the division of the carcass, when Falstaff envisions himself as a poached deer:

> Divide me like a bribed buck, each a
> haunch. I will keep my sides to myself, my shoulders
> for the fellow of the walk [huntsman], and my horns I bequeath
> your husbands. (*MWW* V.v.25–28)

Other pieces were given as gifts or sent to the lord's kitchen, and the pelvic bone was thrown to the crows. This process of butchering was usually bypassed in the case of the smaller roebuck, which was carried home whole except for the feet, which were given to the dogs.

The last stage of the hunt was the *curée*, from which the word "quarry" is derived. This was the formal rewarding of the dogs as an encouragement to them to hunt well the next time. The blood collected in the deerskin was mixed with bread and perhaps some chopped meat from the heart, lungs, or liver, and fed to the dogs after they had bayed again. The party then made its way home, the dogs under the care of their particular huntsman, who would be severely punished if he lost any of "his" dogs. In *The Taming of the Shrew* (Ind.i.16–30), the lord's huntsman has charge of Merriman, Clowder, Silver, Echo, and Bellman, and perhaps others, and after the hunt he is to feed them and to help them overcome their exhaustion. The entire procedure, from start to finish, was accompanied by noises that fueled the hunters' excitement: the horns, the barks and howls of the dogs (*Oth* II.iii.360–61; *TNK* II.iv.11–12; *TA* II.ii.1 s.d., 26; *MND* IV.i.110–27; *TA* II.iii.17–28), the cries of the huntsmen (*2H4* I.ii.191), the snapping of branches and rustling of leaves as men and horses plunged through the forest. When Shakespeare directs that "*a noise of hunting is made within*" (*MWW* V.v.104 s.d.), these are the sounds we should imagine.

Bow and Stable Hunting

The season in which deer could be hunted *par force* was limited. For the hart, or male red deer, the season lasted, according to the *Boke of St. Albans*, from June 24 to September 14. The season for the buck, or male fallow deer, was about the same. At other times of the year, landowners settled for bow and stable hunting, which was a mass drive of harts and hinds (female red deer), and bucks and does (female fallow deer). By Shakespeare's time, fallow deer were almost always hunted in this manner rather than *par force*. The process began with beaters and horsemen (the stable) chasing the game through the park. They were aided in their task by the planned terrain of the park, fences, deer leaps that allowed the deer to move only in one direction, and nets or toils (*LLL* IV.iii.2; *Ham* III.ii.351–53) that blocked certain paths. All these devices helped them to guide the flight toward the stand where the hunters (the bow) waited with their weapons (*RL* 580–81; *LLL* IV.i.24), perhaps hidden behind a blind, or "stalking horse" (*AYLI* V.iv.106). Arrows and crossbow bolts flew in a crowd toward the running deer, and the hunt ended with a mass un-making and *curée* of the slain animals.

In *Love's Labor's Lost*, IV.i and IV.ii, Shakespeare gives us a portrait of a bow and stable hunt and its aftermath. Ferdinand apparently is acting the part of the "stable," for the French princess spots him riding his horse uphill (IV.i.1–2) while she, accompanied by a forester, waits for the deer with her bow:

PRINCESS   Then, forester, my friend, where is the bush
           That we must stand and play the murderer in?

FORESTER   Hereby, upon the edge of yonder coppice,
           A stand where you may make the fairest shoot. (IV.i.7–10)

She emphasizes the importance of killing outright rather than merely wounding the deer, to avoid causing unnecessary pain (IV.i.24–35). The next scene provides a discussion of the hunt's outcome—what was slain and by whom—that must have been, in some respects at least, very much like the sort of talk that took place as the hunters made their way home after a successful day. A similar conversation takes place in *As You Like It* (IV.ii).

Hunting the Hare

The hare was univerally acknowledged to be an enjoyable quarry, for it was quick and clever, given to changing path abruptly. It could be hunted year round and ran uphill so well that Edward Topsell warned against letting it tire the dogs in this fashion. It was hunted *par force*, with dogs alone, though there was a different end to the chase than with the deer.

The hare was selected early in the morning, just after sunrise, when it went to sleep. Once the "muse" or "form," the hare's sleeping place, had been found, the gamekeepers, in Topsell's words, "set the hils and rockes, the rivers and also the brooks with nets and gins." The nets (*MV* I.ii.19–22; *MAAN* II.iii.210), he said, should be "set on this manner, let the rodes be pitched upright, fastning their snares to the tops, raising the net in the middle, and hange a long stone at one side, that when the Hare is in the net she may not go out againe."

Once this was accomplished, the hare was startled from its form, and it ran (*Cor* I.viii.6–7), tail and ears high, away from the dogs, who were uncoupled (*V&A* 674), first one, then another, then all at once, to the sound of horns and the cries, "Avaunt, sire, avaunt!" and "Soho!" The hare bounded through sown fields, flocks of sheep (*V&A* 684), musits (hedge gaps—see *TNK* III.i.97; *V&A* 682) and thickets, trying desperately to evade the pack of harriers or greyhounds at its heels. (When greyhounds were used, hunting purely by sight, the sport was known as "coursing.") Meanwhile, the hunters rode as fast as they could behind the hounds (*V&A* 676–77), blowing their horns and crying (with dogs' names borrowed from Shakespeare), "Io, dogs, there boys, there, io, Ringwood, io, Echo, io, Bellman," and so forth. Hunters were instructed to call the dogs' attention to any of their number who was particularly hot on the scent:

PROSPERO   Hey, Mountain, hey!

ARIEL   Silver! There it goes, Silver!

PROSPERO   Fury, Fury! There, Tyrant, look! Hark, hark! (*Temp* IV.i.255–57)

As the hare tired, first one ear, then the other, drooped. It ran this way, then that (*V&A* 679–81), until finally it came near one of the nets. Ac-

Hares were trapped in nets strung across their favorite paths of flight. From *Adeliche Weydwercke*. Reproduced from the Collections of the Library of Congress.

cording to Topsell, it was driven in "with great cry," whereupon "the keeper of the nets must give token to the hunters by his hollowing voice, after the usual manner of woodmen: *O Oha, O ohe*, that the game is at an end, and then call the Dogs by name." The death was blown on the horn, the dogs restrained, the hare displayed aloft, skinned except for the head, and butchered. It was held high again and the death blown a second time while hounds and hunters alike raised their voices in celebration. Then, as with the deer, the hounds were rewarded with meat, blood, or bread.

Like deer, hares and rabbits were often poached. A simple method was to use dogs to drive the rabbits into their holes. Then nets were placed over the exits and a ferret let loose in the warren or noxious smoke driven into it. The rabbits, fleeing, ran straight into the poachers' nets. It was the job of the warrener (*MWW* I.iv.26), a specialized gamekeeper in charge of the rabbits, to keep the poachers away.

Fox Hunting

Foxes were hunted (*TN* II.v.119–21) not for their meat but for sport and for the pleasure of ridding the countryside of an animal that ate rabbits, hares, and poultry. They were hunted *par force*, with uncoupled hounds and relays, but without a bloodhound. The first step in such a hunt was to "unkennel" (*MWW* III.iii.158) the fox at about midnight the night before the hunt. While the fox was abroad, the huntsmen found the entrances to its den, stuffed them with burning sticks, and covered the holes with dirt (*AW* III.vi.104–6; *Lear* V.iii.23). This deprived the fox of its traditional means of escape. Alternatively, the fox could be hunted in its own den by a terrier, which did not fear to pursue it underground.

Boar Hunting

Boar hunting (*TNK* I.i.77–79, II.i.103–8; *V&A* 410, 587–88, 616–30) was the most dangerous form of hunting, for an enraged boar was fully capable of killing a man or a dog, and unlike the hart, it would turn and attack without first being run to exhaustion. Turberville, fairly plausibly, claims to have seen a pack of fifty dogs attack a boar, with only twelve of the dogs emerging unwounded. The experts held that the boar was ready to charge when it lowered its snout, flattened its ears, ground its tusks, rolled its eyes, and took a few steps forward with ears pricked up again. The goal was to anticipate the charge and drive a special spear, equipped with cross-guards a couple of feet from the point to prevent over-penetration, into the boar just as it surged forward (*V&A* 1112–16). Other methods of making a kill, which minimized the danger, included using archers or crossbowmen to supplement the spearmen, throwing spears en masse instead of thrusting, and driving the boar into a net before attempting the kill. Shakespeare gives a good example of the danger of the boar hunt in the death of Adonis in *Venus and Adonis*; Adonis's hounds, too, suffer in the encounter (913–24). The unmaking of the boar was similar to that of the deer, and the hounds were rewarded in the *fouail*, the equivalent of the *curée*.

Other Prey

Deer, hares, boars, and foxes were not the only animals hunted in England. Otters, considered pests in the rivers just as foxes were considered pests on land, were hunted *par force*, with millers ordered to stop their water wheels so that the dogs could pursue their quarry without fear of injury. Badgers were hunted by common people with terriers. Shakespeare mentions neither of these animals in the context of the hunt, though he does mention the hunting of lions (*T&C* IV.i.19; *Cym* V.iii.38–39; *H8* III.ii.207–9). There were no lions in England, but he may have read accounts of lion hunts in other parts of the world. *See also* Animals; Deer; Dog; Falconry and Fowling.

Hygiene

Dirt was nearly everywhere, and bad smells came with it. Yet the English prided themselves on their cleanliness and did everything they could to avoid foul odors, which they believed could cause disease. How could there have been such an interest in good hygiene on the one hand, and such a failure to achieve it on the other?

One answer was that some of the smells and mess were unavoidable. Human and animal waste, for example, was a fact of life. There were virtually no indoor flush toilets, with the exception of a handful of curiosities very late in the period under discussion. That meant that one had to go outside to use a privy, or "jakes" (*Lear* II.ii.67–69; a pun on this word is "Ajax"—a jakes—in *T&C* III.iii.244–45); anyone who has used an open-seat portable toilet, preferably one without a deodorizer and that has run out of toilet paper in the dead of summer, can verify the noxiousness of the experience. Waste simply fell into the cesspool or "sink" (*T&C* V.i.77–78; *Cor* I.i.123–24) below, and stayed there until the pool was full and had to be covered, and another one dug. Indoors, especially at night, when it was inconvenient to blunder around to the jakes, one used a chamber pot (*Cor* II.i.79), or "jordan" (*2H4* II.iv.34), a basin or jar over which one squatted. The chamber pot was emptied in the morning by a servant. In more lavish homes, there might be a close-stool (*LLL* V.ii.573; *AW* V.ii.16–17)—a chair with a padded open seat and a chamber pot below—hidden in a tiny room off the main bedchamber. Once again, it was the duty of some unfortunate servant to empty the pot outside.

Not everyone followed the rules about where to excrete (*MM* III.ii.111–12). It was considered unhealthy to restrain the impulse to urinate or defecate, and men in particular relieved themselves wherever the need took them. Jack Cade calls London's gutters "the pissing conduit" (*2H6* IV.vi.3), so it seems reasonable to assume that many men urinated in the streets, against buildings and in the gutters. Yet medical experts, even as they urged excretion as necessary, stressed the importance of finding the right place. Andrew Boorde's advice, from his *Dyetary of Helth*, was concerned with proximity, but chiefly as it affected the intensity of foul odors:

> . . . beware of pyssynge in drawghtes; & permyt no common pyssyng place be aboute the howse or mansyon; & let the common howse of easement be over some water, or elles elongated from the howse. And beware of emptynge of pysse-pottes, and pyssing in chymnes [chimneys], so that all evyll and contagyous ayres may be expelled, and clene ayre kept unputryfyed.

Unfortunately, not everyone heeded his advice, and "pyssing in chymnes" was all too common (*1H4* II.i.20–22).

In the country (which is to say, almost everywhere, since towns were infinitesimally smaller than today), human waste was added to the dunghill (*2H6* IV.x.83; *H5* IV.iii.99; *AYLI* I.i.14; *LLL* V.i.75–76; *Lear* III.vii.99; *MWW* I.iii.62) or compost pile, to which stable dung and scraps too humble for even the pigs were also added. The dunghill was usually located as near the house as possible without being intolerably offensive, for it was supplemented every day. It was an absolute necessity, for there was never enough fertilizer on farms, and every bit of manure meant a little more grain the next year, which meant that an extra cow or family member might survive the winter. This was an odor that could not be avoided. In the cities, however, where offal was not jealously hoarded, it was dumped anywhere that was convenient. Sometimes, this meant that it was hurled into the gutters. Often, it meant that one carried it, or paid someone else to carry it, to the ocean or the river, where it was hurled into the water (*Per* IV.vi.178–80).

Cleaning the Body

Another reason for general dirtiness was the difficulty of bathing the entire body at once. For the poorest laborers, it meant a dunking in some cold body of water, and it was this cold—not the bathing itself—that was believed to be unhealthy. The rich, on the other hand, had portable wooden bathtubs that could be brought from the washhouse or scullery into their bedchambers and placed by the fire, plenty of coal to heat the water, and plenty of servants to carry it, pitcher by pitcher, to the tub. Therefore, they could bathe more often, in water made sweet with herbs and using perfumed soap. Public baths had been available for some time, and this should have had a positive effect on the general cleanliness of those living in towns, but the baths were associated with prostitution and licentiousness (*MM* II.i.62–65), and they had gradually fallen out of use. There was a resulting class distinction in the matter of body odor (*TS*

Ind.i.48–58; *AW* V.ii.2–10). The courtier had a sweet "court-odor" (*WT* IV.iv.736), whereas the crowd was "rank" (*Cor* III.i.66), and any genteel person who dared go out in the street must "stand the buffet / With knaves that smell of sweat" (*A&C* I.iv.20–21). For anyone who could afford a tub to wash in or perfumes to cover up his scent, it was unpardonable to smell of sweat (*Cor* IV.vi.131–32; *Cym* I.ii.1–3). The soap used was not very gentle. *The Good Huswifes Jewell* (1587) by Thomas Dawson gave a recipe for soap that called for "half a strike" (anywhere from ¼ to 2 bushels, depending on the region) of ashes and a quart (.95 l) of lime to be boiled in water, to which the "good huswife" was to add 4 pounds (1.8 kg) of tallow and boil until hard.

Even those without bathtubs were expected, if at all possible, to keep their hands (*1H4* II.iv.105; *TA* II.iv.6; *TS* IV.i.138, 142–43) and faces (*Cor* II.iii.62) clean. Water for the cleaning of hands was presented to the master of the house at the beginning of every meal, and the washing of hands and trimming of fingernails (*TN* IV.ii.132) was especially important to table manners, since people ate a great deal with their hands. Knives were present at the table, but forks did not come into general use until James's reign. As for the face, Andrew Boorde recommended wiping the face once a day after combing one's hair. He added that his reader should "wasshe your handes and wrestis [wrists], your face and eyes, and your tethe, with colde water."

There was only so much that could be done about the teeth (*Cor* II.iii.63), for there were no toothbrushes, and those who could afford it liked to eat a great deal of sugar; Paul Hentzner, who saw Elizabeth I in 1598, wrote that she had very black teeth as a result. This was one instance in which being rich was of no help whatsoever, and even a disadvantage. People did the best they could to clean their teeth with their fingernails or with decorative "toothpicker(s)" (*MAAN* II.i.257; *AW* I.i.157–60); the nails were considered a home-grown English approach; the toothpick a fashionable and therefore somewhat suspect foreign import (*WT* IV.iv.757–58; *John* I.i.190–92). The truly fashionable carried not only toothpicks but earpicks for removing wax. Sometimes these were designed to look like sickles or eagles' talons.

Plaque-encrusted teeth could be scraped by a barber, but there was no good substitute for toothpaste, and one recipe, compounded of vinegar, white wine, and honey, would have done more harm than good. As the teeth decayed, they darkened and gave off a foul odor (*JC* I.ii.244; *2GV* III.i.318–23; *Cor* III.iii.121–22; *AYLI* Epi.16–19), eventually falling or being pulled out; Thomas Heywood has a character tell the wise woman in his play *The Wise-Woman of Hogsdon* (1633), "Th'art a good grannam, and but that thy teeth stand like hedge-stakes in thy head, I'd kiss thee." The Shakespearean equivalent is the nurse in *Romeo and Juliet*, who has only four teeth left (I.iii.12–13). Because kissing figured not only in courtship but also in the daily etiquette of visits, and because no one wanted to look at rotting teeth or smell bad breath, white teeth (*LLL* V.ii.333) and fresh breath (*TN* II.iii.53–56; *Oth* V.ii.16; *Cym* IV.ii.223–24; *A&C* V.ii.211–13; *Cor* I.i.60) were highly prized; Boorde recommended chewing anise seed to improve the scent.

Vermin

The lack of everyday bathing and the susceptibility of Renaissance housing and bedding made vermin (*2H4* III.ii.170) a common annoyance, not only to the poor but to anyone who came in contact with an infested body or object. The flea (*LLL* V.ii.690; *TS* IV.iii.110; *1H4* Ii.i.14–22; *H5* II.iii.40–41) was one of the two principal pests. If it could be caught, it was squeezed between the fingernails and pulled apart (*MWW* IV.ii.146–47). For a more general approach, people spread dried wormwood on the floors to drive the fleas out of the house.

Even more infuriating were lice, for they lived on the host in greater profusion and were much harder to catch or to eradicate. Even when the adult lice were removed, their eggs, or nits (*LLL* IV.i.150; *TS* IV.iii.110), remained stuck fast to the head hair, pubic hair, or clothing. They had to be removed one by one with laborious care, hence the phrase "nit-picking" for paying an aggravating amount of attention to tiny details. It was well known that the eggs could be concealed in clothing (*2H4* V.i.35–36; *MWW* I.i.13–18) or passed from one person to another during sexual intercourse or other intimate contact (*Lear* III.ii.27–30). Boorde's *Breviary of Health* blamed infestations on "the corruption of hote humours with sweat, or els of rancknes of the body, or els by unclene kepynge, or lyenge with lousy persons, or els not chaungynge of a mannes sherte, or els lyenge in a lousy bedde." He suggested rubbing a compound of bay oil, mercury, and other ingredients on the body.

Inheritance

England, like most other European nations, emphasized primogeniture (*T&C* I.iii.106; *AYLI* I.i.46–47) in inheritance (*Oth* V.ii.364–66; *Lear* II.ii.16–20), meaning that the firstborn son inherited his father's entire estate. Even with twins, this law applied; whichever twin had emerged first from the womb was the elder, and stood to gain everything (*MWW* II.i.71–72). Ideally, younger sons (*1H4* IV.ii.29) were trained for a profession that enabled them to earn their own living, and daughters were given a substantial dowry at marriage instead of an inheritance. Some regions had their own customs and laws regarding inheritance. For example, a married London freeman was supposed to leave one-third of his property to his widow, another third to his children (to be divided however he wished), and the last third to be shared among anyone else he wished to benefit. In Kent, the practice of gavelkind, in which all sons inherited equally, was still customary. In other counties, boroughkind, which favored the youngest son, prevailed. In most parts of the country, the widow's third was fairly standard. There was little that a man could do to disinherit his first son or widow entirely. He might also be limited in his choices by entail (*3H6* I.i.194, 235; *AW* IV.iii.285)—a legal restriction on the disposal of certain kinds of property, especially land.

In practice, people tried to adjust their wills according to their circumstances. Sometimes, for example, they loved one child more than another, had unmarried daughters, knew that the oldest son did not wish to inherit the family business, or had friends, stepchildren, or distant relatives whom they wished to help. Therefore, some men departed from the norm and willed substantial property to a favored younger son or a single daughter. Wills (*AYLI* I.i.2–3; *TN* I.v.242–47; *MWW* III.iv.57) also usually included small bequests, such as clothing or rings (*AW* V.iii.196–97), to close friends and relatives outside the nuclear family. In some cases, the dying man (or widow—married women could not make wills in their own right) had no son, and then the estate might be left to a daughter (*MAAN* I.i.288, V.i.289; *TNK* II.i.7–9; *MWW* I.i.47–56). Although illegitimate children had no right to inherit (*John* I.i.95), some fathers made provision for them in their wills.

A reasonably typical will, in that it was drawn up for a prosperous shopkeeper and artisan who thus was somewhere in the middle class was that of Johanne Woolfe, a widowed printer who owned a shop at the sign of the Brazen Serpent in St. Paul's Churchyard. She died in 1574, leaving her son and son-in-law

> all the presses, letters, furniture coppies and other necessarie instruments
> and tooles being with in my prynting howse or belonging unto the same

for concerning or belonging to the arte of prynting. And also all the books whatsoever being in my shoppe; my saide dwelling howse or ellswheare and all other my Implements of howsholde at the "Brason Sarpente."

To another son, she left an annuity of £16 per year, provided he kept up his studies at the university; if he failed, the amount was to be reduced. One daughter was left an annuity of £10; another, £6 a year until her husband's death (and £10 a year thereafter). Another annuity was bequeathed to a niece "dyseased in her eies." More distant relatives received bequests of money, plate, goods, gowns, and jewelry, and a sum was set aside for the poor. Finally, she gave instructions for the continuation of her business, authorizing her heirs to lease the shops she had owned and instructing them to honor a commitment to print a specific work for which she had contracted.

Farmers usually left an assortment of seeds, sown fields, tools, and household goods. If they were freeholders, owning their land outright, they could will their land just as they could other property. The situation was more complicated if they were tenants. Copyholders' heirs had to go to the lord of the manor and have their right to rent the land recorded. They paid a fee for this transfer and in exchange got a written copy (hence the term "copyholder") of the lease. *See also* Bastardy; Children; Death; Law; Widow.

Inkle

An inkle (*LLL* III.i.138; *WT* IV.iv.207) was a piece of woven linen tape that could be used for a variety of purposes. Similar tapes of worsted, called caddises, were used as simple garters. Tapes were also sometimes used to close or to decorate items of clothing.

Inn

In 1577, a survey of twenty-seven counties estimated the number of inns in those counties at 2,000. Inns were the only type of overnight accommodation, other than the homes of personal friends, available to travelers. They had evolved out of the medieval monasteries, which had offered beds to pilgrims or other travelers, and subsidized rooms in nearby towns for surplus guests (*AW* III.v.33–35). Because of this ancient association with religious orders, inns were often located near churches, and travelers weary after a day of hard riding (*Mac* III.iii.5–7), if they were unfamiliar with a town, might begin their search for an inn by heading toward the nearest steeple.

Like alehouses, to which they were considered superior (*R2* V.i.13–15), inns hung out pictorial signs to attract customers. The inn was known by whatever image appeared on its sign, such as a centaur (*CE* I.ii 9, 104), garter (*MWW* II.i.173, III.v.set, IV.iii.set, IV.v–vi.set, V.i.set), elephant (*TN* IV.iii.5), pegasus (*TS* IV.iv.5), sagittary (centaur archer—*Oth* I.i.155, I.iii.115), tiger (*CE* III.i.95), saint (*AW* III.v.33–35; *John* II.i.288–89), or castle (*2H6* V.ii.66 s.d.–69). One of the historic inns to which Shakespeare refers is the White Hart, in Southwark (*2H6* IV.viii.24–25), in which Jack Cade briefly resided and in which one of his followers was beheaded.

Inns could be quite grand. They often consisted of multiple timber-framed wings with balconies or windows facing a courtyard. This inn yard was sometimes frequented by itinerant entertainers seeking to earn money by diverting the guests. The medieval tendency toward mass dormitory-style lodgings had given way to individual rooms with keys. There was also a stable, and the first duty of any traveler with a horse was to see that the ostler, or stable manager, saw quickly and honestly to the horse's care and feeding. The ostler in *1 Henry IV*, for example, is ordered to soften the saddle and pad its front end to protect the horse's raw withers (shoulders—II.i.5–7). Ostlers apparently were used to being ordered about by strangers and calmly endured being called "knave" or thief in the hope of earning a paltry tip (*Cor* III.iii.32–33). Their duties included caring not only for visitors' horses but also for those rented by the inns to travelers (*MWW* IV.iii.1–2, 8–10). Inns served food and drink, but they were not supposed to provide drink to local workers; early in the reign of James I, inns were resticted to the "resort, relief, and lodging of wayfaring people," and prohibited from serving alcohol to any except guests, the guests of guests, and laborers eating dinner.

Though inns were some of the best service establishments of the time, they had faults. Inflated prices (*AYLI* III.iii.14) and substandard fodder for the horses (*TNK* V.ii.56–66) were common sources of complaint. It was said of some ostlers that they kept greased hay, making a show of presenting a generous bundle to the horse, which would refuse to eat it. They could then use the same bottle or bundle of hay for the next horse, pocketing the cost of proper feed (*Lear* II.iii.119–23). Shakespeare writes of "mine Host / And his fat Spouse" robbing the poor, weary traveler by beckoning to the tapster "to inflame the reck'ning [bill]" (*TNK* III.v.126–29). The inn guests in *1 Henry IV* list a number of problems with their rooms, notably fleas and a shortage of chamber pots, so that guests are forced to urinate in the fireplace at night (II.i.14–22). *See also* Alehouse; Tavern; Travel.

Inns of Court

The Inns of Court (*2H4* III.ii.13, 23; *2H6* IV.vii.2) were England's third university, serving like Oxford and Cambridge as an institution of higher learning. Located in London, they allowed established lawyers to educate younger colleagues through lectures, discussion, debate, and "moots," or mock trials. Law students lived in one of four inns: Gray's Inn (*2H4* III.ii.34), Lincoln's Inn, the Inner Temple, and the Middle Temple (*1H4* III.iii.207–8; *1H6* II.iv.set, II.v.19). Students who could not achieve membership in one of the four had to settle for one of the lesser Inns of Chancery: Clifford's, Thavie's [David's], Furnival's, Barnard's, Staple's, Clement's (*2H4* III.ii.14), New, or Lion's. The entering students were usually sixteen to twenty years old and as likely to have spent time at a university as not. Some had university degrees, but a degree was not necessary to enter an inn.

For the early part of his studies, a member was an "inner" or "junior" barrister. He sat on the same side of the bar as his fellow juniors during moot courts and listened to the lecture series, or "readings," held three to four mornings a week for two to three weeks in a row. After seven years of membership in his inn, participation in a specified number of moots, and attendance at a specified number of readings, he was called to the bar, meaning that he became an "outer" or "utter" barrister and gained the right to practice law. He was then expected to assist with the education of younger students by giving readings of his own and participating in the moot courts.

All of this applied to common lawyers only. Civil lawyers, a smaller group, studied for nine or ten years at one of the universities. Unlike common lawyers, they were given almost no practical training and participated in no moot courts. Therefore, after becoming doctors of law (*MV* V.i.210; *H8* II.iv.1 s.d.), they went to London to join Doctors' Commons, a professional organization with an extensive library, where they learned actual court procedures. *See also* Law.

Insanity

Shakespeare occasionally uses insanity (*LLL* V.i.25–27) as a plot device, most notably in the cases of Ophelia in *Hamlet*, the jailer's daughter in *The Two Noble Kinsmen*, Edgar and Lear in *King Lear*, Antipholus in *The Comedy of Errors* (IV.iv), Malvolio in *Twelfth Night*, and Christopher Sly in the Induction of *Taming of the Shrew*. The nonsequiturs of his many fools, as crazy as they sound to modern ears, are deliberate juxtapositions of sense and nonsense for the purpose of instructing and entertaining the listeners, and therefore do not fall into the same category. Some of the cases of madness are real, some are false, and all feature apparent or real departures from reasonable behavior.

Insanity then, as now, involved a reversal or distortion of the accepted rules of human behavior and social interaction. This might take the form of seeking to harm oneself or others (*2H6* III.i.347), talking to invisible companions or in a disjointed manner (*TN* I.v.106–7), eating substances normally considered repulsive (*Lear* III.iv.127–32), speaking of oneself in the third person (*Lear* II.iii.20), singing at inappropriate times, failing to recognize well-known faces and names, or mistaking strangers, objects, or animals for friends and relatives. There might be hallucinations or elaborate pretenses, as when the jailer's daughter thinks she is sailing a ship, even though she is on dry land (*TNK* IV.i), or thinks her working-class wooer is the knight Palamon (*TNK* V.ii). The essence of madness was that the madman or madwoman's behavior be incomprehensible to a person considered normal. Thus Sir Thomas More spoke of seeing a mental patient laugh while striking his head repeatedly against a post. It is precisely this detachment from pain and from an understanding of consequences that Constance desires when she expresses her wish to go insane (*John* III.iii.43–60).*

The causes of madness were not fully understood. It was generally accepted that serious emotional trauma, such as the death of a loved one, severe anxiety, or unrequited love, could make a person mad. The causes of the jailer's daughter's insanity, for example, are her hopeless adoration of Palamon, her fear that her father will be executed, and her guilt at having allowed Palamon to escape prison and thus having been the cause of her father's peril (*TNK* III.v). Mental health specialists today would still agree that insanity, whether or not it is caused by extreme emotion, can certainly manifest itself emotionally, perhaps as an obsession with a particular object, person, or activity. It is also possible for the brain to be damaged by injury or illness, and people in the Renaissance recognized both of these types of damage as causes of madness. Two possible culprits, they thought, were fever and a bite from a mad dog (*MWW* IV.ii.119–21). Other supposed causes of madness included demonic possession (*TN* III.iv.8), religious fervor, supernatural noises (*TA* II.iii.104), the phases of the moon (hence lunacy, from *luna*, the Latin word for moon—see *Oth* V.ii.109–11; *WT* II.ii.29; *MWW* IV.ii.19–20), the menstrual cycle (which roughly coincided with the moon's cycle—see *TNK* IV.iii.1–2), the heat of late summer, and a surfeit of the bodily humor called black bile (or melancholy), causes that would not now be recognized as valid. Though doctors often made errors in assessing the causes of insanity, they correctly identified childbirth as a possible trigger for mental illness, and even their errors sometimes made sense; for example, they fixated on religious and demonic causes for mental illness because, in a time deeply concerned with religious strife, madmen often chose religious terms in which to express their delusions (*TNK* IV.iii.18–55; *MND* V.i.4–10).

The people of Shakespeare's time were also correct in identifying the brain as the afflicted organ (*TS* III.ii.162; *TN* IV.ii.118–19); hence their

---

* The Complete Signet Classic Shakespeare combines two scenes in *King John*, so that Constance's wish for madness appears in many other editions of the play in III.iv.

references to the insane as "brainsick" (*2H6* V.i.163; *RL* 175). Other terms for the insane included "mad" (*R&J* IV.v.76; *TA* IV.i.21), "non-come" (from *non compos mentis*, Latin for "not of sound mind"—see *MAAN* III.v.63), and "wood" (*1H6* IV.vii.35; *2GV* II.iii.27). The last term had no linguistic connection to the substance taken from trees, but simply evolved from a similar-sounding Old English word.

There were few effective remedies. Some lunatics were cared for by their families; others simply wandered from town to town, blamed for any increase in local crime, fed perhaps by a few charitable souls, and eventually beaten from the parish as a drain on its resources (*Lear* III.iv.132–33). Still others, if they were thought to be violent (*H8* I.iv.27–30), were locked up and kept in chains. There was little hope of recovery, but they could at least be kept out of sight. One of the principal storehouses for such incurables was the old hospital of St. Mary of Bethlehem, Bedlam for short, which had been used to house the insane since the fourteenth century. Inmates there were kept in dark cells, whipped if disobedient (*AYLI* III.ii.396–98), and exhibited to the public as a form of entertainment. The institution was headed not by a doctor but by anyone with enough influence to be selected by London's Court of Aldermen, so that it was kept as a moneymaking franchise by such tradesmen as a draper, a grocer, and a clothworker. Thus the management was sloppy, the beds (in 1567, at least) nothing but bare boards or straw-stuffed coal sacks, and the building in poor repair. Yet mayors, aristocrats, and aldermen continued to refer inmates to its confines, the charitable continued to support the maintenance of its prisoners, and it became so famous that its name, in Shakespeare's day, was a synonym for both the noun and adjectival forms of "lunatic" (*2H6* III.i.51, V.i.131–32; *John* II.i.183; *H5* V.i.19; *Lear* I.ii.137–39, III.vii.105).

Treatment, when attempted, took various forms. Some thought that music (*R2* V.v.62), familiar surroundings, or a generally peaceful atmosphere might help to restore the mind. Others, who believed in astrological or melancholic causes, prescribed based on the position of the planets or the presumed humoral influence of different herbs. Priests, who were often called upon to treat the insane, tended to favor prayer either by or on behalf of the afflicted person. Clerics on both extreme ends of the religious spectrum—that is, Catholics and Puritans—espoused the expulsion of possession demons through exorcism (*CE* IV.iv.53–56), but this tactic met with disapproval from the mainstream Anglican leadership. The Swiss physician Paracelsus suggested various herbal and mineral medicines or, if all else failed, dunking in cold water. Considering the lack of consensus and the uselessness of most methods of treatment, the general course taken in most of Shakespeare's plays—humoring the afflicted party, even playing along with the hallucinations (*TNK* IV.iii.69–100, V.ii.68–110)—seems kinder than the whippings, bleedings, purgings, and confinements (*R&J*

I.ii.53–56; *TN* III.iv.139–40; *Cor* I.ix.56–58) prescribed by surgeons and magistrates.

Insults

Shakespeare's insults are at times some of the most vivid and lively features of the plays, and they are also one of the most common. Perhaps real people in Tudor and Stuart England did not walk about criticizing each other so bluntly and frequently; certainly it seems unlikely that they did so as eloquently as some of Shakespeare's characters, in the same way that real people today do not think of clever comebacks and putdowns as easily as do characters on well-written sitcoms. But although people may not have uttered strings of epithets like "whoreson caterpillars! Bacon-fed knaves! . . . gorbellied [big-bellied] knaves . . . fat chuffs [misers]" (*1H4* II.ii.85–91) on a daily basis, they must have used many of the terms below. Least likely to have been in common usage are the metaphorical insults, such as Prince Hal's description of the fat Falstaff as "this bed-presser, this horseback-breaker, this huge hill of flesh" and Falstaff's characterization of Hal as a series of thin objects: "you starveling, you eelskin, you dried neat's-tongue [ox-tongue], you bull's pizzle [penis], you stockfish [dried fish] . . . you tailor's yard, you sheath, you bowcase, you vile standing tuck [sword]!" (*1H4* II.iv.244–50) More realistic chains of insults are those like "Boys, apes, braggarts, Jacks, milksops!" (*MAAN* V.i.91) and "whoreson, beetle-headed, flap-eared knave" (*TS* IV.i.146), which rely less on poetry than on remembering a mostly applicable list of derogatory terms.

Most of the insults fall into general categories, such as the group of terms that imply unethical or uncouth behavior. Another group, including "bastard" and "whoreson," accuses the target of illegitimate parentage. A very large group, including "villain" and "wretch," calls the target lowborn or base in manner. Another large group contains words meaning idiot, simpleton, fool, or blockhead. Some insults refer to particular types of behavior, such as obsequiousness, foppish affectation, cowardice, or deceptiveness. All of these terms are directed primarily or exclusively at men. Some modern insults, such as "bastard," were already in use in Shakespeare's day—though the implication of illegitimacy, rather than bad behavior, was at issue. Others, such as "son of a bitch," do not appear in Shakespeare's works, though something like it appears in the term "Thou bitch-wolf's son" in *Troilus and Cressida* (II.i.10).

For women, the opprobrious terms are almost exclusively sexual. Usually, they imply that the woman in question is a prostitute or little better. Into this category fall such insults as drab, giglot, harlot or harlotry, malkin, strumpet (*CE* IV.iv.123), trull (*A&C* III.vi.95), and whore (*TA* IV.ii.71). Other insults focus on women as troublesome or worthless;

in this group we may place baggage, callet, hilding (*AW* III.vi.4), piece, and shrew (*MV* V.i.21).

The first chart below defines many of Shakespeare's insults and gives one citation for each. The second chart lists adjectives commonly found in his barrages of insults, along with terms for men and for women. Readers wishing to compose their own Renaissance-style invective can select a few examples from the appropriate columns and prepare a suitably daunting diatribe. For outstanding Shakespearean examples, see Doll Tearsheet's verbal assault on Pistol (*2H4* II.iv.124–33), Constance's attack on Austria (*John* III.i.41–49), or the long strings of insults in *Romeo and Juliet* (III.v.157–61), *The Taming of the Shrew* (IV.i.114–20, IV.iii.108–12), and *King Lear* (II.ii.16–20).

Insult	Citation	Notes
Asinico	*T&C* II.i.45	Presumably a synonym for "ass"
Ass	*T&C* II.i.45	Presumably a synonym for "ass"
Baggage	*CE* III.i.57	Worthless or immoral woman
Bastard	*H5* III.ii.125	One conceived out of wedlock
Beef-witted	*T&C* II.i.12–13	Stupid
Beggar	*R3* I.ii.42	One who begs for a living; a person of low income and therefore, by the standards of the time, of low character as well
Block	*2GV* II.v.23	Stupid person. The implication is that the target of the insult is as intelligent as a block of wood. Several similar insults, such as loggerhead, make the same comparison.
Capocchia	*T&C* IV.ii.32	Idiot
Caitiff	*Oth* V.ii.317	Miserable wretch; the term originally meant a captive or prisoner
Callet	*WT* II.iii.90–91	Scold; applied only to women
Clotpoll	*Lear* I.iv.47	Blockhead; synonymous with "clodpoll"
Coistrel	*TN* I.iii.39	Literally, a knight's groom; figuratively, a lowborn fellow
Cockney	*TN* IV.i.15	An effeminate fellow, derived from a term for a child overly devoted to its mother
Coxcomb	*MAAN* IV.ii.70, 72	Fool; vain fellow
Crack-hemp	*TS* V.i.45	Person destined to be hanged, a criminal
Cullion	*H5* III.ii.21	Literally, a testicle; figuratively, a low fellow
Cur	*MV* III.iii.18	Common dog, mongrel

Insult	Citation	Notes
Dastard	*1H6* I.iv.111	A sneaking coward
Dog	*TA* IV.ii.77	A base person
Dotard	*TS* V.i.104	Imbecile
Drab	*1H6* V.iv.32	Prostitute, slut. These two latter terms were not synonymous; a "slut" in the late sixteenth and early seventeenth centuries was not a woman of loose morals but one who was dirty or untidy.
Dunghill	*John* IV.iii.87	A term that likens the target to a compost heap
Flirt-gills	*R&J* II.iv.159	Women of inadequate chastity
Giglot	*MM* V.i.349	Lewd or indecently merry girl
Glass-gazing	*Lear* II.ii.16	Vain; a "glass" is a mirror
Goose	*Per* IV.ii.86	Silly or stupid person; sometimes rendered as "gosling"
Greek	*TN* IV.i.18	A cheater at cards, a cunning person, or a merry or immoral person
Gull	*H5* III.vi.67	A dupe, a person easily tricked
Hagseed	*Temp* I.ii.367	Seed of a witch
Harlot	*R&J* IV.ii.14	Prostitute
Hind	*2H6* IV.ii.121	A simple country fellow
Jack	*R3* I.iii.53, 71, 72	Knave
Jackanapes	*AW* III.v.84	This term, often the name of a tame ape or monkey, was used for a person who made himself ridiculous in some way, for example, by putting on airs, performing tricks, or being impertinent.
Jolthead	*2GV* III.i.288	Blockhead
Knave	*CE* III.i.64	Boy, low person, liar, or scoundrel
Loggerhead	*R&J* IV.iv.21	Blockhead
Lown	*Oth* II.iii.91–93	Idler, scoundrel, lowborn man, or boor. A variant of "loon," it was one of the few insults that had specific applications to both men and women; when applied to a woman, it meant "strumpet."
Lozel	*WT* II.iii.107–11	Worthless person, scoundrel
Lubber	*TN* IV.i.14	Lout
Malkin	*Per* IV.iii.34	A proverbial proper name for a lower-class woman; a slut or slattern; a lowborn woman; a rag mop

Insult	Citation	Notes
Mammet	*R&J* III.v.186	Puppet, doll
Mate	*TS* I.i.58	Fellow, companion; not always, but sometimes, contemptuous
Minion	*TS* II.i.13	Mistress, favorite, darling, or servile creature
Miscreant	*1H6* III.iv.44	Heretic, villain
Mongrel	*Lear* I.iv.50	A term of contempt
Mumble-news	*LLL* V.ii.465	Prattler
Noddy	*2GV* I.i.116–25	Simpleton, fool
Peasant	*2GV* IV.iv.43	Since this insult implied low birth, it was especially forceful when applied to someone of good income or family.
Pedascule	*TS* III.i.49	This is not a real word, but a Latinization of the word "pedant." A pedant is a schoolmaster or, in a derogatory sense, one who shows off his learning at inappropriate times. The ending "-cule" is a diminutive, a way of turning "pedant" into a nickname.
Piece	*TNK* III.v.43	Occasionally a term for a man, but more commonly a derogatory term for a woman, expressing contempt and, later, sexual objectification.
Pizzle	*2H4* II.iv.164	Penis
Polecat	*MWW* IV.ii.179	Prostitute
Poltroon	*3H6* I.i.62	Coward
Pussel	*1H6* I.iv.107	A form of the word "pucelle," this term meant a dirty, slatternly woman or a prostitute or courtesan.
Rascal	*1H4* II.ii.5–6	A lowborn or dishonest man
Recreant	*2H6* IV.viii.27	Coward
Rogue	*MWW* II.ii.272	Vagrant, vagabond, dishonest person
Rudesby	*TN* IV.i.52	An insolent or ill-mannered fellow
Ruffian	*2GV* V.iv.60	A brutal criminal
Runnion	*MWW* IV.ii.180	An abusive term for a woman whose meaning is not entirely clear. It appears as "ronyon" in *Macbeth* (I.iii.6).
Saucy	*JC* IV.iii.131	Impertinent
Scroyle	*John* II.i.373	Scoundrel

Insult	Citation	Notes
Sheep-biting	*MM* V.i.356	Doglike
Sir Tyke	*MWW* IV.v.51	Dog
Skainsmate	*R&J* II.iv.160	An insult of unknown meaning
Slave	*Tim* III.vi.98	Low or servile person. In the example cited, sycophants are decried as "Cap-and-knee slaves"—in other words, men who can make a fine show of respect but will not remain loyal.
Slugabed	*R&J* IV.v.2	Lazy person who lies in bed all morning
Sot	*TN* I.v.121	Blockhead
Trojan	*H5* V.i.19	Dissolute fellow, merry companion
Trot	*TS* I.ii.78	Old woman, hag
Turk	*MWW* I.iii.87	Barbarian, savage
Varlet	*Cym* IV.ii.84	Servant or attendant, person of low character
Villain	*MAAN* IV.ii.43, 79	Lowborn person, scoundrel
Wagtail	*Lear* II.ii.69	Sycophant or flatterer. The term comes from the name of a bird that makes a bobbing motion, dipping its head and raising its tail.
Whoreson	*R&J* IV.iv.20	Son of a whore, illegitimately born
Witch	*MWW* IV.ii.179	
Wretch	*1H6* V.iv.7	Miserable, lowborn person

Do-It-Yourself Shakespearean Insults

Adjective	Noun (Male)	Noun (Female)
saucy	lubber	drab
rascally	jack	giglot
scurvy	knave	harlot
whoreson	miscreant	harlotry
unmannered	rascal	malkin
bloody	recreant	strumpet
blasphemous	rogue	trull
incharitable	rudesby	whore
mangy	ruffian	baggage
ignoble	varlet	callet
base	villain	hilding
peevish	bastard	piece

Adjective	Noun (Male)	Noun (Female)
beef-witted	coistrel	shrew
filthy	cullion	
egregious	dastard	
vile	clodpoll	
cullionly	caitiff	
cheating	coxcomb	
moldy	hind	
lack-linen	minion	
lousy	mongrel	
glass-gazing	peasant	
beggarly	goose	
proud	gull	
shallow	loggerhead	
	lubber	
	noddy	
	sot (fool)	
	swain (country bumpkin)	
	wagtail	

Iron

Iron (*T&C* III.ii.177; *MAAN* IV.i.150) was widely used for church-floor tomb slabs, cannons, locks, hinges, door knockers, handles, tools, supports for shop signs, and horseshoes. As steel, it was used in armor and weapons (*Cor* V.vi.149; *Temp* II.i.287; *TNK* II.i.108), and Shakespeare also mentions steel gates (*T&C* III.iii.121–23, S 65) and "poking-sticks" (*WT* IV.iv.227) for the starching and ironing of ruffs. The best iron was imported from Spain or Germany, but some was mined in England wherever the three necessities—ore, timber, and water—were found together. Timber was needed because coal was not a reliable fuel for iron smelting (and would not be until about a century later). The preferred fuel was charcoal, huge amounts of it, produced by charring wood. The great swathes cut into English forests in this period were only partly due to the demands of shipbuilders and carpenters, and greatly due to the vast consumption of charcoal for industrial purposes. Water was required as a source of power. Water wheels in a river or stream ran the bellows that kept the furnace hot and the massive tilt hammer that flattened the metal.

There were two kinds of smelting facilities: bloomeries and blast fur-

Two blacksmiths at work, from *Panoplia*, by Jost Amman. The men wear
leather aprons, as was customary in their trade; like most people who engaged in hard physical labor, they wear simple garments and have stripped
to their shirts above the waist. The flaming forge is visible in the background, and hammers, tongs, files, and an anvil are visible in the foreground. Reproduced from the Collections of the Library of Congress.

naces. Bloomeries were more primitive and inefficient, consisting of a clay-
or stone-lined pit about 2.5 feet (76.2 cm) deep and 2 feet (70 cm) wide
in which the ore was heated for about twelve hours. The resulting "bloom"
weighed about 100 pounds (45.3 kg). Only one bloom at a time could
be produced in a pit. The blast furnace, on the other hand, could produce
iron almost continuously for weeks at a time. The furnace was a square
stone tower, about 18 feet (5.5 m) tall, with a ramp leading to the open

top. Workers dumped cartloads of ore and charcoal into it, and a fire below heated this material. Ash and molten iron gradually made their way to the bottom of the tower, where they were removed at a rate of up to 1 ton (907 metric ton) per day.

In both types of smelting systems, the cast iron produced was brittle and impure. It had to be reheated and hammered several times to improve its plasticity and become wrought iron. The wrought iron was subject to rust (*V&A* 767), so it was often treated with tin, pitch, paint, or varnish to inhibit oxidation. Some iron was bought by armorers, but most of it went to blacksmiths (*John* IV.ii.193–200), whose forges (*H5* V.Cho.23) turned out horseshoes, plow parts, and tools (*2H4* V.i.19–20; *MV* I.ii.39–43; *MWW* III.v.116–17, IV.ii.217–18).